That Old-Time Rock & Roll

A Chronicle of an Era, 1954–63

Richard Aquila

University of Illinois Press
OCM 43615782
Urbana and Chicago

First Illinois paperback, 2000
© 1989, 2000 by Richard Aquila
Reprinted by arrangement with the author
All rights reserved
Manufactured in the United States of America
♾ This book is printed on acid-free paper.

All chart positions and chart data copyright © 1954
through 1963 by Billboard Publications, Inc.
All chart data compiled by the Billboard Research
Department and used with permission.

Library of Congress Cataloging-in-Publication Data
Aquila, Richard, 1946–
That old-time rock & roll : a chronicle of an era,
1954–63 / Richard Aquila.
p. cm.
Originally published: New York : Schirmer Books ;
London : Collier Macmillan Publishers, 1989.
Includes bibliographical references.
ISBN 0-252-06919-6 (pbk. : alk. paper)/
ISBN 978-0-252-06919-2
1. Rock music—To 1961—History and criticism.
2. Rock music—1961–1970—History and criticism.
I. Title: That old time rock and roll. II. Title
ML3534.A68   2000
781.66—dc21
00-028679

P 6 5 4 3 2

That Old-Time Rock & Roll

Music in American Life

A list of books in the series appears at the end of this book.

To my wife, Marie
and my children, Stephen and Valerie

Contents

Preface

In 1961, Little Caesar and the Romans had a hit singing "Those Oldies But Goodies (Remind Me of You)." Their point was well-taken: old songs do often remind us of people, places, or times gone by.

This book is a historical investigation of the old hits and performers from rock's first decade. A source book and history, it explores what "that old time rock & roll" can tell us about the past.

The study begins in 1954—the year when the Chords' "Sh-Boom" and numerous other rhythm and blues records invaded the *Billboard* pop charts, introducing a large white audience to the R & B sound. The book ends in 1963 at the start of a new era in American popular music: the arrival of the Beatles.

Part I traces the rise of rock & roll, describes the various rock styles, explains the relationship of music to culture, and places the music in historical perspective through time lines entitled "Historical Records." Part II contains rock & roll lists which detail the music's main themes, topics, and hit records. Part III is a historical directory with information about virtually every performer who made the charts in rock's early years. (All performers, regardless of style, are included on the assumption that all hit records reflect the listening and buying habits of their audience.) The term "rock charts"—as used in this book—refers to the various hit record listings compiled by individual rock & roll radio stations. These generic rock charts should not be confused with *Billboard's* "Top 100" or "Hot 100" record charts, which were the record industry's official trade listings of top-selling records.

This book is both a history of rock & roll and a history of the times. It explains how early rock reflected American life and thought of the 1950s and early 1960s, providing excellent information about the charter members of the baby boom generation. The music shows that the young generation thought of itself as a distinct group, but still shared many of the adults' values and interests. "That old time rock & roll" suggests Kennedy's America was not much different from Eisenhower's, and the two eras may have more in common than some historians have led us to believe.

Acknowledgments

I wish to thank all those who contributed in some way to this project. Ball State University kindly assisted me with expenses related to the book. I am greatly indebted to Joel Whitburn and *Billboard* for providing detailed chart information for every hit record. Most of my references to chart positions and dates of hit records are based on *Billboard's* Top 100 and Hot 100 chart surveys, as researched and compiled by Joel Whitburn in his excellent work, *Top Pop Singles, 1956–1986* (Record Research, P.O. Box 200, Menomonee Falls, Wisconsin 53051). In a more personal way, others either knowingly or unknowingly, contributed to this book. A long time ago, Dick Biondi and Ruthie Evans taught me the relevance of rock & roll. For thirty years Dan Sawers has been my fellow traveler in the world of rock. My brother, Phil, always reminded me what "real" rock & roll was all about. My parents, Mary and Phil Aquila, provided me with encouragement, love, and opportunity (they also gave me the money to buy a record player, as well as my first '45s—the Hollywood Flames' "Buzz, Buzz, Buzz," Ricky Nelson's "Be Bop Baby," and Danny and the Juniors' "At the Hop"). My kids, Stephen and Valerie, reintroduced me to the joys of discovering rock & roll. And my wife, Marie, both inspired and enabled me to undertake this nontraditional history project. To her, I owe a special thanks. And, of course, I am indebted to thousands of rock & roll performers, particularly Buddy Holly, Bobby Vee, Dion, and Rick Nelson. Their music provided the reason for this book.

Introduction to the Illinois Paperback Edition

History You Can Dance To

Like many baby boomers, I grew up listening and dancing to rock & roll. The music was everywhere: on car radios, at high school dances, in college dorms, at parties, and later on, even at antiwar demonstrations and civil rights marches. Rock changed as our generation did. Elvis Presley gave way to the Beatles; Bob Dylan replaced Chuck Berry as rock & roll's poet laureate. By the mid-1960s, both the music and the times were a-changin'.

The close connection between youth culture and music convinced me that rock & roll was an important phenomenon. As a history graduate student in 1969, I even daydreamed that someday I would write a book about rock & roll's historical significance. But back then, few scholars accepted rock & roll as a serious subject for study. So, I put away my dreams about the music and got down to business writing a doctoral dissertation about a more traditional social history topic—Indians on the early American frontier.

It wasn't until years later when I began teaching courses in American social and cultural history at Ball State University that I had the opportunity to follow through on my dream. By the early 1980s, the history profession had changed greatly. The "new social history"—with its focus on everyday life and ordinary people—had taken the field by storm. Social historians were turning to all sorts of nontraditional historical sources, including rock & roll.

In 1989, I published the first edition of *That Old-Time Rock & Roll: A Chronicle of an Era, 1954–63*. Part rock encyclopedia and part historical monograph, the volume argued that early rock & roll reflected—and sometimes helped shape—youth culture during the Eisenhower/Kennedy years. Prior to my book, only a few other serious studies of rock music had been attempted, notably pioneering works like Carl Belz's *The Story of Rock* (1969); Charlie Gillett's *The Sound of the City: The Rise of Rock and Roll* (1970); Greil Marcus's *Mystery Train: Images of America in Rock 'n' Roll* (1975); and Simon Frith's *Sound Effects: Youth, Leisure, and the Politics of Rock 'n' Roll* (1981).

Most books about rock & roll, however, still took the traditional fan-magazine approach, simply glorifying or trashing rock stars and their music. Equally important, most scholars at the time refused to acknowledge the historical and cultural importance of rock & roll.

I will never forget the response of one of my colleagues in the history department when he first heard that I was writing a book about rock & roll. "Why would you want to do that?" he asked. "Rock & roll isn't history, and it certainly isn't worth your time and effort."

His reaction was not surprising. For over two hundred years, critics have used the same basic arguments against most popular culture: as a mass phenomenon, it lacks artistic value; it debases the audience; it has negative effects on elite culture. Ironically, those very arguments underscore the historical importance of popular culture. Its mass appeal opens a window onto society that we should not ignore.

Rock & roll—one of the most significant developments in popular culture since World War II—is especially important. Like a vast oral history project, the music contains a wealth of information about everyday life and ordinary people. Along with fascinating glimpses of fads, fashions, and politics, it reflects attitudes about religion, race, class, ethnicity, and gender. Hit records have inspired young people to wear blue-suede shoes, do the twist, and give peace a chance.

But these messages are not merely handed down to a passive audience. Just as the music sometimes shapes the behavior of listeners, so the audience can influence the music's contents and direction. For example, John Kay of the rock group Steppenwolf told me that one of his group's biggest hits, "Monster," was inspired by a conversation that he had with a fan about the U.S. government's role in Vietnam.[1]

Studying rock & roll underscores the fact that popular culture is not monolithic. The music contains messages that are sometimes interpreted differently by various groups and subcultures. A good example is Peggy March's 1963 hit, "I Will Follow Him." March told me that while most listeners interpreted the song as a romantic tale about a girl's total devotion to her boyfriend, some believed that the song had religious connotations.[2] Not surprisingly, many of the most successful artists in rock history were those whose appeal spanned the political and cultural spectrum. Elvis Presley, for instance, became a culture hero to both rebellious youths and devout Christians.

Since the late 1980s, numerous scholars have analyzed the social and cultural meaning of rock music. Excellent historical overviews of the music include Jim Miller's *Flowers in the Dustbin: The Rise of Rock and Roll, 1947–1977* (1999); Paul Friedlander's *Rock and Roll: A Social History* (1996); David Szatmary's *A Time to Rock: A Social History of*

Rock 'n' Roll (1996); and Reebee Garofalo's *Rockin' Out: Popular Music in the USA* (1997).

Specific topics have also been explored. Philip Ennis unraveled the roots of rock music in *The Seventh Stream: The Emergence of Rocknroll in American Popular Music* (1992). Joe Stuessy's *Rock and Roll: Its History and Stylistic Development* (1990) concentrated on the music's sound. The importance of gender was the subject of Gillian G. Gaar's *She's a Rebel: The History of Women in Rock & Roll (1992)*. The links between African-American culture and rock music informed studies such as Nelson George's *The Death of Rhythm & Blues* (1988) and Suzanne E. Smith's *Dancing in the Street: Motown and the Cultural Politics of Detroit* (2000).

Many recent scholars have focused on particular musical styles. Among the best are Robert Walser, *Running with the Devil: Power, Gender, and Madness in Heavy Metal Music* (1993); Tricia Rose, *Black Noise: Rap Music and Black Culture in Contemporary America* (1994); and Robert Pruter, *Doowop: The Chicago Scene* (1996).

Cultural studies methodologies have been applied to rock music with varying degrees of success. For example, academic jargon makes Lawrence Grossberg's *We Gotta Get Out of This Place: Popular Conservatism and Postmodern Culture* (1992) almost impenetrable, while George Lipsitz presents a more balanced and nuanced approach in works such as *Time Passages: Collective Memory and American Popular Culture* (1990).

There have been several excellent biographies of rock superstars. Jon Weiner focused on the connections between John Lennon and American history in *Come Together: John Lennon in His Time* (1991) and *Gimme Some Truth: The John Lennon FBI Files* (1999); Peter Guralnick has given us two excellent volumes about the King of Rock & Roll: *Last Train to Memphis: The Rise of Elvis Presley* (1994) and *Careless Love: The Unmaking of Elvis Presley* (1999). In *Scars of Sweet Paradise: The Life and Times of Janis Joplin* (1999), Alice Echols delved into the tragic career of one of rock's greatest female voices; John A. Jackson offered detailed looks at two of rock music's top promoters in *Big Beat Heat: Alan Freed and the Early Years of Rock & Roll* (1991) and *American Bandstand: Dick Clark and the Making of a Rock 'n' Roll Empire* (1997).

Other recent publications provide a useful starting point for scholars and students who want to study the historical and cultural significance of rock music. Anthologies such as *America's Musical Pulse: Popular Music in Twentieth-Century Society* (1992), edited by Kenneth Bindas, and *Present Tense: Rock & Roll and Culture* (1992), edited by Anthony DeCurtis, showcase various scholarly approaches to the music. The various *Billboard* lists compiled by Joel Whitburn (for example, *Joel*

Whitburn's Top Pop Albums, Pop Singles Annual, and *Top Pop Singles*) are essential. They provide comprehensive chart data for all the albums and singles that made the record charts during the rock & roll era.

Other general reference works are also useful. One of the most detailed encyclopedias is *The New Rolling Stone Encyclopedia of Rock & Roll* (1995), edited by Patricia Romanowski and Holly George-Warren. Several publications provide guides to the vast amount of writing about rock & roll: *The Literature of Rock, Vols. 1–3* (1981, 1986, and 1995), edited by Frank Hoffman and B. Lee Cooper; Paul Taylor's *Popular Music since 1955: A Critical Guide to the Literature* (1985); and Gary M. Krebs's *The Rock and Roll Reader's Guide: A Comprehensive Guide to Books by and about Musicians and Their Music* (1997). Also helpful to scholars are Joe Smith's *Off the Record: An Oral History of Popular Music* (1988); Paul D. Grushkin, *The Art of Rock: Posters from Presley to Punk* (1987); and Michael Ochs, *1000 Record Covers* (1996).

During the 1990s, the electronic media also began taking a more serious look at rock music. A ten-part series on the history of rock & roll, coproduced by the BBC and WGBH-TV in Boston, was broadcast on public television. Additional "rockumentaries" were syndicated on cable television.

National Public Radio (NPR) offered a weekly series about the history of rock music that was based on *That Old-Time Rock & Roll.* During the summer of 1993, I was in Ball State University's telecommunications building working on a distance education history class. I happened to run into Stewart Vanderwilt, the general manager of the university's public radio station. "Hey, Richard, how's it going?" he asked. "I just read your new book. It's interesting how you look at history through rock music."

Half-jokingly I replied, "Great, now when's Indiana Public Radio going to start programming some rock & roll instead of just classical music?"

Stewart grinned at me and said, "Funny you should ask. We recently did a survey that showed that the first thing our listeners want is news programming. After that, they want rock music. I'll bet that a show that takes the same approach as your book could attract a lot of listeners. Would you be interested in doing a program that analyzes rock as a reflection of 1950s and 1960s America?"

Vanderwilt didn't have to ask twice. I had been waiting for almost thirty years for someone to ask me that question. Shortly thereafter, Stan Sollars came aboard as producer and engineer, and within a few months our show—*Rock & Roll America*—was on the air locally. We did several specials on National Public Radio in 1995 and 1996. A year later, we signed on to do a weekly series for NPR. Broadcast across the United

States and throughout Europe (as well as in Guam at 3 A.M.), the show was a fixture on NPR for two seasons.

Rock & Roll America programs alternated among four basic approaches. Shows focused on specific performers, various rock styles, the music's history, or particular themes. The program enabled me to interview numerous artists, writers, and disc jockeys from rock & roll's first decade. Their comments underscored the connections between music and history. For example, on one show Pete Seeger explained to our listeners how "We Shall Overcome" became an anthem for the civil rights movement.[3] On another program, Brenda Lee discussed how the music industry's perceptions of women affected her early career, making it hard for her to have creative control over her music.[4] On still another show, Dion recalled the way rock & roll emerged from the rhythm & blues tradition and incorporated elements from country music and white pop.[5]

One of the more interesting interviews I did was with Pat Boone. Though most people don't realize it, he sold more records during the 1950s than any artist on the rock charts with the exception of Elvis Presley. Boone admitted that his cover versions of black rhythm & blues songs such as Little Richard's "Tutti Frutti" or Fats Domino's "Ain't That a Shame" were not as good as the originals. But he insisted that his covers helped open the doors for black artists in an era of segregation. "America [of the mid-1950s] wasn't ready for the earthiness of rock & roll," explained Boone. "There had to be some transition types and transition records. . . . [That's why] I've always referred to myself as the midwife of rock & roll."[6]

Rock & Roll America attracted many listeners on NPR in part because of the serious approach it took to the music. In agreeing to distribute the program, NPR's Andy Trudeau stated, "There is no doubt in my mind that this is exactly the type of program that public radio should be doing on the subject of American pop music of the 1950s through 1970s."[7] The show's executive producer, Stewart Vanderwilt, explained in *NPR Quarterly:* "Our question was, could we create a program that would take the musical genre [our audience] grew up with—and still listens to—and bring to it the same sense of context, perspective, entertainment, and inquiry that they expect from public radio? We aren't simply bringing rock & roll to public radio, we're bringing a public radio sensibility to rock & roll."[8]

By the time *Rock & Roll America* and other serious programs about rock music hit the airwaves in the 1990s, audiences were accustomed to the notion that rock music was worthy of study. Along with numerous scholarly books and articles on the subject, there were other indications that rock music had become mainstream in academia. The authoritative *Encyclopedia of American Social History,* edited by Mary Kupiec Cayton, Elliott J. Gorn, and Peter Williams, included a chapter on rock.[9] Courses on rock & roll history proliferated on college campuses across the country. Sessions devoted to the subject became commonplace at professional meetings of the Organization of American Historians, the American Studies Association, the Popular Culture Association, the American Culture Association, and other scholarly organizations. A journal—*Popular Music and Society*—was created to study the subject. And, rock music studies became a frequent topic of discussion in academia's leading newspaper, the *Chronicle of Higher Education.* The lead sentence in an article entitled "More Scholars Focus on Popular Music as a Key to Examining Culture and History" read: "These days, some of the hottest scholarly debates resound with the beats and melodies of popular music."[10]

Back in 1958, Danny and the Juniors had a Top 20 hit with a song called "Rock and Roll Is Here to Stay." It contained a prophetic line: "Rock and roll will always be, it'll go down in history."[11] Whether rock is still alive is debatable, but clearly the music *has* left its mark on American history. That's why so many academics—and I count myself among them—are interested in analyzing various rock performers, songs, and styles. We hope to unravel the complex ties linking the music, the audience, and the times.

My book *That Old-Time Rock & Roll* tries to place the music in its proper historical context. Unlike most histories of rock & roll, this one argues that the music represents consensus behavior as much as conflict in the 1950s and early 60s. Part 1 provides an overview of the birth and growth of rock & roll; part 2 demonstrates how early rock is linked to both the youth culture and the dominant culture of the Eisenhower/Kennedy era; and part 3 offers a historical encyclopedia of the top singers and songs of rock & roll's first decade. Not only does early rock & roll reveal how teenagers acted and thought, but it provides valuable glimpses of American society and culture in the 1950s and early 1960s. *That Old-Time Rock & Roll* demonstrates that analyzing rock music as a source of history can be both entertaining and informative. Or, as I used to say on my radio show, this is "history you can dance to."

Notes

1. John Kay interview with Richard Aquila, April 25, 1994.
2. Peggy March interview with Richard Aquila, February 10, 1995.
3. Pete Seeger interview with Richard Aquila, May 13, 1994.
4. Brenda Lee interview with Richard Aquila, October 17, 1995.
5. Dion interview with Richard Aquila, October 19, 1995.

6. Pat Boone interview with Richard Aquila, June 25, 1998.

7. Andy Trudeau quoted in "History You Can Dance To . . . ," *WFYI Members' Magazine* (May 1998).

8. Stewart Vanderwilt, "Rock and Roll on Public Radio? What'll Be Next?" *NPR Quarterly* (Summer 1998): 6.

9. Richard Aquila, "Rock Music," in *Encyclopedia of American Social History, Volume III,* ed. Mary Kupiec Cayton, Elliott J. Gorn, and Peter W. Williams (New York: Scribner's, 1993), pp. 1795–1810 .

10. "More Scholars Focus on Popular Music as a Key to Examining Culture and History," *Chronicle of Higher Education,* May 1, 1998, p. A16.

11. Danny and the Juniors, "Rock and Roll Is Here to Stay," music and lyrics by David White, c. 1958.

PART ONE

Rock & Roll's First Decade

1. The Rise of Rock & Roll

The first days of rock & roll have earned a special place in American popular cultural history. "Hound Dog," "Rock Around the Clock," "Peggy Sue," and other songs from that era have become pop music standards. Early stars such as Elvis Presley, Bill Haley, Chuck Berry, Rick Nelson, and Fats Domino have been enshrined in a Hall of Fame. Dick Clark and American Bandstand have become popular icons.

Yet despite the attention paid to rock & roll's first decade, nobody really knows the exact day the music was born. Rock & roll's success has cast a shroud of mystery and legend on its early years. Too many people now claim to be or to know the person who gave birth to the sound. Some trace the roots of rock & roll to the back-country ring shouts of Afro-American slaves. Others find rock prototypes in the "rocking and reeling" spirituals commonly heard in rural black churches of the 1920s and 1930s. Still others locate the roots of rock & roll in black music of the mid-1900s.[1] By then the words "rock" and "roll"—black slang for sexual intercourse—were popping up on numerous records, such as Roy Brown's "Good Rockin' Tonight" (1948), and the Ravens' "Rock All Night Long" (1948). Several songs, like the Boswell Sisters' "Rock and Roll" (1934), and Wild Bill Moore's "We're Gonna Rock, We're Gonna Roll" (1947), used the full phrase. And by the end of 1952, at least two, the Dominoes' "Sixty Minute Man" (1951), and the Clovers' "Ting-a-Ling" (1952), were using the term "rock & roll" to imply both sex and wild partying. (For additional examples, see List #45 in Part II of this book.)

All of these records belonged to a category of music generally known as "rhythm and blues" (R & B). Prior to World War II, record companies referred to blues-oriented songs by black artists as "race music." Even *Billboard*—the music industry's trade magazine—used the distinction for its black market sales chart. But by 1948, with the civil rights movement gaining momentum, the recording industry was embarrassed by the phrase and switched to other names like ebony, sepia, and rhythm and blues. Eventually rhythm and blues caught on as the description of music aimed at the black audience.

The new R & B sound, emphasizing wild singing, suggestive lyrics, and a loud back beat, attracted both black and white listeners. Charlie Gillett, a sociologist as well as noted rock authority, suggests that some whites were drawn to the new black sound because it was different. Unlike traditional white pop music, the R & B "vocal styles were harsh, the songs explicit, [and] the dominant instruments—saxophone, piano, guitar, drums—were played loudly and with an emphatic dance rhythm, the production of the records was crude. The prevailing emotion was excitement."[2]

No doubt the movement of large numbers of blacks to northern metropolitan areas like New York City, Chicago, Cleveland, Buffalo, and Detroit during and after World War II was also greatly responsible for the whites' discovery of rhythm and blues. As blacks migrated northward to jobs in industrial centers, they created new markets for the entertainment industry, particularly small, independent record companies (commonly called "indies") and tiny radio stations hoping to profit from the new audience. Though black performers still found it difficult to break into the segregated, predominantly white, popular music market, their rhythm and blues soon found the way to the radios of many dial-twisting white teenagers, who eagerly listened to the strange new sounds.

As a result, rhythm and blues continued to grow in popularity during the early 1950s. One of the most exciting records to appear was "Rocket 88," by the Ike Turner Band, featuring a lead vocal by Jackie Brenston who normally played sax. Because of its wild electric guitar and focus on cars, many rock experts consider this 1951 song one of the first rock & roll prototypes, despite the fact that it never made *Billboard's* best-selling pop record charts. The following year Fats Domino had a hit with "Going Home" and Lloyd Price released his classic "Lawdy Miss Clawdy."

This 1950s rhythm and blues sound, which later became associated with early rock & roll, soon dominated the R & B charts. Songs like Clyde McPhatter's "Money Honey" (1953), the Midnighters' sexually suggestive "Work with Me, Annie" (1954) and "Annie Had a Baby" (1954), followed by Etta James' equally suggestive reply, "Roll with Me, Henry" (1955), attracted millions of listeners, both black and white. One 1953 R & B record, the Orioles' "Crying in the Chapel," even crossed over to *Billboard's* list of pop singles.

Before long some whites in the music industry began to realize the commercial potential of the new music. In 1951, a white pop singer named Johnny Ray exploded onto the record charts with two R & B influenced hits, "The Little White Cloud That Cried" and "Cry."

Even more significant for the development of rock & roll was the conversion of Bill Haley, a former country and western singer with a group called the Saddlemen, to the new R & B sound. After changing his band's name to Bill Haley and His Comets, he began experimenting with rhythm and blues. Although he was not the only country artist tinkering with R & B (and probably not even the first), Haley became one of the most successful. Two of his early records included cover versions (i.e., imitations of the original black records) of "Rocket 88" and "We're Gonna Rock This Joint Tonight" (both in 1952). In 1953, Haley had his first national hit with "Crazy Man Crazy," which is sometimes considered the first rock & roll song to make *Billboard's* top pop records chart.

Bill Haley later recalled what motivated him to play rhythm and blues: "Around the early fifties the musical world was starved for something new. . . . I felt then that if I could take, say, a Dixieland tune and drop the first and third beats, and accentuate the second and fourth, and add a beat the listeners could clap to as well as dance this would be what they were after." He noted, "From that the rest was easy . . . take everyday sayings like 'Crazy Man Crazy' . . . and apply to what I have just said."[3]

White listeners found Haley's product fresh and intriguing. His music was a blend of black rhythm and blues and white country and western. Even his presentation was different: Haley, with a spit curl in the middle of his forehead and band members in flashy tuxedoes, seemed determined to give the audience a wild show. Like Kansas City's black jazz and blues musicians, they played solos while lying on their backs, jumped in the air, and played their instruments over their heads.

Another white who understood the high energy of the R & B sound was Alan Freed, a disc jockey at WJW in Cleveland, Ohio. Much of what has been written about Freed is distorted, sometimes even fabricated. He claimed to be the father of rock & roll, insisting he coined the phrase in 1951. But the term, as mentioned earlier, had been around in rhythm and blues music since at least the 1930s. (See List #45.) Yet, even if Freed did not invent the phrase "rock & roll," he certainly did much to popularize it.

Exactly when he was turned on to the new R & B sound is debatable. Freed insisted he was an R & B fan by the early 1950s and began to use the phrase "rock & roll" in 1951, which, if true, would substantiate his claim of being the father of rock. But most evidence indicates that Freed didn't pay much attention to the new sound until 1952, by which time many whites, including Bill Haley, were listening to rhythm and blues.

In early 1952, Freed was approached by Leo Mintz, a Cleveland record store owner who told him white teenagers were eagerly buying up all the black R & B records they could get. Freed went to Mintz's store to see for himself, and later described the scene: "I heard the tenor saxophones of Red Prysock and Big Al Sears. I heard the blues-singing, piano-playing Ivory Joe Hunter. I wondered. I wondered for about a week. Then I went to the station manager and talked him into permitting me to follow my classical program with a rock 'n' roll party."[4]

Even though Mintz later insisted Freed wasn't as enthusiastic as he claimed, Freed's importance should not be underestimated. He was the right man at the right moment. He called his show "The Moon Dog Show," later changing it to "The Moon Dog House Rock 'n' Roll Party" (after Todd Rhodes' record, "Blues for Moon Dog"). He was perfect for the "new" unconventional sound. More traditional disc jockeys must have been appalled as Freed howled at the records, screamed along with the music, and banged out a beat with his fists.

Arnold Shaw, who at the time was in the music business and knew Freed, remembers: "Freed possessed the personality, the command of jive talk and even the voice to become its [rock & roll's] supersalesman. An operation on his vocal chords to remove a polyp left him with a gritty hoarseness that made him sound like a blues shouter."[5]

Freed helped popularize the new R & B sound, which he renamed rock & roll, thereby creating a new image for whites who no longer equated it with the old "race music." This in turn got the music played on white radio stations which would not play "race music." Freed and the "new" rock & roll sound were off and running. Both achieved national recognition when Freed's show became syndicated, and he was hired by WINS radio in New York City. Other rock & roll disc jockeys were soon popping up on radio stations across the country. One of the best was George "Hound Dog" Lorenz on WKBW radio in Buffalo, New York. The Hound, a white disc jockey, broadcast live from the ZanziBar, a black lounge, and introduced thousands of white teenagers to the rhythm and blues sound, while howling, "Don't you worry, cats, for the Hound's around . . . Ah oooh, ooh, ooooh!" Lorenz reached a large audience all along the eastern seaboard on WKBW's 50,000 watt radio broadcasts. A Hound Dog fan club and newsletter emerged as testimony to his great popularity.

The radio waves signaled changes in the musical winds. While the so-called "Negro Market" comprised only 5.7 percent of total record sales by late 1953, some major record companies took notice as rhythm and blues and its hybrid offspring, rock & roll, gained momentum in 1954.

A black R & B group, the Crows, broke onto the *Billboard* pop charts early in 1954 with their song "Gee." They were followed shortly thereafter by the Chords' "Sh-Boom" (1954), the first authentic R & B song to make *Billboard's* top ten records chart. Other songs in 1954 like the Midnighters' "Annie Had a Baby," Johnny Ace's "Pledging My Love," and Joe Turner's "Shake, Rattle, and Roll" also attracted a large white audience. To no one's surprise, in April 1954 *Billboard* announced in a special report that "the R & B field has caught the ear of the nation."

Major record companies soon recognized the potential market for R & B songs. Usually their response was to get a white pop singer (with absolutely no rhythm and blues background) to cover the original R & B hit in a more familiar manner, supposedly making it more acceptable to the white audience. For example, as soon as the Chords' "Sh-Boom" hit the record charts, Mercury Records released the Crew Cuts' sanitized, white pop version, which zoomed into the Top 10 within a week.

The pattern was established. Every time a black R & B song on an "indie" hit the charts, it was quickly covered by a white pop performer for a large record company. (For examples of cover records, see List #46.)

The white artists' cover versions were commercial successes for several reasons. For one thing, their versions generally were more acceptable sounding to many whites, who were accustomed to a traditional, white, pop style. Their success also reflects the racism of the day—it was easier for white performers to sell records to the white audience. Also, the major recording companies, with better record distribution capabilities and elliptical connections to disc jockeys, pushed their covers over the originals released on small, independent labels.

Equally important was the fear that R & B records would be too sexually suggestive for the white audience. As a result, cover versions frequently "cleaned up" the lyrics of sexually explicit songs. For example, Etta James' 1955 record, "Roll with Me, Henry," which used the black slang word "roll" for sexual intercourse, became "Dance with Me, Henry," when covered by white pop star Georgia Gibbs in 1955.

Similar changes were made in "Shake, Rattle, and Roll," originally recorded in 1954 by R & B artist Joe Turner, and then covered by Bill Haley and His Comets that same year. Where Joe Turner sang, "Well, you wear low dresses, the sun comes shinin' through/ I can't believe my eyes that all this belongs to you," Bill Haley changed it to "You wear those dresses, your hair done up so nice/ You look so warm, but your heart is cold as ice." Haley simply omitted another suggestive verse sung by Turner: "I said over the hill, and way down underneath/ You make me roll my eyes, and then you make me grit my teeth."[6]

Many radio stations, owned and operated by whites, simply refused to play the rhythm and blues originals, due to economic, social, or cultural considerations. But they were willing to play the white cover versions. What the covers lacked in artistic integrity, they made up for in commercial success. But before long, listeners would want the real thing.

The consciousness of the potential rock audience was raised by a 1955 movie, *The Blackboard Jungle.* Frank Zappa, who became a top rock musician in the late 1960s, recalled, "When the titles flashed, Bill Haley and His Comets started blurching, 'One . . . Two . . . Three O'Clock . . . Four O'Clock Rock. . . .' It was the loudest sound kids had ever heard at that time. . . . Bill Haley . . . was playing the Teenage National anthem and he was LOUD. I was jumping up and down. *Blackboard Jungle,* not even considering that it had the old people winning in the end, represented a strange act of 'endorsement' of the teenage cause."[7]

Haley's song "Rock Around the Clock" (1955) was the vehicle that introduced numerous white youths to rock & roll music. Haley and His Comets had originally covered the R & B song in 1954, but the record went nowhere. When it resurfaced a year later as the theme for *Blackboard Jungle,* it rocketed into the Top 10, remaining there for 19 weeks. By the summer of 1955, rock & roll had arrived, as more radio stations began playing the new music and more R & B artists began selling records to the white teenage audience.

In 1956, the flood gates of popular music came crashing down before a rock tidal wave. Riding the crest were black performers like Chuck Berry, Fats Domino, and Little Richard, who had originally gotten their feet wet in rhythm and blues. And at their head was the man who would be king of rock—Elvis Presley.

Legend has it that in the early 1950s, Sam Phillips, the white owner of Sun Records in Memphis, remarked, "If I could only find a white man who had the negro sound and the negro feel I could make a million dollars." Shortly thereafter a young country boy named Elvis Aaron Presley wandered into the Sun studio to record a song for his mother's birthday present. The rest, as they say in the music business, is history. Presley made Phillips a prophet, and in the process changed the course of American popular music.

Although certainly not the first white country and western performer to sing rhythm and blues, Elvis was the first to successfully blend the raw emotions of R & B with the instruments and feel of country music. Between 1956 and 1958, Presley had the number one record in 45 out of 104 weeks. And before the decade was out, Elvis had indeed become the undisputed king of rock & roll with 18 records that sold one million copies each.[8]

Unlike earlier whites who had recorded black rhythm and blues, Elvis' style was not mere imitation. He had grown up listening to black Mississippi blues singers like Big Bill Broonzy and Big Boy Crudup, and developed a real feel for the music. Rock critic Charlie Gillett insists that Presley "evolved a personal version of this [R & B] style, singing high and clear, breathless and impatient, varying his rhythmic emphasis with a confidence and inventiveness that were exceptional for a white singer. The sound suggested a young man celebrating freedom."[9]

With Elvis leading the way, rock & roll soon established itself as the younger generation's popular music. The media did much to popularize the new sound. Newspapers and magazines did features on rock & roll. Radio promoted the new sound as a way to attract new listeners. Following Alan Freed's lead, disc jockeys developed wild, fast-paced banter to keep pace with the vibrant, new music. "Personality Jocks" like Dick Biondi, Cousin Brucie, Perry Allen, Arnie "Woo Woo" Ginsberg, and Hunter Hancock emerged as the pied pipers of the rock generation. Eventually the rise of Top 40 radio, or sometimes even Top 20, where only the top hits were played over and over again, caught on, lessening the deejay's role. But in the beginning, radio disc jockeys were the high priests for the cult developing around the music.

Television was equally important in popularizing rock & roll. Variety shows hosted by Steve Allen and Ed Sullivan helped introduce Elvis Presley and other rock stars to their audiences. Situation comedies also showcased rock & roll to boost ratings. By 1957, "The Adventures of Ozzie and Harriet" reserved a block of time in each week's episode for Ricky Nelson to sing his latest hit. "The Donna Reed Show," following Nelson's lead, brought in Jimmy Darren to sing his new release, "Good-Bye, Cruel World" (1961), and encouraged regulars Shelley Fabares and Paul Petersen to record pop rock hits of their own. The new music benefited from this exposure. The publicity boosted record sales and polished rock & roll's image. As young and old viewers alike watched Ricky Nelson and other clean-cut teenagers singing on TV in their own living rooms, they became convinced that rock & roll was not that bad after all.

The most influential TV show of all was Dick Clark's "American Bandstand," which premiered on ABC-TV on August 5, 1957.[10]

Critics in recent years have been unkind to Dick Clark. Many claim that he hurt early rock by pushing a homogenized, mass-produced imitation rock & roll, which sometimes has been characterized as schlock-rock or wimp-rock. Others have blasted him for being the quintessential huckster, whose sole purpose in life was to push snake oil remedies for acne or athlete's foot.

Unfortunately this image obscures Clark's extremely significant role in the early days of rock & roll. "American Bandstand," during the late 1950s, was one of the most important vehicles for popularizing rock & roll. Its format was simple. Clark introduced the hit records of the day, and high school kids mostly from South Philadelphia, where the show originated, danced to the music. He usually brought in two guest performers per show who lip-synced their current hits, talked about their careers, and then signed autographs for the kids. Later Clark added dance contests, theme shows, and record reviews, where teens rated new songs ("I give it a 90, it's got a good beat you can dance to.") He even sold mail-order yearbooks so viewers at home could relive the various happenings on the show.

"Bandstand" quickly became one of the hottest shows on TV. Every day nationwide, teenagers rushed home from school to watch their favorite singers and learn new rock & roll dance steps. Before long, "Bandstand" dancers became folk heroes in their own right. As viewers watched them day after day, they got to know the dancers' names; they copied their clothing and hairstyles; they mimicked their "cool" behavior; and they kept track of who was dancing with whom. Some dancers even had their own fan clubs. Viewers identified with couples like Arlene Sullivan and Ken Rossi or Justine Corelli and Bob Clayton. And they paid special attention whenever the camera focused on the "Bandstand" regulars. The show became a live soap opera: would Carol be dancing with Joe today? Did you see Carmen's new sweater? Why aren't Bob and Justine dancing together? Did they really break up? Did you notice Pat's new dance step?

Such strong identification with the "Bandstand" regulars made teen viewers feel like they, too, belonged to this new exclusive club—a subculture based on youth and rock & roll. And by tuning in Clark every afternoon at 3 P.M., teenagers nationwide could attend, if not in person then at least by television hookup, the daily meeting of their peer group.

The critics were right when they said Clark played mostly a softer brand of rock & roll. But it certainly was not all just middle-of-the-road rock. Dick Clark played all the big hits; he brought in black performers to play for the white audience; and his Boy Scout leader looks, coupled with the clean-cut image of his teenage dancers (who were instructed to wear skirts and dresses or coats and ties,) made rock & roll seem safer and less rebellious to both adult and adolescent viewers. In short, Dick Clark and "American Bandstand" broadened the base for rock & roll, and in the process made it more popular than ever before. (For additional information about the relationship between television and rock & roll, see List #33a.)

Full-length motion pictures also contributed to the rising popularity of rock & roll.[11] Some, like *Rock Around the Clock* and *Don't Knock the Rock*, were just "B" movies that showcased as many rock singers as possible. Others, like Elvis Presley's *Love Me Tender, Jailhouse Rock,* or *King Creole,* were relatively big-budget rock & roll movies. Still others tried to cash in on rock trends, such as the Annette Funicello and Frankie Avalon surf movies or films about the twist, e.g., *Twist Around the Clock* (1961) or *Don't Knock the Twist* (1962).

These movies, whatever their quality, served several important functions. They helped shape the public's image of the new music. Some films like *Blackboard Jungle* emphasized rebellious images of youth, sparking territorial, class, or race riots among young viewers. Many adults were appalled at these alleged rock & roll juvenile delinquents. Others were not so alarmed. One news reporter, for example, described a riot in New Jersey as "feverish though harmless."[12]

Most films helped rather than hurt rock & roll's image. Rock performers were usually portrayed as clean-cut American youths, who were simply trying to have fun with their new sound. These movies maintained that rock & rollers were not into drugs, alcohol, or any other un-American activities. Parents were reassured by Frankie Lymon and the Teenagers singing in one film, "I Am Not a Juvenile Delinquent," and by Elvis Presley following the righteous path toward success in *Jailhouse Rock.*

Rock movies also linked rock & roll to the emerging youth culture. By focusing on teen songs and lifestyles, the films contributed to teenagers' feelings of solidarity and made teens feel that their music and culture set them apart from the older generation.

In addition, rock films provided a commercial vehicle to promote rock & roll. They spotlighted performers and their hit records, and allowed many fans who were unable to attend concerts to view rock & rollers on the large screen. (For a list of rock movies, see List #33b.)

2. Rock Styles

During the first decade of rock & roll (1954–1963), three main types of rock music were evident: R & B rock, country rock, and pop rock. Each broad style could, of course, be subdivided into additional categories based on sound, regional variation, or some other distinguishing characteristic. For example, R & B rock included raw, gospel-tinged soul music, as well as polished, pop-sounding motown music. And the R & B rock produced in New Orleans sounded quite different from the R & B rock performed in Chicago. Similarly, the Detroit sound was easily distinguishable from the Philadelphia sound. But, significantly, they all shared a common thread: they were descendents of black rhythm and blues. Put another way, they all belonged to the same musical family. The same is true for the other early rock styles. Despite their individual differences, the performers within each broad category had more in common with each other than they did with those outside their musical family.

Each of the three main styles—R & B rock, country rock, and pop rock—was a variation of the new idiom, rock & roll. It mixed ingredients from rhythm and blues, country and western, and traditional white pop to form a blend that would appeal to teenagers. Within each style performers ranged from talented to untalented, folk to pop, artists to mere imitators. Their recordings spanned a similar spectrum. Some were highly original, with an aesthetic or folk quality that appealed to serious listeners. Others were just quick attempts to cash in on a popular sound and lacked any artistic integrity or value. If taste is a personal matter, then "good" or "bad" music could be found within each style, depending upon one's criteria.

The first style, *R & B rock*, had close ties to traditional rhythm and blues. Many R & B rockers—artists like Fats Domino, Lloyd Price, Bo Diddley, Chuck Berry, the Drifters, and the Coasters—had started their careers in the rhythm and blues field and were influenced by R & B greats like Louis Jordan, Robert Johnson, Howlin' Wolf, or Muddy Waters. (For additional examples of R & B rock performers, see List #1.) When they crossed over to rock, they took their musical stylings with them. R & B rock, like rhythm and blues, featured blues progressions, loud drums accenting a 2–4 beat, and R & B styled combos of honkers and shouters. Vocalists often shouted their lyrics over the constant musical riffs supplied by guitars, bass, drums, and honking tenor saxophones. R & B rockers also utilized the call-and-response pattern commonly found in rhythm and blues, and incorporated gospel harmonies and influences into their music.

Although R & B rock lyrics usually were more pop-oriented and less blatantly sexual than rhythm and blues lyrics, little else was lost in the transition. The new approach still featured the vernacular language, unsophisticated production work, primitive beats, and jive or "cool cat" sound which had given rhythm and blues its original vitality. One variation, doo wop, even continued the street corner harmony sound using human voices to mimic the sounds of instruments. R & B rock was a product of changing demographics. The movement of blacks to northern urban areas helped spawn the music, while the growing acceptance of blacks in society helped popularize it.

Country rock, also called rockabilly, was the second basic rock style. It grew from the field of country and western music, producing country rockers like Elvis Presley, Carl Perkins, Johnny Cash, Jerry Lee Lewis, the Everly Brothers, and Buddy Holly. (See also List #2.) These rockabilly artists, weaned on the sounds of Hank Williams, Lefty Frizzell, Roy Acuff, and other Grand Ole Opry stars, used their country and western musical backgrounds to modify black rhythm and blues.

Country rockers borrowed freely from rhythm and blues. The singers used the shouting style and call-and-response patterns found in R & B, while the musicians played continuously behind the lead singer, emphasizing the second and fourth beat of every measure (unlike traditional white pop which accented beats one and three). Many country rock songs also featured blues progressions, as well as the slurred vocals, lyrics, and jargon associated with rhythm and blues.

But rockabilly artists were not simply imitating the black sound. They added their own touches to the music. Art historian Carl Belz explains that country and western artists who crossed over to rock music "used the beat of the older country generation which was much lighter and quicker than the rhythm and blues beat. In addition, the younger generation kept alive the tradition of the guitar as a folk instrument." Many country rockers also relied on country-inspired vocals and harmonies. For example, both Elvis Presley and Buddy Holly made extensive use of vocal slides, vibratos, glottal stops, and other vocal tricks used by country singers like Hank Williams. The Everly Brothers, on the other hand, relied on pure, Appalachian-style harmonies for their country rock sound. In short, country rock was a hybrid of black rhythm and blues and white country and western. It was, in the words of Carl Perkins, "blues with a country beat."[13]

The new style typified the racial melting pot of southern culture and reflected America's changing society. Just as Brown v. Topeka Board of Education had helped desegregate public schools, country rock was now desegregating the music industry. Well-crafted country rock, with its blend of white country and western and black rhythm and blues, had a true folk quality that set it apart from the homogenized Tin Pan Alley kitsch of the day.

The third type of rock & roll, *pop rock,* was performed mostly by young, white artists influenced by R & B rock, rockabilly, and traditional pop. At its best, pop rock produced high quality rock & roll. It was derivative, without being merely imitative. It borrowed from R & B rock and country rock, yet lended its youthful outlook and vitality. Whether it was Ricky Nelson's southern California brand of rockabilly; Gene Pitney's power pop; the Beach Boys' pop-style harmonies; Dion and the Belmonts' pop-influenced doo wop; or some other pop rock stylist's version of R & B rock, country rock, or traditional pop, well-done pop rock captured the true spirit of rock & roll. It was interpretive and artistic. And like country rock with its southern roots, or R & B rock with its black roots, this brand of pop rock had an authentic folk quality. It was the music of white urban and suburban neighborhoods, "cool" but not overly rebellious, and in tune with white teenage culture.

Less interpretive and artistic was the pop rock style of performers such as Pat Boone, Frankie Avalon, Connie Francis, and other young pop singers who were closer to the Tin Pan Alley stylings of 1940s and 1950s crooners like Perry Como, Eddie Fisher, or Vic Damone. Their records, although sometimes very well produced, lacked the authentic folk quality generally associated with country rock, R & B rock, or interpretive pop rock. They were usually mere imitations of what adult record producers and writers thought rock & roll should sound like. But many members of the rock audience accepted them anyway, since these pop rock artists were young (and therefore part of the baby boom generation), and were singing songs aimed at teen interests and emotions. (For examples of pop rock performers, see List #3.)

Nowadays, the widely accepted belief is that rock & roll was dead artistically by the early 1960s. Some critics have referred to the period 1960–1963 as the years of schlock rock, lamenting that authentic rock & roll was no longer produced. But in reality, all three rock styles continued into the early 1960s, and were just as vital as ever.

Country rock may have suffered the most, as many important artists disappeared from the charts. Buddy Holly died in 1959. Jerry Lee Lewis dropped from view after marrying his 13-year-old distant cousin. Elvis Presley went into the army and came out singing pop

1. Billboard Hot 100 (Courtesy of *Billboard Magazine*)

2. 1954 Fess Parker's portrayal of Davy Crockett on Walt Disney's TV series sparked Crocketmania among young baby boomers. (Courtesy of *Broadcasting Magazine*)

3. 1954 McDonald's began selling its fifteen-cent hamburgers nationally (Courtesy of McDonald's Corporation)

4. 1954 Atomic bomb blast (National Archives)

5. 1955 Pat Boone on Columbia University campus where he was a student (National Archives)

6. 1955 Suburbs, like this one in California, featured nearly identical houses (National Archives)

7. 1956 Little Richard (Courtesy of Vee Jay Records)

8. 1956 Elvis Presley (Courtesy of RCA Records)

9. 1956 President
Dwight D. Eisenhower
(National Archives)

10. 1956 Carl Perkins
(Courtesy of Sun Rec-
ords)

11. 1956 TV's popular "Howdy Doody Show" featured (from left to right) Clarabell, Flub-a-Dub, Howdy Doody, and Buffalo Bob Smith (National Archives)

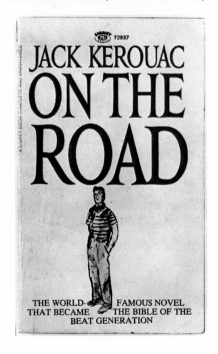

12. 1957 Paperback cover of Jack Kerouac's *On the Road*, which had great impact on the emerging youth culture (Ball State University Photo Service)

13. 1957 Annette and other Mickey Mouse Club Mouseke-
teers became quite popular among baby boomers (© Walt
Disney Productions: Courtesy of *Broadcasting Magazine*)

14. 1957 Edsel automobile (Library of Congress)

15. 1958 Chuck Berry (Courtesy of MCA Records)

16. 1958 The caption on this Ross Lewis cartoon read, "So Russia launched a satellite, but has it made cars with fins yet?" (Courtesy of Milwaukee Public Library)

17. 1958 TV's "77 Sunset Strip" starred Efrem Zimbalist Jr., Edd "Kookie" Byrnes, and Roger Smith (Courtesy of *Broadcasting Magazine*)

18. 1958 Dick Clark and the Top Ten (Courtesy of *Broadcasting Magazine*)

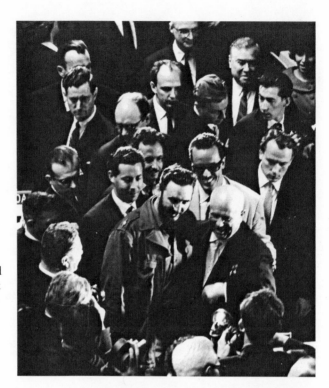

19. 1959 Castro and Khrushchev meet at the United Nations (Library of Congress)

20. 1959 "The Many Loves of Dobie Gillis," a popular situation comedy, starred Dwayne Hickman (right) as Dobie and Bob Denver as his beatnik friend, Maynard G. Krebs (Courtesy of *Broadcasting Magazine*)

21. 1959 Barby doll with original pronged stand (Courtesy of Mattel)

22. 1959 Buddy Holly died in a 1959 plane crash. This is Holly (top row) and his original group, the Crickets (bottom row, left to right: Joe B. Mauldin, Jerry Allison, Niki Sullivan) (Courtesy of MCA Records)

23. 1960 Original cast of the TV sitcom "My Three Sons"; from left to right: William Frawley, Tim Considine, Don Grady, Fred MacMurray, Stanley Livingston (Courtesy of *Broadcasting Magazine*)

24. 1960 U-2 plane like the one piloted by Gary Francis Powers (Department of Defense)

25. 1960
John F. Kennedy
–Richard M.
Nixon Presiden-
tial Debate
(Library of Con-
gress)

26. 1961 President and
Mrs. John F. Kennedy
(National Archives)

27. 1961 "Mr. Ed" was a TV sitcom that featured a talking horse and his owner, Wilbur Post (Alan Young) (Courtesy of *Broadcasting Magazine*)

28. 1961 Roger Maris broke Babe Ruth's home run record, hitting 61 in '61 (Courtesy of *Sporting News*)

29. 1962 Polaris missile fired from submarine (Department of Defense)

30. 1962 "The Adventures of Ozzie and Harriet" (starring, from bottom, Ricky, Ozzie, Harriet, and David Nelson (Courtesy of *Broadcasting Magazine*)

31. 1962 Astronaut John Glenn (Library of Congress)

32. 1963 Martin Luther King Jr. at March on Washington (National Archives)

33. 1963 Civil Defense poster reflected Cold War fears (Courtesy of the Mark Charles Fissel Archives)

34. 1963 Mrs. John F. Kennedy and her children with Robert F. Kennedy at President Kennedy's funeral (National Archives)

oriented middle-of-the-road songs like "It's Now or Never" (1960) and "Fame and Fortune" (1960). Carl Perkins, after a serious automobile crash, was unable to follow up on his rock classic, "Blue Suede Shoes" (1956).

Yet country rock as a style survived in grand fashion. The Everly Brothers continued their success with several impressive hits like "Let It Be Me" (1960), "When Will I Be Loved?" (1960), "Cathy's Clown" (1960), "Walk Right Back" (1961), and "Crying In the Rain" (1962). Roy Orbison achieved new highs for country rock with records such as "Only the Lonely" (1960), "Running Scared" (1961), "Crying" (1961), "Candy Man" (1961), and "Oh, Pretty Woman" (1964). Wanda Jackson had the phenomenal "Let's Have a Party" (1960). Conway Twitty chipped in with "Lonely Blue Boy" (1960) and "C'est Si Bon" (1961). Brenda Lee had a string of hits, including "I'm Sorry" (1960), "Dum Dum" (1961), and the hauntingly beautiful "All Alone Am I" (1962). In addition, a new wave of country artists like Bill Anderson, Jim Reeves, Marty Robbins, Don Gibson, Patsy Cline, Bobby Bare, and Skeeter Davis began crossing over to the rock charts.

R & B rock, likewise, thrived during the alleged dog days of rock & roll. Though many of the earlier stars like Jesse Belvin, Chuck Berry, the Platters, the Chords, the Coasters, Lloyd Price, Fats Domino, and Little Richard faded away, they were replaced by vigorous new talents such as James Brown, Dee Clark, Sam Cooke, the Drifters, Marvin Gaye, the Impressions, Ben E. King, Major Lance, the Miracles, Mary Wells, the Shirelles, the Ronettes, the Marvelettes, and Martha and the Vandellas, to name just a few.

In fact, some of the greatest R & B rock hits of all time came from this so-called schlock rock period: classics like Barrett Strong's "Money" (1960); the Miracles' "Shop Around" (1960) and "You've Really Got a Hold On Me" (1962); the Marvelettes' "Please Mr. Postman" (1961); the Shirelles' "Will You Love Me Tomorrow" (1960); Arthur Alexander's offbeat "You Better Move On" (1962) and "Anna" (1962); the Isley Brothers' "Twist and Shout" (1962); Gene Chandler's "Duke of Earl" (1962); Stevie Wonder's "Fingertips, Pt. 2" (1963); Jimmy Soul's "If You Wanna Be Happy" (1963); Gary U.S. Bonds' raucous "Quarter to Three" (1961) and "New Orleans" (1960); Ben E. King's "Spanish Harlem" (1961) and "Stand By Me" (1961); and Ray Charles' "Georgia On My Mind" (1960), "Hit the Road, Jack" (1961), "I Can't Stop Loving You" (1962), and "You Don't Know Me" (1962).

Pop rock also flourished during the early 1960s. Rick Nelson put out top caliber records like "Travelin' Man" (1961), "Hello Mary

Lou" (1961), and "Down Home" (1963). Gene Pitney demonstrated remarkable range with hits such as "Every Breath I Take" (1961), "Town Without Pity" (1961), "The Man Who Shot Liberty Valence" (1962), and "Only Love Can Break a Heart" (1962). Dion did the classic "Runaround Sue" (1961), and then followed up with numerous other top rockers. Little Peggy March contributed "I Will Follow Him" (1963). The Kingsmen scored big with "Louie Louie" (1963). Del Shannon had "Runaway" (1961) and "Little Town Flirt" (1962). He also became the first American to record a Lennon-McCartney composition, "From Me To You" (1963). Other outstanding pop rock was contributed by the Beach Boys, Leslie Gore, Paul Anka, Bobby Vee, Neil Sedaka, Johnny Tillotson, and Jan and Dean.

As can be seen, rock & roll was still going strong in the early 1960s, reflecting the values, interests, and optimism of teenagers. The music didn't change until its listeners did. And that didn't happen until a tragic day in Dallas in 1963. The bullets that killed President John F. Kennedy on November 22 also shattered the ideals and dreams of many youths. Across the nation, teenagers mourned the tragic death of the man who symbolized the zestful enthusiasm of the American Dream. For many, Kennedy's assassination brought a sudden end to childhood. Teenagers had lost their innocence.[14] After 1963, American youths changed, and so did their music. As the baby boomers began questioning their society and culture, rock & roll was bombarded by forces unleashed by the Beatles and Bob Dylan. And neither American youths nor their music would ever be the same again.

Rock & roll records remain to remind us what life was like in America before Kennedy's assassination. Songs from the three rock styles, *country rock*, *R & B rock*, and *pop rock*, though differing in quality and artistic integrity, are valuable sources of social and cultural history. They all reflected and influenced the beliefs, values, and actions of their listeners.

Similarly, other types of music on the rock & roll charts in the period 1954–1963 were important. Traditional pop, jazz, and country and western, as represented by the records of Frank Sinatra, Andy Williams, Dave Brubeck, and Marty Robbins, sold well to the young audience, showing that teenagers often shared the tastes, dreams, and values of older listeners. And the pop folk stylings of the Kingston Trio, Peter, Paul, and Mary, and the Brothers Four, to name just a few, rapidly gained popularity during these years as the young audience grew older, more sophisticated, and more in step with the idealistic messages of Kennedy's New Frontier. (For specific examples of non-rock & roll performers on the rock charts, see List #4.)

3. Rock & the Baby Boom Generation

In the 1950s and early 1960s, rock & roll belonged almost exclusively to teenagers. Songs like Chuck Berry's "Rock & Roll Music" or Danny and the Juniors' "Rock & Roll Is Here to Stay" reminded youths that rock was their music. They were the rock & roll generation.

They were also the vanguard of the baby boom generation, a demographic bulge in America's population figure. The baby boom began at the end of World War II and continued unabated until 1964. Before it was over, about 76.5 million babies were born, totaling approximately one-third of America's population. The boom was sparked by soldiers hurrying to father babies before rushing off to war; continued by returning vets trying to make up for lost time; and fed by post-war prosperity and a renewed faith in America's future.[15]

By the 1950s, the baby boom generation had emerged as a distinct segment of American society. 1950s teenagers were unique. They were the first generation to be raised on television. They stayed in school for more years than other generations. They were kept in limbo between childhood and adulthood for a longer period. They were taught by progressive educators that they were unique individuals. They grew up in a permissive culture with Freudian psychology and Dr. Spock stressing the importance of childhood. They (or at least their parents) had money, so special products were aimed at them. Their youth was praised by elders accustomed to thinking that technology had made anything "old" obsolete. And they functioned freely, due to increased mobility, changing housing patterns, and the breakdown of the community and the nuclear family.[16]

The baby boom generation certainly was not the first to think it was special. But its sheer numbers and unique qualities provided convincing evidence others lacked. The baby boomers were linked by more than just time and space. They shared a common heritage and destiny, molded by similar historical problems, and shaped by similar experiences, influences, hopes, and dreams.

Rock & roll emerged in the 1950s as the music of the baby boom generation. The cultural role it played was not unusual, for popular music often serves as a means to group identity. British writer Richard Mabey explained that pop music is "concerned with participation, with parties, dances, outings, demonstrations, and any other social gatherings where camaraderie and simple shared emotions are important. . . . The music, in fact, acts as a further binding force on the group, and the observed responses of the other members are a way of clarifying your own."[17]

Other writers likewise have stressed the social and cultural significance of pop music. Sociologist R. Serge Denisoff argued that popular music is a cultural artifact shared by members of a subculture, concluding, "The designation of popular music is more a sociological than a musical definition."[18]

This sociological approach clearly applies to rock & roll, which became a boundary marker for the new youth culture (and its various subcultures) in the 1950s and early 1960s.

The baby boomers rightfully perceived rock & roll as a distinct type of music, perfect for their unique generation. Rock & roll did not sound like traditional pop music. It was more raw and primitive, usually played by small combos featuring guitars, drums, and saxophones. And, significantly, it had a beat kids could dance to. That beat gave rock a special, identifiable sound. Rock & roll, like its forerunner rhythm and blues, stressed the second and fourth beats of a measure, unlike traditional pop music which stressed the first and third beats. Rock also made use of the rhythm and blues' boogie and shuffle (featuring wailing blues notes in the melody and a rolling eight-note figuration in the bass).[19]

Some rock & roll from the 1950s and early 1960s used the expressive vocals and raw emotions associated with rhythm and blues. Other times, vocals by adolescent voices gave the records their identifiable sound. Rock performers also borrowed the rhythm and blues technique of using human voices to serve as musical instruments, establishing a distinct sound known as doo wop. On the 1958 hit record "Get a Job," the Silhouettes sing in doo wop style: "Sha da da da, Sha da da da da/ Yip yip yip yip, yip yip yip yip/ Mum mum mum mum/ Get a job."[20]

Kids did not have to define rock & roll. They knew it when they heard it. As art historian Carl Belz pointed out, "The most persistent feature of rock has been its beat . . . [but] as in the case of jazz, any listener who wants rock defined specifically is probably unable to recognize it."[21]

The new music provided a means to teen solidarity. It gave teens their own dance steps, their own songs, their own nostalgic common past, and their own musical heroes. Rock highlighted the age gap between teenagers and adults, and dealt expressly with the teenage experience. As the baby boomers' music, rock mirrored teen pop culture. There were records about the youths' social lives, buying habits, slang, names, and fads, as well as songs about other teen activities. (For specific examples, see Lists #5–25.)

The rock culture often extended beyond the lyrics. In some cases, the medium was the message. Rock & roll was the music of youth, and the performers were usually just as young as the audience. That provided the music with, at the very least, the appearance of being a folk form. Listeners assumed the performers were speaking directly to them, and for them, because they were all members of the baby boom generation, supposedly sharing similar experiences and values.

The rock culture fed upon itself. Original hit versions of songs became the definitive ones, and listeners cheered performers whose live performances duplicated their original recordings. Teens also made a game out of "their" music. Rock & roll fans quizzed each other about song titles and artists: "Who sang 'Ya Ya'?" (Answer: Lee Dorsey.) "What song is this line from? 'He rocks in the tree tops all night long.'" (Answer: "Rockin' Robin" by Bobby Day.) Teens focused on details: "What label did Ricky Nelson sing most of his hits on?" (Answer: Imperial.) And novices were separated from the pros: "What color was the label Ricky Nelson sang on?" (Answer: usually black, with silver writing and red and yellow striped lines. The more you knew about rock & roll, the more secure was your membership in the rock generation.

Rock & roll, with its sound, styles, and culture (including fashions, hairstyles, dances, etc.), helped promote generational solidarity. This does not mean the rock generation had a monolithic culture. Far from it. Numerous subcultures existed within the youth culture. Like the rest of society, teens divided along economic, racial, cultural, religious, ethnic, and geographic lines. Some liked pop rock; others loved country rock; still others listened only to R & B rock. Sometimes rock & roll even became the locus of confrontation between disparate youth groups struggling for control of the music.[22] But these subcultures were all part of the larger youth culture which was quite distinct from the adult culture. And rock & roll music was one of the main boundaries separating the teenagers from adults.

The teenagers' preoccupation with music was not unusual in the 1950s and early 1960s. Throughout those years more adults than ever were listening to popular and classical music and attending concerts and operas.[23] Teenagers were merely following their parents' lead. But seeing themselves as a unique group, they wanted something different. Rock & roll filled the bill. With its distinctive beat, musical style, artists, hair styles, dance fads, fashion items, and adolescent themes, rock music gave teenagers a new self-image. No doubt, parents' attacks on rock & roll, calling it trash and senseless noise, contributed to the youths' solidarity. A common enemy often serves as a catalyst to bring unity to a community.

In short, rock & roll did much to bring the baby boomers together by making them feel they were a distinct social group, a new youth culture with particular characteristics. The music was "the sound track in the movie version of [the baby boomers'] lives," explained author Landon Y. Jones. "They discovered it, danced to it, romanced to it, went to college to it, got married to it, and someday will presumably be buried to it."[24]

Yet rock was no mere marker for the sociological boundaries of teen identity. It also echoed and shaped the youths' thoughts and actions.

4. Rock: Conflict or Consensus?

Almost from the moment it arrived on the cultural scene, rock & roll was linked to teenage rebellion. Some parents and segments of the establishment even believed the music was outright subversive. Theories about the threatening nature of rock & roll centered on its alleged ties to sexual promiscuity, drugs, miscegenation, perversion, communism, atheism, and criminal activities, as well as its total disregard for conventional mores and institutions. Disc jockeys were fired for playing rock records on the air; rock & roll records were smashed in public displays more than just slightly reminiscent of book burnings; laws were passed banning rock & roll parties; and rock songs like Bill Haley's "Rock Around the Clock" were used in movies depicting juvenile delinquency.[25]

Adult fear of rock & roll probably says more about the paranoia and insecurity of American society in the 1950s and early 1960s than it does about rock & roll. The same adults who feared foreigners because of the expanding Cold War, and who saw the Rosenbergs and Alger Hiss as evidence of internal subversion, often viewed rock & roll as a foreign music with its own sinister potential for corrupting American society.

For many teenagers, rock & roll was not a revolutionary force, nor the means to express generational conflict. It was merely their popular music, more a sign of consensus between the generations than of conflict. A careful analysis of early rock & roll shows that it usually supported and promoted the values and beliefs that dominated American culture in the 1950s and early 1960s.

This does not mean that there were no elements of rebelliousness and protest in rock music. Of course there were. The music's close ties to black rhythm and blues were a direct affront to segregationalist views of the era. The sexuality and uninhibited nature of the music were an assault on the conservative, strait-laced, button-down attitudes of the 1950s and early 1960s. And rock & roll songs like Link Wray's "Rumble" or Ivan's "Wild Child," along with rock dances and fashions, did challenge parental attitudes of propriety. Furthermore, if Marshall McLuhan was right—that the medium is the message—then for many teens rock's driving beat and blaring sound meant outright rebellion. This rebellious side of rock & roll undoubtedly sparked the growth of some teen subcultures which thrived on alienation. (For specific examples of songs that reflected rock's rebellious nature, see List #24.)

At the same time, however, the elements of acquiescence outweighed the elements of rebellion. Most teenagers' adherence to rock & roll music signifies their acceptance, not rejection, of society and culture during the 1950s and early 1960s. The music may have sounded strange to some adult ears, but its message should have sounded quite familiar.

The 1950s and early 1960s are generally viewed as a period of consensus and conformity in American history, an era marked by fears of communism and praise for traditional American values. Rock & roll's treatment of religion, the home, the family, and love of country frequently reflected the era's conservatism. Likewise, commonly-held American myths, folktales, and stereotypes abound in early rock & roll, as do contemporary middle-class rituals involving courtship, marriage, school, and cars.

Rock & roll, for example, reflected America's obsession with religion in the 1950s and early 1960s. The early years of rock coincided with the Cold War era, and for many people religion provided the logical shield against Godless communists. Religion was everywhere. There were billboards praising the Lord, drive-in churches in California, and *Time* and *Newsweek* covers about God and church. Sales of Bibles and other religious books skyrocketed. Hollywood cranked out movies like "The Robe" and "The Ten Commandments." And Congress added "under God" to the pledge of allegiance, as well as "In God We Trust" to our coins.[26]

While adults were watching Bishop Fulton J. Sheen or the Rev. Billy Graham on television, and setting records for church memberships, teenagers were listening to records dealing with God, heaven, and angels. Laurie London's "He's Got the Whole World In His Hands" (1958) assured youths that God was watching over them. Wink Martindale reminded listeners that God was present even on the gambling table in his 1959 song, "The Deck of Cards." Andy Williams sang about miracles in "The Village of St. Bernadette," a 1959 best-seller. Even Elvis, the king of rock & roll, paid homage to a greater king in "Peace in the Valley," a sacred album that reached number three on *Billboard's* record charts in 1957. Some songs, like the Platters' "My Prayer" (1956), Dion and the Belmonts' "A Lover's Prayer" (1959), or Annette's "Oh Dio Mio" (1960), focused on the power of prayer. Others, such as Pat Boone's "A Wonderful Time Up There" (1958), Mark Dinning's "Teen Angel" (1959), or J. Frank Wilson's "Last Kiss" (1964), reflected a firm belief in the afterlife. (For other songs dealing with religion, see List #26.)

Traditional value of home and family is also evident in early rock. "There's no place like home" was the theme of such hits as Pat

Boone's "I'll Be Home" (1956), Roy Orbison's "Blue Bayou" (1963), and Bobby Bare's "Detroit City" (1963). Positive reference to parents appears on such songs as Connie Francis' "Mama" (1960), Roy Orbison's "Mama" (1960) and Paul Petersen's "My Dad" (1962). (For additional examples, see List #27.)

Patriotic sentiments of the 1950s and early 1960s are likewise evident in teenage music. In 1959, as President Eisenhower had informal talks with the Soviet Union's Nikita Khrushchev and Vice President Nixon visited Moscow for an American exhibit, records like Connie Francis' "God Bless America" (1959), the Mormon Tabernacle Choir's "Battle Hymn of the Republic" (1959), and the Tassels' "To a Soldier Boy" (1959) hit the rock charts. By the early 1960s, with President Kennedy guiding the United States through new Cold War entanglements, the rock audience was listening to songs like Johnny Burnette's "God, Country, and My Baby" (1961), the Shirelles' "Soldier Boy" (1962), and Jimmy Dean's "P. T. 109" (1962). The patriotic fervor associated with President Kennedy's New Frontier might also help explain the tremendous popularity of a series of pro-American songs by country singer Johnny Horton. In the late 1950s and early 1960s, Horton hit the charts with records like "The Battle of New Orleans" (1959), "Sink the Bismarck" (1960), "Johnny Freedom" (1960), and "North to Alaska" (1960). His biggest hit, "The Battle of New Orleans," told the story of the common man soldiers who helped Andrew Jackson decisively defeat a British invasion of America during the War of 1812. The victory was one of the finest moments in American military history, and a source of pride for patriotic American teenagers.

Rock & roll itself was 99.9 percent pure American in those days. Usually only American singers made the charts. There were exceptions such as Lonnie Donegan, Rolf Harris, and a few others, but for the most part their hits were novelty records. Real rock & roll was reserved for American artists; foreign performers were viewed as mere imitators. This type of thinking reflected the patriotism of the day, and the generally accepted, ethnocentric notion that foreign products were vastly inferior to American ones. (For more on the relationship between rock music and American politics, see Lists #40–44.)

Rock music reflected traditional American values and beliefs in other ways. Early rock & roll heroes, for example, were very similar to other American heroes of the era. The quintessential teen idol was a white male, good looking, virile, athletic, self-made, honest, sensitive, shy, polite (particularly to his elders and teenage girls), and humble. He had to be cut from the same mold as Jack Armstrong, the All-American boy. Any rock & roller who did not fit that pattern (e.g., blacks, females, or anyone with what could be seen as a physical or character flaw) had a much harder time acquiring hero status.

Ricky Nelson and Elvis Presley were typical rock heroes. Ricky, as seen on TV's "The Adventures of Ozzie and Harriet," came from a middle-class family, looked up to Mom and Dad, played sports, was well-groomed, didn't drink or smoke, and always got the girl through his good looks, boyish charm, and singing ability.

Elvis Presley, despite his reputation as a rebel and loner, was really not that much different. He dressed well, though some parents considered his bright clothes outlandish, and his country-boy shyness, politeness, good looks, and muscles made him the Mickey Mantle of the rock world. Elvis' ties to the pantheon of traditional American heroes were recognized in Bill Parsons' 1958 hit, "The All American Boy," which recounted Elvis' Horatio Alger–like rise to stardom.

Other traditional myths involving the American West, classical figures, rags-to-riches stories, folk tales, or stories about mythical lands or exotic places were also common in rock & roll. (For specific examples, see Lists #28 and #29.)

Rock & roll mirrored common American stereotypes of the 1950s and early 1960s. For example, rock & roll girls were treated as second-class citizens, just as their counterparts in real life were subordinate in all ways to men. Rock songs commonly referred to females as objects of admiration and placed them on pedestals in songs like the Penguins' "Earth Angel" (1954), Johnny Tillotson's "Poetry In Motion" (1960), and Johnny Mastro's "Model Girl" (1961). Other rock & roll hits viewed girls as sex objects, e.g., Buddy Knox's "Party Doll" (1957), Eugene Church's "Pretty Girls Everywhere" (1958), and Eddie Hodges' "Girls Were Made to Love" (1962). Still others described girls as possessions, dependents, or passive objects, e.g., the Fireflies' "You Were Mine" (1959), the Duprees' "You Belong to Me" (1962), the Angels' "My Boyfriend's Back" (1963), and the Cascades' "Shy Girl" (1963). (For additional examples, see List #30a.)

In a similar fashion, stereotypes of males, Indians, regional characters, ethnic groups, and blacks found their way into early rock & roll. (For specific examples, see Lists #30b and #31.) These images show that rock & roll often reflected acceptance, rather than rejection, of middle-class beliefs.

Typical American rituals involving courtship, marriage, school, and automobiles also appear in 1950s and early 1960s rock music. A large percentage of rock songs dealt with teenage love and courtship. The rock & roll generation's version of romance differed little from that of earlier generations, as evidenced by such songs as Paul Anka's "Put Your Head on My Shoulder" (1959), the Danleers' "One Summer Night (We Fell in Love)" (1958), or Cathy Carr's "First Anniversary" (1959). (See also List #16.) And just as older generations had sung about girls like "Marie" and "Laura," rock & rollers had their counterparts in the Crescendos' "Oh, Julie" (1957), Buddy Holly's "Peggy Sue" (1957), or Frankie Avalon's "Dede Dinah" (1958). (For additional examples, see List #15.)

Teenage rock usually echoed sexual standards of the day. Most rock lyrics put forth traditional sentiments about marriage and sex. Teen guilt about innocently staying out past curfew was explained in the Everly Brothers' "Wake Up, Little Susie" (1957) and Ricky Nelson's "It's Late" (1959). (See also List #17a.) Even the adults' propensity toward marriage, as witnessed in the era's growing number of marriages, spilled over into the youth culture. Marriage was idealized in numerous rock hits like the Willows' "Church Bells May Ring" (1956), the Five Satins' "To the Isle" (1957), and Ronnie and the Hi-Lites' "I Wish That We Were Married" (1962). Hit records about going steady, the adolescent version of monogamy, included Tommy Sands' "Going Steady" (1957), Elvis Presley's "Wear My Ring Around Your Neck" (1958), and the Three G's' "Let's Go Steady For the Summer" (1958). (See also List #18.)

Granted, some rock & roll was more sexually explicit than other types of pop music. Sexuality oozed from records such as Mickey and Sylvia's "Love Is Strange" (1956) or the Viscounts' "Harlem Nocturne" (1960). Girl groups like the Ronettes and Shangri-Las had a distinct sexual style. And some rock singers and lyrics were anything but subtle, e.g., Little Richard's "Good Golly, Miss Molly (She Sure Likes to Ball)" (1958). (For other examples, see List #17b.)

But the fact that rock & roll was often more open about sex than many adults were accustomed to during these years does not necessarily mean the music was rebellious. When sexually explicit songs like "Good Golly Miss Molly" or the Kingsmen's "Louie Louie" (1963) came along, the rock audience was often just as stunned as the adults. Teens, just reaching puberty, were titillated by the sounds, but were careful not to tell their parents the lyrics. They knew what they were listening to was taboo. Just as adults could secretly partake in the pleasures of *Lady Chatterley's Lover* or *Peyton Place* and still accept the sexual norms of the day, so could teenagers listen to Little Richard raving about the sexual attributes of "Long Tall Sally" (1956), and still maintain accepted sexual standards.

Another American ritual found in early rock was the traditional battle between American youths and school teachers. Contemporary

Huck Finns and Tom Sawyers did their best to avoid the classroom in songs such as Chuck Berry's "School Days" (1957), Ricky Nelson's "Waitin' in School" (1957), or the Coasters' "Charlie Brown" (1959). And any adult who could remember how exciting it was when school let out for the summer could easily relate to songs like Jerry Keller's "Here Comes Summer" (1959) or Gary U.S. Bonds' "School Is Out" (1961). (See also Lists #11 and #22.)

Rock & roll, like the rest of America in the 1950s and early 1960s, had a love affair with automobiles. By the early 1960s, almost 70 million cars and trucks were on the road—more than one per household. Many of these were designed to appeal to sex and power. There were Edsels with sexually symbolic grills, Oldsmobiles with big, potent engines, and Dodges with long pointed fins.[27]

Songs making use of car imagery raced to the top of the rock charts. For example, Chuck Berry equated sexual pursuit with a drag race in his 1955 hit, "Maybellene." The song has Berry's common man hero "motivatin' over the hill" in his old, but fast, V-8 Ford. All of a sudden he sees his girlfriend, Maybellene, driving by with a rich guy in a brand new, fancy Cadillac Coupe de Ville. The race is on: poor boy versus rich boy, middle class against upper, Ford versus Cadillac. The stakes are high. Sure the girl is the obvious prize, but the race itself is even more important. The virility of the two drivers—in effect the superiority of their respective social classes—is the real contest. For a while, it is too close to call, with the two cars going bumper to bumper at 95 mph. But just as the Cadillac starts to pull away, the V-8 Ford finds new life, as the staying power of the middle-class hero thrusts him forward, forward, forward, until he catches the Caddy at the top of the hill. Exhausted, the Ford's driver asks why Maybellene can't be true, noting that once again she's "doin' the things [she] used to do."[28]

While Berry's middle-class hero may have lost the fickle girl—whose promiscuity would have made her unworthy anyway, according to middle-class sexual standards—he clearly comes away with two moral victories. His personal win reinforced the American belief in the superiority of the common man, while his Ford's victory showed that practical but plain machines (for which America was famous) are technologically superior to fancy ones.

Numerous other rock & roll songs focused on cars. The Playmates sang about the relentless staying power of a big car engine in their 1958 smash, "Beep Beep." Paul Evans explained the advantages of having a large back seat in his 1959 recording, "Seven Little Girls (Sitting in the Backseat Huggin' and Kissin' With Fred)." And the Beach Boys racked up hit after hit with car songs such as "409" (1962), "Shut Down" (1963), and "Little Deuce Coupe" (1963).

Some rock groups, in tune with America's infatuation with the automobile, even named themselves after cars. Perusing the rock charts was like cruising the streets. There were groups called the Cadillacs, El Dorados, Impalas, Fleetwoods, Imperials, and Valiants. There was even one group named the Edsels, who like their Detroit counterpart, had brief success at best. (For additional information about car songs, see List #13.)

The entire rock scene exemplifies the 1950s and early 1960s as an age of affluence, planned obsolescence, and conspicuous consumption. Barrett Strong's 1960 hit, "Money," is a particularly good example that shows teens shared their parents' love of cash. Rejecting the notion that the best things in life are free, Strong concludes he wants money, and that's all he wants.[29]

The latest rock & roll record served the same function for teenagers as the brand new automobile did for adults. Both met Americans' demand for newness and novelty and served as visible symbols of personal progress and success. Record companies issued their products in the millions. And kids bought millions of them. Planned obsolescence was built into the product. With the release of a performer's new record, the previous hit immediately became old and obsolete. The Top 40 record charts reinforced this trend. As many a disc jockey said, "The hits just keep on coming." And the kids just kept on buying.

The record charts reflected another aspect of 1950s culture—the need for statistics. Americans were numbers conscious. They wanted to know: How many? How much? How big? Americans were also flocking to "consumption communities," which according to historian Daniel Boorstin were "invisible new communities [that] were created and preserved by how and what men consumed. . . . The acts of acquiring and using had a new meaning. Nearly all objects from the hats and suits and shoes men wore to the food they ate became symbols and instruments of novel communities. Now men were affiliated less by what they believed than by what they consumed."[30] The Top 10 or Top 40 record charts told teenagers which records were the biggest and best sellers. They also showed teens what records their friends were listening to. By purchasing the same records, any adolescent could gain admission into America's newest consumption community—that of the American teenager.

For many teens buying records was not enough. They also purchased rock styles. Sometimes songs like the Sparkletones' "Black Slacks" (1957) or Carl Perkins' "Blue Suede Shoes" (1956) reflected fashion trends. Other times they caused trends. In either case, they helped sell products. Teens bought anything related to rock & roll. There were Elvis bubble gum cards, Elvis hats, Elvis shoes, Elvis lipstick, Elvis purses, Elvis shirts, and Elvis books. Rock & roll was capitalism at its best, or worst, depending on one's point of view. The materialism of teenagers even became the subject of a 1959 *Life* magazine article, "The U.S. Teen-Age Consumer," which reported that teens spent $10 billion annually on cars, dogs, pimple cream, TV, lipstick, records, and phonographs. By 1963, adolescents were spending $22 billion annually, twice the gross national product of Australia. The selling of the rock culture was big business. Magazines like *Seventeen* were geared to adolescents, as were numerous products ranging from clothing to surfboards to transistor radios. By the mid-1960s, kids were spending $100 million on 45 rpm records alone.[31] Their parents had taught them well. (See Lists #12 and #32.)

The growth of rock & roll shows that youths, like adults, were growing increasingly dependent upon the electronic media. As the 1950s progressed, more and more Americans were watching television and listening to radio. In 1946, only 7,000 TVs could be found in the United States. By 1960, there were 50 million television sets! TV symbolized American affluence and became a solution for the need for mass diversion. Radio served a similar function as mass entertainment for Americans.[32]

Rock & roll's popularity was closely intertwined with television and radio. Rock stars appeared on TV shows such as Dick Clark's "American Bandstand" or the "Ed Sullivan Show." Some songs spoofed TV commercials. Others mentioned specific television shows or characters. Theme songs from popular shows made the rock charts. Some television stars like Ricky Nelson were even able to transfer their popularity over to the rock charts through hit records. (See List #33a.)

Radio stations likewise promoted rock & roll. Radio gave teens the opportunity to hear the new sound. Stations in cities and towns across the country switched to rock formats, which were hectic and fast-paced to keep up with the excitement of the new music. Radio disc jockeys like Alan Freed, Robin Seymore, Russ "the Moose" Siracuse, and Joe Niagara won over thousands of converts to the rock & roll movement. Tom Shannon, a young Buffalo, New York, disc jockey, even wrote his own rock & roll theme song. The promo became so popular that an instrumental version, "Wild Weekend" by the Rockin' Rebels, climbed all the way to number eight on the national record charts in 1963. (The song's distinctive guitar riffs and mention of Buffalo later turned up on John Fogerty's 1985 hit "Rock & Roll Girls.")

Rock & roll songs provide evidence that teenagers and adults were interested in the same things. Rock records, like adult magazines and newspapers, dealt with the American West, Hollywood films, UFOs, monsters, lifestyles, the Beat Generation, the sea, history, alcohol, gambling, food, holidays, vacations, birthdays, trains, travel, and dancing. (For specific examples, see Lists #19–#22, #29, #33–#38, and #41.)

The rock charts also indicate that many teenagers shared their parents' musical tastes. Traditional, old-style pop music by Frank Sinatra, Perry Como, and others continued to sell well. Novelty songs, a long-time staple of the pop music industry, were also grafted onto rock & roll. Jazz, country and western, and folk music also crept onto the rock charts during these years. (For specific examples, see Lists #4 and #47.) Rock songs dealing with recessions, politicians, the space program, and the Cold War demonstrate that teenagers, like adults, were influenced by events in the political arena. (See Lists #39, #42–#44.)

Rock music also makes it clear that teenagers shared their parents' anxieties. Throughout the 1950s and early 1960s, Americans of all ages developed tensions and insecurities over the Cold War, possible nuclear destruction, the speed of social and economic change, new lifestyles, the breakdown of old neighborhoods, the rootlessness resulting from mobility, and the realization that abundance was not enough.[33]

While David Riesman's book *The Lonely Crowd* was explaining loneliness and alienation among adults, rock & roll songs such as the Videls' "Mr. Lonely" (1960) and Paul Anka's "Lonely Boy" (1959) were depicting similar feelings among youth. Other songs allowed alienated or oppressed adolescents to lash out cathartically against society or their imagined enemies. For example, Eddie Cochran's "Summertime Blues" (1958) expressed teenage frustrations with school, parents, work, and the political establishment.[34] (For additional examples of songs dealing with loneliness and alienation, see List #25.)

Lyrics were not the only way to express teen dissatisfaction. Many rock songs contained lyrics that were innocent enough, but when rock performers garbled them or sang them with a lascivious sneer, they took on new meaning. For example, the appearance and slurred vocal deliveries of rock & rollers such as Elvis Presley, Jerry Lee Lewis, and Little Richard combined to communicate adolescent unrest. Ritchie Valens' 1959 hit, "La Bamba," epitomizes what a rock performer could do with seemingly innocent lyrics. With Valens singing in Spanish and playing a wild guitar accompanied by a frenzied beat, the song took on a conspiratorial quality, threatening adults while gaining cult popularity among alienated youths.

Actually, teenage alienation was not a threat to 1950s society; it was symptomatic of the alienation that characterized that society. Rock & roll songs that reflected teen anxieties served as safety valves, letting off adolescent steam caused by the tensions and insecurities of 1950s culture.

Teenagers sometimes used rock & roll as a means to escape from everyday life. Rock artists helped adolescents forget their worries through good-time music like Huey "Piano" Smith and the Clowns' "Rocking Pneumonia and the Boogie Woogie Flu" (1957) or Dickey Doo and the Don'ts' "Nee Nee Na Na Na Na Nu Nu" (1958). (See also List #25c.)

Some songs sought release through humor. While adults listened to Lenny Bruce or Mort Sahl poke fun at American culture, teenagers were listening to rock songs that satirized the space program, communism, and fears about atomic testing, mutants, monsters, UFOs, and technology run amok. (See List #25d.) The need to flee the tense and scary world of the 1950s and early 1960s might also account for the numerous hit records that focused on historical events where good triumphed over evil, or on fantasy worlds that were Gardens of Eden. Other rock songs promised magical cures to teenage problems. (For specific examples, see List #25e.)

Several rock & roll records suggested that death was the ultimate escape from the tragedies of the real world. Jody Reynolds' 1958 hit, "Endless Sleep," was the prototype for the rock songs of the 1950s and 1960s dealing with teenage death. Reynolds sang about his girlfriend's attempt to drown herself after a lovers' quarrel. The macabre lyrics and wail of Reynolds' plaintive voice created a chilling effect as he sang about the dying girl beckoning him to join her in an endless sleep.[35] (For other examples of death rock, see List #25f.)

It is no coincidence that rock & roll became popular in an era of great conformity. Teenagers watched their parents conform in matters regarding politics, religion, and daily living habits. They witnessed the move to the suburbs and the nearly identical tract homes, station wagons, and lifestyles of their families. They learned as their parents pledged their loyalty to democracy, praised God, and avoided being different. They then practiced the conformity the adults preached. Rock & roll forced conformity onto many kids through songs about fashions, slang, and dance styles. (See Lists #12, #14, and #7.) Teenage smoking was encouraged by pictures of rock & rollers with packs of cigarettes tucked in their pockets, or by songs like Dickey Doo and the Don'ts' "Flip Top Box" (1958). Clothing and hair styles worn by rock performers or by "American Bandstand" dancers caught on nationwide. As a style, rock & roll might have seemed alien to parents. But as a process, the rock fad should have been familiar. Teenagers, like adults, were merely trying to conform—as good Americans of the 1950s and early 1960s were inclined to do.

The rise of rock & roll music during this period shows that the Baby Boom generation was emerging as a unique group with a distinct identity. It proves that, to an extent, some kids were rebelling against accepted norms and values. But more important, rock music shows many teenagers were not significantly different from their parents. Much of 1950s and early 1960s rock & roll proves adults and teens shared similar beliefs, values, interests, and pastimes. It also indicates both adults and teens were concerned about the same sources of tensions and insecurities in American life. In short, early rock & roll reveals more consensus than conflict between the generations. The generation gap would not open for another few years.

5. Historical Records

Before turning to specific examples of musical themes and artists, it would be useful to take a look at the music in context of the times through a brief year-by-year recap of the years 1954 through 1963. What follows are "historical records" from rock & roll's first decade.[36]

News

1. Secretary of State John Foster Dulles announces the U. S. policy of "massive retaliation."
2. Senator Joseph McCarthy is discredited in the Army-McCarthy hearings.
3. The French are defeated in Vietnam. Vice-President Nixon urges American intervention.
4. The Supreme Court decision in Brown v. Board of Education of Topeka rules against the "separate but equal" policy in public education.
5. Congress adds "under God" to the pledge to the flag.
6. Thoreau's *Walden* is banned in U. S. Information Service Libraries for being socialistic.
7. United States launches its first Atomic submarine.
8. United States tests its first H-Bomb at Bikini Atoll.

Sports

1. The Cleveland Browns beat the Detroit Lions 56-10 in NFL title game.
2. The Cleveland Indians establish an all-time record by winning 111 games in the American League, before losing to the New York Giants in the World Series.

Life Styles

1. "Davy Crockett" debuts on Walt Disney's TV show, touching off Crockett-mania among youngsters.
2. Frozen TV dinners are introduced.
3. San Francisco bookshop becomes hang out for Beat poets.
4. Pegged pants, duck-tail haircuts, white bucks, flat-tops, and motorcycle jackets gain popularity among teen males.
5. Teenage girls go for poodle skirts, straight skirts, and pastel sweaters.
6. The Beatnik look is in.
7. Disc jockey Alan Freed leaves Cleveland for WINS Radio in New York City.
8. McDonald's launches its national chain, featuring 15¢ hamburgers.

Movies

1. *On the Waterfront*
2. *Rebel Without a Cause*
3. *The Wild One*
4. *The Creature from the Black Lagoon*
5. *Johnnie Guitar*

New TV Shows

1. "The Tonight Show"
2. "Father Knows Best"
3. "Adventures of Rin Tin Tin"
4. "Lassie"
5. "Walt Disney"

Hit Records (Randomly Selected: Yearly rankings of records are included in List #49)

"Shake, Rattle, and Roll"   *Joe Turner*
"Goodnight Sweetheart, Goodnight"   *Spaniels*
  "Sixteen Tons"   *Tennessee Ernie Ford*

"Sh-Boom"   *Chords*
"Earth Angel"   *Penguins*
"Hey There"   *Rosemary Clooney*
"Little Things Mean a Lot"   *Kitty Kallen*
"Three Coins in the Fountain"   *Four Aces*
"Oh, My Papa"   *Eddie Fisher*
"My Lovin' Baby"   *El Dorados*

News

1. Plans are announced to manufacture and use Jonas Salk's polio vaccine.
2. Albert Einstein dies at the age of 76.
3. The minimum wage is raised to $1.00 per hour.
4. New findings indicate possible plant life on Mars. Wave of UFO sightings follows.
5. United States begins supplying economic aid to an independent South Vietnam.
6. The first summit conference between the United States and Soviet Union occurs in Geneva.
7. Actor James Dean dies in car crash.
8. Rosa Parks refuses to give up her bus seat to a white man, leading to the Montgomery, Alabama, bus boycott led by Martin Luther King, Jr.

Sports

1. The Brooklyn Dodgers defeat the Yankees in the World Series, four games to three.
2. The Cleveland Browns win the National Football League title by smashing the Los Angeles Rams 38 to 14.

Life Styles

1. First televised presidential press conference occurs.
2. Panty raids are popular on American campuses.
3. *Village Voice* begins as underground newspaper in New York.
4. Teenage girls help popularize bouffant hair styles, black tights, roll on deodorants, no-smear lipsticks, spiked heels, and pop beads.
5. Teenage male fashions include black denims, pink ties, flattops, and DA's.
6. Pizza gains popularity.
7. Mooning becomes popular teenage craze.
8. First roll-on deodorant introduced.
9. Ann Landers begins her newspaper column.
10. Disneyland opens.

Movies

1. *The Blackboard Jungle*
2. *Marty*
3. *The Rose Tattoo*
4. *Man with the Golden Arm*
5. *East of Eden*

New TV Shows

1. "Alfred Hitchcock Presents"
2. "Cheyenne"
3. "Gunsmoke"
4. "The Millionaire"
5. "The $64,000 Question"

Hit Records

"Rock Around the Clock"   *Bill Haley and His Comets*
"Davy Crockett"   *Bill Hayes*
"Cherry Pink and Apple Blossom White"   *Perez Prado*
"Yellow Rose of Texas"   *Mitch Miller*
"Ain't That a Shame"   *Pat Boone*
"Tweedle Dee"   *La Verne Baker*
"Mr. Sandman"   *Chordettes*
"Bo Diddley"   *Bo Diddley*
"Mystery Train"   *Elvis Presley*
"Maybellene"   *Chuck Berry*

News

1. Soviet troops put down Hungarian revolt.
2. Eisenhower defeats Stevenson for presidency.
3. Britain and France intervene in Middle East war.
4. Secretary of State Dulles says the United States will go to the brink of war to keep peace ("Brinkmanship Policy").
5. U. S. congress authorizes the construction of an interstate super-highway system.
6. Beat poet Allen Ginsberg publishes "Howl."
7. Grace Kelly gives up acting to become Princess of Monaco.
8. Pampers Diapers hit the market.

Sports

1. The Yankees whip the Dodgers four games to three in World Series, as Don Larsen pitches perfect game.
2. The New York Giants stun the Chicago Bears 47 to 7 in the National Football League title game.
3. Michigan State wins the Rose Bowl, but the University of Oklahoma is the number one college team in the country.

Life Styles

1. The James Dean cult grows.
2. Airlines now carrying as many passengers as trains.
3. Drag racing catching on among teens, who are now watching out for the "fuzz."

4. Some teen males wear pegged pants, blue-suede shoes, and long sideburns a la Elvis Presley.
5. Female teen fashions include jeans, sweaters, paperclip chains, and sloppy shirts with photographs on the sleeve. Bobby-sox turned up not down, white bucks, saddle shoes, and Bermuda shorts buckled in back are also in.
6. Girls wear boyfriends' rings on chains to show they are going "steady."
7. "Captain Midnight" decoders are popular.
8. Cars sport long tail fins.
9. TV's "Howdy Doody" begins its 9th season.
10. Instant coffee introduced.

Movies

1. *Around the World in 80 Days*
2. *Friendly Persuasion*
3. *Invasion of the Body Snatchers*
4. *The Ten Commandments*
5. *The King and I*

New TV Shows

1. "Broken Arrow"
2. "Playhouse 90"
3. "To Tell the Truth"
4. "The Gale Storm Show"
5. "Circus Boy"

Hit Records

"Hound Dog"   *Elvis Presley*
"My Prayer"   *Platters*
"The Wayward Wind"   *Gogi Grant*
"Whatever Will Be, Will Be"   *Doris Day*
"Blue Suede Shoes"   *Elvis Presley/Carl Perkins*
"Green Door"   *Jim Lowe*
"Ivory Tower"   *Cathy Carr*
"Standing on the Corner"   *Four Lads*
"Tutti Frutti"   *Little Richard*
"Hot Diggity"   *Perry Como*

News

1. Russians orbit first satellite—"Sputnik 1."
2. UFO sightings are numbered at 414.
3. Ike sends troops to aid desegregation of a Little Rock high school.
4. U. S. troops end occupation of Japan.
5. 4.3 million babies are born in United States—a new record.
6. Congress passes a civil rights act—the first in over 80 years.
7. Soviets launch a dog into space, called "Muttnik" by American wags.
8. Martin Luther King, Jr., helps form the Southern Christian Leadership Conference.
9. New books include Jack Kerouac's *On the Road*; John F. Kennedy's *Profiles in Courage*; Art Linkletter's *Kids Say the Darndest Things*; and Nevil Shute's *On the Beach*.
10. Ford introduces the Edsel.

Sports

1. The Milwaukee Braves, featuring Spahn, Burdette, Aaron, Mathews, and Covington, beat the Yankees in a seven-game World Series.
2. The Detroit Lions maul the Cleveland Browns 59 to 14 to win the National Football League title.
3. Floyd Patterson retains the heavyweight crown by knocking out Pete Rademacher in the 6th round.

Life Styles

1. Sock hops in high school gyms become popular.
2. Sword pins are worn to tell if teens are available or going steady (pointing up means "available").
3. Marilyn Monroe marries Arthur Miller.
4. Girls' fashions feature baggy sweaters, rolled white socks, sack dresses, double pony tails, charm bracelets, Presley lipstick, and Mou-Mous.
5. Teen males go for jeans, shirts with top button left open, collars standing up, and cleats on shoes.
6. Couples seen wearing identical "steady" shirts.
7. TV's "Mickey Mouse Club" begins its third season.

Movies

1. *The Bridge on the River Kwai*
2. *The Three Faces of Eve*
3. *Twelve Angry Men*
4. *Mr. Rock and Roll*
5. *And God Created Woman*

New TV Shows

1. "American Bandstand"
2. "Have Gun Will Travel"
3. "Leave It to Beaver"
4. "Maverick"
5. "The Real McCoys"

Hit Records

"Tammy"   *Debbie Reynolds*
"Love Letters in the Sand"   *Pat Boone*
"It's Not for Me to Say"   *Johnny Mathis*
"Young Love"   *Tab Hunter*
"Little Darlin'"   *Diamonds*
"All Shook Up"   *Elvis Presley*
"Bye Bye Love"   *Everly Brothers*
"Diana"   *Paul Anka*
"Silhouettes"   *Rays*
"Peggy Sue"   *Buddy Holly*

News

1. The United States launches its first successful satellite, Explorer I.
2. Vice President Nixon is jeered and pelted with eggs on his visit to Latin America.
3. The U. S. S. Nautilus, the world's first nuclear sub, completes the first transpolar voyage beneath the Arctic ice pack.
4. Congress appropriates $1 billion to improve educational opportunities at all levels in an effort to close the technology gap between the United States and Soviet Union.
5. Ike reaffirms he will use force to protect Nationalist China from Red China's aggression.
6. Governor Orville Faubus shuts down all Little Rock high schools to evade a Supreme Court desegregation order.
7. The first scheduled jet airliner crosses the Atlantic in 6 hours and 12 minutes.
8. The United States is hit by a major recession.
9. Ike's closest advisor, Sherman Adams, resigns after taking bribes.
10. U. S. churches report largest membership increases since 1950.

Sports

1. The Yankees defeat the Milwaukee Braves in a seven-game World Series, avenging their defeat of the previous year.
2. Two baseball teams, the Dodgers and Giants, announce they are moving to the West coast.
3. The Baltimore Colts win the NFL title game by edging the New York Giants 23 to 17.

4. Floyd Patterson successfully defends his heavyweight title with a TKO of Brian London.

Life Styles

1. The Hula Hoop fad takes America by storm.
2. Teenagers spend $9.5 billion this year on various consumer items.
3. Teen boys like button-down collar shirts, Bermuda shorts, shirt-tails out.
4. Teenage girls go for striped knit pullovers, straight-leg white duck pants, and sneakers.
5. Sack and Chemise dresses don't go over very well.
6. Teen girls wear boyfriends' letter sweaters.
7. Dick Clark's "American Bandstand," in its second season, is one of the hottest shows on TV.
8. Rumbles—street fights—cause problems in urban areas.

Movies

1. *Gigi*
2. *The Defiant Ones*
3. *The Big Country*
4. *Separate Tables*
5. *High School Confidential*

New TV Shows

1. "The Donna Reed Show"
2. "77 Sunset Strip"
3. "The Rifleman"
4. "The Andy Williams Show"
5. "Peter Gunn"

Hit Records

"Nel Blu Dipinto Di Blu (Volare)" *Domenico Modugno*
"It's All in the Game" *Tommy Edwards*
"Patricia" *Perez Prado*
"Little Star" *Elegants*
"Sweet Little Sixteen" *Chuck Berry*
"Witch Doctor" *David Seville*
"Just a Dream" *Jimmy Clanton*
"Tequila" *Champs*
"Get a Job" *Silhouettes*
"Yakety Yak" *Coasters*

News

1. Vice President Nixon debates Khrushchev in Moscow's impromptu "Kitchen Debate."
2. Khrushchev visits the United States and is refused permission to tour Disneyland.
3. Alaska and Hawaii become states.
4. The first seven astronauts are selected.
5. The St. Lawrence Sea Way opens.
6. Rock stars Buddy Holly, Ritchie Valens, and the Big Bopper die in plane crash.
7. Congress investigates rigged TV quiz shows.
8. Last Civil War veteran, a Confederate, dies at the age of 117.
9. Castro takes over in Cuba.
10. First U. S. submarine capable of firing ballistic missiles is launched.

Sports

1. Ingemar Johansson wins heavyweight title by knocking out Floyd Patterson.
2. The Dodgers, now in Los Angeles instead of Brooklyn, beat the Chicago White Sox in the World Series four games to two.
3. The Baltimore Colts defeat the New York Giants 31–16 for NFL title.

Life Styles

1. Beatnik-style poetry readings are the new rage on college campuses.

2. Eye-liner makeup becomes fashionable.
3. Bikini bathing suits are latest craze (named after H-bomb test site).
4. Wool ponchos, bench-warmers, and shaggy dog coats are latest fashion items.
5. Man Tan rub-on sun tan oil hits market.
6. "Sick Jokes" are popular.
7. Polaroid cameras are introduced.
8. Metrecal is advertised to reduce weight.
9. Xerox copiers are sold to public for first time.
10. Barbie Dolls make their first appearance.

Movies

1. *Ben Hur*
2. *The Diary of Anne Frank*
3. *Some Like It Hot*
4. *Room at the Top*
5. *Anatomy of a Murder*

New TV Shows

1. "Adventures in Paradise"
2. "Bonanza"
3. "Many Loves of Dobie Gillis"
4. "The Untouchables"
5. "The Twilight Zone"

Hit Records

"Mack the Knife"   *Bobby Darin*
"Battle of New Orleans"   *Johnny Horton*
"Venus"   *Frankie Avalon*
"Personality"   *Lloyd Price*
"Kansas City"   *Wilbert Harrison*
"A Teenager in Love"   *Dion and the Belmonts*
"Kookie, Kookie (Lend Me Your Comb)"   *Edd Byrnes*
"Lavender Blue"   *Sammy Turner*
"Come Softly to Me"   *Fleetwoods*
"Charlie Brown"   *Coasters*

News

1. Four black students stage the first "sit-in" at a lunch counter in Greensboro, North Carolina, to protest segretation.
2. U. S. pilot Francis Gary Powers and his U-2 spy plane are shot down over the Soviet Union.
3. John F. Kennedy is elected president, narrowly defeating Richard Nixon.
4. Caryl Chessman is executed at San Quentin.
5. The Federal Drug Administration approves the Pill for public sale.
6. The average American income is up to $2,218.
7. 90 percent of all American homes have television.
8. The original Playboy Club opens in Chicago.
9. Dick Clark testifies before Senate Payola hearings.

Sports

1. Bill Mazeroski hits a dramatic ninth inning home run to win the World Series for the Pittsburgh Pirates over the Yankees, four games to three.
2. Floyd Patterson regains his heavyweight title by knocking out Ingemar Johansson in the fifth round.
3. The NFL championship game goes to the Philadelphia Eagles, who defeated the Green Bay Packers 17 to 13.
4. Wilma Rudolph wins three Olympic gold medals.

Life Styles

1. Americans consume 1,050 million pounds of hot dogs.
2. Students for a Democratic Society (SDS) is formed.

3. Pepsi Cola ads acknowledge the baby boom generation with the "For Those Who Think Young" campaign.
4. Barbie and Ken dolls are popular.
5. Fake fur fabrics are popular.
6. Teen girls go for bouffant hairdos.
7. Crewcut hair jelly is sold to teens with flattops.
8. Aluminum cans for beverages become popular.
9. Teens begin dancing the "Twist."

Movies

1. *Never on Sunday*
2. *Spartacus*
3. *Exodus*
4. *Inherit the Wind*
5. *The Apartment*

New TV Shows

1. "My Three Sons"
2. "Route 66"
3. "Surfside Six"
4. "The Andy Griffith Show"
5. "Play Your Hunch"

Hit Records

"Theme from *A Summer Place*"   *Percy Faith*
"The Twist"   *Chubby Checker*
"Itsy Bitsy Teeny Weenie Yellow Polka Dot Bikini"   *Brian Hyland*

"Georgia on My Mind"   *Ray Charles*
"Greenfields"   *Brothers Four*
"New Orleans"   *U.S. Bonds*
"Only the Lonely"   *Roy Orbison*
"Cathy's Clown"   *Everly Brothers*
"Tell Laura I Love Her"   *Ray Peterson*
"Mule Skinner Blues"   *Fendermen*

1961

News

1. United States breaks off diplomatic relations with Castro's Cuba.
2. President Eisenhower's farewell address warns of the growing "military-industrial complex."
3. President John F. Kennedy's inaugural challenges Americans to "ask not what your country can do for you, ask what you can do for your country."
4. The Peace Corps is established.
5. President Kennedy accepts "sole responsibility" for the Bay of Pigs invasion of Cuba.
6. "Freedom Riders" are bussed into the South to promote integration.
7. Astronaut Alan B. Shepard, Jr., becomes the first American in space.
8. The United States sends two army helicopter units to Vietnam.
9. The U. S. government urges the building of fallout shelters.

Sports

1. Roger Maris belts 61 home runs to break Babe Ruth's record of 60 in one season, set in 1927.
2. The New York Yankees destroy the Cincinnati Reds in the World Series four games to one.
3. Ernie Davis, a running back from Syracuse University, wins the Heisman Trophy as outstanding college football player of the year.
4. The Green Bay Packers shut out the New York Giants 37-0 to win the National Football League title.

Life Styles

1. Ray Kroc expands McDonald's to 3,500 outlets.
2. Folk music is new craze on college campuses.
3. Long hair, instead of teased hair, gains popularity among young females.
4. Natural look and less makeup fashionable among teens.
5. Levis now come in white and pastel colors.
6. Skateboarding begins in California.
7. Bed races become popular on campuses, after Delta Chi fraternity members push a starlet on a bed (on wheels) across Nevada desert.
8. Cheap BIC pens (19¢) are introduced.

Movies

1. *Splendor in the Grass*
2. *The Hustler*
3. *Breakfast at Tiffany's*
4. *West Side Story*
5. *The Misfits*

New TV Shows

1. "Ben Casey"
2. "Car 54, Where Are You?"
3. "The Bullwinkle Show"
4. "The Dick Van Dyke Show"
5. "Mr. Ed"

Hit Records

"Raindrops"   *Dee Clark*
"Theme from *Exodus*"   *Ferrante and Teicher*
"Wonderland by Night"   *Bert Kaempfert*
"Runaway"   *Del Shannon*
"Runaround Sue"   *Dion*
"Quarter to Three"   *Gary U.S. Bonds*
"The Lion Sleeps Tonight"   *Tokens*
"Blue Moon"   *Marcels*
"The Way You Look Tonight"   *Lettermen*
"Take Good Care of My Baby"   *Bobby Vee*
"Please Mr. Postman"   *Marvelettes*

News

1. President Kennedy faces the Berlin Crisis.
2. 80 million Americans watch a TV special, "A Tour of the White House With Mrs. John F. Kennedy."
3. Astronaut John Glenn becomes first American to orbit the Earth.
4. The theme for the Seattle World's Fair is "Man in the Space Age."
5. The Supreme Court decides reading a prayer in public schools violates the Constitution.
6. Telstar, a communications satellite, is placed in orbit.
7. Marilyn Monroe dies of an alleged overdose of sleeping pills at the age of 36.
8. The Supreme Court rules that James Meredith, a black, be admitted into the University of Mississippi, a segregated school.
9. The United States forces a showdown with the Soviet Union in the Cuban Missile Crisis.
10. Median family income in the United States is now $5,700.

Sports

1. Bobby Richardson spears a line drive off the bat of Willie McCovey to preserve the Yankees' win in the seventh game of the World Series against the San Francisco Giants.
2. For the second year in a row, the Green Bay Packers win the NFL title by defeating the New York Giants.
3. The University of Cincinnati wins the NCAA college basketball championship.

Life Styles

1. Adults are now doing the Twist, like the kids were last summer.
2. TV's "Ozzie and Harriet" show celebrates 10th anniversary.
3. Albums sell for $4.98 stereo, $3.98 mono.
4. Teen males wear chino slacks and button-down shirts.
5. Teen females like black turtlenecks and black tights.
6. Fringed clothing catches on thanks to the Twist craze.
7. Diet-Rite Cola is introduced.

Movies

1. *Lawrence of Arabia*
2. *The Miracle Worker*
3. *To Kill a Mockingbird*
4. *Advise and Consent*
5. *Whatever Happened to Baby Jane?*

New TV Shows

1. "The Beverly Hillbillies"
2. "Combat"
3. "McHale's Navy"
4. "Password"
5. "I'm Dickens—He's Fenster"

Hit Records

"Moon River"   *Henry Mancini*
"Stranger on the Shore"   *Mr. Acker Bilk*
"The Stripper"   *David Rose*
"Sheila"   *Tommy Roe*
"Twist and Shout"   *Isley Brothers*
"He's a Rebel"   *Crystals*
"Only Love Can Break a Heart"   *Gene Pitney*
"Sherry"   *Four Seasons*
"It Keeps Right On a Hurtin'"   *Johnny Tillotson*
"Scotch and Soda"   *Kingston Trio*
"The Peppermint Twist"   *Joey Dee and the Starlighters*

1963

News

1. President John F. Kennedy assassinated.
2. Massive civil rights demonstrations, led by Martin Luther King, Jr., take place in Birmingham, Alabama.
3. The "Hot Line" is set up between the White House and Kremlin.
4. 250,000 people join the civil rights "March on Washington," where Martin Luther King, Jr., gives "I Have a Dream" speech.
5. Post Office announces the move to Zip Codes.
6. McDonald's sells more than one billion 15¢ hamburgers.

Sports

1. Roger Staubach of the Naval Academy wins the Heisman Trophy in college football.
2. The Chicago Bears win the NFL title by whipping the New York Giants 14–10.
3. Cassius Clay is named Fighter of the Year by Ring Magazine.
4. The Dodgers led by Drysdale, Koufax, and Wills defeat the Yankees in the World Series.

Life Styles

1. Old Tarzan movies become popular on college campuses.
2. Beards are more acceptable on campuses.
3. Surfer style clothing is in.
4. The Jackie Kennedy look featuring pill-box hats, pointed-toe shoes, and softly-curled hair sweeps nation.
5. Playboy Magazine widely read on college campuses.
6. Panty hose and wigs are popular.
7. Folk music big among college and high school youths.

8. Elephant jokes become latest craze.
9. Instamatic cameras become popular.

Movies

1. *Hud*
2. *Beach Party*
3. *Tom Jones*
4. *Bye Bye Birdie*
5. *Cleopatra*

New TV Shows

1. "Hootenanny"
2. "My Favorite Martian"
3. "The Patty Duke Show"
4. "Mr. Novak"
5. "Petticoat Junction"

Hit Records

"Sugar Shack"   *Jimmy Gilmer and the Fireballs*
"Little Town Flirt"   *Del Shannon*
"Surfin' U.S.A."   *Beach Boys*
"Sukiyaki"   *Kyu Sakomoto*
"Louie Louie"   *Kingsmen*
"Be My Baby"   *Ronettes*
"If You Wanna Be Happy"   *Jimmy Soul*
"He's So Fine"   *Chiffons*
"Blowin' in the Wind"   *Peter, Paul, and Mary*
"Rhythm of the Rain"   *Cascades*
"It's My Party"   *Leslie Gore*

PART TWO

Themes, Topics, & Hit Records

The lists in Part II group rock and pop songs to highlight important themes, topics, and hit records. The lists provide examples for each category, but are not meant to be definitive. The year the record was first released is listed after each song title, followed by the performer's name. Most selections are from the period 1954–1963. When relevant and appropriate, records released after 1963 are included.

Lists In Part II

1. Rock & Roll Styles or Genres

● LIST #1: Significant R & B Rock Performers

Hank Ballard and the
  Midnighters
Chuck Berry
Gary U.S. Bonds
Ray Charles
Chords
Dee Clark
Coasters
Sam Cooke
Crystals
Bobby Day
Bo Diddley
Fats Domino
Drifters
Five Satins

Flamingos
Marvin Gaye
Impressions
Isley Brothers
Little Richard
Marvelettes
Miracles
Penguins
Platters
Lloyd Price
Ronettes
Shirelles
Mary Wells
Jackie Wilson
Little Stevie Wonder

● LIST #2: Significant Country Rock Performers

Jimmy Bowen
Dorsey Burnette
Johnny Burnette
Johnny Cash
Buddy Holly and the Crickets
Skeeter Davis
Duane Eddy
Everly Brothers
Dale Hawkins
Johnny Horton
Buddy Knox

Wanda Jackson
Sonny James
Brenda Lee
Jerry Lee Lewis
Roy Orbison
Carl Perkins
Elvis Presley
Jack Scott
Conway Twitty
Gene Vincent

● LIST #3: Significant Pop Rock Performers

Paul Anka	Paul Evans
Frankie Avalon	Fabian
Beach Boys	Fleetwoods
Pat Boone	Four Preps
Freddy Cannon	Four Seasons
Chubby Checker	Connie Francis
Chipmunks	Leslie Gore
Lou Christie	Bill Haley and His Comets
Jimmy Clanton	Brian Hyland
Eddie Cochran	Jan and Dean
Crests	Kingsmen
Crew Cuts	Lettermen
Danny and the Juniors	Ricky Nelson
Bobby Darin	Gene Pitney
Joey Dee and the Starlighters	Bobby Rydell
Diamonds	Neil Sedaka
Dickey Doo and the Don'ts	Del Shannon
Dion and the Belmonts	Johnny Tillotson
Ral Donner	Ritchie Valens
Dovells	Bobby Vee
Elegants	Bobby Vinton

● LIST #4: Other Styles on the Rock Charts

a) Traditional Pop

The rock & roll charts during rock's first decade sometimes reflected quite traditional musical tastes. Old style pop music continued to sell, as evidenced by the continuing success of pop performers like Tony Bennett, Frank Sinatra, Henry Mancini, and others. Some rock artists also recorded pop standards and many rock records resorted to conventional pop formulas: songs about love and romance, marriage, popular names, and angels. All this seems to indicate that many members of the rock & roll audience shared the same tastes and values of adults.

1) *Pop performers on rock charts*

"Mr. Sandman" (1954)   *Chordettes*

"Sincerely" (1955)   *McGuire Sisters*
"Hot Diggity" (1956)   *Perry Como*
"Sugartime" (1957–58)   *McGuire Sisters*
"So Rare" (1957)   *Jimmy Dorsey*
"Chances Are" (1957)   *Johnny Mathis*
"The Twelfth of Never" (1957)   *Johnny Mathis*
"Tea for Two Cha Cha" (1958)   *Tommy Dorsey*
"Catch a Falling Star" (1958)   *Perry Como*
"Return to Me" (1958)   *Dean Martin*
"High Hopes" (1959)   *Frank Sinatra*
"Moon River" (1961)   *Henry Mancini*
"Ramblin' Rose" (1962)   *Nat King Cole*
"I Love You Because" (1963)   *Al Martino*
"Can't Get Used to Losing You" (1963)   *Andy Williams*

2) Rock performers singing pop songs

"Blue Moon" (1956)   *Elvis Presley*
"Mack the Knife" (1959)   *Bobby Darin*
"Won't You Come Home Bill Bailey?" (1960)   *Bobby Darin*
"Clementine" (1960)   *Bobby Darin*
"Where or When" (1960)   *Dion and the Belmonts*
"Volare" (1960)   *Bobby Rydell*
"Clementine" (1960)   *Jan and Dean*
"Lazy River" (1961)   *Bobby Darin*
"That Old Black Magic" (1961)   *Bobby Rydell*
"Blue Moon" (1961)   *Marcels*
"The Way You Look Tonight" (1961)   *Lettermen*
"When I Fall in Love" (1961)   *Lettermen*
"That's All" (1961)   *Bobby Vee*
"Summertime" (1962)   *Rick Nelson*
"Fools Rush In" (1963)   *Rick Nelson*
"Blue Velvet" (1963)   *Bobby Vinton*
"Witchcraft" (1963)   *Elvis Presley*

b) Jazz on the Rock Charts

Jazz was another traditional form of music that made its way onto the rock charts in the years 1954–1963, showing the diversity of the tastes and values within the rock & roll audience. Examples of jazz songs on the rock charts include:

"The Swingin' Shepherd Blues" (1958)   *Moe Koffman Quartette*

"Manhattan Spiritual" (1958)   *Reg Owens*
"Petite Fleur" (1959)   *Chris Barber's Jazz Band*
"Exodus" (1961)   *Eddie Harris*
"Take Five" (1961)   *Dave Brubeck Quartet*
"Walk on the Wild Side" (1962)   *Jimmy Smith*
"Comin' Home Baby" (1962)   *Mel Torme*
"Midnight in Moscow" (1962)   *Kenny Ball and His Jazz Band*

c) Country on the Rock Charts

Country and western songs done by Patsy Cline, Ferlin Husky, Jim Reeves, and other traditional country singers commonly crossed over to the rock & roll charts during the 1950s and early 1960s. The success of country music might be attributed to several things. During these years, country and western music was popular with adults, and this popularity may have spilled over to the younger audience, reflecting similar tastes between members of the rock audience and their parents. The traditional country performers' sound may also have been appealing to many teenagers accustomed to the country-influenced sound of Elvis Presley, the Everly Brothers and other rockabilly artists. Furthermore, the country songs that were the most successful on the rock charts were closer in sound to pop than bluegrass. Finally, the fact that the 1950s and early 1960s were conservative times and country music represented traditional values might also help explain why members of the rock audience were enjoying and buying country and western singles. Examples of country hits on the rock charts include:

"Walkin' After Midnight" (1957)   *Patsy Cline*
"Gone" (1957)   *Ferlin Husky*
"Gotta Travel On" (1958)   *Billy Grammer*
"I Can't Stop Loving You" (1958)   *Don Gibson*
"Oh Lonesome Me" (1958)   *Don Gibson*
"Blue Blue Day" (1958)   *Don Gibson*
"The Three Bells" (1959)   *Browns*
"Battle of New Orleans" (1959)   *Johnny Horton*
"Waterloo" (1959)   *Stonewall Jackson*
"I Ain't Never" (1959)   *Webb Pierce*
"El Paso" (1959)   *Marty Robbins*

"Bonaparte's Retreat" (1959)   *Billy Grammer*
"He'll Have to Go" (1960)   *Jim Reeves*
"Last Date" (1960)   *Floyd Cramer*
"Teensville" (1960)   *Chet Atkins*
"North to Alaska" (1960)   *Johnny Horton*
"Wings of a Dove" (1960)   *Ferlin Husky*
"Please Help Me I'm Falling" (1960)   *Hank Locklin*
"Let's Think About Livin'" (1960)   *Bob Luman*
"Big Iron" (1960)   *Marty Robbins*
"Just One Time" (1960)   *Don Gibson*
"I Fall to Pieces" (1961)   *Patsy Cline*
"Crazy" (1961)   *Patsy Cline*
"On the Rebound" (1961)   *Floyd Cramer*
"Right or Wrong" (1961)   *Wanda Jackson*
"In the Middle of a Heartache" (1961)   *Wanda Jackson*
"Don't Worry" (1961)   *Marty Robbins*
"Just Walk on By" (1961)   *Leroy Van Dyke*
"Hello Walls" (1961)   *Faron Young*
"Sea of Heartbreak" (1961)   *Don Gibson*
"Don't Go Near the Indians" (1962)   *Rex Allen*
"Shame on Me" (1962)   *Bobby Bare*
"Wolverton Mountain" (1962)   *Claude King*
"Detroit City" (1963)   *Bobby Bare*
"500 Miles" (1963)   *Bobby Bare*
"Six Days on the Road" (1963)   *Dave Dudley*

d) Folk Music on the Rock Charts

Folk music also crept onto the rock charts during the late 1950s and early 1960s. The rock & roll audience's acceptance of folk reflected the growing sophistication of the baby boomers, who by the early 1960s were approaching college age. It also mirrored American youths' renewed interest in social and political matters, increasing in part due to the "Quest for a National Purpose" that had captured public attention after Sputnik shocked Americans out of their 1950s complacency. Teenagers' social consciousness was also raised by the more idealistic and activist central government under President Kennedy, as well as the publicity surrounding the expanding Civil Rights Movement. In such an atmosphere, many members of the rock audience eagerly listened to folk songs which reflected the era's idealism and addressed social concerns. The following are some examples of folk records that made the rock charts:

"Marianne" (1957)   *Terry Gilkyson and the Easy Riders*
"Tom Dooley" (1958)   *Kingston Trio*
"Tijuana Jail" (1959)   *Kingston Trio*
"M.T.A." (1959)   *Kingston Trio*
"A Worried Man" (1959)   *Kingston Trio*
"Greenfields" (1960)   *Brothers Four*
"My Tani" (1960)   *Brothers Four*
"The Green Leaves of Summer" (1960)   *Brothers Four*
"Michael" (1961)   *Highwaymen*
"Cottonfields" (1961)   *Highwaymen*
"A Little Bitty Tear" (1961)   *Burl Ives*
"A Dollar Down" (1961)   *Limelighters*
"Funny Way of Laughing" (1962)   *Burl Ives*
"Where Have all the Flowers Gone" (1962)   *Kingston Trio*
"Scotch and Soda" (1962)   *Kingston Trio*
"Lizzie Borden" (1962)   *Chad Mitchell Trio*
"This Land Is Your Land" (1962)   *New Christy Minstrels*
"Lemon Tree" (1962)   *Peter, Paul, and Mary*
"If I Had a Hammer" (1962)   *Peter, Paul, and Mary*
"Walk Right In" (1963)   *Rooftop Singers*
"Tom Cat" (1963)   *Rooftop Singers*
"Hootenanny" (1963)   *Glencoves*
"Greenback Dollar" (1963)   *Kingston Trio*
"The Marvelous Toy" (1963)   *Chad Mitchell Trio*
"Green Green" (1963)   *New Christy Minstrels*
"Puff the Magic Dragon" (1963)   *Peter, Paul, and Mary*
"Blowin' in the Wind" (1963)   *Peter, Paul, and Mary*
"Don't Think Twice It's All Right" (1963)   *Peter, Paul, and Mary*
"Stewball" (1963)   *Peter, Paul, and Mary*

2. Songs About the Youth Culture

● LIST #5: Childhood Themes

Many rock songs, acknowledging that teenagers were not too far removed from childhood, made use of childhood allusions. Numerous records dealt with kids' stories and movies. Others focused on specific childhood interests like candy or cartoons. And some hit records were simply rock & roll versions of childhood songs.

a) Songs Referring to Kids' Stories and Movies

"The Ballad of Davy Crockett" (1955)   *Bill Hayes* (from the Disney movie and TV series "Davy Crockett")

"The Pied Piper" (1957)   *Billy Williams*

"Wringle Wrangle" (1957)   *Fess Parker* (from the Disney film, *Westward Ho the Wagons*)

"Cinderella" (1958)   *Four Preps*

"Little Red Riding Hood" (1958)   *Big Bopper*

"Dinner with Drac" (1958)   *John Zacherle* (referred to various horror movie monsters)

"High Hopes" (1959)   *Frank Sinatra* (from movie, *A Hole In the Head*)

"When You Wish Upon a Star" (1960)   *Dion and the Belmonts* (taken from Disney's movie *Pinocchio*)

"Over the Rainbow" (1960)   *Demensions* (from *The Wizard of Oz*)

"Zip A Dee Doo Dah" (1962)   *Bob B. Soxx and the Blue Jeans* (taken from Disney's *Song of the South*)

"Cinderella" (1962)   *Jack Ross*

"Oliver Twist" (1962)   *Rod McKuen*

"Your Nose Is Gonna Grow" (1962)   *Johnny Crawford* (inspired by the Pinocchio story)

"Alice in Wonderland" (1963)   *Neil Sedaka*

b) Songs About Childhood Interests

Candy

"A Rose and a Baby Ruth" (1956)   *George Hamilton IV*
"Lollipop" (1958)   *Chordettes*
"Candy Man" (1961)   *Roy Orbison*
"Lollipops and Roses" (1962)   *Jack Jones*
"Popsicles and Icicles" (1963)   *Murmaids*
"Candy Girl" (1963)   *Four Seasons*

Cartoons

"I'm a Yogi" (1960)   *Ivy Three (based on Yogi Bear)*
"Alley Oop" (1960)   *Hollywood Argyles*

Some songs also featured characters with cartoon-like voices, e.g., David Seville's "Witch Doctor" (1958); David Seville and the Chipmunks' various Chipmunk recordings; Sheb Wooley's "The Purple People Eater" (1958); and the Nutty Squirrels' "Uh! Oh!" (1959).

Circuses

"The Way of a Clown" (1960)   *Teddy Randazzo*
"Goodbye Cruel World (I'm Off
   to Join the Circus)" (1961)   *Jimmy Darren*
"Merry-Go-Round" (1961)   *Marv Johnson*
"King of Clowns" (1962)   *Neil Sedaka*
"See the Funny Little Clown" (1964)   *Bobby Goldsboro*

Food

"Peanuts" (1957)   *Little Joe and the Thrillers*
"Cherry Pie" (1960)   *Skip and Flip*
"Peanut Butter" (1961)   *Marathons*
"Peppermint Twist" (1961)   *Joey Dee and the Starlighters*
"Mashed Potato Time" (1962)   *Dee Dee Sharp*
"Gravy" (1962)   *Dee Dee Sharp*
"Hot Pastrami" (1963)   *Dartells*
"Hot Pastrami with Mashed Potatoes" (1963)   *Joey Dee and the
                                                  Starlighters*
"On Top of Spaghetti" (1963)   *Tom Glazer and the Children's
                                    Chorus*
"Jelly Bread" (1963)   *Booker T. and the MG's*

Birds and animals

"Two Hound Dogs" (1955)   *Bill Haley and His Comets*
"See You Later Alligator" (1955)   *Bill Haley and His Comets*
"Hound Dog" (1956)   *Elvis Presley*
"Buzz Buzz Buzz" (1957)   *Hollywood Flames*
"Billy Goat" (1957)   *Bill Haley and His Comets*
"Rockin' Robin" (1958)   *Bobby Day*
"Bluebirds Over the Mountain" (1958)   *Ersel Hickey*
"Cha Hua Hua" (1958)   *Pets*
"The Chipmunk Song" (1958)   *Chipmunks (the animals were allegedly doing the singing on this record, as well as on other Chipmunk hits, such as "Alvin's Harmonica," and "Ragtime Cowboy Joe" in 1959; "Alvin's Orchestra," "Alvin For President," and "Rudolph the Red Nosed Reindeer" in 1960; and "The Alvin Twist" in 1962)*
"Uh! Oh! Part 2" (1959)   *Nutty Squirrels (again, the animals were supposedly doing the singing)*
"I Go Ape" (1959)   *Neil Sedaka*
"Bull Dog" (1960)   *Fireballs*
"Pepino the Italian Mouse" (1962)   *Lou Monte*
"Never Love a Robin" (1963)   *Bobby Vee*
"Tie Me Kangaroo Down Sport" (1963)   *Rolf Harris*
"Pepino's Friend Pasqual" (1963)   *Lou Monte*
"Stewball (Was a Race Horse)" (1963)   *Peter, Paul, and Mary*
"Puff the Magic Dragon" (1963)   *Peter, Paul, and Mary*
"Harry the Hairy Ape" (1963)   *Ray Stevens*

Summer camp

"Battle of (Camp) Kookamonga" (1959)   *Homer and Jethro*
"Hello Mudduh, Hello Fadduh" (1963)   *Allan Sherman*

Babies

"Baby Talk" (1959)   *Jan and Dean*
"Baby Sittin' Boogie" (1961)   *Buzz Clifford*

"Baby's First Christmas" (1961) *Connie Francis*
"School Is In" (1961) *Gary U.S. Bonds* (sings about teaching
the baby how to count to four)
"Baby Has Gone Bye Bye" (1962) *George Maharis*
Also, numerous songs have used the word "baby" in their titles,
e.g., Little Richard's "Baby Face" (1958); the Echoes' "Baby
Blue" (1961); the Shirelles' "Baby It's You" (1962); the
Ronettes' "Be My Baby" (1963); Garnett Mimms and the
Enchanters' "Cry Baby" (1963), etc.

Toys and games

"ABCs of Love" (1956) *Frankie Lymon and the Teenagers*
"Leap Frog" (1957) *Chuck Alaimo*
"Let Me Be Your Teddy Bear" (1957) *Elvis Presley*
"Hoola Hoop Song" (1958) *Georgia Gibbs*
"Who's Pushin' Your Swing" (1959) *Gene Vincent*
"Rubber Ball" (1960) *Bobby Vee*
"My Coloring Book" (1962) *Sandy Stewart*
"Daisy Petal Pickin' " (1963) *Jimmy Gilmer & the Fireballs*
"The Marvelous Toy" (1963) *Chad Mitchell Trio*
"Puff the Magic Dragon" (1963) *Peter, Paul, & Mary*

c) Songs Dealing with Childhood Songs and Nursery Rhymes

"Bo Diddley" (1955) *Bo Diddley* (uses "Hush little baby"
rhyme)
"I'm in Love Again" (1956) *Fats Domino* (uses "eenie, meenie,
minee, moe" rhyme)
"Blue Suede Shoes" (1956) *Carl Perkins* (based on children's
rhyme)
"(Twinkle Twinkle) Little Star" (1958) *Elegants*
"Ring-A-Ling-A-Lario" (1959) *Jimmie Rodgers*
"Hush-A-Bye" (1959) *Mystics*
"Cradle of Love" (1960) *Johnny Preston* (based on Mother
Goose)
"(1-2-3) I Shot Mr. Lee" (1960) *Bobbettes* (based on children's
rhyme)
"Rain Rain Go Away" (1962) *Bobby Vinton*

"Roses Are Red" (1962)   *Bobby Vinton*
"Mary's Little Lamb" (1962)   *James Darren*
"Mockingbird" (1963)   *Inez Foxx*
"Lover's Goodbye" (1963)   *Bobby Vee* (based on Brahm's Lullabye)
"Fingertips, Part 2" (1963)   *Little Stevie Wonder* (uses "Mary Had a Little Lamb")
"Hickory, Dick, and Doc" (1964)   *Bobby Vee*

● LIST #6: Adolescent Themes

While some rock records focused on pre-teen themes, others dealt expressly with being a teenager. These show that teens were self-conscious, sometimes painfully so, about their adolescence. Some records referred to youth in general, while other hits aimed at specific age groups within the boom generation. Even performers' names were sometimes geared to the youth market.

a) Songs About Being Young

"Teenage Prayer" (1955)   *Gail Storm*
"Teenage Prayer" (1955)   *Gloria Mann*
"Teen Age Goodnight" (1956)   *Chordettes*
"Young Love" (1956)   *Sonny James*
"A Teenager's Romance" (1957)   *Ricky Nelson*
"High School Romance" (1957)   *George Hamilton IV*
"Teenage Crush" (1957)   *Tommy Sands*
"Young Love" (1957)   *Tab Hunter*
"So Young" (1957)   *Clyde Stacy*
"Teenage Doll" (1958)   *Tommy Sands*
"Ballad of a Teenage Queen" (1958)   *Johnny Cash*
"I'll Wait for You" (1958)   *Frankie Avalon*
"Twixt Twelve and Twenty" (1959)   *Pat Boone*
"Like Young" (1959)   *Andre Previn and David Rose*
"Bobby Sox to Stockings" (1959)   *Frankie Avalon*
"I've Come of Age" (1959)   *Billy Storm*
"Young Ideas" (1959)   *Chico Holiday*
"Almost Grown" (1959)   *Chuck Berry*
"There's No Fool Like a Young Fool" (1959)   *Tab Hunter*

"Teen Beat" (1959)   *Sandy Nelson*
"Teen Commandments" (1959)   *Paul Anka/George Hamilton*
IV/and Johnny Nash
"Teenage Heaven" (1959)   *Eddie Cochran*
"Teenager in Love" (1959)   *Dion and the Belmonts*
"Teensville" (1960)   *Chet Atkins*
"Because They're Young" (1960)   *Duane Eddy*
"Teen Angel" (1960)   *Mark Dinning*
"Young Love" (1960)   *Bobby Vee*
"A Teenager Feels It Too" (1960)   *Denny Reed*
"Lonely Teenager" (1960)   *Dion*
"Young Emotions" (1960)   *Ricky Nelson*
"Dear Lady Twist" (1961)   *Gary U.S. Bonds* (sings "do the
Twist, and you will never get old")
"A Song for Young Love" (1961)   *Lettermen*
"Young World" (1962)   *Rick Nelson*
"Big Girls Don't Cry" (1962)   *Four Seasons*
"Teenage Idol" (1962)   *Rick Nelson*
"Teen Queen of the Week" (1962)   *Freddy Cannon*
"Teenage Cleopatra" (1963)   *Tracy Dey*
"Teenage Heaven" (1963)   *Johnny Cymbal*
"When I Grow Up (To Be a Man)" (1964)   *Beach Boys*

b) Songs About Specific Age Groups

"Seventeen" (1955)   *Fontane Sisters*
"Seventeen" (1955)   *Boyd Bennett*
"She Was Only Seventeen" (1958)   *Marty Robbins*
"Sweet Little Sixteen" (1958)   *Chuck Berry*
"Sixteen Candles" (1958)   *Crests*
"Only Sixteen" (1959)   *Sam Cooke*
"You're Sixteen" (1960)   *Johnny Burnette*
"Happy Birthday, Sweet Sixteen" (1961)   *Neil Sedaka*
"It Hurts To Be Sixteen" (1963)   *Andrea Carroll*

c) Performers' Names Geared to Youth Market

Frankie Lymon and the Teenagers
Six Teens
Royal Teens
Rock-A-Teens

Little Eva
Little Peggy March
Little Stevie Wonder
Little Anthony and the Imperials
Little Willie John
Little Joey and the Flips
Little Joe and the Thrillers
Little Richard
Lolita
Cathy Jean and the Roommates
In addition, many rock & rollers used childish nicknames instead
  of more adult-sounding ones, i.e., there were far more Bobbys,
  Tommys, and Frankies, than there were Bobs, Toms, or Franks.

● LIST #7: Dances and Dancing

At first, teenagers simply did an updated version of the 1940s jitterbug to fast songs, and slow-danced (like their parents' waltz) to
the slow ones. But before long, new dances were invented to go along
with the new music. Kids were soon doing the stroll, the twist, the
slop, the pony, the fly, and a variety of other dances geared to the
young generation and the new rock & roll music.

1955 "When You Dance"   *Turbans*
1956 "Rock & Roll Waltz"   *Kay Starr*
        "Be Bop a Lula"   *Gene Vincent*
        "Blue Jean Bop"   *Gene Vincent*
        "Crazy Legs (Do the Bop)"   *Gene Vincent*
1957 "At the Hop"   *Danny and the Juniors*
        "The Stroll"   *Diamonds*
        "Jingle Bell Rock"   *Bobby Helms*
        "Be Bop Baby"   *Ricky Nelson*
        "Dance To the Bop"   *Gene Vincent*
1958 "Mexican Hat Rock"   *Appelljacks*
        "Rocka-Conga"   *Appelljacks*
        "Tea for Two Cha Cha"   *Tommy Dorsey*
        "The Walk"   *Jimmy McCracklin*
        "Willie and the Hand Jive"   *Johnny Otis*
        "The Freeze"   *Tony and Joe*
        "Hard Times (the Slop)"   *Noble Watts*

"Do You Want to Dance?"   *Bobby Freeman*

"Jeanie, Jeanie, Jeanie"   *Eddie Cochran*

"Splish Splash"   *Bobby Darin*

"Queen of the Hop"   *Bobby Darin*

1959   "Bunny Hop"   *Appelljacks*

"Shimmy Shimmy Ko Ko Bop"   *Little Anthony and the Imperials*

"Midnight Stroll"   *Revels*

"Dance with Me"   *Drifters*

"Record Hop Blues"   *Quarter Notes*

1960   "Finger Poppin' Time"   *Hank Ballard & the Midnighters*

"The Twist"   *Hank Ballard & the Midnighters*

"Let the Little Girl Dance"   *Billy Bland*

"The Twist"   *Chubby Checker*

"The Hucklebuck"   *Chubby Checker*

"(I Do the) Shimmy Shimmy"   *Bobby Freeman*

"Shimmy Like Kate"   *Olympics*

"Save the Last Dance For Me"   *Drifters*

1961   "The Twist"   *Chubby Checker*

"Dear Lady Twist"   *Gary U.S. Bonds*

"Pony Time"   *Chubby Checker*

"Let's Twist Again"   *Chubby Checker*

"The Fly"   *Chubby Checker*

"The Peppermint Twist"   *Joey Dee and the Starlighters*

"The Majestic"   *Dion*

"The Bristol Stomp"   *Dovells*

"Hully Gully Again"   *Little Caesar and the Romans*

"The Fish"   *Bobby Rydell*

"You Can't Sit Down"   *Phil Upchurch Combo*

"The Watusi"   *Vibrations*

"Foot Stomping, Part 1"   *Flares*

1962   "The Percolator Twist"   *Checkmates*

"Twist Twist Senora"   *Gary U.S. Bonds*

"Limbo Rock"   *Champs*

"Do You Love Me (Now That I Can Dance)?"   *Contours*

"Slow Twistin'"   *Chubby Checker*

"Limbo Rock"   *Chubby Checker*

"Twistin' the Night Away"   *Sam Cooke*

"Soul Twist"   *King Curtis*

"Do the Continental"   *Dovells*

"The Alvin Twist"   *Chipmunks*
"The Jitterbug"   *Dovells*
"Bristol Twistin' Annie"   *Dovells*
"Hully Gully Baby"   *Dovells*
"Desafinado (Bossa Nova)"   *Stan Getz and Charlie Byrd*
"The Jam"   *Bobby Gregg and His Friends*
"Potato Peeler"   *Bobby Gregg and His Friends*
"Fly Me to the Moon (Bossa Nova)"   *Joe Harnell*
"Bongo Stomp"   *Little Joey and the Flips*
"The Loco-Motion"   *Little Eva*
"Oliver Twist"   *Rod McKuen*
"Twistin' Postman"   *Marvelettes*
"Let's Dance"   *Chris Montez*
"Meet Me at the Twistin' Place"   *Johnny Morissette*
"Wah Watusi"   *Orlons*
"The Cinnamon Cinder"   *Pastel Six*
"Twist and Shout"   *Isley Brothers*
"The Cha Cha Cha"   *Bobby Rydell*
"I'll Never Dance Again"   *Bobby Rydell*
"Mashed Potato Time"   *Dee Dee Sharp*
"Gravy"   *Dee Dee Sharp*
"Ride! (Your Pony)"   *Dee Dee Sharp*
"Pop Pop Pop Pop-Pie"   *Sherrys*
"Twistin' Matilda"   *Jimmy Soul*
"Loop de Loop"   *Johnny Thunder*
"The Push and Kick"   *Mark Valentino*
"Guitar Boogie Shuffle Twist"   *Virtues*
"Hey Let's Twist"   *Joey Dee & the Starlighters*
1963   "Let's Stomp"   *Bobby Comstock*
"Hot Pastrami"   *Dartells*
"Hot Pastrami With Mashed Potatoes"   *Joey Dee and the Starlighters*
"Blame It on the Bossa Nova"   *Eydie Gorme*
"Let's Turkey Trot"   *Little Eva*
"Monkey Time"   *Major Lance*
"Who Stole the Keeshka?" (Polka)   *Matys Brothers*
"Mickey's Monkey"   *Miracles*
"The Bounce"   *Olympics*
"Bossa Nova Baby"   *Elvis Presley*
"Walkin' the Dog"   *Rufus Thomas*

"The Dog"   *Rufus Thomas*
"You Can't Sit Down"   *Dovells*
"Do the Bird"   *Dee Dee Sharp*

● LIST #8: Rock & Roll

The records themselves sometimes contributed to teenagers' perceptions that rock & roll was unique and the sole property of the youth culture. Some songs glorified rock & roll as the new sound that made traditional pop obsolete. Others focused on rock's distinct sound. Some records alluded to earlier hits, thereby reinforcing in teenagers' minds the historical value and cultural significance of rock & roll. And some just referred to rock & roll in general. All these records reinforced rock & roll's association with youth, thereby providing an important means to teen identity.

a) Song Titles Mentioning Rock

"Rock & Roll Party" (1955)   *Red Prysock*
"Rock Around the Clock" (1955)   *Bill Haley and His Comets*
"Rock and Roll Waltz" (1955)   *Kay Starr*
"R-O-C-K" (1956)   *Bill Haley and His Comets*
"The Saints Rock 'n' Roll" (1956)   *Bill Haley and His Comets*
"Rudy's Rock" (1956)   *Bill Haley and His Comets*
"Rock 'n' Roll Music" (1957)   *Chuck Berry*
"Jailhouse Rock" (1957)   *Elvis Presley*
"Jingle Bell Rock" (1957)   *Bobby Helms*
"Sweet Little Rock and Roller" (1958)   *Chuck Berry*
"Rock 'n' Roll Is Here to Stay" (1958)   *Danny and the Juniors*
"Reelin' and Rockin'" (1958)   *Chuck Berry*
"Hang Up My Rock and Roll Shoes" (1958)   *Chuck Willis*
"Rockin' in the Jungle" (1959)   *Eternals*
"Rock and Roll Cha Cha Cha" (1959)   *Eternals*
"Bongo Rock" (1959)   *Preston Epps*
"Red River Rock" (1959)   *Johnny and the Hurricanes*
"Reveille Rock" (1959)   *Johnny and the Hurricanes*
"Let It Rock" (1960)   *Chuck Berry*
"Rockin' Around the Christmas Tree" (1960)   *Brenda Lee*
"Rocking Goose" (1962)   *Johnny and the Hurricanes*

"If You Were a Rock and Roll Record" (1962)   *Freddy Cannon*
"Limbo Rock" (1962)   *Chubby Checker*

b) Songs Mentioning Rock in Lyrics

"Roll Over Beethoven" (1956)   *Chuck Berry*
"Ready Teddy" (1956)   *Little Richard*
"Rip It Up" (1956)   *Little Richard*
"Jeanie, Jeanie, Jeanie" (1958)   *Eddie Cochran*
"Splish Splash" (1958)   *Bobby Darin*
"Johnny B. Goode" (1958)   *Chuck Berry*
"Purple People Eater" (1958)   *Sheb Wooley*
"Three Stars" (1959)   *Tommy Dee*
"Let's Have a Party" (1960)   *Wanda Jackson*
"Foot Stomping, Part 1" (1961)   *Flares*
"Those Oldies But Goodies" (1961)   *Nino and the Ebb Tides*
"Those Oldies But Goodies" (1961)   *Little Caesar & the Romans*
"Who Put the Bomp?" (1961)   *Barry Mann*
"Mr. Bass Man" (1963)   *Johnny Cymbal*

c) Songs About Specific Aspects of Rock & Roll

"Roll Over Beethoven" (1956)   *Chuck Berry*
"Rock & Roll Music" (1957)   *Chuck Berry*
"Johnny B. Goode" (1958)   *Chuck Berry*
"Dede Dinah" (1958)   *Frankie Avalon*
"The All-American Boy" (1958)   *Bill Parsons*
"Teen Beat" (1959)   *Sandy Nelson*
"More Money For You and Me" (1960)   *Four Preps*
"Who Put the Bomp?" (1961)   *Barry Mann*
"Let There Be Drums" (1961)   *Sandy Nelson*
"Drums Are My Beat" (1962)   *Sandy Nelson*
"Mr. Bass Man" (1963)   *Johnny Cymbal*

● LIST #9: Rock & Roll Martyrs

Not only did rock & roll provide teenagers with heroes, but it also gave them their very own martyrs. The first to develop a cult following was singer Johnny Ace (of "Pledging My Love" fame), when he accidently shot himself while playing Russian Roulette backstage during a concert in 1954. Other early rock & roll performers also died tragic deaths. Weird coincidences sometimes accompanied the deaths. Chuck Willis' last record was "What Am I Living For?" The flip side was "Hang Up My Rock & Roll Shoes." Buddy Holly, prior to his death, had just released "It Doesn't Matter Anymore." And Eddie Cochran, just before his fatal car crash, had recorded a memorial tribute to his friend, Buddy Holly. Every time a rock star died, teenagers joined together to mourn their late idol. In this way, the fallen stars provided an additional means to teen identity and solidarity.

a) Rock Stars Who Passed Away

Johnny Ace—1954, accidental shooting
Chuck Willis—1958, died after surgery
Buddy Holly—1959, plane crash
the Big Bopper—1959, plane crash
Ritchie Valens—1959, plane crash
Jesse Belvin—1960, car crash
Eddie Cochran—1960, car crash
Johnny Horton—1960, car crash
Sam Cooke—1964, shooting victim
Jim Reeves—1964, plane crash

b) Memorial Songs

"Three Stars" (1959)   Tribute to Holly, Valens, and the Big Bopper. Versions were done by Tommy Dee and Eddie Cochran.

"The Great Tragedy" (1959)   Tribute to Holly, Valens, and the Big Bopper, recorded by Hershel Almond.

"The Ballad of Donna and Peggy Sue" (1959)   Tribute to Holly and Valens, recorded by Ray Campi.

"Gold Records in the Snow" (1959)   Tribute to Holly, Valens, and the Big Bopper, recorded by Bennie Barnes.

"Three Young Men" (1959)   Tribute to Holly, Valens, and the Big Bopper, recorded by Lee Davis.

"Tribute To Buddy Holly" (1963)   Mike Berry

"Buddy's Song" (1963)   Bobby Vee (written by Waylon Jennings)

In addition to the singles mentioned above, several albums were released in the early 1960s as tributes to Buddy Holly, including Bobby Vee's *I Remember Buddy Holly* (1963); Jimmy Gilmer's *Buddy's Buddy* (1964); and Tommy Allsup's *The Buddy Holly Songbook* (1965).

● LIST #10: Parties

Most teenagers associated parties with fun, so naturally many rock & roll records dealt with the subject.

"Rock & Roll Party" (1955)   *Red Prysock*
"Party Time" (1957)   *Sal Mineo*
"Splish Splash" (1958)   *Bobby Darin*
"C'mon Everybody" (1958)   *Eddie Cochran*
"Let's Have a Party" (1960)   *Wanda Jackson*
"Quarter to Three" (1961)   *Gary U.S. Bonds*
"Quite a Party" (1961)   *Fireballs*
"Party Lights" (1962)   *Claudine Clark*
"Beach Party" (1962)   *King Curtis*
"Shout! Shout! (Knock Yourself Out)" (1962)   *Ernie Maresca*
"It's My Party" (1963)   *Leslie Gore*

● LIST #11: School

Since a large part of a teenager's life involved going to school, it is not surprising to find numerous records on that topic. Rock & roll songs dealt with both the positive and negative aspects of school. School spirit, a teen microcosm of the era's patriotism, was the subject of several records. High school graduation was another popular subject. Numerous songs focused on social activities which made school worthwhile (particularly boy-girl relations at school), while other records allowed teenagers to vent their frustrations and anger at teachers, principals, and mandatory school attendance.

a) Songs About School in General

"Graduation Day" (1956)   *Four Freshmen*
"Mr. Lee" (1957)   *Bobbettes*
"After School" (1957)   *Randy Starr*
"Hey School Girl" (1957)   *Tom and Jerry* (i.e., Simon & Garfunkel)
"Queen of the Senior Prom" (1957)   *Mills Brothers*
"Walkin' Home from School" (1958)   *Gene Vincent*
"Hey Little Girl (In the High School Sweater)" (1959)   *Dee Clark*

"High School U.S.A." (1959)   *Tommy Facenda*
"Graduation's Here" (1959)   *Fleetwoods*
"See You in September" (1959)   *Tempos*
"Wonderful World" (1960)   *Sam Cooke*
"Angela Jones" (1960)   *Johnny Ferguson*
"Swingin' School" (1960)   *Bobby Rydell*
"Pink Chiffon" (1960)   *Mitchell Torok*
"Valley High" (1961)   *Lettermen*
"School Is In" (1961)   *Gary U.S. Bonds*
"Pomp and Circumstance" (1961)   *Adrian Kimberley*
"It Might As Well Rain Until September" (1962)   *Carole King*
"Roses Are Red" (1962)   *Bobby Vinton*
"The Cheerleader" (1963)   *Paul Petersen*
"Pom Pom Play Girl" (1964)   *Beach Boys*
"Be True To Your School" (1964)   *Beach Boys*
"New Girl in School" (1964)   *Jan and Dean*
"Abigail Beecher (My History Teacher)" (1964)   *Freddy Cannon*

b) Dislike of School

"School Day" (1957)   *Chuck Berry*
"Waitin' in School" (1957)   *Ricky Nelson*
"Back to School Again" (1957)   *Timmie Rogers*
"College Man" (1958)   *Bill Justis*
"Bird Dog" (1958)   *Everly Brothers*
"Summertime Summertime" (1958)   *Jamies*

"C'mon Everybody" (1958)   *Eddie Cochran*
"Charlie Brown" (1959)   *Coasters*
"Here Comes Summer" (1959)   *Jerry Keller*
"Makin' Love" (1959)   *Floyd Robinson*
"Class Cutter" (1959)   *Dale Hawkins*
"I Shot Mr. Lee" (1960)   *Bobbettes*
"School Is Out" (1961)   *Gary U.S. Bonds*
"Stayin' In" (1961)   *Bobby Vee*

● LIST #12: Fashions and Products

Various consumer goods, particularly clothes, were vitally important to the maintenance of teenage subcultures. Rock music reflected the various styles, products, and goods purchased by teenagers seeking status and teen identity. A year-by-year review of rock & roll records provides a veritable catalog of teen fashions, including clothes, shoes, accessories, and hairstyles. Products used by teens were also featured in songs. Some performers actually named themselves after popular items.

a) Songs About Fashions and Fashion Items

1955   "Black Denim Trousers"   *Cheers*
          "Black Denim Trousers"   *Vaughn Monroe*
1956   "Blue Suede Shoes"   *Carl Perkins*
          "Blue Suede Shoes"   *Elvis Presley*
          "Be Bob a Lula"   *Gene Vincent*
          "Blue Jean Bop"   *Gene Vincent*
1957   "Black Slacks"   *Sparkletones*
          "Penny Loafers and Bobby Socks"   *Sparkletones*
          "White Sportcoat and a Pink Carnation"   *Marty Robbins*
          "White Sportcoat and a Pink Carnation"   *Johnny Desmond*
1958   "Chantilly Lace"   *Big Bopper*
          "Jeanie, Jeanie, Jeanie"   *Eddie Cochran*
          "Betty Lou Got a New Pair of Shoes"   *Bobby Freeman*
          "No Chemise Please"   *Gerry Granahan*
          "White Bucks and Saddle Shoes"   *Bobby Pedrick, Jr.*
          "Pink Pedal Pushers"   *Carl Perkins*
          "Short Shorts"   *Royal Teens*

1959	"Lipstick On Your Collar"	*Connie Francis*
	"Bobby Sox To Stockings"	*Frankie Avalon*
	"First Name Initial"	*Annette* (about jewelry)
	"Pointed Toe Shoes"	*Carl Perkins*
	"Tan Shoes and Pink Shoe Laces"	*Dodie Stevens*
1960	"Itsy Bitsy Teenie Weenie Yellow Polka Dot Bikini"	
		Brian Hyland
	"Pink Chiffon"	*Mitchell Torok*
1962	"Venus in Blue Jeans"	*Jimmy Clanton*
	"She Can't Find Her Keys"	*Paul Petersen* (about girls' large purses)
1963	"Betty in Bermudas"	*Dovells*
	"Charms"	*Bobby Vee* (about jewelry)

b) Songs About Hair Styles

Short hair

"My Boy Flat Top" (1955)   *Boyd Bennett*
"Here Comes Summer" (1959)   *Jerry Keller* (mentions flat-tops)

Longer hair

"The All-American Boy" (1958)   *Bill Parsons*
"Kookie Kookie (Lend Me Your Comb)" (1959)   *Edd Byrnes* (with Connie Stevens)

Pony tails

"Chantilly Lace" (1958)   *Big Bopper*
"What Is Love" (1959)   *Playmates*
"Sheila" (1962)   *Tommy Roe*
One group, the Poni-Tails (of "Born Too Late" fame) even named themselves after the popular girls' style.

c) Songs About Products

"The Ballad of Davy Crockett" (1955)   *Bill Hayes* (based on Disney TV show and demand for Crockett-related products)
"Got a Match" (1958)   *Daddy-O's* (about cigarettes)

"Flip Top Box" (1958)   *Dickey Doo and the Don'ts* (about
                        cigarettes)
"Hula Hoop Song" (1958)   *Georgia Gibbs*
"Running Bear" (1959)   *Johnny Preston* (inspired by Dove
                        Soap commercial)
"Big Name Button" (1959)   *Royal Teens*
"Does Your Chewing Gum Lose Its Flavor
  on the Bed Post Overnight?" (1961)   *Lonnie Donegan*
"Transistor Sister" (1961)   *Freddy Cannon*
"Jeremiah Peabody's Polyunsaturated Quick Dissolving Fast
  Action Pleasant Tasting Green and Purple Pills" (1961)
                        Ray Stevens (spoof on commercials)
"The Percolator Twist" (1962)   *Checkmates* (based on Maxwell
                        House Coffee commercial)
"Nick Teen and Al K. Hall" (1963)   *Rolf Harris* (about
                        cigarettes and alcohol)

d) Performers Named After Fashions and Products

Gene Vincent and His Blue Caps
Velours
Poni-Tails
Kuf-Linx

● LIST #13: Cars and Motorcycles

America's fascination with automobiles was reflected in rock &
roll. During the 1950s, more than 67.4 million cars and trucks were
on the road—at least one per household. Since many of these were
designed to appeal to sex and power, rock & roll artists commonly
used cars to symbolize sex, power, success, or rebellion. Some rock
groups even named themselves after cars.

a) Songs About Cars

"Rocket 88" (1951)   *Ike Turner Band*
"Maybellene" (1955)   *Chuck Berry*
"No Money Down" (1956)   *Chuck Berry*
"Race with the Devil" (1956)   *Gene Vincent*
"Transfusion" (1956)   *Nervous Norvous*

"Gas Money" (1958)   *Jan and Arnie*
"Beep Beep" (1958)   *Playmates*
"Seven Little Girls (Sitting in the Backseat)" (1959)   *Paul Evans*

"It's Late" (1959)   *Rick Nelson*
"Teen Angel" (1959)   *Mark Dinning*
"Hot Rod Lincoln" (1960)   *Johnny Bond*
"Hot Rod Lincoln" (1960)   *Charlie Ryan*
"Tell Laura I Love Her" (1960)   *Ray Peterson*
"Stick Shift" (1961)   *Duals*
"409" (1962)   *Beach Boys*
"Shut Down" (1963)   *Beach Boys*
"Little Deuce Coupe" (1963)   *Beach Boys*
"Wide Track" (1963)   *Beach Boys*
"Four on the Floor" (1963)   *Beach Boys*
"Street Machine" (1963)   *Beach Boys*
"Hot Rod Race" (1963)   *Beach Boys*
"Car Trouble" (1963)   *Beach Boys*
"Our Car Club" (1963)   *Beach Boys*
"Ballad of Ole Betsy" (1963)   *Beach Boys*
"Car Crazy Cutie" (1963)   *Beach Boys*
"Cherry Cherry Coupe" (1963)   *Beach Boys*
"Custom Machine" (1963)   *Beach Boys*
"Hey Little Cobra" (1963)   *Rip Chords*
"Six Days on the Road" (1963)   *Dave Dudley*
"Drag City" (1963)   *Jan and Dean*
"I Gotta Drive" (1963)   *Jan and Dean*
"Drag Strip Girl" (1963)   *Jan and Dean*
"Dead Man's Curve" (1963)   *Jan and Dean*
"Sting Ray" (1963)   *Jan and Dean*
"Three Window Coupe" (1964)   *Rip Chords*
"G.T.O." (1964)   *Ronny and the Daytonas*
"Bucket T." (1964)   *Ronny and the Daytonas*
"Three Window Coupe" (1964)   *Jan and Dean*
"Bucket T." (1964)   *Jan and Dean*
"My Mighty G.T.O." (1964)   *Jan and Dean*
"Little Old Lady From Pasadena" (1964)   *Jan and Dean*
"The Anaheim Azusa and Cucamonga Sewing Circle, Book Review and Timing Association" (1964)   *Jan and Dean*
"Last Kiss" (1964)   *J. Frank Wilson*

"Don't Worry Baby" (1964)   *Beach Boys*
"This Car of Mine" (1964)   *Beach Boys*
"Shut Down Part 2" (1964)   *Beach Boys*
"I Get Around" (1964)   *Beach Boys*
"Don't Back Down" (1964)   *Beach Boys*
"Nadine" (1964)   *Chuck Berry*
"No Particular Place to Go" (1964)   *Chuck Berry*

b) Songs About Motorcycles

"Bad Motorcycle" (1958)   *Storey Sisters*
"Motorcycle" (1962)   *Tico and the Triumphs*
"Leader of the Pack" (1964)   *Shangri-Las*
"Little Honda" (1964)   *Hondells*
"Little Honda" (1964)   *Beach Boys*

c) Groups Named After Motor Vehicles

Cadillacs   "Speedoo" (1955)
El Dorados   "Bim Bam Boom" (1956)
Valiants   "This Is the Night" (1957)
Little Anthony and the Imperials   "Tears on My Pillow" (1958)
Impalas   "Sorry" (1959)
Fleetwoods   "Come Softly To Me" (1959)
Duals   "Stick Shift" (1961)
Edsels   "Rama Lama Ding Dong" (1961)
Tico and the Triumphs   "Motorcycle" (1962)
Hondells   "Little Honda" (1964)

● LIST #14: Teenage Slang

Since rock & roll records were aimed at the teen audience, they frequently made use of popular slang and expressions.

a) Slang Terms and Teenage Speech Patterns

Numerous records made use of popular slang. If a girl was pretty, she was considered "tough" (the Kuf-Linx's "So Tough" [1958] and Ace Cannon's "Tuff" [1961]), or a "crazy chick" (Bill Haley and His Comets' "Skinnie Minnie" [1958] and the Royal Teens' "Short Shorts" [1958]). If you didn't know what to say, you were left "breathless" (Jerry Lee Lewis' "Breathless" [1958]). Cars were "wheels" (Edd Byrnes' "Kookie Kookie" [1959]). Kids who were afraid were "chicken" (the Cheers' "Chicken" [1956]). Something you liked was "neat" (Dale Wright's "She's Neat" [1958]), or "crazy" (Bill Haley and His Comets' "Crazy Man Crazy" [1953]). If it was especially neat, it was the "utmost, the very utmost" (Edd Byrnes, "Kookie Kookie" [1959]) or "gone" as in far out (Bill Haley and His Comets' "Crazy Man Crazy" [1953]). If it was really crazy, not to be confused with "neat," it was "kookie" (the Tree Swingers' "Kookie Little Paradise" [1960]). But if it was ugly, it was "raunchy" (Bill Justis, "Raunchy" [1957]). Then again, if it was really ugly, then it was "whupped with an ugly stick" (Bo Diddley, "Say Man" [1959]). If you wanted to tell someone things were okay, you gave him the "high sign" (the Diamonds' "High Sign" [1958]). If something wasn't up to par, it was "rinky dink" (Dave "Baby" Cortez, "Rinky Dink" [1962]). But if it was the ideal place, then it was "where it's at" (Chris Kenner, "I Like It Like That" [1961]). If you didn't get along with someone, that person "bugged you" (Larry Williams' "You Bug Me Baby" [1957]). And if things really got bad, violence erupted in a "rumble" (Link Wray, "Rumble" [1958]). Somebody who was "cool" was a "cat" (Johnny Otis, "Willie and the Hand Jive" [1958] and Carl Perkins, "Blue Suede Shoes" [1956]), or a "daddy-o" (the Sparkletones' "Black Slacks" [1957]). But you had to be careful, because "daddy-o" could also be an insult for a teacher or someone else who was not cool (Bonnie Lou, "Daddy-O" [1955], the Fontane Sisters, "Daddy-O" [1955], or the Coasters' "Charlie Brown" [1959]). Employers were "the man" (Roy Orbison, "Workin' for the Man" [1962]). If you were in love, you got "lovey dovey" (Buddy Knox, "Lovey Dovey" [1960]). And if you were deeply in love, the object of your affections "sent you" (Sam Cooke, "You Send Me" [1957]), or made you want to "rave on this crazy feeling" (Buddy Holly, "Rave On" [1958]). When the romance died, the couple had to "break up" (Neil Sedaka, "Breaking Up Is Hard To Do" [1962]), which might have been caused because one lover "cheated" on the other (the Shields, "You Cheated" [1958]), or perhaps had not shown up for a date, in which case the person waiting was "stood up" (Ricky Nelson, "Stood Up" [1957]). But there was always hope that you could get a date "on the rebound" from broken romance (Floyd Cramer, "On the Rebound" [1961].

Records reflected teenage speech patterns. They showed that teens used colloquial terms like "ain't" (Clarence Henry, "Ain't Got No Home" [1956]), and "ya" (Patience and Prudence, "Gonna Get

Along Without Ya Now" [1956]). They showed that some teens used euphemisms for profanity: "hell" came out as "heck" on songs like the Royal Teens' "Who the Heck Is Harvey?" (1958), and "Jesus" was shortened to "gee" on songs such as Pat Boone's "Gee Whittakers" (1955), the Crows' "Gee" (1954), the Innocents' "Gee Whiz" (1960), and Carla Thomas' "Gee Whiz" (1961).

b) Common Expressions of the Day

"Ain't It a Shame" (1955)   *Fats Domino*
"Ain't That a Shame" (1955)   *Pat Boone*
"See You Later Alligator" (1955)   *Bill Haley and His Comets*
"That'll Be the Day" (1957)   *Buddy Holly & the Crickets*
"Oh Boy" (1957)   *Buddy Holly and the Crickets*
"Think It Over" (1958)   *Buddy Holly and the Crickets*
"How the Time Flies" (1958)   *Jerry Wallace*
"You've Got What It Takes" (1959)   *Marv Johnson*
"Wishful Thinking" (1959)   *Little Anthony & the Imperials*
"Good Timin'" (1960)   *Jimmy Jones*
"Happy Go Lucky Me" (1960)   *Paul Evans*
"Walk, Don't Run" (1960)   *Ventures*
"Tossin' and Turnin'" (1961)   *Bobby Lewis*
"Running Scared" (1961)   *Roy Orbison*
"Take Five" (1961)   *Dave Brubeck*
"Hit the Road, Jack" (1961)   *Ray Charles*
"You Don't Know What You've Got,
  Until You Lose It" (1961)   *Ral Donner*
"You Beat Me to the Punch" (1962)   *Mary Wells*
"You Can't Judge a Book by Its Cover" (1962)   *Bo Diddley*
"Snap Your Fingers" (1962)   *Joe Henderson*
"Hush Your Mouth" (1962)   *Jimmy Reed*
"Sealed With a Kiss" (1962)   *Brian Hyland*

● LIST #15: "Name" Songs

The names given to members of the baby boom generation frequently turned up on rock & roll records. Popular girls' names were particular favorites of song writers, although records focusing on boys' names also made the charts.

a) Songs About Girls' Names

Barbara

"Barbara" (1960)   *Temptations*
"Barbara Ann" (1961)   *Regents*
"Please Don't Ask About Barbara" (1962)   *Bobby Vee*

Betty

"Betty Lou's Got a New Pair of Shoes" (1958)   *Bobby Freeman*
"Betty and Dupree" (1958)   *Chuck Willis*
"Betty My Angel" (1959)   *Jerry Fuller*
"Betty in Bermudas" (1963)   *Dovells*
"A Letter from Betty" (1963)   *Bobby Vee*

Carol

"Carol" (1956)   *Schoolboys*
"Carol" (1958)   *Chuck Berry*
"Oh, Carol" (1959)   *Neil Sedaka*

Cathy

"Kathy-O" (1958)   *Diamonds*
"Cathy's Clown" (1960)   *Everly Brothers*
"Close to Cathy" (1962)   *Mike Clifford*

Diane

"Diana" (1957)   *Paul Anka*
"Dede Dinah" (1958)   *Frankie Avalon*
"Little Diane" (1962)   *Dion*

Donna

"Donna" (1958)   *Ritchie Valens*
"Donna the Prima Donna" (1963)   *Dion*

Jean

"Lean Jean" (1958)   *Bill Haley and His Comets*
"Jeanie, Jeanie, Jeanie" (1958)   *Eddie Cochran*

Jennie

"Jenny Jenny" (1957)   *Little Richard*
"Jennie Lee" (1958)   *Jan and Dean*
"Poor Jenny" (1959)   *Everly Brothers*

Julie

"Oh, Julie" (1957)   *Crescendos*
"How Is Julie" (1962)   *Lettermen*

Linda

"Linda Lu" (1959)   *Ray Sharpe*
"I Saw Linda Yesterday" (1962)   *Dickey Lee*
"Linda" (1963)   *Jan and Dean*

Mary

"Marianne" (1957)   *Easyriders*
"Mary Lou" (1959)   *Ronnie Hawkins*
"Take a Message to Mary" (1959)   *Everly Brothers*
"Hello Mary Lou" (1961)   *Rick Nelson*
"Mary Ann Regrets" (1962)   *Burl Ives*
"Meet Me at Midnight, Mary" (1963)   *Joey Powers*
"What Will My Mary Say?" (1963)   *Johnny Mathis*

Molly

"Good Golly Miss Molly" (1958)   *Little Richard*
"Molly" (1962)   *Bobby Goldsboro*

Patricia

"Patricia" (1958)   *Perez Prado*
"Patty Baby" (1963)   *Freddy Cannon*

Ruby

"Ruby" (1960)   *Ray Charles*
"Ruby Baby" (1963)   *Dion*

Sally

"Long Tall Sally" (1956)   *Little Richard*
"Long Tall Sally" (1956)   *Pat Boone*
"Sally Go 'Round the Roses" (1963)   *Jaynettes*

Sandy

"Sandy" (1959)   *Larry Hall*
"Sandy" (1963)   *Dion*

Sherry

"Sherry" (1962)   *Four Seasons*
"Letter from Sherry" (1963)   *Dale Ward*

Susan

"Wake Up Little Susie" (1957)   *Everly Brothers*
"Susie Q" (1957)   *Dale Hawkins*
"Susie Darlin'" (1958)   *Robin Luke*
"Suzie Baby" (1959)   *Bobby Vee*
"Runaround Sue" (1961)   *Dion*
"Susie Darlin'" (1962)   *Tommy Roe*
"Tra La La La Suzy" (1963)   *Dean and Jean*

Other songs about girls' names

"Be Bop a Lula" (1956)   *Gene Vincent*
"Rosie Lee" (1957)   *Mello-Tones*
"Florence" (1957)   *Paragons*
"Tammy" (1957)   *Debbie Reynolds*
"Shirley" (1957)   *Schoolboys*
"Bernardine" (1957)   *Pat Boone*
"Peggy Sue" (1957)   *Buddy Holly*
"Lucille" (1957)   *Little Richard*
"Short Fat Fanny" (1957)   *Larry Williams*
"Claudette" (1958)   *Everly Brothers*
"Skinny Minnie" (1958)   *Bill Haley and His Comets*
"Dizzy Miss Lizzy" (1958)   *Larry Williams*
"Valerie" (1958)   *Mello-Kings*
"Joanne" (1958)   *Twin-Tones*
"Joanne" (1958)   *Playmates*
"Dottie" (1958)   *Danny and the Juniors*

"Teresa" (1958)   *Eddie Cochran*
"Judy" (1959)   *David Seville*
"Nola" (1959)   *Billy Williams*
"Goodnight Irene" (1959)   *Billy Williams*
"Georgia on My Mind" (1960)   *Ray Charles*
"Angela Jones" (1960)   *Johnny Ferguson*
"Darling Lorraine" (1960)   *Knockouts*
"Corinna Corinna" (1960)   *Ray Peterson*
"Tell Laura I Love Her" (1960)   *Ray Peterson*
"My Girl Josephine" (1960)   *Fats Domino*
"Maria" (1960)   *Johnny Mathis*
"Lucille" (1960)   *Everly Brothers*
"Be Bop a Lula" (1960)   *Everly Brothers*
"Laurie" (1961)   *Bobby Vee*
"Charlena" (1961)   *Sevilles*
"Marie's the Name His Latest Flame" (1961)   *Elvis Presley*
"Jamie" (1962)   *Eddie Holland*
"Gina" (1962)   *Johnny Mathis*
"Sheila" (1962)   *Tommy Roe*
"I've Got Bonnie" (1962)   *Bobby Rydell*
"Gloria" (1962)   *Vito and the Salutations*
"Cindy's Birthday" (1962)   *Johnny Crawford*
"Anna" (1962)   *Arthur Alexander*
"Irene" (1962)   *Bobby Vee*
"Brenda" (1963)   *the Cupids*
"Judy's Turn to Cry" (1963)   *Leslie Gore*
"Marlena" (1963)   *Four Seasons*
"Don't Wanna Think About Paula" (1963)   *Dickey Lee*
"Amy" (1963)   *Paul Petersen*
"Denise" (1963)   *Randy and the Rainbows*
"Maria Elena" (1963)   *Los Indios Tabajaras*
"Wendy" (1964)   *Beach Boys*
"Dawn" (1964)   *Four Seasons*
"Ronnie" (1964)   *Four Seasons*

b) Songs About Boys' Names

"Jim Dandy" (1956)   *Laverne Baker*
"Ready Teddy" (1956)   *Little Richard*
"Eddie My Love" (1956)   *Teen Queens*

"Billy" (1958)   *Kathy Linden*
"Who the Heck Is Harvey?" (1958)   *Royal Teens*
"Goodbye, Jimmy, Goodbye" (1959)   *Kathy Linden*
"Frankie" (1959)   *Connie Francis*
"Joey's Song" (1959)   *Bill Haley and His Comets*
"Oh, Danny Boy" (1959)   *Conway Twitty*
"Tall Paul" (1959)   *Annette*
"Ambrose, Part 5" (1959)   *Linda Laurie*
"Teddy" (1960)   *Connie Francis*
"Big Boy Pete" (1960)   *Olympics*
"Jimmy's Girl" (1961)   *Johnny Tillotson*
"Norman" (1961)   *Sue Thompson*
"Hit the Road, Jack" (1961)   *Ray Charles*
"Michael (Row the Boat Ashore)" (1961)   *Highwaymen*
"Big John" (1961)   *Shirelles*
"Frankie and Johnny" (1961)   *Brook Benton*
"James Hold the Ladder Steady" (1962)   *Sue Thompson*
"Johnny Jingo" (1962)   *Hayley Mills*
"Johnny Angel" (1962)   *Shelley Fabares*
"Johnny Loves Me" (1962)   *Shelley Fabares*
"Johnny Get Angry" (1962)   *Joanie Sommers*
"Just Tell Her Jim Said Hello" (1962)   *Elvis Presley*
"Bobby's Girl" (1962)   *Marcie Blane*
"My One and Only Jimmy Boy" (1963)   *Girlfriends*
"Willie Can" (1963)   *Sue Thompson*
"Ronnie, Call Me When You Get a Chance" (1963)   *Shelley Fabares*
"Frankie and Johnny" (1963)   *Sam Cooke*
"Wait 'Til My Bobby Gets Home" (1963)   *Darlene Love*

● LIST #16: Love and Courtship

Naturally, teen romance and dating were the subjects of innumerable records. Some rock & rollers sang about the glories of teenage love. Others about love gone wrong. Still others focused on unrequited love, teenagers' longing for romance, or teen dating patterns. Most of these records indicate that the rock & roll version of love and romance differed very little from that of earlier generations. The following records are just a few examples of rock songs about love and courtship.

"Pledging My Love" (1955)   *Johnny Ace*
"Heartbreak Hotel" (1956)   *Elvis Presley*
"I Want You, I Need You, I Love You" (1956)   *Elvis Presley*
"Love Me Tender" (1956)   *Elvis Presley*
"A Teenager's Romance" (1957)   *Ricky Nelson*
"Have I Told You Lately That I Love You?" (1957)   *Ricky Nelson*
"Gone" (1957)   *Ferlin Husky*
"Bye Bye Love" (1957)   *Everly Brothers*
"Long Lonely Nights" (1957)   *Lee Andrews and the Hearts*
"Poor Little Fool" (1958)   *Ricky Nelson*
"Lonesome Town" (1958)   *Ricky Nelson*
"You Are My Destiny" (1958)   *Paul Anka*
"I'll Wait for You" (1958)   *Frankie Avalon*
"For Your Precious Love" (1958)   *Jerry Butler*
"It's All in the Game" (1958)   *Tommy Edwards*
"This Little Girl of Mine" (1958)   *Everly Brothers*
"Devoted to You" (1958)   *Everly Brothers*
"Just a Dream" (1958)   *Jimmy Clanton*
"Big Man" (1958)   *Four Preps*
"Tears on my Pillow" (1958)   *Little Anthony & the Imperials*
"Put Your Head on My Shoulder" (1959)   *Paul Anka*
"Venus" (1959)   *Frankie Avalon*
"Why" (1959)   *Frankie Avalon*
"This Should Go On Forever" (1959)   *Rod Bernard*
"First Anniversary" (1959)   *Cathy Carr*
"The Big Hurt" (1959)   *Miss Toni Fisher*
"Mr. Blue" (1959)   *Fleetwoods*
"I Want to Be Wanted" (1960)   *Brenda Lee*
"I'm Sorry" (1960)   *Brenda Lee*
"Only the Lonely" (1960)   *Roy Orbison*
"Puppy Love" (1960)   *Paul Anka*
"Mission Bell" (1960)   *Donnie Brooks*
"He Will Break Your Heart" (1960)   *Jerry Butler*
"A Million to One" (1960)   *Jimmy Charles*
"The Way You Look Tonight" (1961)   *Lettermen*
"When I Fall in Love" (1961)   *Lettermen*
"Crying" (1961)   *Roy Orbison*
"Running Scared" (1961)   *Roy Orbison*
"Moon River" (1961)   *Jerry Butler*

"There's a Moon Out Tonight" (1961)   *Capris*
"Please Love Me Forever" (1961)   *Cathy Jean & the Roommates*
"Look in my Eyes" (1961)   *Chantels*
"Heart and Soul" (1961)   *Cleftones*
"Rain Drops" (1961)   *Dee Clark*
"Runaway" (1961)   *Del Shannon*
"Girl of My Best Friend" (1961)   *Ral Donner*
"Jimmy's Girl" (1961)   *Johnny Tillotson*
"Come Back Silly Girl" (1962)   *Lettermen*
"All Alone Am I" (1962)   *Brenda Lee*
"Till Death Do Us Part" (1962)   *Bob Braun*
"So This Is Love" (1962)   *Castells*
"Crying in the Rain" (1962)   *Everly Brothers*
"I Sold My Heart to the Junkman" (1962)   *Blue Belles*
"Heartbreaker" (1962)   *Dean Christie*
"When a Boy Falls in Love" (1963)   *Mel Carter*
"Every Day I Have to Cry" (1963)   *Steve Alaimo*
"You Don't Have to Be a Baby to Cry" (1963)   *Caravelles*
"Rhythm of the Rain" (1963)   *Cascades*
"Two Faces Have I" (1963)   *Lou Christie*

● LIST #17: Sex and Morality

Rock & roll music, like the teen culture and adult culture in general, both accepted and rejected traditional sexual attitudes and morals. Some rock songs echoed the 1950s standards of sexual behavior. For example, teen guilt and worries about innocently having stayed out past curfews were the subjects of the Everly Brothers' "Wake Up Little Susie" (1957) and Ricky Nelson's "It's Late" (1959). Other songs, such as the Kingsmen's "Louie Louie" (1963) or Little Richard's "Long Tall Sally" (1956) clearly overstepped the era's bounds of sexual propriety.

a) Traditional Attitudes

"Wake Up Little Susie" (1957)   *Everly Brothers*
"You're So Square (Baby I Don't Care)" (1958)   *Elvis Presley*
"It's Late" (1959)   *Ricky Nelson*
"Please Help Me I'm Falling" (1960)   *Hank Locklin*
"Sacred" (1961)   *Castells*

"That's Old Fashioned" (1962)   *Everly Brothers*
"Go Away Little Girl" (1962)   *Steve Lawrence*
"Please Don't Ever Change" (1962)   *Crickets*
"What Will Mary Say" (1963)   *Johnny Mathis*
See also List #18 (songs about marriage and going steady).

b) Non-Traditional Attitudes

"Work With Me Annie" (1954)   *Hank Ballard & the Midnighters*
"Annie Had a Baby" (1954)   *Hank Ballard & the Midnighters*
"Love Is Strange" (1956)   *Mickey and Sylvia*
"Long Tall Sally" (1956)   *Little Richard*
"Rip It Up" (1956)   *Little Richard*
"Fever" (1956)   *Little Willie John*
"Be Bop a Lula" (1956)   *Gene Vincent*
"Whole Lot of Shakin' Going On" (1957)   *Jerry Lee Lewis*
"Great Balls of Fire" (1957)   *Jerry Lee Lewis*
"Party Doll" (1957)   *Buddy Knox*
"(Annie's Been Workin') The Midnight Shift" (1957)   *Buddy Holly*
"Good Golly Miss Molly" (1958)   *Little Richard*
"Fever" (1958)   *Peggy Lee*
"Breathless" (1958)   *Jerry Lee Lewis*
"Reelin' and Rockin' " (1958)   *Chuck Berry*
"One Night With You" (1958)   *Elvis Presley*
"That's My Desire" (1958)   *Dion and the Belmonts*
"Sweet Nothins" (1959)   *Brenda Lee*
"Will You Love Me Tomorrow" (1960)   *Shirelles*
"Last Night" (1961)   *Mar-Keys*
"I Love How You Love Me" (1961)   *Paris Sisters*
"The Stripper" (1962)   *David Rose*
"Louie Louie" (1963)   *Kingsmen*

● LIST #18: Marriage and Going Steady

Even the adults' propensity toward marriage, as witnessed in the rising marriage rates during the 1950s, spilled over into the youth culture. Numerous rock & roll hits idealized marriage. Hit records about going steady—the adolescent version of monogamy—were also common.

a) Marriage

"Church Bells May Ring" (1956)   *Willows*
"From a School Ring to a Wedding Ring" (1956)   *Rover Boys*
"To the Aisle" (1957)   *Five Satins*
"I'll Wait for You" (1958)   *Frankie Avalon*
"Now We're One" (1958)   *Buddy Holly*
"Down the Aisle of Love" (1958)   *Quin-Tones*
"The Wedding" (1958)   *June Valli*
"A House, a Car, and a Wedding Ring" (1958)   *Dale Hawkins*
"The Big Bopper's Wedding" (1958)   *Big Bopper*
"I Got a Wife" (1959)   *Mark IV*
"I'm Gonna Get Married" (1959)   *Lloyd Price*
"Where Were You on Our Wedding Day" (1959)   *Lloyd Price*
"Primrose Lane" (1959)   *Jerry Wallace*
"The Hawaiian Wedding Song" (1959)   *Andy Williams*
"Alimony" (1959)   *Frankie Ford*
"Mountain of Love" (1960)   *Harold Dorman*
"Angela Jones" (1960)   *Johnny Ferguson*
"Tell Laura I Love Her" (1960)   *Ray Peterson*
"When We Get Married" (1961)   *Dreamlovers*
"Three Steps to the Altar" (1961)   *Shep and the Limelites*
"Make Believe Wedding" (1961)   *Castells*
"Life's Too Short" (1962)   *Lafayettes*
"Most People Get Married" (1962)   *Patti Page*
"Hey Paula (I Want To Marry You)" (1962)   *Paul and Paula*
"I Wish That We Were Married" (1962)   *Ronnie & the Hi-Lites*
"James (Hold the Ladder Steady)" (1962)   *Sue Thompson*
"What Will Mary Say" (1963)   *Johnny Mathis*
"Meet Me At Midnight Mary" (1963)   *Joey Powers*
"Chapel of Love" (1964)   *Dixie Cups*

b) Going Steady

"Eddie My Love" (1956)   *Teen Queens*
"Going Steady" (1957)   *Tommy Sands*
"Wear My Ring" (1957)   *Gene Vincent*
"White Bucks and Saddle Shoes" (1958)   *Bobby Pedrick Jr.*
"Wear My Ring (Around Your Neck)" (1958)   *Elvis Presley*
"Believe What You Say" (1958)   *Ricky Nelson*
"Well . . . All Right" (1958)   *Buddy Holly*

"Let's Go Steady for the Summer" (1958)   *Three G's*
"Teen Angel" (1959)   *Mark Dinning*
"Too Young to Go Steady" (1960)   *Connie Stevens*
"This Time" (1961)   *Troy Shondell*
"It's My Party" (1963)   *Leslie Gore*
"Let's Go Steady Again" (1963)   *Neil Sedaka*

● LIST #19: The Beat Generation

America's interest in the Beat Generation left its imprint on early rock & roll. During the 1950s and early 1960s, the public learned about "beatniks" through magazine articles and television shows. Before long, kids were imitating the media's stereotyped images of the Beats.

"Crazy Man Crazy" (1953)   *Bill Haley and His Comets*
"Bongo Rock" (1959)   *Preston Epps*
"Bongo Bongo Bongo" (1960)   *Preston Epps*
"Beatnik Fly" (1960)   *Johnny and the Hurricanes*
"Bongo Stomp" (1962)   *Little Joey and the Flips*

● LIST #20: Surfing

By the early 1960s, the surfing fad had taken America by storm. Youngsters on the west coast bought surf boards and caught the waves. Elsewhere, teens purchased sidewalk surf boards and hit the pavement. There were numerous beach party movies revolving around surfing. And teenagers wore jackets, jams, and other items geared to surfing. Rock music both reflected and affected the growth of the surf craze.

"Let's Go Trippin'" (1961)   *Dick Dale and the Deltones*
"Surfin'" (1962)   *Beach Boys*
"Surfin' Safari" (1962)   *Beach Boys*
"Surfer's Stomp" (1962)   *Marketts*
"Balboa Blue" (1962)   *Marketts*
"Beach Party" (1962)   *Dave York*
"Beach Party" (1962)   *King Curtis*
"Surfin' U.S.A." (1963)   *Beach Boys*

"Surfer Girl" (1963)   *Beach Boys*
"Pipeline" (1963)   *Chantays*
"Surf City" (1963)   *Jan and Dean*
"The Lonely Surfer" (1963)   *Jack Nitzsche*
"Wipe Out" (1963)   *Surfaris*
"Surfer Joe" (1963)   *Surfaris*
"Surfin' Bird" (1963)   *Trashmen*
"Catch a Wave" (1963)   *Beach Boys*
"Sidewalk Surfin'" (1963)   *Jan and Dean*

● LIST #21: Food

Perusing the rock charts of the 1950s and early 1960s was at times like going down an isle in a supermarket. Most of the era's popular foods also made tantalizing topics for rock & roll records.

"Cherry Pie" (1954)   *Marvin and Johnny*
"Peanuts" (1957)   *Little Joe and the Thrillers*
"Forty Cups of Coffee" (1957)   *Bill Haley and His Comets*
"Ginger Bread" (1958)   *Frankie Avalon*
"Lollipop" (1958)   *Chordettes*
"Fried Onions" (1958)   *Lord Rockingham XI*
"Cherry Pie" (1960)   *Skip and Flip*
"Peanut Butter" (1961)   *Marathons*
"Does Your Chewing Gum Lose Its Flavor on the Bed Post Overnight?" (1961)   *Lonnie Donegan*
"Peppermint Twist" (1961)   *Joey Dee and the Starlighters*
"Mashed Potato Time" (1962)   *Dee Dee Sharp*
"Gravy" (1962)   *Dee Dee Sharp*
"Green Onions" (1962)   *Booker T. and the MG's*
"Who Stole the Keeshka?" (1963)   *Matys Brothers*
"Hot Pastrami" (1963)   *Dartells*
"Hot Pastrami with Mashed Potatoes" (1963)   *Joey Dee and the Starlighters*
"Hooka Tooka (My Soda Crackers)" (1963)   *Chubby Checker*
"On Top of Spaghetti" (1963)   *Tom Glazer and the Children's Chorus*
"Hot Cakes (1st Serving)" (1963)   *Dave "Baby" Cortez*
"Bread and Butter" (1964)   *Newbeats*

● LIST #22: Holidays, Vacations, and Birthdays

These occasions provided much to sing about, as evidenced by the numerous records focusing on them.

a) Christmas Records

"Jingle Bell Rock" (1957)   *Bobby Helms*
"Santa and the Satellite" (1957)   *Buchanan and Goodman*
"The Chipmunk Song" (1958)   *Chipmunks*
"Happy Reindeer" (1958)   *Dancer, Prancer, and Nervous*
"Donde Está Santa Claus" (1958)   *Augie Rios*
"Little Drummer Boy" (1958)   *Harry Simeone Chorale*
"Rudolph the Red Nosed Reindeer" (1960)   *Chipmunks*
"Rockin' Around the Christmas Tree" (1960)   *Brenda Lee*
"Jingle Bell Rock" (1961)   *Bobby Rydell & Chubby Checker*
"Santa Claus Is Coming to Town" (1962)   *Four Seasons*
"Santa Claus Is Watching You" (1962)   *Ray Stevens*
"Little Saint Nick" (1964)   *Beach Boys*
"The Man with All the Toys" (1964)   *Beach Boys*
Numerous rock stars also put out Christmas albums, e.g., Elvis Presley, Bobby Vee, and the Beach Boys.

b) Songs About Birthdays

"Happy Happy Birthday Baby" (1957)   *Tune Weavers*
"Sixteen Candles" (1958)   *Crests*
"Happy Birthday Sweet Sixteen" (1961)   *Neil Sedaka*
"Happy Birthday Blues" (1961)   *Kathy Young & the Innocents*
"Cindy's Birthday" (1962)   *Johnny Crawford*
"Birthday Party" (1963)   *Pixies Three*

c) Songs About Vacations

"Summertime" (1957)   *Sam Cooke*
"Summertime Summertime" (1958)   *Jamies*
"Summertime Blues" (1958)   *Eddie Cochran*
"Here Comes Summer" (1959)   *Jerry Keller*
"Sea Cruise" (1959)   *Frankie Ford*
"Summer's Gone" (1960)   *Paul Anka*
"School Is Out" (1961)   *Gary U.S. Bonds*

"Summertime" (1961)　*Marcels*
"Vacation" (1962)　*Connie Francis*
"Summertime" (1962)　*Rick Nelson*
"Wonderful Summer" (1963)　*Robin Ward*

● LIST #23:　Miscellaneous Teen Activities

Rock & roll records dealt with almost every imaginable aspect of teen culture.

Swimming and baseball

"Summertime Summertime" (1958)　*Jamies*
"Here Comes Summer" (1959)　*Jerry Keller*
"School Is Out" (1961)　*Gary U.S. Bonds*

Baby sitting

"Baby Sittin' Boogie" (1961)　*Buzz Clifford*
"School Is In" (1961)　*Gary U.S. Bonds*

Kissing

"One Kiss" (1957)　*Eddie Cochran*
"Seven Little Girls Sitting in the Backseat (Hugging and Kissing with Fred)" (1959)　*Paul Evans*
"Kissin' Time" (1959)　*Bobby Rydell*
"Kissin' Game" (1961)　*Dion*
"One Last Kiss" (1961)　*Bobby Vee*
"Save Your Kisses" (1962)　*Tommy Roe*
"Please Don't Kiss Me Again" (1963)　*Charmettes*
"Last Kiss" (1964)　*J. Frank Wilson*
"Kiss Me Sailor" (1964)　*Diane Renay*

Amusement parks

"Merry-Go-Round" (1961)　*Marv Johnson*
"Palisades Park" (1962)　*Freddy Cannon*
"I Saw Linda Yesterday" (1962)　*Dickey Lee*
"County Fair" (1962)　*Beach Boys*

Concert sing-a-longs

"Hootenanny" (1963)   *Glencoves*
"Soul Hootenanny" (1964)   *Gene Chandler*

Hanging around soda shops

"Waitin' in School" (1957)   *Ricky Nelson*
"An Empty Cup, A Broken Date" (1957)   *Buddy Holly and the Crickets*
"Little Queenie" (1959)   *Chuck Berry*
"If I Didn't Have a Dime to Play the Jukebox" (1962)   *Gene Pitney*

Needing gas money

"Gas Money" (1958)   *Jan and Arnie*
"Summertime Blues" (1958)   *Eddie Cochran*

Hitch-hiking

"Hitch-Hike" (1963)   *Marvin Gaye*

Walking

"I'm Walkin'" (1957)   *Fats Domino*
"I'm Walkin'" (1957)   *Ricky Nelson*
"Walkin' with Mr. Lee" (1958)   *Lee Allen*
"Walkin' Home from School" (1958)   *Gene Vincent*
"I Want to Walk You Home" (1959)   *Fats Domino*
"Angela Jones" (1960)   *Johnny Ferguson*
"Bashful Bob" (1960)   *Bobby Vee*
"Walkin' to New Orleans" (1960)   *Fats Domino*
"Walkin' with My Angel" (1961)   *Bobby Vee*

Movie theaters or drive-ins

"Sittin' in the Balcony" (1957)   *Eddie Cochran*
"Drive-In Show" (1957)   *Eddie Cochran*
"Wake Up Little Susie" (1957)   *Everly Brothers*
"Sad Movies" (1961)   *Sue Thompson*
"Those Lazy-Hazy-Crazy Days of Summer" (1963)   *Nat King Cole*

"All Summer Long" (1964)   *Beach Boys*

Love letters

"P.S. I Love You" (1953)   *Hilltoppers*
"I'm Gonna Sit Right Down and Write Myself a Letter"
(1957)   *Billy Williams*
"Love Letters in the Sand" (1957)   *Pat Boone*
"A Letter to an Angel" (1958)   *Jimmy Clanton*
"See You in September" (1959)   *Tempos*
"Please Mr. Postman" (1961)   *Marvelettes*
"It Might As Well Rain Until September" (1962)   *Carole King*
"Love Letters" (1962)   *Ketty Lester*
"Sealed with a Kiss" (1962)   *Brian Hyland*
"Letter from Sherry" (1963)   *Dale Ward*

Dear John letters

"Dear One" (1962)   *Larry Finegan*
"A Letter From Betty" (1963)   *Bobby Vee*

Telephone calls

"Ring My Phone" (1957)   *Tommy Sands*
"Waitin' in School" (1957)   *Ricky Nelson*
"Chantilly Lace" (1958)   *Big Bopper*
"Anonymous Phone Call" (1962)   *Bobby Vee*
"Do You Love Me?" (1962)   *Contours*
"Beachwood 4-5789" (1962)   *Marvelettes*
"Don't Hang Up" (1962)   *Orlons*

Saying goodnight

"Goodnight, Sweetheart, Goodnight" (1954)   *Spaniels*
"Don't Say Goodnight" (1957)   *Valentines*
"Goodnight My Love" (1957)   *McGuire Sisters*
"Goodnight My Love" (1959)   *Ray Peterson*
"Goodnight Irene" (1959)   *Billy Williams*
"Save Your Kisses" (1962)   *Tommy Roe*
"She Can't Find Her Keys" (1963)   *Paul Petersen*
"Goodnight My Love" (1963)   *Fleetwoods*
"Please Don't Kiss Me Again" (1963)   *Charmettes*

Self-consciousness about height and weight

"Long Tall Sally" (1956)   *Little Richard*
"Short Fat Fanny" (1957)   *Larry Williams*
"Bony Moronie" (1957)   *Larry Williams*
"Lean Jean" (1958)   *Bill Haley and His Comets*
"Skinnie Minnie" (1958)   *Bill Haley and His Comets*
"Tall Paul" (1959)   *Annette*
"Cut Across Shorty" (1960)   *Eddie Cochran*

Journals

"The Diary" (1958)   *Neil Sedaka*

High school rings

"From a School Ring to a Wedding Ring" (1956)   *Rover Boys*
"Wear My Ring" (1957)   *Gene Vincent*
"Wear My Ring Around Your Neck" (1958)   *Elvis Presley*
"Teen Angel" (1959)   *Mark Dinning*

High school sweaters

"Hey Little Girl (In the High School Sweater)" (1959)   *Dee Clark*

The Lettermen wore high school sweaters when performing.

Importance of teen friendship

"Girl of My Best Friend" (1961)   *Ral Donner*
"The Crowd" (1962)   *Roy Orbison*
"Be True to Your School" (1963)   *Beach Boys*
"I Get Around" (1964)   *Beach Boys*

Importance of having one's own room

"Teenage Heaven" (1958)   *Eddie Cochran*
"In My Room" (1963)   *Beach Boys*

● LIST #24: Teenage Rebellion

Rock & roll has often been viewed as a rebellious music that stood in contrast to the conformity and consensus of the 1950s and early 1960s. Many songs and styles provide evidence that rock music did have a rebellious side.

a) Sexually Suggestive Songs

"Shake, Rattle, and Roll" (1954)   *Joe Turner*
"Shake, Rattle, and Roll" (1954)   *Bill Haley and His Comets*
"Work with Me Annie" (1954)   *Hank Ballard and the Midnighters*
"Sexy Ways" (1954)   *Hank Ballard and the Midnighters*
"Annie Had a Baby" (1954)   *Hank Ballard & the Midnighters*
"Roll with Me, Henry (The Wallflower)" (1955)   *Etta James*
"Love Is Strange" (1956)   *Mickey and Sylvia*
"Rip It Up" (1956)   *Little Richard*
"Long Tall Sally" (1956)   *Little Richard*
"Fever" (1956)   *Little Willie John*
"I'm in Love Again" (1956)   *Fats Domino*
"Be Bop a Lula" (1956)   *Gene Vincent*
"In the Still of the Night" (1956)   *Five Satins*
"(Annie's Been Workin') The Midnight Shift" (1957)   *Buddy Holly*
"Whole Lot of Shakin' Going On" (1957)   *Jerry Lee Lewis*
"Great Balls of Fire" (1957)   *Jerry Lee Lewis*
"Party Doll" (1957)   *Buddy Knox*
"One Night (With You)" (1958)   *Elvis Presley*
"Reelin' and Rockin'" (1958)   *Chuck Berry*
"Good Golly Miss Molly" (1958)   *Little Richard*
"Breathless" (1958)   *Jerry Lee Lewis*
"Fever" (1958)   *Peggy Lee*
"That's My Desire" (1958)   *Dion and the Belmonts*
"Chantilly Lace" (1958)   *Big Bopper*
"Shimmy, Shimmy Ko-Ko-Bop" (1959)   *Little Anthony and the Imperials*
"I'm Ready" (1959)   *Fats Domino*
"Hey Little Girl" (1959)   *Dee Clark*
"Mio Amore" (1960)   *Flamingos*
"I Love How You Love Me" (1961)   *Paris Sisters*
"Last Night" (1961)   *Mar-Keys*
"Louie Louie" (1963)   *Kingsmen*

b) Against Authority or Expected Behavior

"Yakety Yak" (1958)   *Coasters*
"Get a Job" (1958)   *Silhouettes*
"Summertime Blues" (1958)   *Eddie Cochran*
"C'mon Everybody" (1958)   *Eddie Cochran*
"Charlie Brown" (1959)   *Coasters*
"Alimony" (1959)   *Frankie Ford*
"Nag" (1961)   *Halos*
"Workin' For the Man" (1962)   *Roy Orbison*
"Patches" (1962)   *Dickey Lee*
"Give Us Your Blessings (Don't Make Us Run Away)"
(1963)   *Ray Peterson*
"Midnight Mary" (1963)   *Joey Powers*

c) Against Traditional Pop Music

"Crazy Man Crazy" (1953)   *Bill Haley and His Comets*
"Rock Around the Clock" (1955)   *Bill Haley & His Comets*
"Roll Over Beethoven" (1956)   *Chuck Berry*
"Rock & Roll Music" (1957)   *Chuck Berry*
"That Is Rock & Roll" (1959)   *Coasters*

d) Juvenile Delinquency

"Rock Around the Clock" (1955)   *Bill Haley & His Comets*
"Jailhouse Rock" (1957)   *Elvis Presley*
"Bad Boy" (1957)   *Jive Bombers*
"Leroy's Back in Jail Again" (1958)   *Jack Scott*
"Bad Motorcycle" (1958)   *Storey Sisters*
"Rumble" (1958)   *Link Wray*
"Real Wild Child" (1958)   *Ivan*
"C'mon Everybody" (1958)   *Eddie Cochran*
"Ambrose, Part 5" (1959)   *Linda Laurie*
"Take a Message to Mary" (1959)   *Everly Brothers*
"Bad Boy" (1960)   *Marty Wilde*
"I'm Here to Get My Baby Out of Jail" (1962)   *Everly Brothers*
"Motorcycle" (1962)   *Tico and the Triumphs*
"He's a Rebel" (1962)   *Crystals*

"He's a Bad Boy" (1963)   *Carole King*
"Leader of the Pack" (1964)   *Shangri-Las*

e) Other Rebellious Behavior (e.g., Non-Conformist Clothes, Slang, etc.)

"Daddy-O" (1955)   *Bonnie Lou*
"Black Slacks" (1957)   *Sparkletones*
See also List #11b (anti-school songs), List #12 (songs about wild teen fashions and products), and List #14 (songs about slang).

● LIST #25: Alienation, Anxieties, and Death

The 1950s and early 1960s were anxious years for Americans of all ages. Teenagers, like adults, had to cope with international crises, new lifestyles, and rapid economic and social change. Their tensions and insecurities are evident in various types of rock and pop songs. There were records about loneliness, alienation, and oppression. Some songs provided release through humorous, happy, or carefree music, while others promised escape through magic, alcohol, or make-believe worlds. Several records dealt with death, the ultimate escape from life's worries.

a) Loneliness

"Angels in the Sky" (1955)   *Crew Cuts*
"Heartbreak Hotel" (1956)   *Elvis Presley*
"Walkin' After Midnight" (1957)   *Patsy Cline*
"Lonely Chair" (1957)   *Lloyd Price*
"An Empty Cup, a Broken Date" (1957)   *Buddy Holly & the Crickets*
"Little Star" (1958)   *Elegants*
"Gee" (1958)   *George Hamilton IV*
"Lonesome Town" (1958)   *Ricky Nelson*
"Lonely Teardrops" (1958)   *Jackie Wilson*
"No One Knows" (1958)   *Dion and the Belmonts*
"Don't Pity Me" (1958)   *Dion and the Belmonts*
"Lonely Boy" (1959)   *Paul Anka*
"Lonely Street" (1959)   *Andy Williams*
"Mr. Lonely" (1960)   *Videls*

"Lonely Teenager" (1960)   *Dion*
"Lonely Blue Boy" (1960)   *Conway Twitty*
"Lonely Blue Nights" (1960)   *Rosie*
"Lonely Man" (1961)   *Elvis Presley*
"Lonely Boy, Lonely Guitar" (1963)   *Duane Eddy*
"Mr. Lonely" (1964)   *Bobby Vinton*

b) Alienation and Oppression

"Summertime Blues" (1958)   *Eddie Cochran*
"Yakety Yak" (1958)   *Coasters*
"Get a Job" (1958)   *Silhouettes*
"Bad Motorcycle" (1958)   *Storey Sisters*
"Wild Child" (1958)   *Ivan*
"Rumble" (1958)   *Link Wray*
"Well . . . All Right" (1958)   *Buddy Holly*
"Charlie Brown" (1959)   *Coasters*
"Workin' for the Man" (1962)   *Roy Orbison*
"I Was Born to Cry" (1962)   *Dion*
"He's a Rebel" (1962)   *Crystals*
"Leader of the Pack" (1964)   *Shangri-Las*

c) Escape Through Good Time Music

"Buzz Buzz Buzz" (1957)   *Hollywood Flames*
"Rocking Pneumonia and the Boogie Woogie Flu"
(1957)   *Huey Smith and the Clowns*
"Rockin' Robin" (1958)   *Bobby Day*
"Don't You Just Know It?" (1958)   *Huey Smith & the Clowns*
"Nee Nee Na Na Na Na Nu Nu" (1958)   *Dickey Doo & the
Don'ts*
"Baby Talk" (1959)   *Jan and Dean*

d) Escape Through Humor and Satire

"Flying Saucer" (1956)   *Buchanan and Goodman*
"The Creature" (1957)   *Buchanan and Ancell*
"Witch Doctor" (1958)   *David Seville*
"The Chipmunk Song" (1958)   *Chipmunks*
"Purple People Eater" (1958)   *Sheb Wooley*

"Green Mosquito" (1958)   *Tune Rockers*
"The Blob" (1958)   *Five Blobs*
"Russian Bandstand" (1959)   *Spencer and Spencer*
"The Astronaut" (1961)   *Jose Jiminez*
See also List #48 (novelty records).

e) Escape Through Fantasy Worlds, Magic, or Alcohol

Fantasy worlds

"Stranded in the Jungle" (1956)   *Cadets*
"Rockin' in the Jungle" (1959)   *Eternals*
"Enchanted Sea" (1959)   *Islanders*
"Quiet Village" (1959)   *Martin Denny*
"Utopia" (1960)   *Frank Gari*
"Shangri-La" (1964)   *Vic Dana*

Magic

"I Put a Spell on You" (1956)   *Screamin' Jay Hawkins*
"Witch Doctor" (1958)   *David Seville*
"Love Potion #9" (1959)   *Clovers*
"Gypsy Woman" (1961)   *Impressions*
"Fortune Teller" (1962)   *Bobby Curtola*
"Aladdin" (1962)   *Bobby Curtola*
"Gypsy Woman" (1963)   *Rick Nelson*
"Gypsy Cried" (1963)   *Lou Christie*

Alcohol

"Tequila" (1958)   *Champs*
"Alligator Wine" (1958)   *Screamin' Jay Hawkins*
"Cherry Berry Wine" (1961)   *Charlie McCoy*
"Scotch and Soda" (1962)   *Kingston Trio*
For additional songs about alcohol, see List #37.

f) Songs About Death (i.e., Death Rock)

"Endless Sleep" (1958)   *Jody Reynolds*
"Tom Dooley" (1958)   *Kingston Trio*
"Teen Angel" (1959)   *Mark Dinning*
"Running Bear" (1959)   *Johnny Preston*
"Tell Laura I Love Her" (1960)   *Ray Peterson*

"Ebony Eyes" (1961)   *Everly Brothers*
"Moody River" (1961)   *Pat Boone*
"Patches" (1962)   *Dickey Lee*
"End of the World" (1963)   *Skeeter Davis*
"Give Us Your Blessing" (1963)   *Ray Peterson*
"Last Kiss" (1964)   *J. Frank Wilson*
"Leader of the Pack" (1964)   *Shangri-Las*
"I Can Never Go Home Any More" (1965)   *Shangri-Las*
"I Want My Baby Back" (1965)   *Jimmy Cross* (Note: This record was released after 1964, which is the cut-off point for this study, but in many ways it was the low point of Death Rock. It parodied the genre, telling the story of a guy who wanted his dead girl friend back. In the last verse, he digs her up, climbs into the coffin with her, closes the lid, and sings triumphantly "I got my baby back.)"

3. Songs About American Society and Culture

● **LIST #26: Religious Themes**

In some ways, rock & roll was neither rebellious nor revolutionary. Rock music themes often reflected patterns or beliefs held by Americans of all ages. For example, rock & roll records, with their numerous references to God, angels, and religion, mirrored America's preoccupation with religion during the 1950s and early 1960s.

a) Songs Mentioning God or Religious Themes

"Crying in the Chapel" (1953)   *Orioles*
"A Sunday Kind of Love" (1953)   *Harptones*
"Teenage Prayer" (1955)   *Gloria Mann*
"My Prayer" (1956)   *Platters*
"Church Bells May Ring" (1956)   *Willows*
"Race with the Devil" (1956)   *Gene Vincent*
"Peace in the Valley" (1957)   *Elvis Presley*
"Shrine of St. Cecelia" (1957)   *Faron Young*
"Sinner Man" (1958)   *Tommy Sands*
"Maybe" (1958)   *Chantels*
"Guess Things Happen That Way" (1958)   *Johnny Cash*
"The Little Drummer Boy" (1958)   *Harry Simeone Chorale*
"A Wonderful Time Up There" (1958)   *Pat Boone*
"Little Star" (1958)   *Elegants*
"He's Got the Whole World in His Hands" (1958)   *Laurie London*
"Ten Commandments of Love" (1958)   *Moonglows*
"The Teen Commandments" (1958)   *Paul Anka/Johnny Nash/ and George Hamilton IV*
"Lucky Devil" (1959)   *Carl Dobkins Jr.*
"A Prayer and a Jukebox" (1959)   *Little Anthony and the Imperials*
"The Village of St. Bernadette" (1959)   *Andy Williams*
"The Little Drummer Boy" (1959)   *Johnny Cash*

106

"The Three Bells" (1959)   *Browns*
"Tall Oak Tree" (1959)   *Dorsey Burnett*
"Three Stars" (1959)   *Tommy Dee*
"Deck of Cards" (1959)   *Wink Martindale*
"The Battle Hymn of the Republic" (1959)   *Mormon
                                                        Tabernacle Choir*
"A Lover's Prayer" (1959)   *Dion and the Belmonts*
"Tell Laura I Love Her" (1960)   *Ray Peterson*
"Wings of a Dove" (1960)   *Ferlin Husky*
"O Dio Mio" (1960)   *Annette*
"Adam and Eve" (1960)   *Paul Anka*
"Mission Bell" (1960)   *Donnie Brooks*
"Three Steps to Heaven" (1960)   *Eddie Cochran*
"Ebony Eyes" (1961)   *Everly Brothers*
"Bless You" (1961)   *Tony Orlando*
"I Dreamed of a Hillbilly Heaven" (1961)   *Tex Ritter*
"God, Country, and My Baby" (1961)   *Johnny Burnette*
"Sacred" (1961)   *Castells*
"Little Altar Boy" (1961)   *Vic Dana*
"100 Pounds of Clay" (1961)   *Gene McDaniels*
"Let There Be Drums" (1961)   *Sandy Nelson*
"Thou Shalt Not Steal" (1962)   *John D. Loudermilk*
"Conscience" (1962)   *James Darren*
"Teenage Heaven" (1963)   *Johnny Cymbal*
"You're the Devil in Disguise" (1963)   *Elvis Presley*
"Dominique" (1963)   *Singing Nun*
"Give Us Your Blessing" (1963)   *Ray Peterson*
"Last Kiss" (1964)   *J. Frank Wilson*
"Thou Shalt Not Steal" (1964)   *Dick and Dee Dee*
"Chapel of Love" (1964)   *Dixie Cups*

b) Songs Alluding to Angels

"Earth Angel" (1954)   *Penguins*
"Angels in the Sky" (1955)   *Crew-Cuts*
"My Special Angel" (1958)   *Bobby Helms*
"Angel Baby" (1958)   *Dean Martin*
"A Letter to an Angel" (1958)   *Jimmy Clanton*
"The Angels Listened In" (1959)   *Crests*
"Teen Angel" (1959)   *Mark Dinning*

"Angel Face" (1959)   *James Darren*
"Blue Angel" (1960)   *Roy Orbison*
"Angel Baby" (1960)   *Rosie and the Originals*
"Rockin' Little Angel" (1960)   *Ray Smith*
"Earth Angel" (1960)   *Johnny Tillotson*
"Devil or Angel" (1960)   *Bobby Vee*
"Little Angel" (1960)   *Eddie Cochran*
"Angel on My Shoulder" (1961)   *Shelby Flint*
"Pretty Little Angel Eyes" (1961)   *Curtis Lee*
"Walkin' with My Angel" (1961)   *Bobby Vee*
"Oh, My Angel" (1962)   *Bertha Tillman*
"Come On Little Angel" (1962)   *Belmonts*
"Johnny Angel" (1962)   *Shelley Fabares*
"Look Homeward Angel" (1964)   *Monarchs*
"Death of an Angel" (1964)   *Kingsmen*

● LIST #27: Home and Parents

Too often, rock is seen merely as a music of alienation and rebellion. In reality, many records that made the rock charts sang praises of traditional values involving the home and hearth.

a) Songs About "Home Sweet Home"

"A Thousand Miles Away" (1956)   *Heartbeats*
"I'll Be Home" (1956)   *Pat Boone*
"A House, a Car, and a Wedding Ring" (1958)   *Dale Hawkins*
"House of Love" (1959)   *Scott Garrett*
"Lonely Teenager" (1960)   *Dion*
"My Home Town" (1960)   *Paul Anka*
"Daddy's Home" (1961)   *Shep and the Limelites*
"Comin' Home Baby" (1962)   *Mel Tormé*
"Six Days on the Road" (1963)   *Dave Dudley*
"500 Miles" (1963)   *Bobby Bare*
"Detroit City" (1963)   *Bobby Bare*
"Blue Bayou" (1963)   *Roy Orbison*
"Hello Muddah Hello Fadduh" (1963)   *Allan Sherman*
"In My Room" (1963)   *Beach Boys*

b) Songs Praising Parents

"Teenager's Mother" (1956)   *Bill Haley and His Comets*
"Mama" (1960)   *Roy Orbison*
"Mama" (1960)   *Connie Francis*
"Your Maw Said You Cried" (1961)   *Kenny Dino*
"Mama Said" (1961)   *Shirelles*
"Mama Sang a Song" (1962)   *Walter Brennan*
"My Dad" (1962)   *Paul Petersen*
"Mama Didn't Lie" (1963)   *Jan Bradley*
"Walk Like a Man" (1963)   *Four Seasons*

● LIST #28: Myths and Popular Images

Commonly held American myths and popular beliefs found their way into early rock & roll. Some songs were odes to classical subjects like Cupid or Venus, while others focused on more contemporary myths involving rags-to-riches themes or the myth of the common man. Folk tales and exotic places also provided material for many rock songs.

a) Classical Myths

"Arrow of Love" (1957)   *Six Teens* (inspired by Cupid myth)
"That'll Be the Day" (1957)   *Buddy Holly and the Crickets*
                              (mentions Cupid)
"Stupid Cupid" (1958)   *Connie Francis*
"Venus" (1959)   *Frankie Avalon*
"Cupid" (1961)   *Sam Cooke*
"Venus in Blue Jeans" (1962)   *Jimmy Clanton*

b) Rags to Riches Myth

"All-American Boy" (1958)   *Bill Parsons*
"Ballad of a Teenage Queen" (1958)   *Johnny Cash*
"Johnny B. Goode" (1958)   *Chuck Berry*
"I'm Gonna Be a Wheel Someday" (1959)   *Fats Domino*
"North to Alaska" (1960)   *Johnny Horton*
"Bye Bye Johnny" (1960)   *Chuck Berry*
"Duke of Earl" (1962)   *Gene Chandler*

"Ballad of Jed Clampett" (1962)   *Flatt and Scruggs*
"Follow That Dream" (1962)   *Elvis Presley*
"Only in America" (1963)   *Jay and the Americans*
"You Never Can Tell" (1964)   *Chuck Berry*

c) Folk Tales (or Pseudo-Folk Tales)

"Endless Sleep" (1958)   *Jody Reynolds*
"Tom Dooley" (1958)   *Kingston Trio*
"M.T.A." (1959)   *Kingston Trio*
"Mona Lisa" (1959)   *Carl Mann*
"Mona Lisa" (1959)   *Conway Twitty*
"Love Potion #9" (1959)   *Clovers*
"Teen Angel" (1959)   *Mark Dinning*
"Dutchman's Gold" (1960)   *Walter Brennan*
"When You Wish Upon a Star" (1960)   *Dion and the Belmonts*
"Tell Laura I Love Her" (1960)   *Ray Peterson*
"Big Bad John" (1961)   *Jimmy Dean*
"Moody River" (1961)   *Pat Boone*
"Your Nose Is Gonna Grow" (1962)   *Johnny Crawford*
"Lizzie Borden" (1962)   *Chad Mitchell Trio*
"Old Rivers" (1962)   *Walter Brennan*
"P.T. 109" (1962)   *Jimmy Dean*
"Patches" (1962)   *Dickey Lee*
"Give Us Your Blessing" (1963)   *Ray Peterson*
"End of the World" (1963)   *Skeeter Davis*
"Rag Doll" (1964)   *Four Seasons*
"Just Like Romeo and Juliet" (1964)   *Reflections*

d) Mythical Lands and Exotic Places

"Stranded in the Jungle" (1956)   *Jayhawks*
"Shangri-La" (1957)   *Four Coins*
"Quiet Village" (1959)   *Martin Denny*
"The Enchanted Sea" (1959)   *Islanders*
"Rockin' in the Jungle" (1959)   *Eternals*
"Shimmy, Shimmy Ko-Ko-Bop" (1959)   *Little Anthony and the Imperials*
"Calcutta" (1960)   *Lawrence Welk*
"Kookie Little Paradise" (1960)   *Tree Swingers*
"Utopia" (1960)   *Frank Gari*

"Yellow Bird" (1961)   *Arthur Lymon*
"Halfway to Paradise" (1961)   *Tony Orlando*
"The Lion Sleeps Tonight" (1961)   *Tokens*
"Village of Love" (1962)   *Nathaniel Mayer*
"B'wa Nina" (1962)   *Tokens*
"A Swingin' Safari" (1962)   *Billy Vaughn*
"Mecca" (1963)   *Gene Pitney*
"Shangri-La" (1964)   *Vic Dana*
See also songs about the American West (List #29).

● LIST #29: The American West

Americans have long been fascinated by the West, and teenagers of the 1950s and early 1960s were no different. While adults were watching TV westerns like "Gunsmoke" and attending western movies like *The Searchers* and *Shane*, teens were listening to rock & roll records dealing with the American West. Some of the songs merely dealt with traditional cowboy and Indian themes, while others, such as the Beach Boys' songs about California, picked up on traditional, mythic images of the West as a land of opportunity and happiness—a Garden of Eden. Occasionally rock stars joined hands with the establishment to make western movies. Ricky Nelson played "Colorado," a young gunslinger, in the John Wayne film *Rio Bravo*. And Elvis Presley played a hero torn between Indians and whites in the western *Flaming Star*.

"Ramrod" (1958)   *Duane Eddy*
"Western Movies" (1958)   *Olympics*
"Zorro" (1958)   *Chordettes*
"El Paso" (1959)   *Marty Robbins*
"Big Iron" (1959)   *Marty Robbins*
"Raw-Hide" (1959)   *Link Wray*
"Kansas City" (1959)   *Wilbert Harrison*
"Ragtime Cowboy Joe" (1959)   *Chipmunks*
"Don't Take Your Guns to Town" (1959)   *Johnny Cash*
"Red River Rock" (1959)   *Johnny and the Hurricanes*
"Running Bear" (1959)   *Johnny Preston*
"One Hour Ahead of the Posse" (1959)   *Sam Cooke*
"Ballad of the Alamo" (1960)   *Marty Robbins*
"Ballad of the Alamo" (1960)   *Bud and Travis*

"Please Mr. Custer" (1960)   *Larry Verne*
"Dutchman's Gold" (1960)   *Walter Brennan*
"The Magnificent Seven" (1960)   *Al Caiola*
"Mule Skinner Blues" (1960)   *Fendermen*
"North to Alaska" (1960)   *Johnny Horton*
"Bad Man Blunder" (1960)   *Kingston Trio*
"San Antonio Rose" (1961)   *Floyd Cramer*
"Bonanza" (1961)   *Al Caiola*
"Cowboy Jimmy Joe" (1961)   *Lolita*
"Big Bad John" (1961)   *Jimmy Dean*
"Apache" (1961)   *Jorgen Ingmann*
"(Ghost Riders) In the Sky" (1961)   *Ramrods*
"I Dreamed of a Hillbilly Heaven" (1961)   *Tex Ritter*
"Flaming Star" (1961)   *Elvis Presley*
"Don't Go Near the Indians" (1962)   *Rex Allen*
"Surfin' Safari" (1962)   *Beach Boys*
"Ten Little Indians" (1962)   *Beach Boys*
"Deep in the Heart of Texas" (1962)   *Duane Eddy*
"Ballad of Paladin" (1962)   *Duane Eddy*
"The Man Who Shot Liberty Valance" (1962)   *Gene Pitney*
"Surf City" (1963)   *Jan and Dean*
"Abilene" (1963)   *George Hamilton IV*
"Surfin' U.S.A." (1963)   *Beach Boys*
"Surfer Girl" (1963)   *Beach Boys*
"Long Tall Texan" (1963)   *Murray Kellum*
"Gunslinger" (1963)   *Bo Diddley*
"Lone Teen Ranger" (1963)   *Jerry Landis*
"Ringo" (1964)   *Lorne Greene*
"California Sun" (1964)   *Rivieras*

● LIST #30: Gender

a) Songs About Women

During the years 1954–1963, women were in many ways second-class citizens, lacking political, economic, and social equality with males. The feminine mystique which was in full bloom by the late 1950s contained several important elements: females existed to please males, have babies, keep house, be attractive, be subservient, provide comfort, be passive, and follow a man's lead in all matters.

Women were seen as objects, possessions, and playthings. Although rock & roll may have been revolutionary in some ways, it was outright conservative in its attitudes toward women. Sexual stereotypes of the 1950s and early 1960s abound in early rock & roll.

Women as objects of admiration: princesses, perfect creatures, etc.

"Earth Angel" (1954)   *Penguins*
"Queen of the Senior Prom" (1957)   *Mills Brothers*
"Living Doll" (1959)   *Cliff Richard*
"Venus" (1959)   *Frankie Avalon*
"Mona Lisa" (1959)   *Carl Mann*
"Mona Lisa" (1959)   *Conway Twitty*
"Pineapple Princess" (1960)   *Annette*
"Poetry in Motion" (1960)   *Johnny Tillotson*
"Image of a Girl" (1960)   *Safaris*
"Princess" (1961)   *Frank Gari*
"Princess, Princess" (1961)   *Johnny Tillotson*
"Model Girl" (1961)   *Johnny Mastro*
"Bless You" (1961)   *Tony Orlando*
"Portrait of My Love" (1961)   *Steve Lawrence*
"There's Got to Be a Girl" (1961)   *Lettermen*
"Little Girl (You're My Miss America)" (1962)   *Beach Boys*
"Venus in Blue Jeans" (1962)   *Jimmy Clanton*
"Teenage Cleopatra" (1963)   *Tracey Dey*
"I Wish I Were a Princess" (1963)   *Little Peggy March*
"Surfer Girl" (1963)   *Beach Boys*
For records about girls who were angels and heaven-sent, see List #26

Women as sex objects

"Long Tall Sally" (1956)   *Little Richard*
"Fever" (1956)   *Little Willie John*
"Great Balls of Fire" (1957)   *Jerry Lee Lewis*
"Party Doll" (1957)   *Buddy Knox*
"Little Bitty Pretty One" (1957)   *Thurston Harris*
"The Girl Can't Help It" (1957)   *Little Richard*
"Short Fat Fanny" (1957)   *Larry Williams*
"Bony Moronie" (1957)   *Larry Williams*
"Wiggle Wiggle" (1958)   *Accents*

"Chantilly Lace" (1958)   *Big Bopper*
"Pretty Girls Everywhere" (1958)   *Eugene Church*
"Short Shorts" (1958)   *Royal Teens*
"Breathless" (1958)   *Jerry Lee Lewis*
"Good Golly Miss Molly" (1958)   *Little Richard*
"Reelin' and Rockin'" (1958)   *Chuck Berry*
"Hey Little Girl" (1959)   *Dee Clark*
"Pretty Blue Eyes" (1959)   *Steve Lawrence*
"Shimmy, Shimmy Ko-Ko-Bop" (1959)   *Little Anthony and the
                                        Imperials*
"What Is Love?" (1959)   *Playmates*
"Dream Lover" (1959)   *Bobby Darin*
"Please Help Me I'm Falling" (1960)   *Hank Locklin*
"Sailor" (1960)   *Lolita*
"Calendar Girl" (1960)   *Neil Sedaka*
"Mr. Sandman" (1961)   *Bobby Vee*
"Pretty Little Angel Eyes" (1961)   *Curtis Lee*
"That's What Girls Are Made For" (1961)   *Spinners*
"Girls Were Made to Love" (1962)   *Eddie Hodges*
"Sweet Dream Baby" (1962)   *Roy Orbison*
"Go Away Little Girl" (1962)   *Steve Lawrence*
"Surf City" (1963)   *Jan and Dean*
"Surfer Girl" (1963)   *Beach Boys*

Women as possessions

"Dungaree Doll" (1955)   *Eddie Fisher*
"Party Doll" (1957)   *Buddy Knox*
"You Were Mine" (1959)   *Fireflies*
"Shop Around" (1960)   *Miracles*
"Baby Blue" (1961)   *Echoes*
"100 Pounds of Clay" (1961)   *Gene McDaniels*
"Travelin' Man" (1961)   *Rick Nelson*
"Bobby's Girl" (1962)   *Marcie Blane*
"You Belong to Me" (1962)   *Duprees*
"A Woman Is a Man's Best Friend" (1962)   *Teddy and the
                                             Twilights*

Women as dependents or passive objects

"Tammy" (1957)   *Debbie Reynolds*
"I Met Him on a Sunday" (1958)   *Shirelles*

"This Little Girl of Mine" (1958) *Everly Brothers*
".The Answer to a Maiden's Prayer" (1959) *June Valli*
"Little Bitty Girl" (1960) *Bobby Rydell*
"Will You Love Me Tomorrow" (1960) *Shirelles*
"One Boy" (1960) *Joanie Sommers*
"I've Told Every Little Star" (1961) *Linda Scott*
"Big John" (1961) *Shirelles*
"Baby It's You" (1961) *Shirelles*
"Be My Boy" (1961) *Paris Sisters*
"I Love How You Love Me" (1961) *Paris Sisters*
"Triangle" (1961) *Janie Grant*
"Daddy's Home" (1961) *Shep and the Limelites*
"Right or Wrong (I'll Stay With You)" (1961) *Wanda Jackson*
"If I Cried Every Time You Hurt Me" (1961) *Wanda Jackson*
"Where the Boys Are (Is Where I Want To Be)" (1961) *Connie Francis*
"Beechwood 4-5789 (You Can Call Me Up and Get a Date Any Old Time)" (1962) *Marvelettes*
"Dutchess of Earl" (1962) *Pearlettes*
"When the Boys Get Together" (1962) *Joanie Sommers*
"He Hit Me (And It Felt Like a Kiss)" (1962) *Crystals*
"He Knows I Love Him Too Much" (1962) *Paris Sisters*
"She Cried" (1962) *Jay and the Americans*
"Tell Him" (1962) *Exciters*
"Johnny Angel" (1962) *Shelley Fabares*
"Johnny Loves Me" (1962) *Shelley Fabares*
"Big Girls Don't Cry" (1962) *Four Seasons*
"I Will Follow Him" (1963) *Little Peggy March*
"Foolish Little Girl" (1963) *Shirelles*
"What Does a Girl Do?" (1963) *Shirelles*
"I Adore Him" (1963) *Angels*
"You Don't Have to Be a Baby To Cry" (1963) *Caravelles*
"My Boyfriend's Back" (1963) *Angels*
"Wait 'Til My Bobby Gets Home" (1963) *Darlene Love*
"Today I Met the Boy I'm Gonna Marry" (1963) *Darlene Love*
"Shy Girl" (1963) *Cascades*
"Then He Kissed Me" (1963) *Crystals*
"Da Doo Ron Ron" (1963) *Crystals*
"Ronnie, Call Me When You Get a Chance" (1963) *Shelley Fabares*

"Follow the Boys" (1963)   *Connie Francis*
"When the Boy's Happy (the Girl's Happy Too)" (1963)   *Four Pennies*

"My One and Only Jimmy Boy" (1963)   *Girlfriends*
"It's My Party" (1963)   *Leslie Gore*
"Judy's Turn to Cry" (1963)   *Leslie Gore*
"Blue Navy Blue" (1964)   *Diane Renay*
"Kiss Me Sailor" (1964)   *Diane Renay*
"That's the Way Boys Are" (1964)   *Leslie Gore*

Women as wenches, wretches, and shrews

"Get a Job" (1958)   *Silhouettes*
"Hard Headed Woman" (1958)   *Elvis Presley*
"Ambrose, Part 5" (1959)   *Linda Laurie*
"You Talk Too Much" (1960)   *Joe Jones*
"Devil or Angel" (1960)   *Bobby Vee*
"Wild One" (1960)   *Bobby Rydell*
"Nag" (1961)   *Halos*
"Mother-in-Law" (1961)   *Ernie K-Doe*
"Runaround Sue" (1961)   *Dion*
"Hats Off to Larry" (1961)   *Del Shannon*
"Devil Woman" (1962)   *Marty Robbins*
"Little Town Flirt" (1962)   *Del Shannon*
"Mean Woman Blues" (1963)   *Roy Orbison*
"Donna the Prima Donna" (1963)   *Dion*
"You're the Devil in Disguise" (1963)   *Elvis Presley*
"She's a Fool" (1963)   *Leslie Gore*

Women as aggressive persons

"Fever" (1958)   *Peggy Lee*
"Teach Me, Tiger" (1959)   *April Stevens*
"Wild One" (1960)   *Bobby Rydell*
"This Is It" (1962)   *Jay and the Americans*
"Come Back Silly Girl" (1962)   *Lettermen*
"Girls Grow Up Faster than Boys" (1963)   *Cookies*
"You Don't Own Me" (1963)   *Leslie Gore*
"Snap Your Fingers" (1963)   *Joe Henderson*
"Little Old Lady from Pasadena" (1964)   *Jan and Dean*
"Fun Fun Fun" (1964)   *Beach Boys*

(Some female performers also had an implicit sexuality in their acts, e.g., Mary Wells, the Shirelles, the Paris Sisters, the Ronettes, the Marvelettes, Martha and the Vandellas, and the Shangri-Las.)

Women as upholders of traditional values

"You're So Square" (1958)   *Elvis Presley*
"That's Old Fashioned" (1962)   *Everly Brothers*
"Please Don't Ever Change" (1962)   *Crickets*

b) Songs About Men

If rock & roll records treated females as passive, submissive, and emotional playthings, their flip side idealized males as aggressive, dominant individuals. The *guys* asked the girls for a date. *They* did the telephoning. *They* initiated every move in the romance. Teenage males dominated their world, just as adult males dominated the rest of society. Images of these macho men who are lovers and fighters pop up time after time on rock & roll records.

Men as lovers

"Love Me" (1956)   *Elvis Presley*
"Party Doll" (1957)   *Buddy Knox*
"Gotta Travel On" (1958)   *Billy Grammer*
"Teach Me, Tiger" (1959)   *April Stevens*
"Handy Man" (1960)   *Jimmy Jones*
"Shop Around" (1960)   *Miracles*
"Will You Love Me Tomorrow" (1960)   *Shirelles*
"Travelin' Man" (1961)   *Rick Nelson*
"The Wanderer" (1961)   *Dion*
"Everybody Loves a Lover" (1962)   *Shirelles*
"Two Lovers" (1962)   *Mary Wells*
"Little Black Book" (1962)   *Jimmy Dean*
"He's So Fine" (1963)   *Chiffons*
"I Adore Him" (1963)   *Angels*
"A Fine Fine Boy" (1963)   *Darlene Love*
"Then He Kissed Me" (1963)   *Crystals*
"Don't Say Goodnight and Mean Goodbye" (1963)   *Shirelles*

Men as tough guys

"Blue Suede Shoes" (1956)   *Carl Perkins*
"Blue Suede Shoes" (1956)   *Elvis Presley*
"Bad Motorcycle" (1958)   *Storey Sisters*
"Wild Child" (1958)   *Ivan*
"Ambrose, Part 5" (1959)   *Linda Laurie*
"I'm a Man" (1959)   *Fabian*
"Turn Me Loose" (1959)   *Fabian*
"Tiger" (1959)   *Fabian*
"Battle of New Orleans" (1959)   *Johnny Horton*
"North to Alaska" (1960)   *Johnny Horton*
"Big Iron" (1960)   *Marty Robbins*
"Stayin' In" (1961)   *Bobby Vee*
"Big John" (1961)   *Shirelles*
"Big Bad John" (1961)   *Jimmy Dean*
"He's a Rebel" (1962)   *Crystals*
"Duke of Earl" (1962)   *Gene Chandler*
"He Hit Me (And It Felt Like a Kiss)" (1962)   *Crystals*
"Steel Men" (1962)   *Jimmy Dean*
"Soldier Boy" (1962)   *Shirelles*
"Johnny Get Angry" (1962)   *Joanie Sommers*
"Wait Til My Bobby Gets Home" (1963)   *Darlene Love*
"My Boyfriend's Back" (1963)   *Angels*
"Ringo" (1964)   *Lorne Greene*
"Leader of the Pack" (1964)   *Shangri-Las*
"Blue Navy Blue" (1964)   *Diane Renay*
"Kiss Me Sailor" (1964)   *Diane Renay*

● LIST #31: Ethnic and Racial Stereotypes

Ethnic and racial stereotypes from the 1950s and early 1960s can be found in rock & roll. Indians were portrayed as comic book characters, often complete with stereotypical chants and tom-toms. Hispanics were ridiculed for their accents or linked to bullfighting, tequila, or romantic "hot Latin" images. Arabs became the brunt of rock & roll jokes using every available stereotype, including camels, Arabian nights, accents, sand dunes, slurs, and stupid sheiks.

Other ethnic or racial stereotypes can also be found in early rock & roll. Records focused on Polish food, French and Italian lovers, and the broken English spoken by some ethnics and immigrants. Ironically, even blacks, who contributed greatly to the birth of rock & roll, suffered as rock & roll stereotypes. Blacks were often portrayed as comic figures (e.g., the Coasters' records). Songs noted their alleged fondness of watermelon ("Watermelon Man"), spending money ("Duke of Earl"), and uninhibited dancing and sexual behavior ("Shimmy Shimmy Ko-Ko-Bop").

a) Indians

"Running Bear" (1959)   *Johnny Preston*
"Half-Breed" (1959)   *Marvin Rainwater*
"Please Mr. Custer" (1960)   *Larry Verne*
"Flaming Star" (1961)   *Elvis Presley*
"Don't Go Near the Indians" (1962)   *Rex Allen*
"Apache" (1962)   *Jorgen Ingmann*
"Ten Little Indians" (1962)   *Beach Boys*

b) Hillbillies

"I Dreamed of Hillbillie Heaven" (1961)   *Tex Ritter*
"Wolverton Mountain" (1962)   *Claude King*
"I'm the Girl from Wolverton Mountain" (1962)   *Jo Ann Campbell*
"Ballad of Jed Clampett" (1962)   *Flatt & Scruggs*

c) Hispanics

"Torero" (1958)   *Renato Carosone*
"Tequila" (1958)   *Champs*
"The Tijuana Jail" (1958)   *Kingston Trio*
"El Matador" (1958)   *Kingston Trio*
"Donde Esta Santa Claus" (1958)   *Augie Rios*
"La Bamba" (1958)   *Ritchie Valens*
"Torquay" (1959)   *Fireballs*
"Vaquero" (1960)   *Fireballs*
"Too Much Tequila" (1960)   *Champs*
"Pepe" (1960)   *Duane Eddy*
"The Astronaut" (1961)   *Jose Jiminez*
"Spanish Harlem" (1961)   *Ben E. King*

"Mexico" (1961)   *Bob Moore*
"Twist Twist Senora" (1962)   *Gary U.S. Bonds*
"Lonely Bull" (1962)   *Herb Alpert & the Tijuana Brass*
"Spanish Lace" (1962)   *Gene McDaniels*
"Happy Jose" (1962)   *Jack Ross*
"Speedy Gonzales" (1962)   *Pat Boone*
"Little Latin Lupe Lu" (1963)   *Righteous Brothers*
"Mexican Drummer Man" (1964)   *Herb Alpert & the Tijuana Brass*
"Little Latin Lupe Lu" (1964)   *Kingsmen*
West Side Story   This soundtrack album was extremely popular throughout the early 1960s.

d) Blacks

"Witch Doctor" (1958)   *David Seville*
"Charlie Brown" (1959)   *Coasters*
"Shimmy Shimmy Ko-Ko-Bop" (1959)   *Little Anthony and the Imperials*
"Duke of Earl" (1962)   *Gene Chandler*
"Dutchess of Earl" (1962)   *Pearlettes*
"Watermelon Man" (1963)   *Mongo Santamaria*

e) Other Ethnic or Racial Stereotypes

"Geisha Girl" (1957)   *Hank Locklin*
"Sheik of Araby" (1958)   *Lou Monte*
"Chanson D'Amour" (1958)   *Art and Dotty Todd*
"Lazy Mary" (1958)   *Lou Monte*
"Ciao Ciao Bambina" (1959)   *Jackie Noguez*
"C'est Si Bon" (1960)   *Conway Twitty*
"Ahab the Arab" (1962)   *Ray Stevens*
"Pepino the Italian Mouse" (1962)   *Lou Monte*
"Parisian Girl" (1962)   *Crickets*
"Don't Go Near the Eskimos" (1962)   *Ben Colder*
"Who Stole the Keeshka?" (1963)   *Matys Brothers*
"Pepino's Friend Pasqual" (1963)   *Lou Monte*
"Sukiyaki" (1963)   *Kyu Sakamoto*
"Dominique" (1963)   *the Singing Nun*
"Me Japanese Boy" (1964)   *Bobby Goldsboro*

● LIST #32: Money

Rock & roll was born in an age of affluence. The 1950s witnessed American liberation from the bonds of depression and war. And Americans celebrated by spending money—lots of it. American youths were no different from adults. They, too, were interested in money and materialism, as evidenced by numerous records.

"Money Honey" (1956)   *Elvis Presley*
"Rip It Up" (1956)   *Little Richard*
"Money Tree" (1956)   *Patience and Prudence*
"Chantilly Lace" (1958)   *Big Bopper*
"Teenage Heaven" (1958)   *Eddie Cochran*
"Gas Money" (1958)   *Jan and Arnie*
"Yakety Yak" (1958)   *Coasters*
"Summertime Blues" (1958)   *Eddie Cochran*
"I'm Gonna Be a Wheel Someday" (1959)   *Fats Domino*
"Money" (1960)   *Barrett Strong*
"More Money for You and Me" (1961)   *Four Preps*
"Busted" (1963)   *Ray Charles*
"Money" (1964)   *Kingsmen*

For additional songs dealing with materialistic concerns, see
   Lists #12 and #13.

● LIST #33: Rock Music and the Media

a) Television

Rock music and television had a steady relationship during the 1950s and early 1960s. After all, the rock generation was the first to grow up with TV, so naturally there was much cross-breeding.

TV show themes on the rock charts

"Ballad of Davy Crockett" (1955)   *Bill Hayes*
"Peter Gunn" (1959)   *Ray Anthony*
"77 Sunset Strip" (1959)   *Don Ralke*
"Mr. Lucky" (1960)   *Henry Mancini*
"Peter Gunn" (1960)   *Duane Eddy*
"Bonanza" (1961)   *Al Caiola*
"Theme from 'Dr. Kildare' (Three Stars)" (1962)   *Richard Chamberlain*

"Ballad of Jed Clampett" (1962)   *Flatt and Scruggs*
"Route 66 Theme" (1962)   *Nelson Riddle*
"Theme from 'Ben Casey'" (1962)   *Val Jean*
"Ballad of Paladin" (1962)   *Duane Eddy*
"Bonanza" (1962)   *Johnny Cash*
"Out of Limits" (1963)   *Marketts*

TV performers on rock charts

Ricky Nelson   *"I'm Walking" (1957) and other hits*
Fess Parker   *"Wringle Wrangle" (1957)*
Tommy Sands   *"Teenage Crush" (1957) and others*
Dean Martin   *"Return to Me" (1958) and others*
Edd Byrnes   *"Kookie Kookie" (1959)*
Roger Smith   *"Beach Time" (1959)*
Annette   *"Tall Paul" (1959) and others*
Walter Brennan   *"Dutchman's Gold" (1960) and others*
Burl Ives   *"A Little Bitty Tear" (1961) and others*
Jose Jiminez   *"The Astronaut" (1961)*
Johnny Crawford   *"Cindy's Birthday" (1962) and others*
Richard Chamberlain   *"Theme From 'Dr. Kildare' (Three Stars)" (1962)*
Shelley Fabares   *"Johnny Angel" (1962) and others*
Paul Petersen   *"My Dad" (1962)*
Vince Edwards   *"Why Did You Leave Me?" (1962)*
George Maharis   *"Teach Me Tonight" (1962)*

Songs about TV shows

"Searchin'" (1957)   *Coasters*
"Zorro" (1958)   *Chordettes*
"I'm a Yogi" (1959)   *Ivy Three*
"The Touchables" (1961)   *Dickie Goodman*
"Ben Crazy" (1962)   *Dickie Goodman*
"Dr. Ben Basey" (1962)   *Mickey Shorr and the Cut Ups*
"Calling Dr. Casey" (1962)   *John D. Loudermilk*

Songs about TV commercials

"Flip Top Box" (1961)   *Dickey Doo and the Don'ts*
"Jeremiah Peabody's Poly Unsaturated Quick Dissolving Fast Acting Pleasant Tasting Green and Purple Pills" (1961)   *Ray Stevens*

"That Greasy Kid Stuff" (1962)   *Janie Grant*
"Percolator Twist" (1962)   *Billy Joe and the Checkmates*

Rock & roll on television

Various variety shows, such as the "Ed Sullivan Show," "Steve
  Allen's Tonight Show," and the "Perry Como Show,"
  sometimes spotlighted rock & roll performers.
Dick Clark's "American Bandstand" (many local TV stations
  copied Clark's show, e.g., in Buffalo, New York, there were two
  different programs, Pat Fagan's "Dance Party" and Rick Azar's
  "Buffalo Bandstand."
Dick Clark's "Saturday Night Show."
Situation comedies sometimes included a segment where teens
  would play rock & roll, e.g., "Ozzie and Harriet" (featured
  Ricky Nelson's singing), the "Donna Reed Show," "My Three
  Sons."

b) Movies

Rock & roll of the 1950s and early 1960s reflects that teenagers,
like adults, were interested in Hollywood and movies. Just as adults
expected to see their favorite stars in movies, teenagers took it for
granted that they would be able to see their rock idols on the silver
screen. And many rock stars took it for granted that films would be
the next logical step in their careers. Before the 1950s decade was
out, rock artists were commonly appearing in films like *Rock Around
the Clock* and *Don't Knock the Rock*, which served as vehicles to showcase a caravan of rock stars. And by 1963, individual teen idols like
Elvis Presley, Ricky Nelson, Frankie Avalon, Fabian, Bobby Vee, Annette, and Connie Francis had already attempted to establish careers
as movie stars. Hollywood and rock & roll were intertwined in other
ways. Some songs and performers' names alluded to movies or the
movie industry. Themes from Hollywood films commonly made the
rock charts. Rock & roll singers sometimes recorded sound tracks for
movies. And rock & rollers tapped movies for material for hit records.

Songs and group names referring to movies or movie industry

"Searchin'" (1957)   *Coasters*
"That'll Be the Day" (1957)   *Buddy Holly and the Crickets*
                               (inspired by a line from John
                               Wayne's *The Searchers*)

"Sittin' in the Balcony" (1957)   *Eddie Cochran*
"Drive-In Show" (1957)   *Eddie Cochran*
"Wake Up Little Susie" (1957)   *Everly Brothers*
"Ballad of a Teenage Queen" (1958)   *Johnny Cash*
"The Blob" (1958)   *Five Blobs*
"Dinner with Drac" (1958)   *John Zacherle*
"Western Movies" (1958)   *Olympics*
"Zorro" (1958)   *Chordettes*
"Along Came Jones" (1959)   *Coasters*
"The Mummy" (1959)   *Bob and Dor McFadden*
"Sailor" (1960)   *Lolita* (performer named after movie)
"Sad Movies Make Me Cry" (1961)   *Sue Thompson*
"Better Tell Him No" (1961)   *Starlets* (their name)
"Little Hollywood Girl" (1962)   *Crickets*
"Little Hollywood Girl" (1962)   *Tommy Roe*

Songs from movies that made the rock charts

(From movies of the same name except as indicated)

"Rock Around the Clock" (1955)   *Bill Haley and His Comets*
(from *Blackboard Jungle*)
"Friendly Persuasion" (1956)   *Pat Boone*
"Love Me Tender" (1956)   *Elvis Presley*
"Poor Boy" (1956)   *Elvis Presley* (from *Love Me Tender*)
"Loving You" (1957)   *Elvis Presley*
"Let Me Be Your Teddy Bear" (1957)   *Elvis Presley* (from
Loving You)
"Jailhouse Rock" (1957)   *Elvis Presley*
"Treat Me Nice" (1957)   *Elvis Presley* (from *Jailhouse Rock*)
"Around the World" (1957)   *Mantovani*
"Wringle Wrangle" (1957)   *Fess Parker* (from *Westward Ho*)
"Tammy" (1957)   *Debbie Reynolds* (from *Tammy and the
Bachelor*)
"It's Not for Me to Say" (1957)   *Johnny Mathis* (from *Lizzie*)
"All the Way" (1957)   *Frank Sinatra* (from *The Joker Is Wild*)
"April Love" (1957)   *Pat Boone*
"The Ballad of Thunder Road" (1958)   *Robert Mitchum*
"A Certain Smile" (1958)   *Johnny Mathis*
"Hard Headed Woman" (1958)   *Elvis Presley* (from *King Creole*)
"Don't Ask Me Why" (1958)   *Elvis Presley* (from *King Creole*)

"High Hopes" (1959)   *Frank Sinatra* (from *A Hole in the Head*)
"The Magnificent Seven" (1960)   *Al Caiola*
"Never on Sunday" (1960)   *Don Costa*
"Over the Rainbow" (1960)   *Demensions* (from *The Wizard of Oz*)
"Because They're Young" (1960)   *Duane Eddy*
"Theme from *A Summer Place*" (1960)   *Percy Faith*
"Theme from *The Apartment*" (1960)   *Ferrante and Teicher*
"Theme from *Exodus*" (1960)   *Ferrante and Teicher*
"North to Alaska" (1960)   *Johnny Horton*
"Theme from *The Sundowners*" (1960)   *Mantovani*
"Maria" (1960)   *Johnny Mathis* (from *West Side Story*)
"One Boy" (1960)   *Joanie Sommers* (from *Bye Bye Birdie*)
"Pepe" (1960)   *Duane Eddy*
"Wild in the Country" (1961)   *Elvis Presley*
"Lonely Man" (1961)   *Elvis Presley* (from *Wild In the Country*)
"Flaming Star" (1961)   *Elvis Presley*
"Can't Help Falling in Love" (1961)   *Elvis Presley* (from *Blue Hawaii*)
"Rock-a-Hula Baby" (1961)   *Elvis Presley* (from *Blue Hawaii*)
"Moon River" (1961)   *Jerry Butler* (from *Breakfast At Tiffany's*)
"Never on Sunday" (1961)   *Chordettes*
"Ring of Fire" (1961)   *Duane Eddy*
"One Last Kiss" (1961)   *Bobby Vee* (from *Bye Bye Birdie*)
"Wooden Heart" (1961)   *Joe Dowell* (from *G.I. Blues*)
"Tonight" (1961)   *Ferrante and Teicher* (from *West Side Story*)
"Where the Boys Are" (1961)   *Connie Francis*
"Exodus" (1961)   *Eddie Harris*
"Moon River" (1961)   *Henry Mancini* (from *Breakfast at Tiffany's*)
"Let's Get Together" (1961)   *Hayley Mills*
"Town Without Pity" (1961)   *Gene Pitney*
"The Exodus Song" (1961)   *Pat Boone*
"Zip-a-Dee Doo Dah" (1962)   *Bob B. Soxx and the Blue Jeans* (from *Song of the South*)
"The Man Who Shot Liberty Valance" (1962)   *Gene Pitney* (inspired by film of the same name)
"Walk on the Wild Side" (1962)   *Jimmy Smith*

"Follow That Dream" (1962)   *Elvis Presley*

"King of the Whole Wide World" (1962)   *Elvis Presley* (from
                                                Kid Galahad)

"Return to Sender" (1962)   *Elvis Presley* (from *Girls! Girls!
                                    Girls!*)

"More" (1963)   *Vic Dana* (from *Mondo Cane*)

"Toys in the Attic" (1963)   *Jack Jones*

"Wives and Lovers" (1963)   *Jack Jones*

"Days of Wine and Roses" (1963)   *Henry Mancini*

"Days of Wine and Roses" (1963)   *Andy Williams*

"Charade" (1963)   *Henry Mancini*

"More" (1963)   *Kai Winding* (from *Mondo Cane*)

"One Broken Heart For Sale" (1963)   *Elvis Presley* (from *It
                                    Happened At the World's
                                    Fair*)

"Bossa Nova Baby" (1963)   *Elvis Presley* (from *Fun in
                                    Acapulco*)

"Love with the Proper Stranger" (1964)   *Jack Jones*

"Pink Panther Theme" (1964)   *Henry Mancini*

"Kissin' Cousins" (1964)   *Elvis Presley*

"Viva Las Vegas" (1964)   *Elvis Presley*

"What'd I Say" (1964)   *Elvis Presley* (from *Viva Las Vegas*)

Rock & roll movies

1956   *Blackboard Jungle*
         Love Me Tender
         Rock Around the Clock
         Don't Knock the Rock
         Shake, Rattle, and R-O-C-K
         The Girl Can't Help It

1957   *The Big Beat*
         Don't Knock the Rock
         Jailhouse Rock
         Jamboree
         Loving You
         Mister Rock 'n' Roll
         Rock Around the World
         Rock Pretty Baby
         Rock, Rock, Rock

1958	Go, Johnny, Go
	High School Confidential
	Hot Rod Gang
	King Creole
	Let's Rock
1959	College Confidential
	All the Young Men
	G.I. Blues
	Flaming Star
1961	Blue Hawaii
	Hey Let's Twist
	Teenage Millionaire
	Twist Around the Clock
	Wild in the Country
1962	Follow That Dream
	Girls! Girls! Girls!
	It's Trad, Dad
1963	Beach Party
	Bye Bye Birdie
	Fun In Acapulco
	It Happened At the World's Fair
	Kid Galahad
	Live It Up

c) Rock Songs Made Into Commercials

Rock songs and television commercials have always been intertwined. Many early rock hits such as Dickey Doo and the Don'ts' "Flip Top Box" (1958) and Billy Joe and the Checkmates' "Percolator Twist" (1962) were based on commercials. And by the 1980s, as the baby boomers approached middle age, the rock & roll songs of their youth increasingly were being used in TV commercials. This marked a major change. Rather than basing the song on a popular commercial (as was the trend in the 1950s and early 1960s), the commercial was now being based on a popular song. The numerous ads using old rock & roll hits provide evidence of the aging of the baby boom generation. They show that advertisers and ad executives now realize that nostalgic songs are the perfect way to catch the attention of this new segment of middle-age consumers. They also indicate that rock & roll music has been absorbed by the mainstream culture. Yesterday's rock classics are today's pop standards. The following is a list of rock & roll hits that have been used in 1980s commercials. (The commercial is preceded by a bullet.)

"Shake Rattle & Roll" (1954)   *Bill Haley and His Comets*
   • McDonald's Hamburger Commercial
"Goodnight, Sweetheart, Goodnight" (1954)   *Spaniels*
   • New Trail Granola Bars Commercial
"Only You" (1955)   *Platters*
   • Red Lobster Seafood commercial
   • Wendy's Hamburger commercial
"Rock Around the Clock" (1955)   *Bill Haley and His Comets*
   • Olympic Fitness Center: "Gonna jog around the track tonight"
   • Shield Soap commercial
"Tutti-Frutti" (1955)   *Little Richard*
   • Bon Bon Fruit Scoops
"(You've Got) The Magic Touch" (1956)   *Platters*
   • Hyatt Hotel commercial
"Love Me Tender" (1956)   *Elvis Presley*
   • Love Me Tender Dog Chunks commercial
"Let the Good Times Roll" (1956)   *Shirley and Lee*
   • Scott Tissue commercial
"Slippin' and Slidin'" (1956)   *Little Richard*
   • Baby Magic Oil commercial
"Why Do Fools Fall In Love?" (1956)   *Frankie Lymon & the Teenagers*
   • American Greeting Cards commercial
"Great Balls of Fire" (1957)   *Jerry Lee Lewis*
   • Burger King commercial
"Let Me Be Your Teddy Bear" (1957)   *Elvis Presley*
   • Teddy Graham Cereal commercial
"Whole Lot of Shakin' Going On" (1957)   *Jerry Lee Lewis*
   • Dairy Association commercial for real cheese
   • Burger King commercial: "Whole lot of breakfast going on"
"Little Darlin'" (1957)   *Diamonds*
   • Hi-C Fruit Drink commercial
   • Kentucky Fried Chicken: "Chicken Littles"
"Oh Boy!" (1957)   *Buddy Holly and the Crickets*
   • Buick commercial: "Oh Buick!"
"Come Go with Me" (1957)   *Dell-Vikings*
   • Kentucky Fried Chicken commercial

"At the Hop" (1957)   *Danny and the Juniors*
- Turner Broadcasting commercial for Atlanta Hawks basketball team: "At the Hoop"
- Smooshies toy commercial

"For Your Love (I Would Do Anything)" (1958)   *Ed Townsend*
- Jeweler's Association commercial for gold jewelry

"Short Shorts" (1958)   *Royal Teens*
- Nair Leg Hair Removal Cream commercial

"Chantilly Lace" (1958)   *Big Bopper*
- Mercury commercial

"Good Golly Miss Molly" (1958)   *Little Richard*
- Dolly Madison Cupcakes commercial: "Good Golly, it's Dolly"

"It's So Easy" (1958)   *Buddy Holly*
- Fantastik cleaning solution
- Toyota Tercel commercial

"Get a Job" (1958)   *Silhouettes*
- Chicago Tribune Want Ads commercial
- Quaker Granola Dip commercial: "Get a Dip"

"Summertime Summertime" (1958)   *Jamies*
- McDonald's Hamburger commercial
- Chico-San Rice Cakes commercial
- Ken-L Ration Dog Food commercial
- Mazda car commercial

"Tequila" (1958)   *Champs*
- Tequita wine cooler

"I Wonder Why" (1958)   *Dion and the Belmonts*
- Hi-C Fruit Drink commercial

"Summertime Blues" (1958)   *Eddie Cochran*
- Hi-C Fruit Drink commercial
- Cedar Point, Ohio, Amusement Park commercial
- Nestle's Toll House Cookies commercial
- NBC Television: "NBC's Got the Cure for the Summertime Blues"

"Do You Wanna Dance?" (1958)   *Bobby Freeman*
- Mercury Sable commercial

"Splish Splash" (1958)   *Bobby Darin*
- GTE Flip Phone
- Liquid Drano commercial

"La Bamba" (1958)   *Ritchie Valens*
- Subaru car commercial

- Pop Secret pop corn commercial

"He's Got the Whole World in His Hands" (1958)   *Laurie London*

- Radio Shack cellular phone: "You've Got the Whole World in Your Hands"

"Yakety Yak" (1958)   *Coasters*

- Coppertone Sun Tan Lotion: "Yakety yak, summertime's back"

"Betty Lou Got a New Pair of Shoes" (1958)   *Bobby Freeman*

- Deer Foam Slippers commercials

"Breathless" (1958)   *Jerry Lee Lewis*

- Liquid Sunlight dish detergent commercial

"Put Your Head On My Shoulder" (1959)   *Paul Anka*

- Head and Shoulders Shampoo commercial

"Personality" (1959)   *Lloyd Price*

- Light and Elegant diet food: " 'Cause it's light and elegant"
- K-Mart photo department
- Chevrolet Spectrum commercial

"Mack the Knife" (1959)   *Bobby Darin*

- McDonald's Hamburger commercial

"Kansas City" (1959)   *Wilbert Harrison*

- Chicago car dealer commercial: "Chevy City"

"Dedicated to the One I Love" (1959 and 1961)   *Shirelles*

- Nutra-Grain Cereal commercial

"Shout!" (1959)   *Isley Brothers*

- "Win, Lose, or Draw" TV show prom.
- Shout stain remover commercial

"Itsy Bitsy Teenie Weenie Yellow Polka Dot Bikini" (1960)

Brian Hyland

- Epilady Electric Shaver commercial

"What'd I Say" (1959)   *Ray Charles*

- Water Pik commercial

"Wonderful World" (1960)   *Sam Cooke*

- Public service anti-drug commercial

"Calendar Girl" (1960)   *Neil Sedaka*

- Purina Cat Chow

"The Twist" (1960 and 1961)   *Chubby Checker*

- Skil Power Screw Driver commercial
- Hardee's commercial for soft ice cream cones
- Super pretzels commercial

"Peanut Butter" (1961)   *Marathons*

- Peter Pan Peanut Butter commercial

"Mama Said" (1961)   *Shirelles*
  • Mercury Topaz commercial
"Barbara Ann" (1961)   *Regents*
  • Nabisco Granola Dips commercial
"Don't Hang Up" (1962)   *Orlons*
  • Sprint telephone service commercial
"I Remember You" (1962)   *Frank Ifield*
  • "George Bush for President Commercial"—1988: aimed at
      Jimmy Carter's administration
"Big Girls Don't Cry" (1962)   *Four Seasons*
  • No Nonsense Panty Hose commercial
"Sealed with a Kiss" (1962)   *Brian Hyland*
  • Zip-Lock Freezer Bags
"The Loco-Motion" (1962)   *Little Eva*
  • Quaker Peanut Whipps Granola Bars commercial
"The Stripper" (1962)   *David Rose*
  • Hardee's Hamburger commercial
"Duke of Earl" (1962)   *Gene Chandler*
  • Liquid Vanish toilet bowl cleaner commercial
"Surfin' U.S.A." (1963)   *Beach Boys*
  • Nurf Ball commercial: "Nurfin' U.S.A."
  • Quaker Chewy Granola commercial
"Hello Stranger" (1963)   *Barbara Lewis*
  • McDonald's commercial
"Just One Look" (1963)   *Doris Troy*
  • Toyota commercial
"Be My Baby"(1963)   *Ronettes*
  • Mercury Topaz commercial
"Wipe Out" (1963)   *Surfaris*
  • Stri-Dex acne medication commercial
"Da Doo Ron Ron" (1963)   *Crystals*
  • Energizer Batteries
"Tie Me Kangaroo Down, Sport" (1963)   *Rolf Harris*
  • Wallaby Squirt commercial
"The Bird's the Word" (1963)   *Trashmen*
  • Nintendo commercial
"My Boyfriend's Back" (1963)   *Angels*
  • Chunky candy commercial
"He's So Fine" (1963)   *Chiffons*
  • Hi-C Fruit Drink

"Hello Muddah, Hello Fadduh!" (1963)   *Allan Sherman*
   • Downy fabric softener commercial
"Bread and Butter" (1964)   *Newbeats*
   • Quaker Rice Cakes
"Pretty Woman" (1964)   *Roy Orbison*
   • Tone soap commercial
"High Heel Sneakers" (1964)   *Tommy Tucker*
   • Fresh Start laundry detergent

● LIST #34: The Supernatural

Many Americans were fascinated by the occult during the 1950s and early 1960s. The country's preoccupation with UFOs and monsters surfaced in rock songs.

"Rockin' Ghost" (1956)   *Archie Bleyer*
"I Put a Spell on You" (1956)   *Screamin' Jay Hawkins*
"Flying Saucers Rock & Roll" (1957)   *Billy Lee Riley*
"Flying Saucer" (1957)   *Buchanan and Goodman*
"Could This Be Magic?" (1957)   *Dubs*
"The Blob" (1958)   *Five Blobs*
"Dinner with Drac" (1958)   *John Zacherle*
"The Mummy" (1959)   *Bob and Dor McFadden*
"Midnight Stroll" (1959)   *Revels*
"This Magic Moment" (1960)   *Drifters*
"Gypsy Woman" (1961)   *Impressions*
"Blue Ghost" (1962)   *Tommy Roe*
"Fortune Teller" (1962)   *Bobby Curtola*
"The Monster Mash" (1962)   *Bobby "Boris" Pickett*
"Monster's Holiday" (1962)   *Bobby "Boris" Pickett*
"Magic Wand" (1962)   *Don & Juan*
"The Gypsy Cried" (1963)   *Lou Christie*
"Gypsy Woman" (1963)   *Rick Nelson*
See also "death rock" songs (List #25f).

● LIST #35: The Sea

For whatever psychological reasons, people have long been fascinated by oceans; beach-going is a well-established American pastime. Hit records on the rock charts reflected these interests in the sea and boating.

"Ship of Love" (1955)   *Nutmegs*
"Marianne" (1957)   *Terry Gilkyson and the Easyriders*
"Sail Along Silvery Moon" (1957)   *Billy Vaughn*
"Deep Blue Sea" (1957)   *Jimmy Dean*
"Endless Sleep" (1958)   *Jody Reynolds*
"Sea Cruise" (1959)   *Frankie Ford*
"Sea of Love" (1959)   *Phil Phillips*
"The Enchanted Sea" (1959)   *Islanders*
"The Enchanted Sea" (1959)   *Martin Denny*
"Harbor Lights" (1960)   *Platters*
"Red Sails in the Sunset" (1960)   *Platters*
"Beyond the Sea" (1960)   *Bobby Darin*
"Sea of Heartbreak" (1961)   *Don Gibson*
"Underwater" (1961)   *Frogmen*
"Stranger on the Shore" (1962)   *Mr. Acker Bilk*
See also songs about surfing (List #20).

● LIST #36: Cities and Suburbs

a) Songs About Urban and Suburban Lifestyles

"Silhouettes" (1957)   *Rays* (about identical tract homes)
"City Lights" (1959)   *Ivory Joe Hunter*
"Spanish Harlem" (1960)   *Ben E. King*
"Harlem Nocturne" (1960)   *Viscounts*
"My Home Town" (1960)   *Paul Anka*
"Town Without Pity" (1961)   *Gene Pitney*
"Up on the Roof" (1962)   *Drifters*
"Uptown" (1962)   *Crystals*
"Uptown" (1962)   *Roy Orbison*
"My Block" (1963)   *Chiffons*
"On Broadway" (1963)   *Drifters*
"Surf City" (1963)   *Jan and Dean*
"Drag City" (1963)   *Jan and Dean*
"Under the Boardwalk" (1964)   *Drifters*
"Dancing in the Street" (1964)   *Martha and the Vandellas*
"Little Boxes" (1964)   *Pete Seeger* (tract homes)

b) Songs About Cities

"When the Swallows Come Back to Capistrano" (1957)   *Pat Boone*

"Philadelphia U.S.A." (1958)   *Nu Tornados*

"Manhattan Spiritual" (1958)   *Reg Owens*

"Sweet Little Sixteen" (1958)   *Chuck Berry* (mentions various cities)

"M.T.A." (1959)   *Kingston Trio* (about Boston)

"Tucumcari" (1959)   *Jimmie Rodgers*

"El Paso" (1959)   *Marty Robbins*

"Kansas City" (1959)   *Wilbert Harrison*

"Kansas City" (1959)   *Rocky Olson*

"High School U.S.A." (1959)   *Tommy Facenda* (mentions various cities)

"Tallahassee Lassie" (1959)   *Freddy Cannon*

"Kissin' Time" (1959)   *Bobby Rydell* (mentions various cities)

"Way Down Yonder in New Orleans" (1959)   *Freddy Cannon*

"Okefenokee" (1959)   *Freddy Cannon*

"Battle of New Orleans" (1959)   *Johnny Horton*

"Miami" (1959)   *Eugene Church*

"Harlem Nocturne" (1960)   *Viscounts*

"Spanish Harlem" (1960)   *Ben E. King*

"Calcutta" (1960)   *Lawrence Welk*

"Walkin' to New Orleans" (1960)   *Fats Domino*

"Chattanooga Shoe Shine Boy" (1960)   *Freddy Cannon*

"Chattanooga Choo Choo" (1960)   *Ernie Fields*

"New Orleans" (1960)   *Gary U.S. Bonds*

"San Antonio Rose" (1961)   *Floyd Cramer*

"Bristol Stomp" (1961)   *Dovells*

"Calcutta" (1961)   *Four Preps*

"Lookin' for Love" (1962)   *Bobby Vee* (mentions various cities)

"Midnight in Moscow" (1962)   *Kenny Ball and His Jazz Band*

"I Left My Heart in San Francisco" (1962)   *Tony Bennett*

"Abilene" (1963)   *George Hamilton IV*

"Kansas City" (1963)   *Trini Lopez*

"Mecca" (1963)   *Gene Pitney*

"Twenty Four Hours from Tulsa" (1963)   *Gene Pitney*

"Detroit City" (1963)   *Bobby Bare*

"Memphis" (1963)   *Lonnie Mack*

"Honolulu Lulu" (1963)   *Jan and Dean*

"Marching Through Madrid" (1963)   *Herb Alpert and the*
Tijuana Brass

"Viva Las Vegas" (1964)   *Elvis Presley*

"Little Old Lady From Pasadena" (1964)   *Jan and Dean*

"Memphis" (1964)   *Johnny Rivers*

● LIST #37: Alcohol and Gambling

Teenagers, like adults, were also interested in these activities, which became common subjects on the rock charts.

a) Alcohol

"W-P-L-J (White Port and Lemon Juice)" (1955)   *Four Deuces*

"I Put a Spell on You" (1956)   *Screamin' Jay Hawkins*

"Tequila" (1958)   *Champs*

"Alligator Wine" (1958)   *Screamin' Jay Hawkins*

"Too Much Tequila" (1960)   *Champs*

"One Mint Julep" (1961)   *Ray Charles*

"Cherry Berry Wine" (1961)   *Charlie McCoy*

"Tequila Twist" (1962)   *Champs*

"A Steel Guitar and a Glass of Wine" (1962)   *Paul Anka*

"Scotch and Soda" (1962)   *Kingston Trio*

"Nick Teen and Al K. Hall" (1963)   *Rolf Harris*

b) Gambling

"Deck of Cards" (1959)   *Wink Martindale*

"From a Jack to a King" (1962)   *Ned Miller*

"Stewball" (1963)   *Peter, Paul, and Mary*

● LIST #38: Trains

Since trains have long captured the public's fancy, it is not surprising that songs using trains for romantic and mysterious imagery have turned up on the rock charts.

"Woo Woo Train" (1955)   *Valentines*

"Mystery Train" (1955)   *Elvis Presley*

"Rock Island Line (1956) *Lonnie Donegan*
"Click Clack" (1958) *Dickey Doo and the Don'ts*
"Midnight Special" (1960) *Paul Evans*
"Down By the Station" (1960) *Four Preps*
"Night Train" (1960) *Viscounts*
"Train of Love" (1960) *Annette*
"Chattanooga Choo Choo" (1960) *Ernie Fields*
"Chattanooga Choo Choo" (1962) *Floyd Cramer*
"Night Train" (1962) *James Brown*

● LIST #39: Work

Since folk and pop music have traditionally dealt with daily activities such as work, it is not surprising that the subject would be explored by rock & roll singers, too.

"Blue Monday" (1956) *Fats Domino*
"Rip It Up" (1956) *Little Richard*
"Summertime Blues" (1958) *Eddie Cochran*
"Yakety Yak" (1958) *Coasters*
"Get a Job" (1958) *Silhouettes*
"Got a Job" (1958) *Miracles*
"Gas Money" (1958) *Jan and Arnie*
"Let It Rock" (1960) *Chuck Berry*
"Chain Gang" (1960) *Sam Cooke*
"Big Bad John" (1961) *Jimmy Dean*
"School Is In" (1961) *Gary U.S. Bonds*
"Workin' for the Man" (1962) *Roy Orbison*
"Steel Men" (1962) *Jimmy Dean*
"Busted" (1963) *Ray Charles*
"That Lucky Old Sun" (1963) *Ray Charles*

4. Songs about American Politics

● LIST #40: Patriotism and Freedom

The 1950s and early 1960s witnessed consensus in American political opinion. Most Americans were proud of their freedom, boastful of their nation's accomplishments, and patriotic toward their flag and institutions. These feelings are reflected in many of the hit records on the rock charts.

"Ballad of Davy Crockett" (1955)   *Bill Hayes*
"Gotta Travel On" (1958)   *Billy Grammer* (freedom)
"God Bless America" (1959)   *Connie Francis*
"Battle of New Orleans" (1959)   *Johnny Horton*
"Johnny Reb" (1959)   *Johnny Horton*
"Battle Hymn of the Republic" (1959)   *Mormon Tabernacle Choir*
"To a Soldier Boy" (1959)   *Tassels*
"I'm Gonna Be a Wheel Someday" (1959)   *Fats Domino*
"Sink the Bismarck" (1960)   *Johnny Horton*
"Johnny Freedom" (1960)   *Johnny Horton*
"North to Alaska" (1960)   *Johnny Horton*
"Ballad of the Alamo" (1960)   *Bud and Travis*
"There's a Star Spangled Banner Waving Somewhere, #2 (Ballad of Francis Powers)" (1960)   *Red River Dave*
"God, Country, and My Baby" (1961)   *Johnny Burnette*
"Sound Off" (1961)   *Titus Turner*
"The Wanderer" (1961)   *Dion* (about individual freedom)
"Travelin' Man" (1961)   *Rick Nelson* (individual freedom)
"The Astronaut" (1961)   *Jose Jiminez*
"If I Had a Hammer" (1962)   *Peter, Paul, and Mary*
"P.T. 109" (1962)   *Jimmy Dean*
"My Daddy Is President" (1962)   *Little Jo Ann*
"Soldier Boy" (1962)   *Shirelles*
"Duke of Earl" (1962)   *Gene Chandler*
"Up on the Roof" (1962)   *Drifters*
"Blowin' in the Wind" (1963)   *Peter, Paul, and Mary*
"Only in America" (1963)   *Jay and the Americans*

"In the Summer of His Years" (1963)   *Connie Francis* (tribute to President Kennedy)

"Navy Blue" (1964)   *Diane Renay*
"Kiss Me Sailor" (1964)   *Diane Renay*

● LIST #41: History

Interest in American history was running at high tide in the 1950s and early 1960s. With the United States locked in a Cold War struggle against the Soviet Union, many Americans looked to the past for ideological strength and justification. The patriotic fervor associated with President Kennedy's New Frontier might also help explain the series of pro-American and historical songs that reached the rock charts in these years.

"Ballad of Davy Crockett" (1955)   *Bill Hayes*
"Battle of New Orleans" (1959)   *Johnny Horton*
"Bonaparte's Retreat" (1959)   *Billy Grammer*
"Johnny Reb" (1959)   *Johnny Horton*
"El Paso" (1959)   *Marty Robbins*
"Big Iron" (1959)   *Marty Robbins*
"Waterloo" (1959)   *Stonewall Jackson*
"Good Timin'" (1960)   *Jimmy Jones*
"Sink the Bismarck" (1960)   *Johnny Horton*
"Johnny Freedom" (1960)   *Johnny Horton*
"North to Alaska" (1960)   *Johnny Horton*
"Commanche" (1960)   *Johnny Horton*
"Ballad of the Alamo" (1960)   *Bud and Travis*
"Please Mr. Custer" (1960)   *Larry Verne*
"Mr. Livingston" (1960)   *Larry Verne*
"Battle of Gettysburg" (1961)   *Fred Darian*
"The Burning of Atlanta" (1962)   *Claude King*

● LIST #42: Space and the Space Program

One of the federal government's major accomplishments during the John F. Kennedy administration was legislation launching America's space program. Americans of all ages got caught up in the race for space, as they cheered on Alan Shepard, John Glenn, and other astronauts. Records on the rock charts reflected this fascination with space.

"Flying Saucer" (1956)   *Buchanan and Goodman*
"Flying Saucer the Second" (1957)   *Buchanan and Goodman*
"Flying Saucers Rock and Roll" (1957)   *Billy Lee Riley*
"Santa and the Satellite" (1957)   *Buchanan and Goodman*
"Purple People Eater" (1958)   *Sheb Wooley*
"Jupiter C" (1959)   *Pat and the Satellites* (also their name)
"The Clouds" (1959)   *the Spacemen* (also their name)
"The Little Space Girl" (1959)   *Jesse Lee Turner*
"The Astronaut" (1961)   *Jose Jiminez*
"Fly Me to the Moon (Bossa Nova)" (1962)   *Joe Harnell*
"Telstar" (1962)   *Tornadoes*
"Baja" (1963)   *Astronauts* (their name)
"Martian Hop" (1963)   *Ran-Dells*

● LIST #43: John F. Kennedy

Americans admired the charm, wit, and ability of President Kennedy. Youths found it particularly easy to relate to the zestful, 43-year-old Kennedy, who was the youngest person ever elected to the presidency. JFK's great popularity, engaging personality, youthful image, good looks, and war-hero reputation made him the ideal subject for several hit records on the rock charts.

"Alvin for President" (1960)   *Chipmunks* (parody of the
                                           Kennedy/Nixon election)
"P.T. 109" (1962)   *Jimmy Dean*
"My Daddy Is President" (1962)   *Little Jo Ann*
The First Family (1962)   *Vaughn Meader* (best-selling comedy
                                       album about Kennedy and his
                                       family)
"In the Summer of His Years" (1963)   *Connie Francis* (tribute
                                                 to JFK)

● LIST #44: The Cold War

Like other events in the news, relations with the Soviet Union influenced rock & roll. In 1958 Nikita Khrushchev demanded the return of West Berlin to East Germany. Tensions increased in 1959 and grew ominous when the Soviets shot down an American spy plane over Russian territory in 1960. The following year, the Russians threatened to allow East Germany to annex West Berlin. In response,

President Kennedy called up National Guard units and asked Congress for an additional $3.2 billion in defense funds. The Soviets then erected the Berlin Wall to separate West and East Berlin permanently. In 1962 the Cuban Missile Crisis brought the United States and Soviet Union eyeball to eyeball. The Soviets blinked first, allowing both to look away from possible nuclear war.

These Cold War events were not lost on the rock audience, as evidenced by the numerous records dealing with Cold War topics. The great publicity given to events in Germany, along with President Kennedy's famous 1962 speech in which he declared that like all free men, "Ich bin ein Berliner" ("I am a Berliner"), might also help explain the proliferation of rock hits sung in German or performed by German artists. American disdain for the allegedly immoral and godless communists may have contributed to the popularity of rock & roll records concerned with patriotic themes, religion, and traditional morals and values. Folk and country artists further reinforced America's claim to justice and freedom as their songs made the rock charts (see Lists #4c and 4d). The records on the charts show that many teenagers supported America 100 percent in the Cold War struggle against the Soviet Union.

"Sh-Boom" (1954)   *Chords* (title of the song inspired by the atomic bomb blast)

"Summertime Blues" (1958)   *Eddie Cochran* (talks about taking problems to the United Nations)

"Russian Bandstand" (1959)   *Spencer and Spencer*

"There's a Star Spangled Banner Waving Somewhere, No. 2 (Ballad of Francis Powers)" (1960)   *Red River Dave*

"Greetings (This Is Uncle Sam)" (1961)   *Valadiers*

"Guided Missiles (Aimed At My Heart)" (1961)   *Cuff-Links*

"Midnight in Moscow" (1962)   *Kenny Ball and His Jazz Band*

"Mr. Khrushchev" (1962)   *Bo Diddley*

"Dear Ivan" (1962)   *Jimmy Dean*

"West of the Wall" (1962)   *Miss Toni Fisher*

"Cruel War" (1962)   *Peter, Paul, and Mary*

"If I Had a Hammer" (1962)   *Peter, Paul, and Mary*

"Where Have All the Flowers Gone" (1962)   *Peter, Paul, and Mary*

"Where Have All the Flowers Gone" (1962)   *Kingston Trio*

"The End of the World" (1963)   *Skeeter Davis* (uses apocalyptic imagery of Cold War era)

"Hard Rain's A-Gonna Fall" (1963)   *Bob Dylan*
"Talking World War III Blues" (1963)   *Bob Dylan*
"Masters of War" (1963)   *Bob Dylan*
"With God On Our Side" (1964)   *Bob Dylan*

- Numerous songs recorded in German or performed by German artists also began appearing around the time of the Berlin Crisis, e.g., Ivo Robic's "Morgen" (1959); Lolita's "Sailor" (1960); Bert Kaempfert's "Wonderland by Night" (1960); Joe Dowell's "Wooden Heart" (1961); and Wayne Newton's "Danke Schoen" (1963)
- Songs with patriotic themes were common on the rock charts (for examples, see Lists # 40–43).
- Numerous songs about religion, which may have been viewed as a response to the godless communists, also made the rock charts (see List #26).
- Numerous hit records supported traditional values and morals, perhaps as a defense against communism's alleged immorality (see Lists #16–18 and #27).

5. Miscellaneous Records

● **LIST #45: Early R & B Songs Mentioning "Rock & Roll"**

Disc jockey Alan Freed is often given credit for coining the phrase "rock & roll" in 1951 or 1952. But the words "rock" and "roll" had long been used by black rhythm and blues artists as slang for sexual intercourse. Even the full phrase, "rock and roll," was used by R & B singers long before Freed arrived on the scene. The following includes examples of rhythm and blues songs that used the words "rock" and "roll" long before the rise of rock & roll music.

"Rocking and Rolling" (1939)   *Bob Robinson*
"Rock and Roll" (1934)   *Boswell Sisters*
"Rockin' Rollin' Mama" (1939)   *Buddy Jones*
"Cherry Red" (1939)   *Joe Turner*
"We're Gonna Rock, We're Gonna Roll" (1947)   *Wild Bill Moore*
"Rocking At Midnight" (1948)   *Roy Brown*
"Good Rockin' Tonight" (1948)   *Roy Brown*
"Rock All Night" (1948)   *Ravens*
"All She Wants to Do Is Rock" (1949)   *Wynonie Harris*
"Rock and Roll" (1949)   *Wild Bill Moore*
"Rock and Roll" (1950)   *John Lee Hooker*
"Rockin' with Red" (1950)   *Piano Red*
"Rockin' Blues" (1950)   *Little Esther*
"We're Gonna Rock" (1951)   *Gunter Lee Carr*
"Sixty Minute Man" (1951)   *Dominos*

● **LIST #46: Cover Records of Rhythm and Blues and Early R & B Rock Songs**

In the 1950s, many major record companies employed white singers to cover (i.e., rerecord) rhythm and blues hits or early R & B rock songs originally performed by black artists. This practice reflects the economic, political, social, and cultural realities of the day, which discriminated against blacks in both the music industry and the country as a whole. Later, the process of covering hit records be-

142

came commonplace as both white and black performers rerecorded earlier rock & roll hits. (Please note: On the following list, song titles are arranged alphabetically. The original artists are in italics, cover artists in roman type.)

"Ain't Got No Home"	*Clarence "Frogman" Henry* (1956)
	Buddy Holly (1956)
"Ain't It a Shame"	*Fats Domino* (1955)
	Pat Boone (1955) (became "Ain't' That a Shame)
	Four Seasons (1963)
"At My Front Door"	*El Dorados* (1955)
	Pat Boone (1955)
"Blue Monday"	*Fats Domino* (1956)
	Buddy Holly (1956)
	Crickets (1963)
"Blueberry Hill"	*Fats Domino* (1956)
	Elvis Presley (1957)
	the Lettermen (1961)
"Bo Diddley"	*Bo Diddley* (1955)
	Buddy Holly (1956)
	Bobby Vee (1962)
"Brown Eyed Handsome Man"	*Chuck Berry* (1956)
	Buddy Holly (1956)
	Bobby Vee (1964)
"Cherry Pie"	*Marvin and Johnny* (1954)
	Skip and Flip (1960)
"Church Bells May Ring"	*Willows* (1956)
	Diamonds (1956)
"Corrina Corrina"	*Joe Turner* (1956)
	Ray Peterson (1960)
"Crying in the Chapel"	*Orioles* (1953)
	June Valli (1953)
"Devil or Angel"	*Clovers* (1956)
	Bobby Vee (1960)
"Earth Angel"	*Penguins* (1955)
	Crew Cuts (1955)
	Johnny Tillotson (1960)
"Eddie My Love"	*Teen Queens* (1956)
	McGuire Sisters (1956)
	Fontane Sisters (1956)
	Chordettes (1956)

"Fever"	*Little Willie John* (1956)
	Peggy Lee (1958)
	Elvis Presley (1960)
"Goodnight, My Love"	*Jesse Belvin* (1956)
	McGuire Sisters (1957)
	Ray Peterson (1959)
	Fleetwoods (1963)
"Goodnight, Sweetheart, Goodnight"	*Spaniels* (1954)
	McGuire Sisters (1954)
"Good Rockin' Tonight"	Two R & B versions: *Roy Brown* (1948)
	and *Wynonie Harris* (1948)
	Elvis Presley (1954)
	Buddy Holly (1956)
	Pat Boone (1959)
"Gum Drop"	*Charms* (1954)
	Crew Cuts (1955)
"Hearts of Stone"	*Charms* (1954)
	Fontane Sisters (1954)
"Hound Dog"	*"Big Mama" Thornton* (1953)
	Elvis Presley (1956)
"I Almost Lost My Mind"	*Ivory Joe Hunter* (1950)
	Pat Boone (1956)
"I Feel So Bad"	*Chuck Willis* (1954)
	Elvis Presley (1961)
"I Hear You Knockin'"	*Smiley Lewis* (1955)
	Gale Storm (1955)
"I'll Be Home"	*Flamingos* (1956)
	Pat Boone (1956)
"I'm in Love Again"	*Fats Domino* (1956)
	Fontane Sisters (1956)
	Ricky Nelson (1957)
"I'm Walkin'"	*Fats Domino* (1957)
	Ricky Nelson (1957)
"In the Still of the Night"	*Five Satins* (1956)
	Dion (1961)
	Santo and Johnny (1964)
"It's Too Late"	*Chuck Willis* (1956)
	Buddy Holly & the Crickets (1957)

"Ka-Ding-Dong"	*G-Cleffs* (1956)
	Diamonds (1956)
	Hilltoppers (1956)
"Ko Ko Mo"	*Gene and Eunice* (1955)
	Crew Cuts (1955)
	Perry Como (1955)
"Lawdy Miss Clawdy"	*Lloyd Price* (1952)
	Elvis Presley (1956)
	Gary Stites (1960)
"Ling Ting Tong"	*Charms* (1954)
	Five Keys (1954)
	Buddy Knox (1961)
"Little Darlin'"	*Gladiolas* (1957)
	Diamonds (1957)
"Long Lonely Nights"	*Lee Andrews and the Hearts* (1957)
	Bobby Vee (1961)
"Long Tall Sally"	*Little Richard* (1956)
	Pat Boone (1956)
	Elvis Presley (1956)
	Eddie Cochran (1958)
"Louie Louie"	*Richard Berry* (1956)
	Kingsmen (1963)
	Paul Revere and the Raiders (1963)
"Love Is Strange"	*Mickey and Sylvia* (1956)
	Buddy Holly (1959)
"Love Love Love"	*Clovers* (1956)
	Diamonds (1956)
	Bobby Vee (1962)
"Lovey Dovey"	*Clovers* (1954)
	Buddy Knox (1961)
"Milk Cow Blues"	*Kokomo Arnold* (1935)
	Elvis Presley (1955)
	Eddie Cochran (1958)
	Ricky Nelson (1961)
"Money Honey"	*Clyde McPhatter & the Drifters* (1953)
	Elvis Presley (1956)
"My Baby Left Me"	*Arthur "Big Boy" Crudup* (1950)
	Elvis Presley (1956)

"Mystery Train"	*Little Jr. Parker's Blue Flames* (1953)
	Elvis Presley (1954)
"One Night"	*Smiley Lewis* (1956)
	Elvis Presley (1958)
"Pledging My Love"	*Johnny Ace* (1954)
	Theresa Brewer (1955)
	Bobby Vee (1961)
"Ready Teddy"	*Little Richard* (1956)
	Elvis Presley (1956)
	Buddy Holly (1957)
"Rip it Up"	*Little Richard* (1956)
	Bill Haley and His Comets (1956)
	Elvis Presley (1956)
	Buddy Holly (1956)
"Rock Around the Clock"	*Sonny Dae* (1954)
	Bill Haley and His Comets (1954)
"Rocket 88"	*Jackie Brenston (and the Ike Turner Band)* (1951)
	Bill Haley and His Comets (1952)
"Roll with Me Henry (The Wallflower)	*Etta James* (1955)
	Georgia Gibbs (1955)
	(Gibbs' version was called "Dance With Me, Henry")
"See Saw"	*Moonglows* (1956)
	Don Cornell (1956)
"Shake, Rattle, and Roll"	*Joe Turner* (1954)
	Bill Haley & His Comets (1954)
	Elvis Presley (1956)
	Buddy Holly (1956)
"Sh-Boom"	*Chords* (1954)
	Crew Cuts (1954)
"Since I Met You Baby"	*Ivory Joe Hunter* (1956)
	Bobby Vee (1960)
"Sincerely"	*Moonglows* (1954)
	McGuire Sisters (1955)
	Bobby Vee (1960)
"Slippin' and Slidin'"	*Little Richard* (1956)
	Buddy Holly (1959)
"A Story Untold"	*Nutmegs* (1955)
	Crew Cuts (1955)

"That's All Right"	*Arthur "Big Boy" Crudup* (1947)
	Elvis Presley (1954)
"Ting-A-Ling"	*Clovers* (1952)
	Buddy Holly (1956)
"Tutti Frutti"	*Little Richard* (1955)
	Pat Boone (1956)
	Elvis Presley (1956)
"Tweedle Dee"	*Laverne Baker* (1954)
	Georgia Gibbs (1955)
"Valley of Tears"	*Fats Domino* (1957)
	Buddy Holly (1957)
"We're Gonna Rock This Joint"	*Gunter Lee Carr* (1951)
	Bill Haley & His Comets (1952)
"When You Dance"	*Turbans* (1955)
	Lou Christie (1963)
"Why Do Fools Fall in Love"	*Frankie Lymon and the Teenagers* (1956)
	Diamonds (1956)
	Gale Storm (1956)
"Witchcraft"	*Spiders* (1956)
	Elvis Presley (1963)
"Wisdom of a Fool"	*Five Keys* (1957)
	Bobby Vee (1961)

● **LIST #47: Novelty Songs on the Rock Charts**

Novelty songs, a longtime staple of the pop music industry, continued to appeal to the rock & roll audience, as evidenced by numerous novelty hits on the rock charts during the 1950s and early 1960s.

"Transfusion" (1956) *Nervous Norvous*
"Ape Call" (1956) *Nervous Norvous*
"The Old Philosopher" (1956) *Eddie Lawrence*
"The Flying Saucer" (1957) *Buchanan and Goodman*
"Stranded in the Jungle" (1957) *Cadets*
"The Creature" (1957) *Buchanan and Ancell*
"Flying Saucer the Second" (1957) *Buchanan and Goodman*
"Santa and the Satellite" (1957) *Buchanan and Goodman*
"Shiek of Araby" (1958) *Lou Monte*
"Beep Beep" (1958) *Playmates*
"Witch Doctor" (1958) *David Seville*

"The Chipmunk Song" (1958)   *Chipmunks*
"Purple People Eater" (1958)   *Sheb Wooley*
"The Purple People Eater Meets the Witch Doctor" (1958)   *Joe South*
"Yakety Yak" (1958)   *Coasters*
"Green Mosquito" (1958)   *Tune Rockers*
"Splish Splash" (1958)   *Bobby Darin*
"Nee Nee Na Na Na Na Nu Nu" (1958)   *Dickey Doo & the Don'ts*
"Dinner with Drac" (1958)   *John Zacherle*
"Lazy Mary" (1958)   *Lou Monte*
"I Got a Wife" (1959)   *Mark IV*
"Uh Oh-Part 2" (1959)   *Nutty Squirrels*
"Midnight Stroll" (1959)   *Revels*
"Russian Bandstand" (1959)   *Spencer and Spencer*
"Charlie Brown" (1959)   *Coasters*
"Along Came Jones" (1959)   *Coasters*
"Gzachstahagen" (1959)   *Wildcats*
"Love Potion #9" (1959)   *Clovers*
"Happy Reindeer" (1959)   *Dancer, Prancer, and Nervous*
"Battle of (Camp) Kookamonga" (1959)   *Homer and Jethro*
"The Mummy" (1959)   *Bob and Dor McFadden*
"Rockin' in the Jungle" (1959)   *Eternals*
"Alvin's Harmonica" (1959)   *Chipmunks*
"Ragtime Cowboy Joe" (1959)   *Chipmunks*
"Kookie Kookie" (1959)   *Edd Byrnes (with Connie Stevens)*
"Poison Ivy" (1959)   *Coasters*
"My Girl" (1959)   *Floyd Robinson*
"I'm a Hog for You" (1959)   *Coasters*
"Run, Red, Run" (1959)   *Coasters*
"Mr. Custer" (1960)   *Larry Verne*
"Mr. Livingston" (1960)   *Larry Verne*
"Delaware" (1960)   *Perry Como*
"Itsy Bitsy Teenie Weenie Yellow Polka Dot Bikini" (1960)   *Brian Hyland*
"Alvin's Orchestra" (1960)   *Chipmunks*
"Alvin for President" (1960)   *Chipmunks*
"Rudolph the Red Nosed Reindeer" (1960)   *Chipmunks*
"Kookie Little Paradise" (1960)   *Jo Ann Campbell*
"Jeremiah Peabody's Poly Unsaturated Quick Dissolving Fast

Acting Pleasant Tasting Green and Purple Pills" (1961) *Ray Stevens*

"Little Egypt" (1961) *Coasters*

"Does Your Chewing Gum Lose Its Flavor on the Bed Post Overnight?" (1961) *Lonnie Donegan*

"More Money for You and Me" (1961) *Four Preps*

"The Astronaut" (1961) *Jose Jiminez*

"Small Sad Sam" (1961) *Phil McLean*

"Who Put the Bomp" (1961) *Barry Mann*

"The Touchables" (1961) *Dickie Goodman*

"The Touchables in Brooklyn" (1961) *Dickie Goodman*

"Pepino the Italian Mouse" (1962) *Lou Monte*

"Monster Mash" (1962) *Bobby "Boris" Pickett*

"Dr. Ben Basey" (1962) *Mickey Shorr and the Cut-Ups*

"Ben Crazy" (1962) *Dickie Goodman*

"Speedy Gonzales" (1962) *Pat Boone*

"Ahab the Arab" (1962) *Ray Stevens*

"The Alvin Twist" (1962) *Chipmunks*

"Don't Go Near the Eskimos" (1962) *Ben Colder*

"Santa Claus Is Watching You" (1962) *Ray Stevens*

"My Boomerang Won't Come Back" (1962) *Charlie Drake*

"Speed Ball" (1963) *Ray Stevens*

"Still No. 2" (1963) *Ben Colder*

"Who Stole the Keeshka?" (1963) *Matys Brothers*

"Pepino's Friend Pasqual" (1963) *Lou Monte*

"Martian Hop" (1963) *Ran-Dells*

"Hello Madduh, Hello Fadduh" (1963) *Allan Sherman*

"Harry the Hairy Ape" (1963) *Ray Stevens*

"On Top of Spaghetti" (1963) *Tom Glazer and the Children's Chorus*

"Surfin' Bird" (1963) *Trashmen*

"Tie Me Kangaroo Down Sport" (1963) *Rolf Harris*

● **LIST #48: Instrumentals on the Rock Charts**

"Honky Tonk (Pts. 1 and 2)" (1956) *Bill Doggett*

"Ram-Bunk-Shush" (1957) *Bill Doggett*

"Raunchy" (1957) *Bill Justis*

"Sail Along Silvery Moon" (1957) *Billy Vaughn*

"Hard Times (the Slop) (1957)   *Noble Watts*
"Till" (1957)   *Roger Williams*
"Walking with Mr. Lee" (1958)   *Lee Allen and His Band*
"Weekend" (1958)   *Kingsmen*
"Mexican Hat Rock" (1958)   *Appelljacks*
"Tequila" (1958)   *Champs*
"Topsy (Part II)" (1958)   *Cozy Cole*
"Rebel Rouser" (1958)   *Duane Eddy*
"Ramrod" (1958)   *Duane Eddy*
"Cannonball" (1958)   *Duane Eddy*
"College Man" (1958)   *Bill Justis*
"Patricia" (1958)   *Perez Prado*
"Teasin'" (1958)   *Quaker City Boys*
"The Green Mosquito" (1958)   *Tune Rockers*
"Rumble" (1958)   *Link Wray and His Raymen*
"Petite Fleur" (1959)   *Chris Barber's Jazz Band*
"The Happy Organ" (1959)   *Dave "Baby" Cortez*
"Quiet Village" (1959)   *Martin Denny*
"Yep" (1959)   *Duane Eddy*
"Forty Miles of Bad Road" (1959)   *Duane Eddy*
"Bongo Rock" (1959)   *Preston Epps*
"In the Mood" (1959)   *Ernie Fields*
"Torquay" (1959)   *Fireballs*
"Rockin' Crickets" (1959)   *Hot Toddys*
"Crossfire" (1959)   *Johnny and the Hurricanes*
"Red River Rock" (1959)   *Johnny and the Hurricanes*
"Reveille Rock" (1959)   *Johnny and the Hurricanes*
"Teen Beat" (1959)   *Sandy Nelson*
"Jupiter-C" (1959)   *Pat and the Satellites*
"Only You" (1959)   *Frank Pourcel and His French Fiddles*
"The Lonely One" (1959)   *Duane Eddy*
"Some Kind-a Earthquake" (1959)   *Duane Eddy*
"Bonnie Come Back" (1959)   *Duane Eddy*
"Like Young" (1959)   *Andre Previn and David Rose*
"Woo Hoo" (1959)   *Rock-A-Teens*
"Sleepwalk" (1959)   *Santo and Johnny*
"Tall Cool One" (1959)   *Wailers*
"Raw-Hide" (1959)   *Link Wray and His Raymen*
"Smokie, Part 2" (1960)   *Bill Black Combo*
"White Silver Sands" (1960)   *Bill Black Combo*

"Last Date" (1960)   *Floyd Cramer*

"Because They're Young" (1960)   *Duane Eddy*

"Theme from *A Summer Place*" (1960)   *Percy Faith*

"Exodus" (1960)   *Ferrante and Teicher*

"Beatnik Fly" (1960)   *Johnny and the Hurricanes*

"Wonderland by Night" (1960)   *Bert Kaempfert*

"Pepe" (1960)   *Duane Eddy*

"Caravan" (1960)   *Santo and Johnny*

"Walk Don't Run" (1960)   *Ventures*

"Perfidia" (1960)   *Ventures*

"Harlem Nocturne" (1960)   *Viscounts*

"Night Train" (1960)   *Viscounts*

"Calcutta" (1960)   *Lawrence Welk*

"Bumble Boogie" (1961)   *B. Bumble and the Stingers*

"Take Five" (1961)   *Dave Brubeck*

"Tuff" (1961)   *Ace Cannon*

"Stick Shift" (1961)   *Duals*

"Quite a Party" (1961)   *Fireballs*

"Underwater" (1961)   *Frogmen*

"Pomp and Circumstance" (1961)   *Adrian Kimberley*

"Asia Minor" (1961)   *Ko Ko Mo*

"Yellow Bird" (1961)   *Arthur Lymon*

"Moon River" (1961)   *Henry Mancini*

"Last Night" (1961)   *Mar-Keys*

"Mexico" (1961)   *Bob Moore*

"Let There Be Drums" (1961)   *Sandy Nelson*

"Ghost Riders in the Sky" (1961)   *Ramrods*

"Wheels" (1961)   *String-a-Longs*

"You Can't Sit Down" (1961)   *Phil Upchurch Combo*

"Ram-Bunk-Shush" (1961)   *Ventures*

"Let's Go Trippin'" (1961)   *Dick Dale and His Del-Tones*

"Dance with the Guitar Man" (1962)   *Duane Eddy*

"Midnight In Moscow" (1962)   *Kenny Ball and His Jazz Band*

"Nut Rocker" (1962)   *B. Bumble and the Stingers*

"Stranger on the Shore" (1962)   *Mr. Acker Bilk*

"Green Onions" (1962)   *Booker T. and the MG's*

"Limbo Rock" (1962)   *Appelljacks*

"Rinky-Dink" (1962)   *Dave "Baby" Cortez*

"Alley Cat" (1962)   *Bent Fabric*

"Surfer's Stomp" (1962)   *Marketts*

" 'Route 66' Theme" (1962)   *Nelson Riddle*
"Wild Weekend" (1962)   *Rockin' Rebels*
"The Stripper" (1962)   *David Rose*
"Let's Go" (1962)   *Routers*
"Telstar" (1962)   *Tornadoes*
"Theme From 'Ben Casey' " (1962)   *Valjean*
"A Swingin' Safari" (1962)   *Billy Vaughn*
"Soul Twist" (1962)   *King Curtis*
"El Watusi" (1963)   *Ray Baretto*
"Pipe Line" (1963)   *Chantays*
"Memphis" (1963)   *Lonnie Mack*
"Out of Limits" (1963)   *Marketts*
"The Lonely Surfer" (1963)   *Jack Nitzsche*
"Our Winter Love" (1963)   *Bill Purcell*
"Yakety Sax" (1963)   *Boots Randolph*
"Watermelon Man" (1963)   *Mongo Santamaria*
"Wipe Out" (1963)   *Surfaris*
"Washington Square" (1963)   *Village Stompers*
"More" (1963)   *Kai Winding*

● LIST #49: Rock & Roll's Greatest Hits, 1954–1963

Throughout the history of rock & roll, records have been charted, compared, graphed, bulleted, starred, and otherwise ranked in popularity. "American Bandstand" had its weekly Top 10. Radio stations their Top 20, 30, or even 40. And *Billboard* its Top 100 or Hot 100. There seems to be a long tradition—a pop culture obligation—to rank listeners' favorite hits. After all, this is America where "one man one vote" is the law of the land, particularly when it comes to popular culture.

What follows is my ballot for the greatest hits of rock & roll's first decade. After noting important prototypes of early rock & roll, I have selected the top songs of each year, 1954 through 1963, as well as the Top 40 hits for the entire decade. Each record is listed in the year that it peaked on the charts. Included are records representing all styles. Critics sometimes dismiss some pop rock, pop, and folk that made the rock charts during these years, claiming that those songs do not qualify as rock & roll. But many of those records were widely accepted by members of the rock audience. It is, therefore, only fitting that those songs be included as notable and representative hits of the era.

My choices are based on more than just personal taste. I have considered record sales, jukebox plays, TV and radio air time, aesthetic quality, and overall popularity, as well as historical value and cultural significance. No doubt many will disagree with my rankings, but to quote a Rick Nelson hit, "Fools rush in where wise men fear to go. . . ."

Roots of Rock & Roll

1. "Crazy Man Crazy" (1953)   *Bill Haley and His Comets*
2. "Lawdy Miss Clawdy" (1952)   *Lloyd Price*
3. "Sixty Minute Man" (1951)   *Dominoes*
4. "Money Honey" (1953)   *Clyde McPhatter & the Drifters*
5. "A Sunday Kind of Love" (1953)   *Harptones*
6. "Hound Dog" (1953)   *Big Mama Thornton*
7. "Crying in the Chapel" (1953)   *Orioles*
8. "Shake a Hand" (1953)   *Faye Adams*
9. "Ting-a-Ling" (1952)   *Clovers*
10. "Baby It's You" (1953)   *Spaniels*
11. "We're Gonna Rock This Joint" (1952)   *Bill Haley and His Comets*
12. "Rockin' Chair" (1951)   *Fats Domino*
13. "Rocket 88" (1951)   *Jackie Brenston (and the Ike Turner Band)*
14. "Don't Deceive Me" (1953)   *Chuck Willis*
15. "Have Mercy Baby" (1952)   *Billy Ward and the Dominoes*
See also List #45, rhythm and blues songs mentioning "rock & roll."

Top Songs, Year by Year

1954

1. "Shake, Rattle, and Roll"   *Joe Turner*
2. "Goodnight, Sweetheart, Goodnight"   *Spaniels*
3. "Earth Angel"   *Penguins*
4. "That's All Right"   *Elvis Presley*
5. "Sh-Boom"   *Chords*
6. "Cherry Pie"   *Marvin and Johnny*
7. "Annie Had a Baby"   *Hank Ballard and the Midnighters*
8. "Gee"   *Crows*
9. "Shake, Rattle, and Roll"   *Bill Haley and His Comets*
10. "Work With Me, Annie"   *Hank Ballard and the Midnighters*
11. "Lovey Dovey"   *Clovers*
12. "Sh-Boom"   *Crew Cuts*
13. "I Feel So Bad"   *Chuck Willis*

14. "Reconsider Baby"   *Lowell Fulson*
15. "Mambo Baby"   *Ruth Brown*

1955

1. "Bo Diddley"   *Bo Diddley*
2. "Mystery Train"   *Elvis Presley*
3. "Rock Around the Clock"   *Bill Haley and His Comets*
4. "Maybellene"   *Chuck Berry*
5. "See You Later, Alligator"   *Bill Haley and His Comets*
6. "Pledging My Love"   *Johnny Ace*
7. "I Hear You Knockin'"   *Smiley Lewis*
8. "Ain't It a Shame"   *Fats Domino*
9. "Seventeen"   *Boyd Bennett*
10. "Story Untold"   *Nutmegs*
11. "Tweedle Dee"   *Laverne Baker*
12. "Ballad of Davy Crockett"   *Bill Hayes*
13. "Roll With Me, Henry"   *Etta James*
14. "Baby, Let's Play House"   *Elvis Presley*
15. "Only You"   *Platters*
16. "I Forgot to Remember to Forget"   *Elvis Presley*
17. "Ain't That a Shame"   *Pat Boone*
18. "Black Denim Trousers"   *Cheers*
19. "At My Front Door"   *El Dorados*
20. "Hearts of Stone"   *Charms*
21. "Sincerely"   *Moonglows*
22. "I Got a Woman"   *Ray Charles*
23. "Smokey Joe's Cafe"   *Robins*
24. "My Babe"   *Little Walter*
25. "Daddy O"   *Bonnie Lou*

1956

1. "Hound Dog"   *Elvis Presley*
2. "In the Still of the Night"   *Five Satins*
3. "Blue Suede Shoes"   *Carl Perkins*
4. "Blue Suede Shoes"   *Elvis Presley*
5. "Heartbreak Hotel"   *Elvis Presley*
6. "Long Tall Sally"   *Little Richard*
7. "Be Bop a Lula"   *Gene Vincent and His Blue Caps*
8. "Tutti Frutti"   *Little Richard*
9. "Rip It Up"   *Little Richard*
10. "Don't Be Cruel"   *Elvis Presley*
11. "Ready Teddy"   *Little Richard*
12. "I'm in Love Again"   *Fats Domino*

13. "Roll Over Beethoven"   *Chuck Berry*
14. "I Want You, I Need You, I Love You"   *Elvis Presley*
15. "Since I Met You Baby"   *Ivory Joe Hunter*
16. "Fever"   *Little Willie John*
17. "Let the Good Times Roll"   *Shirley and Lee*
18. "Speedo"   *Cadillacs*
19. "When You Dance"   *Turbans*
20. "Eddie My Love"   *Teen Queens*
21. "Why Do Fools Fall in Love"   *Frankie Lymon and the Teenagers*
22. "Stranded in the Jungle"   *Cadets*
23. "The Great Pretender"   *Platters*
24. "It's Too Late"   *Chuck Willis*
25. "Blue Moon"   *Elvis Presley*
26. "Singin' the Blues"   *Guy Mitchell*
27. "Love Me Tender"   *Elvis Presley*
28. "I Walk the Line"   *Johnny Cash*
29. "Tonight You Belong to Me"   *Patience and Prudence*
30. "Gonna Get Along Without You Now"   *Patience and Prudence*
31. "Money Honey"   *Elvis Presley*
32. "My Baby Left Me"   *Elvis Presley*
33. "My Prayer"   *Platters*
34. "Church Bells May Ring"   *Willows*
35. "I Almost Lost My Mind"   *Pat Boone*
36. "I Put a Spell on You"   *Screamin' Jay Hawkins*
37. "I'll Be Home"   *Pat Boone*
38. "Friendly Persuasion"   *Pat Boone*
39. "My Blue Heaven"   *Fats Domino*
40. "Ka Ding Dong"   *Diamonds*

1957

1. "Peggy Sue"   *Buddy Holly*
2. "Whole Lotta Shakin' Going On"   *Jerry Lee Lewis*
3. "Keep a Knockin'"   *Little Richard*
4. "Bony Moronie"   *Larry Williams*
5. "Bye Bye Love"   *Everly Brothers*
6. "Rock and Roll Music"   *Chuck Berry*
7. "Love Is Strange"   *Mickey and Sylvia*
8. "Diana"   *Paul Anka*
9. "That'll Be the Day"   *Buddy Holly and the Crickets*
10. "Little Darlin'"   *Diamonds*
11. "Young Love"   *Sonny James*
12. "Blueberry Hill"   *Fats Domino*
13. "Jingle Bell Rock"   *Bobby Helms*

14. "Silhouettes"   *Rays*
15. "All Shook Up"   *Elvis Presley*
16. "School Days"   *Chuck Berry*
17. "Jailhouse Rock"   *Elvis Presley*
18. "Happy Happy Birthday Baby"   *Tuneweavers*
19. "Susie Q"   *Dale Hawkins*
20. "Little Bitty Pretty One"   *Thurston Harris*
21. "Over the Mountain"   *Johnnie and Joe*
22. "Come Go with Me"   *Dell Vikings*
23. "Be Bop Baby"   *Ricky Nelson*
24. "I'm Walkin'"   *Fats Domino*
25. "I'm Walkin'"   *Ricky Nelson*
26. "Searchin'"   *Coasters*
27. "Jenny Jenny"   *Little Richard*
28. "Raunchy"   *Bill Justis*
29. "Gone"   *Ferlin Husky*
30. "Peanuts"   *Little Joe and the Thrillers*
31. "Black Slacks"   *Joe Bennett and the Sparkletones*
32. "Kisses Sweeter Than Wine"   *Jimmie Rodgers*
33. "Walkin' After Midnight"   *Patsy Cline*
34. "April Love"   *Pat Boone*
35. "Short Fat Fanny"   *Larry Williams*
36. "Let Me Be Your Teddy Bear"   *Elvis Presley*
37. "C. C. Rider"   *Chuck Willis*
38. "You Send Me"   *Sam Cooke*
39. "Honeycomb"   *Jimmie Rodgers*
40. "Ain't Got No Home"   *Clarence "Frogman" Henry*

1958

1. "Get a Job"   *Silhouettes*
2. "Great Balls of Fire"   *Jerry Lee Lewis*
3. "Summertime Blues"   *Eddie Cochran*
4. "At the Hop"   *Danny and the Juniors*
5. "You Cheated"   *the Shields*
6. "Yakety Yak"   *Coasters*
7. "Good Golly Miss Molly"   *Little Richard*
8. "Buzz Buzz Buzz"   *Hollywood Flames*
9. "Book of Love"   *Monotones*
10. "Johnny B. Goode"   *Chuck Berry*
11. "All I Have to Do Is Dream"   *Everly Brothers*
12. "It's Only Make Believe"   *Conway Twitty*
13. "Little Star"   *Elegants*
14. "We Belong Together"   *Robert and Johnny*

15. "Tequila"   *Champs*
16. "Splish Splash"   *Bobby Darin*
17. "Poor Little Fool"   *Ricky Nelson*
18. "Witch Doctor"   *David Seville*
19. "Willie and the Hand Jive"   *Johnny Otis*
20. "Short Shorts"   *Royal Teens*
21. "Dede Dinah"   *Frankie Avalon*
22. "Chantilly Lace"   *Big Bopper*
23. "Do You Want to Dance?"   *Bobby Freeman*
24. "Susie Darlin'"   *Robin Luke*
25. "I Wonder Why"   *Dion and the Belmonts*
26. "For Your Precious Love"   *Jerry Butler and the Impressions*
27. "To Know Him Is to Love Him"   *Teddy Bears*
28. "Maybe"   *Chantels*
29. "One Summer Night"   *Danleers*
30. "Jo Ann"   *Twin-Tones*
31. "Rumble"   *Link Wray and His Raymen*
32. "One Night"   *Elvis Presley*
33. "Sweet Little Sixteen"   *Chuck Berry*
34. "Rockin' Robin"   *Bobby Day*
35. "La-Do-Dada"   *Dale Hawkins*
36. "Waitin' in School"   *Ricky Nelson*
37. "Stood Up"   *Ricky Nelson*
38. "Jennie Lee"   *Jan and Arnie*
39. "The Stroll"   *Diamonds*
40. "Endless Sleep"   *Jody Reynolds*

1959

1. "What'd I Say"   *Ray Charles*
2. "Shout"   *Isley Brothers*
3. "La Bamba"   *Ritchie Valens*
4. "A Teenager in Love"   *Dion and the Belmonts*
5. "Mary Lou"   *Ronnie Hawkins*
6. "There Goes My Baby"   *Drifters*
7. "Come Softly to Me"   *Fleetwoods*
8. "Stagger Lee"   *Lloyd Price*
9. "Lonely Teardrops"   *Jackie Wilson*
10. "Sixteen Candles"   *Crests*
11. "Donna"   *Ritchie Valens*
12. "Sleep Walk"   *Santo and Johnny*
13. "Believe Me"   *Royal Teens*
14. "Hushabye"   *Mystics*
15. "Hey Little Girl"   *Dee Clark*

16. "Sea of Love"   *Phil Phillips*
17. "I've Had It"   *the Bell Notes*
18. "Mr. Blue"   *Fleetwoods*
19. "Kansas City"   *Wilbert Harrison*
20. "Battle of New Orleans"   *Johnny Horton*
21. "Personality"   *Lloyd Price*
22. "Charlie Brown"   *Coasters*
23. "Sea Cruise"   *Frankie Ford*
24. "Teen Beat"   *Sandy Nelson*
25. "Tallahassee Lassie"   *Freddy Cannon*
26. "Tell Him No"   *Travis and Bob*
27. "Sorry (I Ran All the Way Home)"   *Impalas*
28. "Cross Fire"   *Johnny and the Hurricanes*
29. "Bongo Rock"   *Preston Epps*
30. "The Happy Organ"   *Dave "Baby" Cortez*
31. "Love Potion #9"   *Clovers*
32. "Lovers Never Say Goodbye"   *Flamingos*
33. "So Fine"   *Fiestas*
34. "I Only Have Eyes for You"   *Flamingos*
35. "Since I Don't Have You"   *Skyliners*
36. "Waterloo"   *Stonewall Jackson*
37. "Tragedy"   *Thomas Wayne*
38. "Ballad of a Girl and Boy"   *Graduates*
39. "C'mon Everybody"   *Eddie Cochran*
40. "Goodbye Baby"   *Jack Scott*

1960

1. "New Orleans"   *Gary "U.S." Bonds*
2. "Let's Have a Party"   *Wanda Jackson*
3. "Only the Lonely"   *Roy Orbison*
4. "Harlem Nocturne"   *Viscounts*
5. "Handy Man"   *Jimmy Jones*
6. "Money"   *Barrett Strong*
7. "Are You Lonesome Tonight"   *Elvis Presley*
8. "Cathy's Clown"   *Everly Brothers*
9. "Georgia on My Mind"   *Ray Charles*
10. "Muleskinner Blues"   *Fendermen*
11. "The Twist"   *Chubby Checker*
12. "He Will Break Your Heart"   *Jerry Butler*
13. "What in the World's Come Over You"   *Jack Scott*
14. "El Paso"   *Marty Robbins*
15. "Sweet Nothin's"   *Brenda Lee*
16. "Running Bear"   *Johnny Preston*

17. "Tonight's the Night" *Shirelles*
18. "Tell Laura I Love Her" *Ray Peterson*
19. "Teen Angel" *Mark Dinning*
20. "Why Do I Love You So" *Johnny Tillotson*
21. "Good Timin'" *Jimmy Jones*
22. "You Got What It Takes" *Marv Johnson*
23. "You Talk Too Much" *Joe Jones*
24. "Sandy" *Larry Hall*
25. "I'm Sorry" *Brenda Lee*
26. "Fannie Mae" *Buster Brown*
27. "Poetry in Motion" *Johnny Tillotson*
28. "Blue Angel" *Roy Orbison*
29. "Finger Poppin' Time" *Hank Ballard and the Midnighters*
30. "Where or When" *Dion and the Belmonts*
31. "Mountain of Love" *Harold Dorman*
32. "Image of a Girl" *Safaris*
33. "Walk Don't Run" *Ventures*
34. "A Thousand Stars" *Kathy Young and the Innocents*
35. "Stay" *Maurice Williams and the Zodiacs*
36. "Think" *James Brown*
37. "Love You So" *Ron Holden*
38. "Angela Jones" *Johnny Ferguson*
39. "Mr. Lonely" *Videls*
40. "Please Mr. Custer" *Larry Verne*

1961

1. "Quarter to Three" *Gary "U.S." Bonds*
2. "Runaway" *Del Shannon*
3. "Runaround Sue" *Dion*
4. "Will You Love Me Tomorrow" *Shirelles*
5. "Last Night" *Mar-Keys*
6. "Travelin' Man" *Rick Nelson*
7. "The Lion Sleeps Tonight" *Tokens*
8. "Angel Baby" *Rosie and the Originals*
9. "Pretty Little Angel Eyes" *Curtis Lee*
10. "I Love How You Love Me" *Paris Sisters*
11. "Raindrops" *Dee Clark*
12. "Every Breath I Take" *Gene Pitney*
13. "Rubber Ball" *Bobby Vee*
14. "Shop Around" *Miracles*
15. "Ya Ya" *Lee Dorsey*
16. "Girl of My Best Friend" *Ral Donner*
17. "Blue Moon" *Marcels*

18. "Candy Man"   *Roy Orbison*
19. "The Way You Look Tonight"   *Lettermen*
20. "Wonderland By Night"   *Bert Kaempfert*
21. "Please Mr. Postman"   *Marvelettes*
22. "Look in My Eyes"   *Chantels*
23. "Marie's the Name (His Latest Flame)"   *Elvis Presley*
24. "Hats Off to Larry"   *Del Shannon*
25. "Run to Him"   *Bobby Vee*
26. "Take Good Care of My Baby"   *Bobby Vee*
27. "Dedicated to the One I Love"   *Shirelles*
28. "Cupid"   *Sam Cooke*
29. "Crying"   *Roy Orbison*
30. "Hit the Road, Jack"   *Ray Charles*
31. "Hello Mary Lou"   *Rick Nelson*
32. "Tossin' and Turnin' "   *Bobby Lewis*
33. "There's a Moon Out Tonight"   *Capris*
34. "Barbara Ann"   *Regents*
35. "Baby Blue"   *Echoes*
36. "Mother In Law"   *Ernie K-Doe*
37. "Let's Twist Again"   *Chubby Checker*
38. "I Like It Like That"   *Chris Kenner*
39. "The Mountain's High"   *Dick and DeeDee*
40. "Corrina Corrina"   *Ray Peterson*

1962

1. "Twist and Shout"   *Isley Brothers*
2. "Sheila"   *Tommy Roe*
3. "Shout! Shout! Knock Yourself Out!"   *Ernie Maresca*
4. "Baby It's You"   *Shirelles*
5. "The Wanderer"   *Dion*
6. "He's a Rebel"   *Crystals*
7. "Do You Love Me?"   *Contours*
8. "Let's Dance"   *Chris Montez*
9. "I Can't Stop Loving You"   *Ray Charles*
10. "Only Love Can Break a Heart"   *Gene Pitney*
11. "Soldier Boy"   *Shirelles*
12. "Sherry"   *Four Seasons*
13. "Big Girls Don't Cry"   *Four Seasons*
14. "Palisades Park"   *Freddy Cannon*
15. "Duke of Earl"   *Gene Chandler*
16. "You Don't Know Me"   *Ray Charles*
17. "It Keeps Right On a Hurtin' "   *Johnny Tillotson*
18. "Can't Help Falling in Love"   *Elvis Presley*

19. "Peppermint Twist"   *Joey Dee and the Starlighters*
20. "Norman"   *Sue Thompson*
21. "Shout"   *Joey Dee and the Starlighters*
22. "You Better Move On"   *Arthur Alexander*
23. "Anna"   *Arthur Alexander*
24. "Walkin' with My Angel"   *Bobby Vee*
25. "Scotch and Soda"   *Kingston Trio*
26. "Where Have All the Flowers Gone"   *Kingston Trio*
27. "She Cried"   *Jay and the Americans*
28. "When I Fall In Love"   *Lettermen*
29. "Come Back Silly Girl"   *Lettermen*
30. "The Twist"   *Chubby Checker*
31. "The Loco-Motion"   *Little Eva*
32. "Let's Go"   *Routers*
33. "Surfin' Safari"   *Beach Boys*
34. "All Alone Am I"   *Brenda Lee*
35. "Roses Are Red"   *Bobby Vinton*
36. "Happy Birthday Sweet Sixteen"   *Neil Sedaka*
37. "Patches"   *Dickey Lee*
38. "Monster Mash"   *Bobby "Boris" Pickett*
39. "Ahab the Arab"   *Ray Stevens*
40. "Johnny Angel"   *Shelley Fabares*

1963

1. "Louie Louie"   *Kingsmen*
2. "Surfin' U.S.A."   *Beach Boys*
3. "Be My Baby"   *Ronettes*
4. "Fingertips, Part 2"   *Little Stevie Wonder*
5. "If You Wanna Be Happy"   *Jimmy Soul*
6. "Da Doo Ron Ron"   *Crystals*
7. "Then He Kissed Me"   *Crystals*
8. "He's So Fine"   *Chiffons*
9. "Little Deuce Coupe"   *Beach Boys*
10. "Blowin' in the Wind"   *Peter, Paul, and Mary*
11. "Surfer Girl"   *Beach Boys*
12. "Surfer Joe"   *Surfaris*
13. "Surf City"   *Jan and Dean*
14. "The End of the World"   *Skeeter Davis*
15. "Rhythm of the Rain"   *Cascades*
16. "Go Away Little Girl"   *Steve Lawrence*
17. "Wipe Out"   *Surfaris*
18. "It's My Party"   *Leslie Gore*
19. "Be True to Your School"   *Beach Boys*

20. "Bring It On Home to Me"   *Sam Cooke*
21. "I Will Follow Him"   *Little Peggy March*
22. "Wild Weekend"   *Rockin' Rebels*
23. "You Really Got a Hold on Me"   *Miracles*
24. "The Monkey Time"   *Major Lance*
25. "Ruby Baby"   *Dion*
26. "Blue on Blue"   *Bobby Vinton*
27. "You Can't Sit Down"   *Dovells*
28. "Little Town Flirt"   *Del Shannon*
29. "Mockingbird"   *Inez Foxx*
30. "Sally Go 'Round the Roses"   *Jaynettes*
31. "Puff the Magic Dragon"   *Peter, Paul, and Mary*
32. "Denise"   *Randy and the Rainbows*
33. "Mickey's Monkey"   *Miracles*
34. "Walk Right In"   *Rooftop Singers*
35. "Hey Girl"   *Freddie Scott*
36. "Walkin' the Dog"   *Rufus Thomas*
37. "On Broadway"   *Drifters*
38. "Only in America"   *Jay and the Americans*
39. "Everybody"   *Tommy Roe*
40. "Zip-A-Dee-Doo-Dah"   *Bob B. Soxx and the Blue Jeans*

Rock's Top Forty

1. "Hound Dog" (1956)   *Elvis Presley*
2. "Louie Louie" (1963)   *Kingsmen*
3. "Peggy Sue" (1957)   *Buddy Holly*
4. "Whole Lotta Shakin' Going On" (1957)   *Jerry Lee Lewis*
5. "Quarter to Three" (1961)   *Gary U.S. Bonds*
6. "In the Still of the Night" (1956)   *Five Satins*
7. "Twist and Shout" (1962)   *Isley Brothers*
8. "Get a Job" (1958)   *Silhouettes*
9. "Runaway" (1961)   *Del Shannon*
10. "Blue Suede Shoes" (1956)   *Carl Perkins/Elvis Presley*
11. "Keep a Knockin" (1957)   *Little Richard*
12. "What'd I Say" (1959)   *Ray Charles*
13. "Shout" (1959)   *Isley Brothers*
14. "Shake, Rattle, and Roll" (1954)   *Joe Turner*
15. "Bony Moronie" (1957)   *Larry Williams*
16. "Great Balls of Fire" (1958)   *Jerry Lee Lewis*
17. "Heartbreak Hotel" (1956)   *Elvis Presley*
18. "Long Tall Sally" (1956)   *Little Richard*
19. "Be Bop a Lula" (1956)   *Gene Vincent and His Blue Caps*

20. "Summertime Blues" (1958)   *Eddie Cochran*
21. "Surfin' U.S.A." (1963)   *Beach Boys*
22. "Runaround Sue" (1961)   *Dion*
23. "Will You Love Me Tomorrow?" (1961)   *Shirelles*
24. "Bye Bye Love" (1957)   *Everly Brothers*
25. "New Orleans" (1960)   *Gary U.S. Bonds*
26. "Last Night" (1961)   *Mar-Keys*
27. "La Bamba" (1959)   *Ritchie Valens*
28. "A Teenager in Love" (1959)   *Dion and the Belmonts*
29. "Be My Baby" (1963)   *Ronettes*
30. "Mary Lou" (1959)   *Ronnie Hawkins*
31. "At the Hop" (1958)   *Danny and the Juniors*
32. "Da Doo Ron Ron" (1963)   *Crystals*
33. "You Cheated" (1958)   *Shields*
34. "Yakety Yak" (1958)   *Coasters*
35. "Good Golly Miss Molly" (1958)   *Little Richard*
36. "Rock and Roll Music" (1957)   *Chuck Berry*
37. "Buzz Buzz Buzz" (1958)   *Hollywood Flames*
38. "Book of Love" (1958)   *Monotones*
39. "Johnny B. Goode" (1958)   *Chuck Berry*
40. "School Days" (1957)   *Chuck Berry*

PART THREE

The Performers, A to Z

This section comprises an historical encyclopedia of virtually every performer—pop, folk, and rock—who made the record charts between 1954 and 1963. Each entry includes information about the performers and hit records, including the title of each hit, its record label, the number the song peaked at on the *Billboard* charts, and the record's year of release (a [+] following the year indicates the record peaked on the charts the year following its first appearance). Unless otherwise indicated, all chart information is based on *Billboard*'s Top 100 chart (covering the years 1955 through 1958) or Hot 100 chart (covering the years after 1958), as compiled by Joel Whitburn's *Record Research*. Whenever possible, the entry also explains how the performer reflected and/or affected the times.[1]

My purpose here is to show how performers and their hit records fit the overall patterns of rock & roll. It is not to compile a listing of every record made by each artist. Although I have tried to be as comprehensive as possible, space limitations sometimes prevented me from listing every hit of every performer. For complete data about every record or biographical information about each artist, please consult Joel Whitburn's *Top Pop Singles, 1955–1986* or *Billboard* magazine.

ABBOTT, BILLY, & THE JEWELS This pop rock group had a minor hit in 1963 with "Groovy Baby" (Parkway, #55, 1963), a song referring to popular teenage slang.

THE ACCENTS Their only hit was "Wiggle, Wiggle" (Brunswick, #51, 1958+). The song assured girls that a well-placed wiggle would even show through a sack dress, the popular fashion of the day. The song reflects clothing styles and sexist attitudes of the day.

ADDERLEY, CANNONBALL This jazz musician's R & B-influenced "African Waltz" (Riverside, #41, 1961) reflects the growing interest in Afro-American culture by the early 1960s. He would have even greater success later on with his instrumental hit, "Mercy, Mercy, Mercy" (Capitol, #11, 1967).

ACE, JOHNNY His "Pledging My Love" (Duke, 1955), a number one record on rhythm and blues charts, was one of the first R & B songs to become popular among white teenagers. The song was later covered by numerous rock performers, including teen idols Johnny Tillotson and Bobby Vee. Ace's death in 1954, while playing Russian Roulette just prior to going out on stage, contributed to the legend that grew around him.

ADAMS, FAYE This rhythm and blues singer had a big hit, "Shake a Hand" (Herald, 1953) on the rhythm and blues charts in 1953.

ALAIMO, CHUCK This saxophonist's "Leap Frog" (MGM, #92, 1957) barely made the charts in 1957. His pop rock song about a childhood game is a good example of how some rock songs focused on pre-teen themes.

ALAIMO, STEVE A pop rock performer who enjoyed moderate success in the early 1960s. His best-known hits offer good glimpses of musical trends of the day. "Mashed Potatoes" (Checker, #81, 1962) was an unsuccessful attempt to tie into the dance craze of 1961. "Every Day I Have To Cry" (Checker, #46, 1963) found Alaimo trying to copy the increasingly popular R & B rock style, while "Michael" (Checker, #100, 1963) was a minor hit trying to cash in on the folk sound made popular by acts such as Peter, Paul, and Mary. Steve Alaimo eventually found his niche as a pop vocalist and regular on Dick Clark's "Where the Action Is," a popular TV show of the mid to late 1960s.

ALEXANDER, ARTHUR He barely dented the top record charts in 1962 with two songs he wrote, "You Better Move On" (Dot, #24, 1962) and "Anna" (Dot, #68, 1962). Yet, artistically, the songs were two of the year's best, and were later recorded by the Rolling Stones and Beatles, respectively. His success shows the lingering influence of the R & B sound on 1960s' rock music.

ALLEN, LEE, AND HIS BAND He began as a saxophone player on several Fats Domino records. In 1957 he recorded an instrumental, "Walkin' With Mr. Lee" (Ember, #54, 1958), which became a minor hit in early 1958.

ALLEN, REX He first achieved fame with a country and western radio show out of Chicago in the late 1940s. By the early 1950s, he was making Grade B westerns for Republic Studios. In 1962 he had a Top 20 record on the rock charts with "Don't Go Near the Indians" (Mercury, #17, 1962). The song mirrors the public's fascination with the American West during the early 1960s when TV westerns were extremely popular. It also reflects stereotypes of Indians, and shows the continuing influence of country and western on pop music.

ALLEN, RICHIE His only hit was "Stranger From Durango" (Imperial, #90, 1960). The song tried to capitalize on the popularity of movie and TV westerns in the early 1960s.

THE ALLISONS This pop rock group had a minor hit in 1963 with "Surfer Street" (Tip, #93, 1963). The song reflected the surfing fad of the day.

ALPERT, HERB, AND THE TIJUANA BRASS In 1962 this group reached number six on the *Billboard* charts with "The Lonely Bull" (A & M, #6, 1962). Alpert, co-founder of A & M Records, did well throughout the 1960s and 1970s with pop-oriented records like "Whipped Cream" (A & M, #68, 1965); "Taste of Honey" (A & M, #7, 1965); "Zorba the Greek" (A & M, #11, 1965); "Tijuana Taxi" (A & M, #38, 1965); "What Now My Love" (A & M, #24, 1966); "Spanish Flea" (A & M, #27, 1966); "The Work Song" (A & M, #18, 1966); and "Mame" (A & M, #19, 1966). His biggest hit, "This Guy's In Love With You" (A & M, #1, 1968) was done without the Tijuana Brass. His tremendous success proves that old-fashioned, middle-of-the-road pop appealed to the rock audience throughout the 1960s.

ANDERSON, BILL His "Still" (Decca, #8, 1963) was one of the biggest hits of 1963, peaking at number eight on the charts. It is a good example of the pop-influenced country and western music that was appealing to the rock & roll audience in the early 1960s.

ANDREWS, LEE, AND THE HEARTS This R & B rock group from Philadelphia enjoyed brief success in the late 1950s with three hits which were throwbacks to the old rhythm and blues sound of the early 1950s: "Long Lonely Nights" (Chess, #45, 1957); "Tear Drops" (Chess, #20, 1957); and "Try the Impossible" (United Artists, #33, 1958).

THE ANGELS These three pretty, white girls from New Jersey had several hits in the early 1960s copying the sound of the Shirelles and other black girl groups. Their biggest hit was "My Boyfriend's Back" (Smash, #1, 1963). The song reflected attitudes of the day which held that girls had to be submissive and dependent upon males. "My Boyfriend's Back," along with other Angel hits like " 'Til" (Caprice, #14, 1961 +); "Cry Baby Cry" (Caprice, #38, 1962); and "I Adore Him" (Smash, #25, 1963), provide a good example of 1960s mass-produced pop rock.

ANITA AND THE SO & SO'S These were the Anita Kerr Singers. Their pop rock hit, "Joey Baby" (RCA, #91, 1962), is a good example of a rock song dealing with a popular teenage name.

ANKA, PAUL One of the most talented pop rock stars of the late 1950s. Coming out of Ottawa, Canada, he first hit the charts at age 16 with "Diana" in 1957. Hit after hit followed throughout rock's first decade. Though considered a rock & roller, Anka was actually closer to the old-style pop singers. Like the Sinatras, Comos, and Bennetts of the previous generation, Anka crooned out ballads about love, romance, and traditional values. His success shows that many members of the rock & roll audience had values and tastes similar to adults. Anka eventually moved completely toward pop music, writing "My Way" for Frank Sinatra, and the theme song for Johnny Carson's "Tonight Show." His biggest hits include:

"Diana"	ABC	#2	1957
"You Are My Destiny"	ABC	#7	1958
"Crazy Love"	ABC	#19	1958
"Let the Bells Keep Ringing"	ABC	#30	1958

"Midnight"	ABC	#69	1958
"(All of a Sudden) My Heart Sings"	ABC	#15	1958 +
"I Miss You So"	ABC	#33	1959
"Lonely Boy"	ABC	#1	1959
"Put Your Head on My Shoulder"	ABC	#2	1959
"It's Time to Cry"	ABC	#4	1959
"Puppy Love"	ABC	#2	1960
"My Home Town"	ABC	#8	1960
"Hello Young Lovers"	ABC	#23	1960
"Summer's Gone"	ABC	#11	1960
"The Story of My Love"	ABC	#16	1961
"Tonight My Love, Tonight"	ABC	#13	1961
"Dance on Little Girl"	ABC	#10	1961
"Love Me Warm and Tender"	RCA	#12	1962
"A Steel Guitar and a Glass of Wine"	RCA	#13	1962
"Eso Beso"	RCA	#19	1962
"Love Makes the World Go 'Round"	RCA	#26	1963
"Remember Diana"	RCA	#39	1963
"Goodnight My Love"	RCA	#27	1969
"Jubilation"	Buddah	#65	1972
"(You're) Having My Baby"	United Artists	#1	1974
"One Man Woman/One Woman Man"	United Artists	#7	1974 +
"I Don't Like to Sleep Alone"	United Artists	#8	1975
"There's Nothing Stronger Than Our Love"	United Artists	#15	1975
"Times of Your Life"	United Artists	#7	1975 +

ANKA, PAUL, GEORGE HAMILTON IV, AND JOHNNY NASH
These three pooled their talents for a hit record in 1958, "The Teen Commandments" (ABC, #29, 1958). The song, an inspirational pep talk aimed at teens, is a good example of how many early rock hits focused on religious themes and traditional values. This type of song reflects that many teenagers shared the adult values of the day which stressed religion.

ANNETTE (FUNICELLO)   It seems that almost every middle-class American teenage boy loved, or at least lusted for, this young girl, who first became a TV star on Walt Disney's "Mickey Mouse Club." In 1959 and 1960 she had hits with pop rock geared to adolescent interests. Her biggest hits included "Tall Paul" (Disneyland, #7, 1959); "Jo-Jo the Dog-Faced Boy" (Vista, #73, 1959);

"First Name Initial" (Vista, #20, 1959); "Oh Dio Mio" (Vista, #10, 1960); "Train of Love" (Vista, #36, 1960); and "Pineapple Princess" (Vista, #11, 1960). Later, Annette starred with Frankie Avalon in a series of Beach Party movies during the surfing fad of the early 1960s.

ANN-MARGARET In 1961 her Hollywood star was on the rise with movies, Las Vegas performances, and even one hit record, "I Just Don't Understand" (RCA, #17, 1961). She later went on to star in *Bye Bye Birdie*, a 1963 movie that satirized rock's teen idols.

ANTHONY, RAY This trumpet player and his orchestra recorded "Peter Gunn" (Capitol, #8, 1959), the theme song for a popular TV show of the same name. Its success can be attributed to two things: the popularity of the television show and the continuing appeal of the 1940s Big Band sound.

THE APPALACHIANS By the early 1960s, the term "Appalachia" was synonymous with President Kennedy's New Frontier programs to aid one of the most poverty-stricken areas in the country. Trying to capitalize on this name recognition and the rising folk sound, this group had minor success with a folk version of Larry Williams' classic, "Bony Moronie" (ABC, #62, 1963).

THE APPELLJACKS Led by Dave Appell, this pop-rock instrumental group had a series of hits, including "Mexican Hat Rock" (Cameo, #16, 1958); "Rocka-Conga" (Cameo, #38, 1958); and "Bunny Hop" (Cameo, #70, 1959). The songs, which became quite popular on "American Bandstand," reflect teen interest in new dance crazes.

THE AQUATONES These six performers from Long Island are a good example of the one-hit artists that abounded during the early years of rock & roll. In 1958 they came out of nowhere on a small independent label and had one medium-sized hit with pop rock appeal, "You" (Fargo, #21, 1958). By the end of the year, they were nowhere again.

ATKINS, CHET This country and western guitarist had several minor hits on the rock charts, including "Boo Boo Stick Beat" (RCA, #49, 1959); "One Mint Julep" (RCA, #82, 1960); and "Teensville" (RCA, #73, 1960). His greatest contribution to rock & roll came as A&R chief for RCA-Victor, supervising Elvis Presley's early hits.

AUDREY Her minor hit, "Dear Elvis (Pages 1 & 2)" (Plus, #87, 1956), reflected the Elvismania sweeping the United States in 1956.

AVALON, FRANKIE One of the original pop rockers of the late 1950s. Coming out of South Philadelphia, he was closely associated with Dick Clark and made numerous appearances on "American Bandstand." He appealed mostly to adolescent girls and parents who saw him as a nice, clean-cut kid (unlike the more sexual Elvis). He had a long string of hits, beginning with the now classic "Dede Dinah" in 1958. Avalon's great success reflects the growing market for both pop singers and lyrics that appealed to teenagers. In the early 1960s, Avalon also starred with Annette Funicello in several Beach Party movies dealing with that era's surfing craze. His greatest hits included:

"Dede Dinah"	Chancellor	#7	1958
"Ginger Bread"	Chancellor	#9	1958
"I'll Wait for You"	Chancellor	#15	1958
"Venus"	Chancellor	#1	1959
"Bobby Sox to Stockings"	Chancellor	#8	1959
"A Boy Without a Girl"	Chancellor	#10	1959
"Just Ask Your Heart"	Chancellor	#7	1959
"Why"	Chancellor	#1	1959
"Swingin' on a Rainbow"	Chancellor	#36	1959+
"Don't Throw Away All Those Teardrops"	Chancellor	#22	1960
"Where Are You"	Chancellor	#32	1960
"Tuxedo Junction"	Chancellor	#82	1960
"Togetherness"	Chancellor	#26	1960
"You Are Mine"	Chancellor	#26	1962

BACHARACH, BURT This pop musician and composer (who often wrote with Hal David) had one minor hit, "Saturday Sunshine" (Kapp, #93, 1963). But he wrote or co-wrote numerous other hits for performers like Gene Pitney ("The Man Who Shot Liberty Valance," "Only Love Can Break a Heart," and "Twenty Four Hours From Tulsa"); Bobby Vee ("Be True To Yourself"); the Shirelles ("Baby, It's You"); the Five Blobs ("The Blob"); Sam Cooke ("Wonderful World"); Jackie DeShannon ("What the World Needs Now"); and Dionne Warwick ("Anyone Who Had a Heart," "Walk On By," and many others).

BAEZ, JOAN If Bob Dylan was the king of the folk movement, then Baez was the queen. Though her singles seldom made the charts, her albums were best-sellers in the mid and late 1960s. Her recording of "We Shall Overcome" associated her with civil rights, while many other songs made her a champion of the peace movement. Her music also reflected the rising popularity of folk, as well as the growing sophistication of the rock & roll generation. Her only singles to make the Top 40 were "The Night They Drove Old Dixie Down" (Vanguard, #3, 1971) and "Diamonds and Rust" (A & M, #35, 1975).

BAKER, LaVERN   An early R & B performer who enjoyed great success with hits like "Tweedle Dee" (Atlantic, #22 on the *Billboard* "Best Seller Chart," 1954); "Jim Dandy" (Atlantic, #22, 1956); and "I Cried a Tear" (Atlantic, #6, 1958).

BALL, KENNY, AND HIS JAZZMEN   The title of this British jazz group's instrumental hit, "Midnight in Moscow" (Kapp, #2, 1962), reflected America's preoccupation with the Soviet Union in 1962, a year that witnessed the Cuban Missile Crisis and other Cold War tensions.

BALLARD, HANK, AND THE MIDNIGHTERS   One of the truly outstanding R & B groups of the mid 1950s, they went on to only medium success in rock & roll. Their R & B hits like "Work with Me, Annie" (Federal, 1954); "Sexy Ways" (Federal, 1954); and "Annie Had a Baby" (Federal, 1954) are excellent examples of the sexuality of early rhythm and blues. Their biggest rock hits were dance-oriented songs like "Finger Poppin' Time" (King, #7, 1960) and "Let's Go, Let's Go, Let's Go" (King, #6, 1960). Ballard also wrote and recorded "The Twist," which later became a smash hit for Chubby Checker.

BARBER'S JAZZ BAND, CHRIS   They had a sleeper with "Petite Fleur" (Laurie, #5, 1959), an exotic instrumental that mixed dixieland music with a French theme. Its success proved that a well-done pop record could sell quite well to some members of the rock audience.

BARE, BOBBY   His country and western–influenced hits in the early 1960s included "Shame on Me" (RCA, #23, 1962); "Detroit City" (RCA, #16, 1963); and "500 Miles Away from Home" (RCA, #10, 1963). His success can be attributed to the down home, folk-like quality of the songs, which set them apart from many of the more pop-oriented, mass-produced records of the time. Bobby Bare's first national hit had been in 1958, with "The All-American

Boy," a song about Elvis Presley's rise to fame. This record, which reached number two on the charts, was erroneously credited to Bill Parsons. *See* Bill Parsons.

BARRETTO, RAY This jazz percussionist had one hit record, "El Watusi" (Tico, #17, 1963). The song had a novel refrain and an interesting sound which mixed ingredients from Latin music and rhythm and blues. It reflected the growing Afro-American consciousness of the day.

BARRY AND THE TAMBERLANES This pop-rock group enjoyed brief success with "I Wonder What She's Doing Tonight" (Valiant, #21, 1963), written by pop musician Barry De Vorzon. The lyrics reflected teen interests in romance and broken hearts.

B. BUMBLE AND THE STINGERS They had two instrumental hits, "Bumble Boogie" (Rendezvous, #21, 1961), which was based on Rimsky-Korsakov's "Flight of the Bumble Bee"; and "Nutrocker" (Rendezvous, #23, 1962), based on Tchaikovsky's "The Nutcracker." Both are perfect examples of how classical music could be drastically altered simply by adding electric guitars and a rock & roll beat.

BEACH BOYS Comprised of Brian Wilson, Carl Wilson, Dennis Wilson, Mike Love, and Al Jardine, the Beach Boys were arguably the most significant pop rock group of the early and mid 1960s. Their blend of tight harmonies, soaring falsettos, catchy tunes, and teen-oriented lyrics provided them with an impressive string of hit singles and albums. Back in the early 1960s, many teenagers were optimistic, fun-loving, and carefree, and the Beach Boys' music fit the mood. They were unsurpassed at recording songs about subjects teenagers loved. Throughout the early and mid 1960s, they had numerous hits singing about surfing, fun in the sun, cars, dating, school, dancing, and other adolescent activities.

But by 1965 the Beach Boys were having trouble keeping up with the rapidly changing times. The rock audience had grown up and left the Beach Boys behind. Brian Wilson, their talented writer, producer, lead singer, and creative genius, initially met the challenge with his brilliant creation, "Good Vibrations," and the critically acclaimed album, *Pet Sounds* (1966). But unable to write the meaningful lyrics that the more sophisticated rock audience demanded by the late 1960s, Brian Wilson eventually slipped into drugs and depression. And with him tumbled the

35. *Teensville* album cover (Ball State University Photo Service)

36. Jerry Butler (Courtesy of Vee Jay Records)

37. Ray Charles (National Archives)

38. Dee Clark (Courtesy of Vee Jay Records)

39. Joey Dee and the Starlighters contributed to the Twist craze (Ball State University Photo Service)

40. Bo Diddley (Courtesy of MCA Records)

41. Dion (Ball State University Photo Service)

42. The Eldorados (Courtesy of Vee Jay Records)

Beach Boys. After 1967, they only occasionally broke into the Top 20, mostly with nostalgic surf items like "Do It Again" (1968).

If the Beach Boys' initial success reflected the naîveté and hedonism of American teens in the early 1960s, their eventual demise mirrored the growing sophistication and changing interests of college students by the late 1960s, when protesting replaced surfing as a popular pastime.

The Beach Boys later enjoyed a comeback with an album of nostalgic hits, *Endless Summer* (1974), followed by numerous sellout concerts and tours in the 1970s and 1980s. Shortly after being inducted into the Rock & Roll Hall of Fame, they even made it back to the *Billboard* charts in 1988 with a hit single, "Ko Ko Mo," from the Tom Cruise film *Cocktail*. But, for the most part, the Beach Boys' recent popularity is based on their reputation as one of rock & roll's supergroups of the 1960s. The fact that original Beach Boy records are still selling nearly 30 years after their original release shows that rock & roll, when well done, has a timeless folk quality. It also suggests that aging Baby Boomers are trying to hold on to their youth by listening to nostalgic Beach Boys' hits. The Beach Boys' greatest hits include:

"Surfin Safari"	Capitol	#14	1962
"409"	Capitol	#76	1962
"Surfin' U.S.A."	Capitol	#3	1963
"Shut Down"	Capitol	#23	1963
"Surfer Girl"	Capitol	#7	1963
"Little Deuce Coupe"	Capitol	#15	1963
"Be True to Your School"	Capitol	#6	1963
"In My Room"	Capitol	#23	1963
"Fun Fun Fun"	Capitol	#5	1964
"I Get Around"	Capitol	#1	1964
"Don't Worry Baby"	Capitol	#24	1964
"When I Grow Up (To Be a Man)"	Capitol	#9	1964
"Wendy"	Capitol	#44	1964
"Little Honda"	Capitol	#65	1964
"Dance Dance Dance"	Capitol	#8	1964
"Do You Wanna Dance?"	Capitol	#12	1965
"Please Let Me Wonder"	Capitol	#52	1965
"Help Me Rhonda"	Capitol	#1	1965
"California Girls"	Capitol	#3	1965
"The Little Girl I Once Knew"	Capitol	#20	1965 +
"Barbara Ann"	Capitol	#2	1966
"Sloop John B"	Capitol	#3	1966
"Wouldn't It Be Nice?"	Capitol	#8	1966

"God Only Knows"	Capitol	#39	1966
"Good Vibrations"	Capitol	#1	1966
"Heroes and Villains"	Brother	#12	1967
"Wild Honey"	Capitol	#31	1967
"Darlin'"	Capitol	#19	1967 +
"Do It Again"	Capitol	#20	1968
"I Can Hear Music"	Capitol	#24	1969
"Rock and Roll Music"	Brother	#5	1976
"The Beach Boys' Medley"	Capitol	#12	1981
"Come Go with Me"	Caribou	#18	1981 +
"Getcha Back"	Caribou	#26	1985
"California Dreamin'"	Capitol	#57	1986

THE BEAU-MARKS These four musicians hailed from Canada and had one American hit, a solid rock & roll song entitled "Clap Your Hands" (Shad, #45, 1960). Despite its plodding beat, the record still had enough of a folk quality to generate some excitement among members of the rock audience who were getting tired of the formula pop rock of the early 1960s.

THE BELL NOTES This Long Island quintet's only big hit was "I've Had It" (Time, #6, 1959), an interesting rock & roll song which featured teen-oriented lyrics and a superb plunking guitar riff. Their follow-ups, "Old Spanish Town" (Time, #76, 1959) and "Shortnin' Bread" (Madison, #96, 1960), barely made the charts.

BELLUS, TONY He made the rock charts with "Robbin' the Cradle" (NRC, #25, 1959). Its musical blend of pop rock and country and western appealed to many members of the teen audience, as did the lyrics which dealt with a fellow in love with a much younger girl—a common fantasy for many young girls.

THE BELMONTS They started their career as the latter half of Dion and the Belmonts. After their lead singer, Dion, left for a solo career, the Belmonts (Angelo D'Aleo, Fred Milano, and Carlo Mastrangelo) decided to try it on their own. Although they never came close to matching Dion's success, they did record some excellent pop rock in the early 1960s. Their biggest hits were "Tell Me Why" (Sabina, #18, 1961) and "Come On Little Angel" (Sabina, #28, 1962). *See also* Dion and the Belmonts.

BELVIN, JESSE Got his start in the rhythm and blues field in the late 1940s and early 1950s. After co-writing the Penguins' classic

R & B rock hit, "Earth Angel" (1954), he went on to have two national hits of his own: "Goodnight My Love" (Modern, 1956), which became disc jockey Alan Freed's closing theme on his nightly show over WINS-Radio in New York City; and "Guess Who" (RCA, #31, 1959). He died in a car crash in 1960.

BENNETT, BOYD This pop rock musician struck a responsive chord in the rising youth culture of the 1950s with his two teen-oriented hits, "Seventeen" (King, #17, 1955) and "My Boy Flat Top" (King, #39, 1955).

BENNETT, JOE, AND THE SPARKLETONES Good example of pop rock of the late 1950s. Their hits, "Black Slacks" (ABC, #17, 1957) and "Penny Loafers and Bobby Socks" (ABC, #43, 1957), mirror fashions of the day. "Black Slacks" used typical teenage expressions like "cool breeze," "crazy little mama," "hep-cat," "cool daddy-o," and "rarin' to go."

BENNETT, TONY Though definitely not a rock performer, his hit recordings of "I Left My Heart In San Francisco" (Columbia, #19, 1962) and "I Wanna Be Around" (Columbia, #14, 1963) clearly show that many members of the so-called rock generation were also buying and enjoying traditional pop music, which suggests that teens might not have been as rebellious or different as many adults thought.

BENTON, BROOK This R & B rock artist from South Carolina put together a long string of hits, beginning with "It's Just a Matter of Time" in 1959, and ending with "Rainy Night in Georgia" in 1970. His long-term success shows the continuing popularity of R & B rock. His hits included:

"It's Just a Matter of Time"	Mercury	#3	1959
"Endlessly"	Mercury	#12	1959
"Thank You Pretty Baby"	Mercury	#16	1959
"So Many Ways"	Mercury	#6	1959
"The Ties That Bind"	Mercury	#37	1960
"Kiddio"	Mercury	#7	1960
"The Same One"	Mercury	#16	1960
"For My Baby"	Mercury	#28	1961
"Think Twice"	Mercury	#11	1961
"The Boll Weevil Song"	Mercury	#2	1961
"Frankie and Johnny"	Mercury	#20	1961

"Revenge"	Mercury	#15	1961 +
"Shadrack"	Mercury	#19	1962
"Lie to Me"	Mercury	#13	1962
"Hotel Happiness"	Mercury	#3	1962 +
"I Got What I Wanted"	Mercury	#28	1963
"My True Confession"	Mercury	#22	1963
"Rainy Night in Georgia"	Mercury	#4	1970

BENTON, BROOK, AND DINAH WASHINGTON   These two R & B rock performers joined forces for two hits: "Baby (You've Got What It Takes)" (Mercury, #5, 1960) and "A Rockin' Good Way" (Mercury, #7, 1960).

BERNARD, ROD   His only big hit was "This Should Go On Forever" (Argo, #20, 1959). The pop rock sound and teen-oriented lyrics appealed to Baby Boomers, who had just reached high school age.

BERRY, CHUCK   Emerging from the rhythm and blues tradition, Chuck Berry became one of rock & roll's first and greatest superstars. He combined potent images of the urban and teen cultures with folk-quality lyrics and a driving R & B beat to produce high quality hits, such as "Rock & Roll Music" (1957) and "Johnny B. Goode" (1958). Themes of the 1950s focusing on the automobile, teenage lifestyles, music, romance, and success abound in his music. In the mid 1960s, with the Beatles and other British rock stars acknowledging his influence, Berry returned to the rock charts with several hits. In 1972, he got his first number one song with "My Ding-A-Ling." But something was missing despite his success. Chuck Berry—the second time around—was no longer in step with his audience. By the late 1960s and early 1970s, the rock audience had grown more sophisticated and introspective about various social and political causes. When that happened, Chuck Berry was unable to keep pace and became more a nostalgia item than folk poet. His music became a testimonial to a living legend, rather than a true reflection of the times. Berry was inducted into the Rock & Roll Hall of Fame in 1985. Among his greatest hits are classics such as:

"Maybellene"	Chess	#42	1955
"Roll Over Beethoven"	Chess	#29	1956
"School Days"	Chess	#5	1957
"Rock & Roll Music"	Chess	#8	1957
"Sweet Little Sixteen"	Chess	#2	1958
"Johnny B. Goode"	Chess	#8	1958

"Carol"	Chess	#18	1958
"Sweet Little Rock & Roll"	Chess	#47	1958
"Jo Jo Gun"	Chess	#83	1958
"Almost Grown"	Chess	#32	1959
"Little Queenie"	Chess	#80	1959
"Back in the U.S.A."	Chess	#37	1959
"Let It Rock"	Chess	#64	1960
"Too Pooped to Pop"	Chess	#42	1960
"Nadine"	Chess	#23	1964
"No Particular Place to Go"	Chess	#10	1964
"You Never Can Tell"	Chess	#14	1964
"Promised Land"	Chess	#41	1964 +
"My Ding-A-Ling"	Chess	#1	1972
"Reelin' & Rockin'"	Chess	#27	1972 +

THE BIG BOPPER In real life he was J. P. Richardson, a Texas dee-jay. His novelty song, "Chantilly Lace" (Mercury, #6, 1958), became one of the biggest hits of 1958, because of its rapid-fire, jive-talk lyrics. Listeners found the Big Bopper's delivery hilarious, and various lines of the song—such as the lascivious opening line, "Hellooo Baby, you know what I like!"—became faddish with teenagers. His only other hits, "Little Red Riding Hood" (Mercury, #72, 1958) and "Big Bopper's Wedding" (Mercury, #38, 1958), followed the same formula. The Big Bopper achieved legendary status in the world of rock after he died in a 1959 plane crash, along with Buddy Holly and Ritchie Valens.

BILK, MR. ACKER This British clarinetist with the funny name had a number one hit with a jazz-influenced instrumental, "Stranger on the Shore" (Atco, #1, 1962). It was a throwback to the Big Band sound of the 1940s, showing the continuing pop influence on rock & roll.

BILLY JOE AND THE CHECKMATES Their instrumental "Percolator Twist" (Dore, #10, 1962) featured a xylophone mimicking the sound of coffee perking. Based on a popular coffee commercial, the song reflects television's impact and the new dance craze that was sweeping the nation.

BILLY AND LILLIE Billy Ford and Lillie Bryant enjoyed brief success with "La Dee Dah" (Swan, #9, 1957) and "Lucky Ladybug" (Swan, #14, 1958). Their style shows how rhythm and blues was becoming more pop and teen oriented by the late 1950s.

BLACK, JEANNE She made the rock charts with "He'll Have to Stay" (Capitol, #4, 1960), which was the reply to Jim Reeve's earlier hit, "He'll Have to Go" (1960). Both songs are prime examples of the middle-of-the-road country and western music that appealed to the teen audience in the early 1960s.

BLACK'S COMBO, BILL Bill Black got his start in the late 1950s as the bass player in Elvis Presley's early back-up band. He later formed his own combo and achieved success with instrumental hits such as "Smokie, Part 2" (Hi, #17, 1959); "White Silver Sands" (Hi, #9, 1960); "Josephine" (Hi, #18, 1960); "Don't Be Cruel" (Hi, #11, 1960); and "Blue Tango" (Hi, #16, 1960). His sound, which incorporated white pop and subdued country and western, shows how musicians were mixing different types of music during the 1950s and 1960s.

BLAND, BILLY His "Let the Little Girl Dance" (Old Town, #7, 1960) was one of the more interesting hits of 1960. It reflected the continuing popularity of R & B rock, as well as teen interest in dancing and romance.

BLAND, BOBBY "BLUE" This great rhythm and blues performer from Tennessee had difficulty transferring his popularity over to the rock or pop charts. His only hits to crack the Top 20 were "Turn on Your Love Light" (Duke, #28, 1961) and "Call On Me" (Duke, #22, 1963).

BLANE, MARCIE Everything from her name to her one hit record, "Bobby's Girl" (Seville, #3, 1962), epitomizes the early 1960s. Her name—Marcie—along with her sweet, clean-cut sounding voice, indicates the type of role model chosen by many teen girls. The blatantly sexist lyrics, relegating the girl's existence to a mere appendage of the boy's, also provide a good reflection of the times. The record's slick production work is an excellent example of the mass-produced pop rock style so popular in the early 1960s.

BLEYER, ARCHIE He had one minor pop rock hit, "The Rockin' Ghost" (Cadence, #61, 1956). His greatest contribution to rock & roll came as the founder and musical director of Cadence Records, a label that signed performers like the Everly Brothers and Johnny Tillotson.

THE BLUE-BELLES This R & B rock group had one big hit, "I Sold My Heart To the Junkman" (Newtown, #15, 1962). Their lead singer, Patti LaBelle, later found greater fame as the lead singer for LaBelle ("Lady Marmalade" in 1975), and as a solo rhythm and blues performer in the 1980s.

THE BOBBETTES This quintet of girls, ranging from age 11 to 15, had a hit with "Mr. Lee" (Atlantic, #6, 1957), a song about their school principal. They followed up with "I Shot Mr. Lee" (Triple X, #52, 1960). Both were bouncy dance songs with which high-schoolers could identify.

BOB B. SOXX & THE BLUE JEANS This R & B rock group was produced by Phil Spector. Their biggest and most memorable hit was "Zip-A-Dee-Doo-Dah" (Philles, #8, 1962). The record, based on a song from Walt Disney's film *Song of the South,* clearly showed what rock & roll artists could do with pop material. Spector's production work and the group's authentic rhythm and blues feel made this record one of the outstanding releases of 1962. Their other two hits, "Why Do Lovers Break Each Other's Hearts" (Philles, #38, 1963) and "Not Too Young to Get Married" (Philles, #63, 1963), are good examples of how the rhythm and blues sound could be combined with teen-oriented lyrics to appeal to the white, teenage audience.

BOND, JOHNNY He started out as a country and western performer, making movies with Gene Autry and Tex Ritter. He recorded "Hot Rod Lincoln" (Republic, #26, 1960), which beat out Charlie Ryan's version of the song in a race up the rock charts. Both records attracted teenagers interested in drag racing and hot cars.

BONDS, GARY "U.S." I can still remember hearing "New Orleans" (Legrand, #6, 1960) for the first time in 1960. It was a wild party record—the greatest sound to hit the airwaves in a long, long time. Like others, I was confused by the performers' or performer's name. Many people thought the U.S. Bonds were a group. Only later did we find that it was one guy, Gary Anderson, singing on multi-track recordings. For two years he released smash after smash, including "Quarter to Three" (Legrand, #1, 1961); "School Is Out" (Legrand, #5, 1961); "School Is In" (Legrand, #28, 1961); "Dear Lady Twist" (Legrand, #9, 1961 +); "Twist, Twist Senora" (Legrand, #9, 1962); and "Seven Day Weekend"

(Legrand, #27, 1962). Bonds' songs, reflecting teen attitudes of the early 1960s, clearly show that authentic R & B rock was still very much alive in the early 1960s. Gary "U.S." Bonds later made a brief comeback in the early 1980s, with rock superstar Bruce Springsteen producing hits like "This Little Girl" (EMI, #11, 1981) and "Out of Work" (EMI, #21, 1982).

BOOKER T. & THE MG'S The house band for Stax Records throughout the 1960s, this R & B rock group had one major hit, "Green Onions" (Stax, #3, 1962), in the early years of rock & roll. The group went on to further success with hit singles like "Groovin'" (Stax, #21, 1967); "Soul Limbo" (Stax, #17, 1968); "Hang 'Em High" (Stax, #9, 1968+); and "Time Is Tight" (Stax, #6, 1969). Their long-term success shows the enduring popularity of rhythm and blues–influenced instrumental records.

BOONE, PAT With five number one records, he was truly one of the giants in early rock music. His success gave a conservative respectability to rock & roll, for Boone symbolized the traditional values of white, middle-class America in the 1950s and early 1960s. He dressed properly in white bucks, coats, ties, and sweaters; he was a God-fearing family man, with a pretty young blond wife and daughters; and he was squeaky-clean, from his peach fuzz face to his short, well-combed hair. His songs—even his covers of black R & B hits—were done in a traditional white pop style. And he even wrote a book, *Twixt Twelve and Twenty*, that advised teenagers to maintain traditional morals and love of God. Boone's great success is evidence of the continuity between the 1940s crooner style and 1950s pop rock. It also shows that the values of many 1950s teenagers were, for the most part, remarkably similar to those of their parents. His hits that made the Top 30 charts included:

"Ain't That a Shame"	Dot	#21	1955
"At My Front Door"	Dot	#7	1955
"No Other Arms"	Dot	#26	1955
"Gee Whittakers!"	Dot	#27	1955+
"Tutti Frutti"	Dot	#12	1956
"I'll Be Home"	Dot	#5	1956
"Long Tall Sally"	Dot	#18	1956
"I Almost Lost My Mind"	Dot	#1	1956
"Chains of Love"	Dot	#20	1956
"Friendly Persuasion"	Dot	#8	1956

"Don't Forbid Me"	Dot	#1	1956
"Why Baby Why"	Dot	#6	1957
"I'm Waiting Just for You"	Dot	#27	1957
"Love Letters in the Sand"	Dot	#1	1957
"Bernardine"	Dot	#23	1957
"Remember You're Mine"	Dot	#20	1957
"There's a Gold Mine in the Sky"	Dot	#28	1957
"April Love"	Dot	#1	1957
"A Wonderful Time Up There"	Dot	#10	1958
"It's Too Soon to Know"	Dot	#13	1958
"Sugar Moon"	Dot	#11	1958
"If Dreams Came True"	Dot	#12	1958
"For My Good Fortune"	Dot	#23	1958
"With the Wind and Rain in Your Hair"	Dot	#21	1959
"For a Penny"	Dot	#23	1959
"Twixt Twelve and Twenty"	Dot	#17	1959
"The Fool's Hall of Fame"	Dot	#29	1959
"Welcome New Lovers"	Dot	#18	1960
"Moody River"	Dot	#1	1961
"Big Cold Wind"	Dot	#19	1961
"Speedy Gonzales"	Dot	#6	1962

BOWEN, JIMMY An early rockabilly artist, his biggest hit was "I'm Stickin' With You" (Roulette, #14, 1957). He later focused on the production end of the record business, eventually becoming president of MCA Records.

BOYCE, TOMMY He had one minor hit in late 1962 with a teen-oriented pop rock song, "I'll Remember Carol" (RCA, #80, 1962). He later achieved greater success as part of Tommy Boyce and Bobby Hart. The duo had two hits in the late 1960s, "I Wonder What She's Doing Tonight" (A & M, #8, 1967) and "Alice Long" (A & M, #27, 1968), and wrote several hits for the Monkees.

BRADLEY, JAN Her excellent R & B rock hit, "Mama Didn't Lie" (Chess, #14, 1963), shows that many teens actually looked up to their parents in the early 1960s, refuting the stereotype that all teens were juvenile delinquents or rebellious toward their parents.

BRAUN, BOB This pop performer had a hit with a saccharine ballad called "Till Death Do Us Part" (Decca, #26, 1962). The song, about marriage and everlasting love, reflected the traditional values of some members of the youth culture. Braun later went on to present his middle-of-the-road pop music on his own syndicated talk show, originating from WLW-TV in Cincinnati, Ohio.

BRENNAN, WALTER   Old Grandpa McCoy from TV's "The Real McCoys" transferred his popularity to the rock charts with "Dutchman's Gold" (Dot, #30, 1960); "Old Rivers" (Liberty, #5, 1962); and "Mama Sang a Song" (Liberty, #38, 1962). His success is a tribute to his lovable television character, and evidence of the continuing acceptance by the teen audience of the traditional values and themes he sang about.

BROOKS, DONNIE   1960 was his year. He had two hits, "Mission Bell" (Era, #7, 1960) and "Doll House" (Era, #31, 1960), both of which appealed to teens who liked middle-of-the-road pop rock.

THE BROTHERS FOUR   These guys were fraternity brothers at the University of Washington, and their success with folk songs like "Greenfields" (Columbia, #2, 1960); "My Tani" (Columbia, #50, 1960); and "Frogg" (Columbia, #32, 1961) was an indication of things to come. As the Baby Boom generation grew older, it turned increasingly toward the simple, pure, yet more sophisticated folk sound.

BROWN, BUSTER   His "Fannie Mae" (Fire, #38, 1960) was a minor, but highly significant hit. It was a throwback to early R & B rock, and later was re-recorded by numerous rock groups, including Joey Dee and the Starlighters (of Twist fame). The song became one of the true classics of rock & roll.

BROWN, JAMES   This rhythm and blues shouter from Little Richard's home town of Macon, Georgia, had several fine hits in the early 1960s with his group the Famous Flames. But his rise to superstardom occurred after 1964, when his songs reflected whites' growing acceptance of black culture, the emergence of black pride, and the continuing importance of authentic rhythm and blues music in rock. Inducted into the Rock & Roll Hall of Fame in 1985, his best-sellers include:

"Try Me"	Federal	#48	1958+
"Think"	Federal	#33	1960
"Night Train"	King	#35	1962
"Prisoner of Love"	King	#18	1963

"Papa's Got a Brand New Bag"	King ·	#8	1965
"I Got You (I Feel Good)"	King	#3	1965
"It's a Man's Man's Man's World"	King	#8	1966
"Cold Sweat (Part I)"	King	#7	1967
"I Got the Feelin'"	King	#6	1968
"Licking Stick-Licking Stick (Part 1)"	King	#14	1968
"Say It Loud, I'm Black and I'm Proud"	King	#10	1968
"Mother Popcorn"	King	#11	1969
"Get Up (I Feel Like Being a) Sex Machine (Part 1)"	King	#15	1970
"Super Bad"	King	#13	1970
"Hot Pants"	People	#15	1971
"Get on the Good Foot (Part 1)"	Polydor	#18	1972
"Living in America"	Scotti Bros.	#4	1985+

BROWN, MAXINE She had two R & B influenced hits: "All in My Mind" (Nomar, #19, 1961) and "Funny" (Nomar, #25, 1961).

BROWN, ROY One of the early rhythm and blues greats, whose New Orleans sound influenced the rise of rock & roll. One of his greatest R & B songs was "Good Rockin' Tonight" (1948), later covered by Elvis Presley, Buddy Holly, and Pat Boone. He achieved only minor success on the rock charts with "Party Doll" (Imperial, #89, 1957) and "Let the Four Winds Blow" (Imperial, #29, 1957).

BROWN, RUTH She came out of the rhythm and blues field in the early 1950s to record hits like "Lucky Lips" (Atlantic, #26, 1957); "This Little Girl's Gone Rockin'" (Atlantic, #24, 1958); and the now classic "Shake a Hand" (Atlantic, #97, 1962).

THE BROWNS This country and folk influenced group had three big hits: "The Three Bells" (RCA, #1, 1959); "Scarlet Ribbons" (RCA, #13, 1959); and "The Old Lamplighter" (RCA, #5, 1960). Their success indicates that many members of the rock & roll audience also appreciated records that had an old-fashioned sound or appealed to traditional values. The Browns' soft harmonies also foreshadowed the coming of country and folk rock. Jim Ed Brown went on to become a popular country and western artist for RCA Records.

BROWN'S TUNETOPPERS, AL Their only hit, "The Madison" (Amy, #23, 1960), was a tribute to a dance fad of the day.

BRUBECK QUARTET, DAVE This jazz quartet's biggest hit was "Take Five" (Columbia, #25, 1961), which demonstrated that great numbers of young Americans wanted something other than just rock & roll. Brubeck, who toured college campuses throughout the 1950s and 1960s, proved that jazz could sell to the rock audience, a lesson learned well by younger musicians who would later fuse jazz with rock during the late 1960s and early 1970s.

BRYANT, ANITA A former Miss America runner-up from Oklahoma turned pop singer, she had several pop rock hits on the charts in 1959 and 1960, including "Till There Was You" (Carlton, #30, 1959); "Paper Roses" (Carlton, #5, 1960); "In My Little Corner of the World" (Carlton, #10, 1960); and "Wonderland By Night" (Carlton, #18, 1960).

BRYANT, RAY This jazz pianist had one hit, a pop rock song about a new dance, "Madison Time" (Columbia, #30, 1960).

BUCHANAN & GOODMAN They hit the best-selling charts with novelty records that incorporated snips of hit songs into a spoken script that sounded like a news report. Their biggest hit was "The Flying Saucer" (Luniverse, #7, 1956). Their follow-ups, "Flying Saucer the Second" (Luniverse, #19, 1957) and "Santa & the Satellite" (Luniverse, #32, 1957), followed the same formula to success. Their records reflect the public's interest in flying saucers and the emerging space program.

BUD AND TRAVIS They had one minor hit, "Ballad of the Alamo" (Liberty, #64, 1960), the theme from the movie, *The Alamo*. The single tried to capitalize on the popularity of historical songs such as Johnny Horton's "Battle of New Orleans" (1959) or Stonewall Jackson's "Waterloo" (1959). The entire genre reflects American patriotic interests of the day and anticipates Kennedy's New Frontier.

BURKE, SOLOMON This R & B rock artist had a string of minor hits throughout the 1960s. His biggest was "Just Out of Reach" (Atlantic, #24, 1961).

BURNETTE, DORSEY His only two hits were country-influenced songs like "Tall Oak Tree" (Era, #23, 1960) and "Hey Little One" (Era, #48, 1960). "Tall Oak Tree," which dealt with God and creation, showed that teenagers of the era were still concerned with religion and traditional values. He also co-wrote, with his brother Johnny, hits for Ricky Nelson like "Waitin' In School" and "Believe What You Say."

BURNETTE, JOHNNY   The brother of Dorsey Burnette, he became a minor teen idol in the early 1960s. His first hit was "Dreamin'" (Liberty, #11, 1960), a country and western–influenced song that dealt with teenage romance. He followed up with other solid pop rock hits, such as "You're Sixteen" (Liberty, #8, 1960), a song that later became a big hit for Ringo Starr in the late 1970s; "Little Boy Sad" (Liberty, #17, 1961); and "God, Country, and My Baby" (Liberty, #18, 1961), a song that reflected teenage concerns about the Cold War.

BUTLER, JERRY   He began his career with Curtis Mayfield's Chicago-based R & B rock group, the Impressions. Butler's first solo hit was "For Your Precious Love" (Falcon, #11, 1958), a hauntingly beautiful ballad that became one of rock's greatest hits. He followed up with other top-notch singles like "He Will Break Your Heart" (Vee Jay, #7, 1960); "Find Another Girl" (Vee Jay, #27, 1961); "Moon River" (Vee Jay, #11, 1961); and "Make It Easy on Yourself" (Vee Jay, #20, 1962). He later came back in the late 1960s with "Hey Western Union Man" (Mercury, #16, 1968), "Only the Strong Survive" (Mercury, #4, 1969), and "What's the Use of Breaking Up" (Mercury, #20, 1969).

BYRNES, EDD   He first caught the public's attention as the hip, jive-talking car hop on "77 Sunset Strip," one of TV's most successful private eye shows of the late 1950s and early 1960s. In 1959 he jive-talked his way to two hit records. "Kookie, Kookie (Lend Me Your Comb)" (Warner Brothers, #4, 1959) was based on Kookie's habit of constantly combing his hair, like many teenagers of the time, and featured Byrnes in a duet with Connie Stevens. It became a smash hit, as teenagers began using hip phrases or words from the song, such as "ginchy," "you're the utmost, the very utmost," or prefacing words with "like" (as in "like wow" or "like fantastic"). Byrnes then followed up with "Like I Love You" (Warner Brothers, #42, 1959). Both records reflect the teen culture of the era and demonstrate television's significant impact on the youth culture.

THE CADETS This R & B rock group had a hit record with "Stranded in the Jungle" (Modern, #18, 1956), a novelty song that showed how rhythm and blues became more pop-oriented by the mid-1950s to appeal to the larger white audience. *See also* the Jacks.

THE CADILLACS Like many groups in the mid-1950s, they were named after a car, trying to take advantage of the public's fascination with automobiles. Their biggest hits were "Speedo" (Josie, #30, 1955 +), which was lead singer Earl Carroll's nickname, and "Peek-A-Boo" (Josie, #28, 1958 +), two classic examples of R & B rock.

CAIOLA, AL This guitarist's two instrumental hits, "The Magnificent Seven" (United Artists, #35, 1960) and "Bonanza" (United Artists, #19, 1961), reflect America's fascination with the American West during the early 1960s. Both were themes from westerns, one a movie and the other a popular TV show.

CAMPBELL, GLEN He had two minor hits in the early 1960s, "Turn Around, Look At Me" and "Too Late to Worry, Too Blue to Cry." As a studio musician, he also played guitar occasionally for both the Beach Boys and the Champs. His greatest success came in the late 1960s and 1970s with an impressive string of hits, his own TV show, and appearances in movies. His best-selling records include:

"Turn Around, Look At Me"	Crest	#62	1961
"Too Late to Worry, Too Blue to Care"	Capitol	#76	1962
"The Universal Soldier"	Capitol	#45	1965
"Gentle on My Mind"	Capitol	#62	1967
"By the Time I Get to Phoenix"	Capitol	#26	1967
"Hey Little One"	Capitol	#54	1968
"I Wanna Live"	Capitol	#36	1968
"Dreams of the Everyday Housewife"	Capitol	#32	1968
"Wichita Lineman"	Capitol	#3	1968 +
"Let It Be Me" (with Bobbie Gentry)	Capitol	#36	1969
"Galveston"	Capitol	#4	1969
"Where's the Playground Susie"	Capitol	#26	1969
"Try a Little Kindness"	Capitol	#23	1969
"Honey Come Back"	Capitol	#19	1970
"All I Have to Do Is Dream" (with Bobbie Gentry)	Capitol	#27	1970

"It's Only Make Believe"	Capitol	#10	1970
"Rhinestone Cowboy"	Capitol	#1	1975
"Country Boy (You Got Your Feet in LA)"	Capitol	#11	1975+
"Southern Nights"	Capitol	#1	1977

CAMPBELL, JO-ANN   This pop singer had two novelty hits on the charts. Her first, "Kookie Little Paradise" (ABC, #61, 1960), was a minor hit in 1960. Her biggest, "I'm the Girl From Wolverton Mountain" (Cameo, #38, 1962), was the answer song to Claude King's 1962 hit "Wolverton Mountain."

CANNON, ACE   This sax player and his band found success with "Tuff" (Hi, #17, 1961+) and "Blues Stay Away From Me" (Hi, #36, 1962), instrumentals with an authentic R & B rock feel.

CANNON, FREDDY   Nicknamed "Boom Boom," he had numerous hits between 1959 and 1965. Overall, his music exemplifies the formula pop rock manufactured for the teen audience in the early 1960s. On his best records, such as "Tallahassie Lassie" and "Palisades Park," Cannon exhibited a dynamic, high-energy approach that accurately captured the spirit of rock & roll. But at his worst, on records like "Chattanooga Shoe Shine Boy" or "Jump Over," Cannon's style was just a poor imitation of rock & roll. Cannon's records provide good examples of both the peaks and valleys of early 1960s pop rock. Among his biggest hits were:

"Tallahassee Lassie"	Swan	#6	1959
"Okefenokee"	Swan	#43	1959
"Way Down Yonder in New Orleans"	Swan	#3	1959+
"Chattanooga Shoe Shine Boy"	Swan	#34	1960
"Jump Over"	Swan	#28	1960
"Humdinger"	Swan	#59	1960
"Happy Shades of Blue"	Swan	#83	1960
"Buzz Buzz A-Diddle It"	Swan	#51	1961
"Transistor Sister"	Swan	#35	1961
"Palisades Park"	Swan	#3	1962
"Patty Baby"	Swan	#65	1963
"Abigail Beecher"	Warner Brothers	#16	1964
"Where the Action Is"	Warner Brothers	#13	1965

THE CAPRIS   They had one glorious hit, "There's a Moon Out Tonight" (Old Town, #3, 1961+). The ballad blended white pop with an R & B style, and struck a responsive chord among youths looking for romance.

THE CARAVELLES   These two girls from England only had one big hit, "You Don't Have to Be a Baby to Cry" (Smash, #3, 1963). The record was pure pop in lyrics and sound, yet appealed greatly to many members of the rock & roll audience.

CAROSONE, RENATO   His only hit was "Torero" (Capitol, #19, 1958). This instrumental mixed Mexican instrumentation and R & B rock to produce one of the strangest sounds on the rock charts in 1958. Later songs, such as the Kingston Trio's "El Matador" (1960) and Herb Alpert and the Tijuana Brass' "Lonely Bull" (1962), would also make use of the bull and matador motif found in "Torero."

CARR, CATHY   She was a pop singer out of the same mold as other mid-1950s singers like Theresa Brewer, Patti Page, and Jo Stafford. Yet two of her hits, "Ivory Tower" (Fraternity, #6, 1956) and "First Anniversary" (Roulette, #42, 1959), sold quite well to the rock & roll audience. Teens could relate to her bouncy, youthful voice, as well as her romantic lyrics.

CARROLL, ANDREA   Had one hit, "It Hurts to Be Sixteen" (Big Top, #45, 1963). The record, with its blatant appeal to teenage angst, epitomizes slick pop rock of the early 1960s.

CARTER, MEL   Though he came out of a Gospel music background, his style and sound was straight pop. His biggest hits, "When a Boy Falls in Love" (Derby, #44, 1963); "Hold Me, Thrill Me, Kiss Me" (Imperial, #8, 1965); and "Band of Gold" (Imperial, #32, 1966), all reflect traditional attitudes toward romance and marriage.

THE CASCADES   This California group had a smash hit with "Rhythm of the Rain" (Valiant, #3, 1963), a teen-oriented tearjerker with a very catchy melody. They followed up with "Shy Girl" (Valiant, #91, 1963) and "The Last Leaf" (Valiant, #60, 1963), two minor hits which are equally good examples of the era's pop rock style.

CASH, JOHNNY   He was part of the Sun Records' stable, which included other rockabilly artists like Elvis Presley, Carl Perkins, and Jerry Lee Lewis (sometimes referred to as Sun's "million dollar quartet"). Cash's particular brand of rockabilly was always closer to country and western than rock & roll. His big hits on the

Sun label included "I Walk the Line" (Sun, #19, 1956); "Ballad of a Teenage Queen" (Sun, #16, 1958); "Guess Things Happen That Way" (Sun, #11, 1958); and "The Ways of a Woman in Love" (Sun, #24, 1958). Later on, he switched to Columbia and achieved additional success with "Don't Take Your Guns to Town" (Columbia, #32, 1959); "Ring of Fire" (Columbia, #17, 1963); "Folsom Prison Blues" (Columbia, #32, 1968); and "A Boy Named Sue" (Columbia, #2, 1969).

THE CASTELLS A perfect example of the polished pop rock style that was so popular in the early 1960s. This California quartet's harmonies, reminiscent of 1950s pop music, combined with a soft rock beat to earn them hits with ballads like "Sacred" (Era, #20, 1961) and "So This Is Love" (Era, #21, 1962). Both songs reflected traditional values of the day.

CATHY JEAN AND THE ROOMMATES This New York group had one hit record, the now classic "Please Love Me Forever" (Valmor, #12, 1961). A throwback to the 1950s R & B rock sound, it had a desperate, emotional, folk quality that appealed to teenagers in love.

CHAMBERLAIN, RICHARD TV's Dr. Kildare proved he could transfer his bedside manner to girls in the rock audience with hits such as "Theme from 'Dr. Kildare'" (MGM, #10, 1962); "Love Me Tender" (MGM, #21, 1962); and "All I Have to Do Is Dream" (MGM, #14, 1963). Chamberlain's style was straight pop, showing that old-style crooners could still sell records in the pop market, if the material was geared to the youth culture. In Chamberlain's case, one of his hits was the theme from his popular TV show, which attracted a large teen audience. The others were covers of earlier hits by Elvis Presley and the Everly Brothers.

THE CHAMPS This talented instrumental group's biggest hit was "Tequila" (Challenge, #1, 1958). They also enjoyed some success with "El Rancho Rock" (Challenge, #30, 1958); "Too Much Tequila" (Challenge, #30, 1960); and "Limbo Rock" (Challenge, #40, 1962). Their R & B–influenced music was up beat and designed to appeal to teenage dancers.

CHANDLER, GENE His smash hit, "The Duke of Earl" (Vee Jay, #1, 1962), was a slickly produced version of the 1950s doo wop sound. Its lyrics proudly proclaimed that nothing could stop the "Duke of Earl" from accomplishing his goals. Chandler's appearance —in a top hat and tails, carrying a cane—reinforced the song's rags to riches message. The record reflects positive American feelings of the early 1960s, and the growing black consciousness of the era's emerging Civil Rights Movement.

CHANNEL, BRUCE His record, "Hey! Baby" (Smash, #1, 1962), featuring Delbert McClinton on harmonica, was one of the biggest hits of 1962. Like many popular songs of the early 1960s, it was bouncy, upbeat, and perfect for dancing. And like many songs of the era, it was also pure fluff and highly forgettable.

THE CHANTAYS This California-based band had one hit, "Pipeline" (Dot, #4, 1963), an instrumental that echoed the California surf sound.

THE CHANTELS This all-girl group came out of New York in the late 1950s with a delicate, high-pitched rhythm and blues sound. Their biggest hits, "Maybe" (End, #15, 1958) and "Look in My Eyes" (Carlton, #14, 1961), had a classic R & B rock sound.

CHARLES, JIMMY His only big hit, "A Million to One" (Promo, #5, 1960), was a teen ballad about unrequited love, with just the right amount of rhythm and blues mixed in. It was the kind of record that was perfect for a "lady's choice" dance at teen record hops.

CHARLES, RAY Anyone who thinks rock & roll was dead by the late 1950s or early 1960s should listen to Ray Charles' music. During those years he had hit after hit, including classics like "What'd I Say" (1959); "Georgia on My Mind" (1960); "Hit the Road, Jack" (1961); "I Can't Stop Loving You" (1962); and "You Don't Know Me" (1962). Charles blended rhythm and blues, gospel, country and western, and pop to create some of the finest hit records in the history of rock music. His success is a tribute to the mixing of white and black musical styles that had been going on at the grass roots level since at least the 1920s. Ray Charles became a charter member of the Rock & Roll Hall of Fame in 1985. His biggest hits include:

"What'd I Say"	Atlantic	#6	1959
"One Mint Julep"	Impulse	#8	1961
"Georgia on My Mind"	ABC	#1	1960

"Ruby"	ABC	#28	1960
"Hit the Road, Jack"	ABC	#1	1961
"Unchain My Heart"	ABC	#9	1961
"Hide 'nor Hair"	ABC	#20	1962
"I Can't Stop Loving You"	ABC	#1	1962
"Born to Lose"	ABC	#41	1962
"You Don't Know Me"	ABC	#2	1962
"You Are My Sunshine"	ABC	#7	1962
"Your Cheating Heart"	ABC	#29	1962
"Don't Set Me Free"	ABC	#20	1963
"Take These Chains from My Heart"	ABC	#8	1963
"No One"	ABC	#21	1963
"Without Love There Is Nothing"	ABC	#29	1963
"Busted"	ABC	#4	1963
"That Lucky Old Sun"	ABC	#20	1963 +
"Crying Time"	ABC	#6	1965 +
"Together Again"	ABC	#19	1966
"Let's Go Get Stoned"	ABC	#31	1966
"Here We Go Again"	ABC	#15	1967
"Yesterday"	ABC	#25	1967
"Eleanor Rigby"	ABC	#35	1968

THE CHARMETTES They had a minor hit with "Please Don't Kiss Me Again" (Kapp, #100, 1963), which was patterned after the sound of the Shirelles and other R & B rock girl groups.

THE CHARMS *See* Otis Williams and the Charms.

CHECKER, CHUBBY Born Ernest Evans, his stage name was a take-off on Fats Domino, and his sound and style imitated R & B rock. His first hit, "The Class," featured Checker's impressions of Fats Domino, the Coasters, Elvis, and the Chipmunks. Most of his other hits dealt with various teen dances, like the Pony, the Hucklebuck, the Fly, the Limbo Rock, and of course, the Twist. His recording of Hank Ballard's "The Twist" became a number one record in both 1960 and 1961! The success of these dance songs shows that American teens, like adults, were looking for good times. When "The Twist" was first released in 1960, it was just a teen hit and dance craze. But the following year, it caught on as a dance fad among adults, too. This was the first time that the Baby Boom culture had spread to the adult world, but it was an indication of things to come. Checker's biggest hits included:

"The Class"	Parkway	#38	1959
"The Twist"	Parkway	#1	1960
"The Hucklebuck"	Parkway	#14	1960
"Pony Time"	Parkway	#1	1961
"Dance the Mess Around"	Parkway	#24	1961
"Let's Twist Again"	Parkway	#8	1961
"The Fly"	Parkway	#7	1961
"The Twist"	Parkway	#1	1961+
"Slow Twistin'"	Parkway	#3	1962
"Dancin' Party"	Parkway	#12	1962
"Limbo Rock"	Parkway	#2	1962
"Popeye the Hitchhiker"	Parkway	#10	1962
"Let's Limbo Some More"	Parkway	#20	1962
"Twenty Miles"	Parkway	#15	1962
"Birdland"	Parkway	#12	1963
"Twist It Up"	Parkway	#25	1963
"Loddy Lo"	Parkway	#12	1963
"Hooka Tooka"	Parkway	#17	1963+
"Hey Bobba Needle"	Parkway	#23	1964
"Let's Do the Freddie"	Parkway	#40	1965

THE CHEERS The actor Bert Convy was one of this group's three members. Their biggest hit was "Black Denim Trousers" (Capitol, #13, 1955), which focused on rebellious teenagers and their wild clothing styles.

THE CHIFFONS Their soft rhythm and blues sound fit their soft name. Like other girl groups of the early 1960s, such as the Shirelles and Marvelettes, the Chiffons had an authentic and sexy R & B rock sound. Their three biggest hits were "He's So Fine" (Laurie, #1, 1963); "One Fine Day" (Laurie, #5, 1963); and "Sweet Talkin' Guy" (Laurie, #10, 1966). They also recorded under the name "The Four Pennies." *See also* The Four Pennies.

THE CHIMES This pop rock group from Brooklyn enjoyed their greatest success with a traditional ballad, "Once In Awhile" (Tag, #11, 1960).

THE CHIPMUNKS These three characters—Simon, Theodore, and Alvin . . . ALVIN!!!—were the creation of pop artist David Seville (whose real name was Ross Bagdasarian). He introduced them to the rock audience in a novelty Christmas record called "The Chipmunk Song" (Liberty, #1, 1958). Seville used multi-track recordings of his own voice speeded up to create the silly Chipmunk voices. Teenagers loved the record, which became an annual Christmas hit for the next four years in a row. Other Chipmunks hits soon followed: "Alvin's Harmonica" (Liberty, #3, 1959); "Ragtime Cowboy Joe" (Liberty, #16, 1959); "Alvin's Orchestra" (Liberty, #33, 1960); "Rudolph the Red-Nosed Reindeer" (Liberty, #21, 1960); and there was even "The Alvin Twist" (Liberty, #40, 1962). These hits show the continuing popularity of the novelty song tradition, even in rock & roll. The Chipmunks became a full-time business for David Seville and his family. By the 1980s the Chipmunks had their own Saturday morning cartoon series and had recorded a series of albums spoofing rock and pop music. *See also* David Seville.

THE CHORDETTES They began as an all-girl pop group from Sheboygan, Wisconsin, in the late 1940s. By the mid-1950s they were recording records aimed at the teen audience, such as "Mr. Sandman" (Cadence, 1954); "Eddie My Love" (Cadence, #18, 1956); "Born to Be with You" (Cadence, #5, 1956); "Lay Down Your Arms" (Cadence, #16, 1956); "Teen Age Goodnight" (Cadence, #45, 1956); "Just Between You and Me" (Cadence, #19, 1957); "Lollipop" (Cadence, #2, 1958); "Zorro" (Cadence, #17, 1958); "No Other Arms, No Other Lips" (Cadence, #27, 1959); and "Never on Sunday" (Cadence, #13, 1961).

THE CHORDS This group was comprised of five rhythm and blues singers from New York City. In 1954, they wrote and recorded the original version of "Sh-Boom" (Cat, #9, 1954), which many consider to be the first rock & roll song. Unfortunately for the Chords, their record was covered by the Crew Cuts, a white pop group from Canada, and the cover version became the bigger hit on the national record charts, reflecting both the prejudice and market realities of the day.

CHRISTIE, DEAN He had one minor hit, "Heartbreaker" (Select, #87, 1962), a pop rock song that reflected teen attitudes toward romance, and stereotypes of girls as heartbreakers.

CHRISTIE, LOU This pop rocker enjoyed great success in 1963 with "The Gypsy Cried" (Roulette, #24, 1963); "Two Faces Have I" (Roulette, #6, 1963); and "How Many Teardrops" (Roulette, #46, 1963). His style, which relied on the high falsettos found in 1950s doo wop, is a good example of how white pop rock was greatly influenced by black rhythm and blues. Later in the 1960s, he found additional success with hits such as "Lightnin' Strikes" (MGM, #1, 1965 +); "Rhapsody in the Rain" (MGM, #16, 1966); and "I'm Gonna Make You Mine" (Buddah, #10, 1969).

CHURCH, EUGENE He had one of the all-time great R & B rock hits, "Pretty Girls Everywhere" (Class, #36, 1958). The song, reflecting teenage males' insatiable desires for teenage females, parodied the "water, water everywhere, but not a drop to drink" theme. It also reflected stereotypes of the era, which treated girls as mere sex objects.

CLANTON, JIMMY His first and biggest hit was "Just a Dream" in 1958. Clanton is an excellent example of the clean-cut teen idols of the late 1950s and early 1960s. He was well-groomed, and had a big smile, careful coiffure, and numerous sweaters. His non-threatening image and teen pop style appealed to the white, middle-class, suburban teen audience. His biggest hits included:

"Just a Dream"	Ace	#4	1958
"A Letter to An Angel"	Ace	#25	1958
"My Own True Love"	Ace	#33	1959
"Go Jimmy Go"	Ace	#5	1959 +
"Another Sleepless Night"	Ace	#22	1960
"Venus in Blue Jeans"	Ace	#7	1962

CLARK, CLAUDINE Her only hit came with "Party Lights" (Chancellor, #5, 1962), an R & B rock song that featured frantic singing about teenage social life.

CLARK, DEE An R & B rocker whose biggest hits included "Nobody But You" (Abner, #21, 1958 +); "Just Keep It Up" (Abner, #18, 1959); "Hey Little Girl" (Abner, #20, 1959); and "Raindrops" (Vee Jay, #2, 1961). His records blended a rhythm and blues sound with lyrics about school and romance.

THE CLASSICS This Brooklyn quartet's biggest hit was "Till Then" (Music Note, #20, 1963), a good example of the soft, pop rock sound of the early 1960s.

THE CLEFTONES They came out of a rhythm and blues background to achieve some success in the late 1950s and early 1960s. Their biggest hit was "Heart and Soul" (Gee, #18, 1961).

CLIFFORD, BUZZ A pop rock performer of the early 60s. His only hit, "Baby Sittin' Boogie" (Columbia, #6, 1961), dealt with the problems of baby-sitting for little kids. Babysitting was a common source of income for teenage girls in the early 1960s, but as this record shows, the job could interfere with teen romance.

CLIFFORD, MIKE His hit record, "Close to Cathy" (United Artists, #12, 1962), reflects both the slick, commercial pop-rock style of the early 1960s, as well as teenagers' romantic concerns.

CLINE, PATSY This legendary country & western singer made the pop charts with hits such as "Walkin' After Midnight" (Decca, #17, 1957); "I Fall to Pieces" (Decca, #12, 1961); "Crazy" (Decca, #9, 1961); and "She's Got You" (Decca, #14, 1962). Her success shows that country music was still very much alive on the rock charts in the early 1960s.

THE CLOVERS This rhythm and blues group, which had 13 top R & B hits from 1951 through 1955, found success on the rock charts with "Love, Love, Love" (Atlantic, #30, 1956) and "Love Potion #9" (United Artists, #23, 1959). The latter song later become an even bigger hit for the Searchers, a British rock group whose lackluster imitation reached number three on the charts in 1964.

THE COASTERS This R & B rock group had a string of excellent novelty hits in the 1950s and early 1960s. Two of their biggest, "Yakety Yak" and "Charlie Brown," focused on teen-adult conflict. While others, such as "Searchin'" and "Along Came Jones," alluded to movie or TV screen heroes. Their records, featuring upbeat dance music and funny lyrics, were the perfect blend of black rhythm and blues and white pop novelty lyrics. The Coasters were elected to the Rock & Roll Hall of Fame in 1986. *See also* Leiber & Stoller.

"Young Blood"	Atco	#8	1957
"Searchin'"	Atco	#5	1957
"Yakety Yak"	Atco	#1	1957
"Charlie Brown"	Atco	#2	1959
"Along Came Jones"	Atco	#9	1959
"Poison Ivy"	Atco	#7	1959
"Run Red Run"	Atco	#36	1959
"Little Egypt"	Atco	#23	1961

COCHRAN, EDDIE This country-influenced pop rocker (who was inducted into the Rock & Roll Hall of Fame in 1986) combined the looks of Elvis with the rebel image of James Dean. His biggest hit was "Summertime Blues," a 1958 rocker which reflected teenage frustrations about work, parents, and the adult establishment. The song became a rock & roll classic and was later recorded by numerous other performers, including the Beach Boys, Blue Cheer, the Who, Bobby Vee, and the Crickets. Cochran died in a car crash while on tour in England in 1960.

"Sittin' in the Balcony"	Liberty	#18	1957
"Drive-In Show"	Liberty	#82	1957
"Jeannie Jeannie Jeannie"	Liberty	#94	1958
"Summertime Blues"	Liberty	#8	1958
"C'mon Everybody"	Liberty	#35	1958 +
"Somethin' Else"	Liberty	#58	1959

COLE, COZY He came out of the jazz-band tradition, having played drums with Cab Calloway, Benny Goodman, and Artie Shaw. He made the pop charts in 1958 with "Topsy, Part II" (Love, #3, 1958); "Topsy, Part I" (Love, #27, 1958); and "Topsy, Part III" (Love, #36, 1958), all of which are good examples of the close relationship between early rock, rhythm and blues, and jazz.

COLE, NAT KING He was one of the few blacks to consistently make *Billboard*'s pop charts prior to the coming of rock & roll. No doubt his early success can be attributed to his traditional, white pop singing style. His popularity continued throughout the first decade of rock & roll with hits such as "Ramblin' Rose" (Capitol, #2, 1962); "Dear Lonely Hearts" (Capitol, #13, 1962); "Those Lazy-Hazy-Crazy Days of Summer" (Capitol, #6, 1963); and "That Sunday, That Summer" (Capitol, #12, 1963). His continued success in the 1960s shows that the teen audience could also appreciate the traditional offerings of one of pop music's elder statesmen.

COMO, PERRY He was about as far as one could get from the teenage rock & roll audience in terms of age, appearance, style, and sound. But he was able to reach the rock audience with hits such as "Juke Box Baby" (RCA, #10, 1956); "Catch a Falling Star" (RCA, #9, 1958); and "Delaware" (RCA, #22, 1960). No doubt the fact that he was recording for RCA, a major company with marketing clout, helps explain his success. But his hits also show that many teenagers enjoyed pop as much as rock.

COMSTOCK, BOBBY This pop rocker never quite made it to the top, although he did enjoy moderate success with "Tennessee Waltz" (Blaze, #52, 1959) and "Let's Stomp" (Lawn, #57, 1963), two songs aimed at teen dances.

THE CONTOURS This R & B rock group from Detroit only had one hit that cracked *Billboard*'s Top 30, but it became one of rock & roll's greatest hits: "Do You Love Me?" (Gordy, #3, 1962). The song, written by Motown's Berry Gordy, Jr., shows how important dancing and rock & roll were in the teen culture. "Do You Love Me?" later became a hit for the Dave Clark Five in 1964, and then became a hit again for the Contours almost 25 years later, when the original hit version appeared in the movie soundtrack of *Dirty Dancing*.

COOKE, SAM One of rock & roll's superstars from the late 1950s and early 1960s, whose soft R & B rock style anticipated soul music of the late 1960s. Sam Cooke was one of the few performers of his day who wrote and recorded his own material, and his songs eventually were covered by numerous other artists, including Buddy Holly, Cat Stevens, Rod Stewart, Art Garfunkel, the Animals, and Johnny Rivers. His greatest hits, such as "You Send Me," "Wonderful World," or "Twistin' the Night Away," were solid blends of rhythm and blues and gospel, and had lyrics aimed at teen audiences. Sam Cooke was elected to the Rock & Roll Hall of Fame in 1985. His hits included:

"You Send Me"	Keen	#1	1957
"I Love You for Sentimental Reasons"	Keen	#43	1957+
"Love You Most of All"	Keen	#26	1958
"Everybody Like to Cha Cha Cha"	Keen	#31	1959
"Only Sixteen"	Keen	#28	1959
"Wonderful World"	Keen	#12	1960
"Chain Gang"	RCA	#2	1960
"Cupid"	RCA	#17	1961
"Twistin' the Night Away"	RCA	#9	1962
"Having a Party"	RCA	#17	1962
"Bring It On Home to Me"	RCA	#13	1962
"Nothing Can Change This Love"	RCA	#12	1962
"Send Me Some Lovin'"	RCA	#13	1963
"Another Saturday Night"	RCA	#10	1963
"Frankie and Johnny"	RCA	#14	1963
"Little Red Rooster"	RCA	#11	1963

"Good News"	RCA	#11	1964
"Good Times"	RCA	#11	1964
"Shake"	RCA	#7	1965

THE COOKIES They began as backup singers for pop artists like Carole King and Neil Sedaka. Later, they found success on their own with three hits that blended elements of pop rock and R & B rock: "Chains" (Dimension, #17, 1962); "Don't Say Nothin' Bad" (Dimension, #7, 1963); and "Girls Grow Up Faster Than Boys" (Dimension, #33, 1963 +).

THE CORSAIRS They had one of the more unusual records on the charts in 1961 and 1962: "Smoky Places" (Tuff, #12, 1961 +). The song, with its rhythm and blues feel and soft drum role, caught the attention of members of the rock & roll audience searching for a different sound.

CORTEZ, DAVE "BABY" His three biggest hits, "The Happy Organ" (Clock, #1, 1959); "The Whistling Organ" (Clock, #61, 1959); and "Rinky Dink" (Chess, #10, 1962), are excellent examples of instrumental R & B rock.

CRAMER, FLOYD This country and western piano player, one of Nashville's top studio musicians, first hit the rock charts with "Last Date" (RCA, #2, 1960) and "On the Rebound" (RCA, #4, 1961), two songs that alluded to teenage dating. He also had a hit with "San Antonio Rose" (RCA, #8, 1961).

CRAWFORD, JOHNNY Best known as the son on TV's "Rifleman" series, he had hit records with "Cindy's Birthday" (Del Fi, #8, 1962); "Your Nose Is Gonna Grow" (Del Fi, #14, 1962); "Rumors" (Del Fi, #12, 1962); and "Proud" (Del Fi, #29, 1963). His recording career fits a pattern common in the early 1960s: a successful teenage television star would be chosen to record a song geared to the teen market. Image and marketing—rather than singing ability or any real feel for rock & roll—were usually responsible for the performer's success. The success of this type of mass-produced pop rock reflects the power of the media, as well as the fact that the teen audience could easily be manipulated to purchase any records they perceived as being teen-oriented, regardless of quality or artistic integrity.

THE CRESCENDOS This Nashville group's only hit was a teenage lament, "Oh, Julie" (Nasco, #5, 1957). The record is a perfect example of rock & roll "name" songs, i.e., songs that focused on common names found among teenagers. It also is an excellent example of the primitive lyrics and music of early pop rock. *See also* Dale Ward.

THE CRESTS With two blacks, one Hispanic, and an Italian-American lead singer, they were one of the few integrated groups in rock & roll. Their sound, which mixed elements of R & B with pop, earned them success with songs about teen romance, like "Sixteen Candles" (Coed, #2, 1958+); "Six Nights a Week" (Coed, #28, 1959); "The Angels Listened In" (Coed, #22, 1959); "Step by Step" (Coed, #14, 1960); and "Trouble in Paradise" (Coed, #20, 1960). Their lead singer, Johnny Maestro, went on to later success with the Brooklyn Bridge, which had one smash hit in 1968, "Worst That Could Happen."

THE CREW CUTS These four white pop singers from Toronto first achieved success by covering black rhythm and blues songs like "Sh-Boom" (Mercury, 1954); "Earth Angel" (Mercury, 1955); and "Ko Ko Mo" (Mercury, 1955). Other hits included "Seven Days" (Mercury, #20, 1956) and "Young Love" (Mercury, #24, 1957). The great success of their stiff, pop rock versions of doo wop songs can be attributed to several things. Some members of the pop and rock audience may have preferred the white, pop covers, because they were more familiar-sounding than the rhythm and blues originals. Others may have opted for the covers due to other social and cultural prejudices. In some cases, listeners simply did not have access to the original records. Major record companies like Mercury, with better means of distribution and marketing, pushed the covers at the expense of the originals. Even radio stations, because of social, cultural, or economic considerations, often played only white cover versions of black rhythm and blues hits.

CREWE, BOB Although he had a minor hit with "The Whiffenpoof Song" (Warwick, #96, 1960), most of his success came as a song writer (his first hit was the Rays' "Silhouettes") and producer for the Four Seasons.

THE CRICKETS *See* Buddy Holly and the Crickets.

THE CROWS These four rhythm and blues singers scored big in 1954 with "Gee" (Rama, #17, 1954). The song, which received a great deal of play on white radio stations and made *Billboard*'s Top 20, is regarded as one of the first "rock & roll" records.

THE CRYSTALS   The creative force behind this all-black girl group from Brooklyn was Phil Spector, a white, rock & roll production whiz from Los Angeles. Their biggest hits included "There's No Other" (Philles, #20, 1961 +); "Uptown" (Philles, #13, 1962); "He's a Rebel" (Philles, #1, 1962); "He's Sure the Boy I Love" (Philles, #11, 1962 +); "Da Doo Ron Ron" (Philles, #3, 1963); and "Then He Kissed Me" (Philles, #6, 1963). The songs mixed a rhythm and blues feel with teen-oriented lyrics and high energy production work. They represent some of the finest rock & roll records of all time. Ironically, the lead singer on most of the Crystals' hits, Darlene Love, wasn't even a member of the group. Spector was recording her as a solo act and used her as a studio musician to sing lead on "He's a Rebel" and several other songs. The Crystals' hits are perfect examples of what came to be known as Phil Spector's "Wall of Sound": layer after layer of instruments, voices, and other noises to create a total sound effect. *See also* Phil Spector.

CURTIS, KING   This R & B rock musician played the tenor sax and gained fame for his studio work on records by the Coasters, Buddy Holly, and other early rock performers. His solo records never even dented *Billboard*'s Hot 100, perhaps because he tried to cover too much musical ground in diverse records like "Soul Twist" (Enjoy, 1962); "Beach Party" (Capitol, 1962); and "Harper Valley P.T.A." (Atco, 1968).

CURTOLA, BOBBY   This Canadian pop singer had two minor hits on the American charts, "Fortune Teller" (Del Fi, #41, 1962) and "Aladdin" (Del Fi, #92, 1962). Both songs were straight pop rock and reflected teenage interests in the early 1960s.

CYMBAL, JOHNNY   Had a hit in 1963 called "Mr. Bass Man" (Kapp, #16, 1963). The song was a pop rock tribute to rock & roll bass singers and an excellent parody of the doo wop sound. In 1968, singing under the name "Derek," Cymbal returned to the rock charts with "Cinnamon" (Bang, #11, 1968 +).

THE DADDY-O's   This pop rock group made *Billboard*'s Top 40 with their hit, "Got a Match" (Cabot, #40, 1958). The song's title alluded to teens bumming matches off their friends to light up cigarettes. The group's name and song reflect "hip" teen culture of the late 1950s.

DALE, DICK, AND THE DEL-TONES   They were a by-product of the surfing fad of the early 1960s. They came out of California with their surf jackets, wind-blown hair, and surf sound to record several minor hits, the biggest of which was "Let's Go Trippin'" (Del-tone, #60, 1961 +). They also appeared in several of the Frankie Avalon and Annette "Beach Party" movies. Their music reflects the new surfing fad, as well as America's fascination with the California Dream.

DALE & GRACE   Dale Houston and Grace Broussard made the charts with two middle-of-the-road pop rock ballads, "I'm Leaving It Up to You" (Montel, #1, 1963) and "Stop and Think It Over" (Montel, #8, 1964).

DANA, VIC   This young, pop vocalist from Buffalo, New York, enjoyed moderate success in the early and mid-1960s with records like "Little Altar Boy" (Dolton, #45, 1961 +); "More" (Dolton, #42, 1963); "Shangri-La" (Dolton, #27, 1964); "Red Roses for a Blue Lady" (Dolton, #10, 1965); and "I Love You Drops" (Dolton, #30, 1966). His hits show that, throughout the 1960s, many members of the rock audience still appreciated traditional pop songs which dealt with conventional themes and values.

DANCER, PRANCER, AND NERVOUS   Had one hit, "The Happy Reindeer" (Capitol, #34, 1959), which copied the sound of the Chipmunks' Christmas songs.

THE DANLEERS   This R & B rock group from Brooklyn had one of 1958's biggest hits, "One Summer Night" (Mercury, #16, 1958). The romantic ballad quickly became a doo wop classic.

DANNY AND THE JUNIORS   This pop rock group had two of rock & roll's greatest hits: "At the Hop" (ABC, #1, 1957 +) and "Rock and Roll Is Here to Stay" (ABC, #19, 1958). "At the Hop" started a new dance craze on "American Bandstand," while "Rock and Roll Is Here to Stay" became a teen anthem, covered by almost every nostalgia group since the 1970s. Ironically, neither song was written by teenagers. Both were written and produced by adults, and then sung by Danny and the Juniors, young vocalists from Philadelphia, who did a credible job copying the doo wop sound. In fact, the flip side of "At the Hop," a slow ballad called "Sometimes," is one of the best doo wop records to come out of the 1950s. The group later had additional hits with "Dottie" (ABC, #41, 1958) and "Twistin' U.S.A." (Swan, #27, 1960).

DANTE AND THE EVERGREENS This California-based pop rock group had one big hit, "Alley-Oop" (Madison, #15, 1960), a novelty song about the cartoon cave-man, Alley Oop. Unfortunately for Dante's group, the song was also recorded by the Hollywood Argyles, whose version became the number one record in the country.

DARIN, BOBBY His career provides a virtual mirror of the diverse musical styles and tastes from the various eras of rock & roll. When he first hit the rock charts in 1958 with songs like "Splish Splash," "Dream Lover," and "Queen of the Hop," he could rock with the best of them. Singing under the name, "The Rinky-Dinks," he even recorded a solid R & B rock song called "Early in the Morning." But then, he steered more toward middle-of-the-road music with pop standards such as "Mack the Knife," "Clementine," and "Won't You Come Home, Bill Bailey," becoming a young version of Frank Sinatra, complete with tux and snapping fingers. By 1962, with the Ray Charles sound on the rise, Bobby Darin got soul and began cranking out R & B and country and western influenced hits like "What'd I Say" and "You're the Reason I'm Living." In the mid-1960s, he tried his hand at popular Broadway hits such as "Hello Dolly" and "Mame." And when folk rock and protest music became the vogue by the late 1960s, Darin began recording songs like "If I Were a Carpenter" and "The Girl That Stood Beside Me." Some members of the rock audience might view Darin as just another pop performer who tried to cash in on the latest musical trend. But Bobby Darin was no dilettante. He may have had eclectic musical tastes, but he was a sincere pop rock artist, with a distinct interpretive style, which he applied to all his recordings. As a result, many of his records now stand among some of the greatest hits in rock & roll history. Darin's best-selling records included:

"Splish Splash"	Atco	#3	1958
"Queen of the Hop"	Atco	#9	1958
"Early in the Morning" (sung under the name "the Rinky-Dinks")	Atco	#24	1958

"Dream Lover"	Atco	#2	1959
"Mack the Knife"	Atco	#1	1959
"Beyond the Sea"	Atco	#6	1960
"Clementine"	Atco	#21	1960
"Won't You Come Home, Bill Bailey"	Atco	#19	1960
"I'll Be There"	Atco	#79	1960
"Artificial Flowers"	Atco	#20	1960
"Lazy River"	Atco	#14	1961
"Nature Boy"	Atco	#40	1961
"You Must Have Been a Beautiful Baby"	Atco	#5	1961
"Irresistible You"	Atco	#15	1961+
"Multiplication"	Atco	#30	1961+
"What'd I Say"	Atco	#24	1962
"Things"	Atco	#3	1962
"Baby Face"	Atco	#46	1962
"If a Man Answers"	Capitol	#32	1962
"You're the Reason I'm Living"	Capitol	#3	1963
"18 Yellow Roses"	Capitol	#10	1963
"Milord"	Atco	#45	1964
"Hello Dolly"	Capitol	#79	1965
"Mame"	Atlantic	#53	1966
"If I Were a Carpenter"	Atlantic	#8	1966
"The Girl That Stood Beside Me"	Atlantic	#66	1966
"Lovin' You" ("Amy" on flip side)	Atlantic	#32	1966
"The Lady Came from Baltimore"	Atlantic	#62	1967
"Darling Be Home Soon"	Atlantic	#93	1967

DARREN, JAMES This baby-faced actor was a media creation. His first hit, "Gidget" (Colpix, #41, 1959), came from the teen movie in which he co-starred. He then introduced his next big hit, "Good-Bye Cruel World" (Colpix, #3, 1961) on TV's "Donna Reed Show." The song quickly zoomed to the top of the charts. His follow up hits included nonsensical pop songs like "Her Royal Majesty" (Colpix, #6, 1962); "Conscience" (Colpix, #11, 1962); "Mary's Little Lamb" (Colpix, #39, 1962); "Hail to the Conquering Hero" (Colpix, #97, 1962); and "Pin a Medal on Joey" (Colpix, #54, 1963). These songs, some of the worst hit records ever palmed off to the public as rock & roll, show that some teens in the early 1960s would buy any pop record that was marketed as rock music.

THE DARTELLS They capitalized on Dee Dee Sharp's "Mashed Potatoes," and did a similar-sounding record, "Hot Pastrami" (Dot, #11, 1963). What does it reflect about the times? Simply that kids in this era of the Twist were looking for new dance hits, sometimes the sillier the better.

DAVIS, SAMMY, JR. This pop performer hit the rock charts with "What Kind of Fool Am I?" (Reprise, #17, 1962) and "The Shelter of Your Arms" (Reprise, #17, 1963), both of which showed that traditional pop still appealed to teens.

DAVIS, SKEETER This pretty young blond from Kentucky (with a country twang to go with her folksy name) had several excellent country rock hits in the early 1960s. Her first song to make the Top 30 was "My Last Date With You" (RCA, #26, 1960). Her next hit, the hauntingly sad "The End of the World" (RCA, #2, 1963), reflected the apocalyptic mood of a nation that had just been through the Cuban Missile Crisis. Her last big hit was a romantic ballad written by Carole King, "I Can't Stay Mad at You" (RCA, #7, 1963). Skeeter Davis later recorded an entire album of Buddy Holly songs, *Skeeter Davis Sings Buddy Holly* (RCA, 1967), as a tribute to the late country-rock great.

DAY, BOBBY Even if he had not recorded on the Class label, he still would have been a class act, with authentic R & B rockers like "Little Bitty Pretty One" (Class, #57, 1957); "Rockin' Robin" (Class, #2, 1958); and "Over and Over" (Class, #41, 1958). His music, upbeat and infectious, epitomizes R & B rock dance songs.

DEAN, JIMMY Pork sausage isn't Jimmy Dean's only claim to fame. In the early 1960s this Texan hit the rock charts with several pop hits. His biggest seller was "Big Bad John" (Columbia, #1, 1961), a pop hit with a country and western flavor that struck a responsive chord among hardworking, patriotic, middle-class Americans. He followed up with additional hits that reflected other traditional American values. "Dear Ivan" (Columbia, #24, 1962), which came out in the midst of heightening Cold War tensions between the United States and Soviet Union, was an open letter to the Russian people asking for peace and understanding. "To a Sleeping Beauty" (Columbia, #26, 1962) focused on parental love for children. "The Cajun Queen" (Columbia, #22, 1962) dealt with folklore of a particular American region. "P.T. 109" (Columbia, #8, 1962) was a tribute to John F. Kennedy, the nation's young and heroic new president, while "Steelmen" (Columbia, #41, 1962) sang praises to hardworking blue-collar Americans. His songs reflect the patriotism and values of many Americans in the early 1960s.

DEAN & JEAN Welton Young and Brenda Lee Jones achieved minor success with "Tra La La La Suzy" (Rust, #35, 1963) and "Hey Jean, Hey Dean" (Rust, #32, 1964), two R & B–influenced hits.

DEE, JOEY, & THE STARLIGHTERS Unlike most rock artists of the early 1960s, this group achieved its initial success as a live band, not a recording group. The band happened to be playing one night in 1961 at the Peppermint Lounge on New York City's West 45th Street when several high society celebrities came in to dance the Twist. (The dance craze had been popular among teens the previous year.) After newspaper photographers took pictures of these adults doing the Twist, the dance quickly became a national sensation—for the second time. But this time around adults, as well as teenagers, were twisting. The Starlighters capitalized on the phenomenon by releasing a record called "The Peppermint Twist" (Roulette, #1, 1961+), which zoomed to the top of the charts. For more than a year they were one of the hottest rock groups around, with a best-selling live album and dance hits like "Hey, Let's Twist" (Roulette, #20, 1962); "Roly Poly" (Roulette, #74, 1962); "Shout" (Roulette, #6, 1962); "What Kind of Love Is This" (Roulette, #18, 1962); and "Hot Pastrami With Mashed Potatoes" (Roulette, #36, 1963). Their music reflected a renewed interest in rhythm and blues, and one of the biggest dance crazes of the century. It also indicated that the fads of the youth culture were beginning to affect the larger, mainstream American culture.

DEE, JOHNNY This man, who in reality was John D. Loudermilk, had minor success with "Sittin' in the Balcony" (Colonial, #38, 1957), a cover version of an Eddie Cochran song which dealt with teenagers kissing in movie theaters. *See also* John D. Loudermilk.

DEE, TOMMY In February 1959, three major rock stars—Buddy Holly, Ritchie Valens, and the Big Bopper—were killed in a plane crash. Shortly thereafter, Tommy Dee eulogized them in a hit single, "Three Stars" (Crest, #11, 1959), a maudlin tribute complete with a heavenly chorus. The song was one of the first indications that martyrdom was being awarded to the dead rock & rollers. Eventually, all three would develop a cult following.

THE DE JOHN SISTERS They had one minor hit, "Straighten Up and Fly Right" (Sunbeam, #73, 1958), a novelty song that received some air play on "American Bandstand."

THE DELL VIKINGS With two white and three black members, this group was one of the few integrated acts in rock & roll. Their biggest hits were "Come Go with Me" (Dot, #5, 1957) and "Whispering Bells" (Dot, #9, 1957), two classic examples of 1950s doo wop.

THE DEMENSIONS Their only big hit, "Over the Rainbow" (Mohawk, #16, 1960), clearly reflects the pop side of early 1960s rock & roll.

DENNY, MARTIN His instrumental group had one of the biggest hits of 1959 with "Quiet Village" (Liberty, #4, 1959), an exotic novelty record complete with bird calls and other jungle sounds. His only other major hit was "The Enchanted Sea" (Liberty, #28, 1959), another recording with a strange, Polynesian feel.

DEY, TRACEY She had a minor hit with "Teenage Cleopatra" (Liberty, #75, 1963), which reflected female stereotypes of the early 1960s.

THE DIAMONDS This pop rock group from Canada had several major hits in the early days of rock & roll. Their greatest success came in 1957 with "Little Darlin'," a doo wop classic originally recorded by the Gladiolas, and "The Stroll," which became a big dance fad on "American Bandstand." The Diamonds' music is a good example of music mass produced for the teen market: it mimicked authentic R & B rock, and had lyrics geared to teen interests. Some of their biggest hits included:

"Why Do Fools Fall in Love"	Mercury	#16	1956
"The Church Bells May Ring"	Mercury	#20	1956
"Love, Love, Love"	Mercury	#30	1956
"Ka-Ding-Dong"	Mercury	#35	1956
"Soft Summer Breeze"	Mercury	#34	1956
"Little Darlin'"	Mercury	#2	1957
"The Stroll"	Mercury	#5	1957+
"High Sign"	Mercury	#38	1958
"She Say (Oom Dooby Doom)"	Mercury	#18	1959
"One Summer Night"	Mercury	#22	1961

DICK AND DEEDEE At their best, these two white pop rock singers produced memorable R & B influenced hits like "The Mountain's High" (Liberty, #2, 1961) and "Turn Around" (Warner Brothers,

#27, 1963 +). At their worst, they turned in tepid, if not embarrassing, attempts at rock & roll, such as "Tell Me" (Liberty, #22, 1962); "Young and In Love" (Warner Brothers, #17, 1963); and "Thou Shalt Not Steal" (Warner Brothers, #13, 1964 +).

DIDDLEY, BO   A pioneer of R & B Rock, he was elected to the Rock & Roll Hall of Fame in 1986. His 1955 classic rhythm and blues hit, "Bo Diddley," had a driving African rhythm and ham-bone beat, which greatly influenced Elvis Presley, Buddy Holly, and the Rolling Stones, to name just a few. To this day the song "Bo Diddley," though recorded more than 30 years ago, sounds fresh and contemporary. Other big hits included "Say Man" (Checker, #20, 1959) and "You Can't Judge a Book By the Cover" (Checker, #48, 1962).

DINNING, MARK   His only big hit was "Teen Angel" (MGM, #1, 1959 +). The song epitomizes what some rock historians have labelled "Death Rock." The lyrics of this pop rock tearjerker, aimed directly at teenagers, dealt with high school romance, class rings, cars, and the promise of eternal love. Adolescents, filled with insecurities about growing up, dating, and life in general, ate up this rock & roll version of romantic tragedy.

DINO, KENNY   He only had one hit, "Your Ma Said You Cried in Your Sleep Last Night" (Musicor, #24, 1961), but what a song it was! Definitely one of the best of 1961. Dino sounded like a young Elvis Presley, while the song's teen lyrics and music built to a climax, reminiscent of Roy Orbison's best records. It was the sleeper rock & roll hit of the year, and later influenced the sound of the Dave Clark Five's big hit of 1964, "Bits and Pieces."

DION   After two years as the lead singer with Dion and the Belmonts, he took the solo route in 1960 and found great success. His velvety-smooth, melodic voice allowed him to glide effortlessly from R & B rock to pop ballads to urban blues to folk. His greatest hits of the early 1960s all had teen-oriented lyrics combined with a touch of rhythm and blues. Perhaps he is best known for three songs: "Runaround Sue," a classic rock & roll shouter from 1961 that warned teen males to keep away from teases like Sue; "The Wanderer," an R & B influenced hit in 1961 that proclaimed teenage freedom; and "Abraham, Martin, and John," a folk rock hit in 1968 which reflected the nation's despair over assassinations. Dion—one of the most talented pop rockers from the 1950s and 1960s—was elected to the Rock & Roll Hall of Fame in 1988. Among his greatest hits are:

"Lonely Teenager"	Laurie	#12	1960
"Havin' Fun"	Laurie	#42	1960
"Kissin' Game"	Laurie	#82	1961
"Runaround Sue"	Laurie	#1	1961
"The Wanderer"	Laurie	#2	1961 +
"The Majestic"	Laurie	#36	1961 +
"Lovers Who Wander"	Laurie	#3	1962
"(I Was) Born to Cry"	Laurie	#42	1962
"Little Diane"	Laurie	#8	1962
"Love Came to Me"	Laurie	#10	1962
"Sandy"	Laurie	#21	1963
"Ruby Baby"	Columbia	#2	1963
"This Little Girl"	Columbia	#21	1963
"Donna the Prima Donna"	Columbia	#6	1963
"Drip Drop"	Columbia	#6	1963
"Johnny B. Goode"	Columbia	#71	1964
"Abraham, Martin, & John"	Laurie	#4	1968
"Purple Haze"	Laurie	#63	1969
"Both Sides Now"	Laurie	#91	1969

See also Dion and the Belmonts.

DION AND THE BELMONTS These four Italian-American boys, named after the Bronx streetcorner they used to sing on, proved that white teenagers could capture the feel of R & B rock. Their first hit came in 1958 with "I Wonder Why," a fast-paced doo wop record complete with tight harmonies and soaring falsettos. Their harmony sound earned them additional hits, including "A Teenager in Love," which became a teen anthem in 1959. They were one of rock's super groups of the late 1950s and early 1960s. Their biggest hits included:

"I Wonder Why"	Laurie	#22	1958
"No One Knows"	Laurie	#19	1958
"Don't Pity Me"	Laurie	#40	1958 +
"A Teenager in Love"	Laurie	#5	1959
"Where or When"	Laurie	#3	1959 +
"When You Wish Upon a Star"	Laurie	#30	1960
"In the Still of the Night"	Laurie	#38	1960

See also Dion; The Belmonts.

THE DIXIEBELLES This black, all-girl group from Memphis enjoyed brief success with pop-influenced songs like "Down At Papa Joe's" (Sound Stage, #9, 1963) and "Southtown, U.S.A." (Soundstage, #15, 1964).

DOBKINS, CARL, JR. He had two big hits, "My Heart Is an Open Book" (Decca, #3, 1959) and "Lucky Devil" (Decca, #25, 1959+). Both songs had a country rock feel and were geared toward teen romance.

DOGGETT, BILL Living proof that you didn't have to be young to be a hit with the rock & roll audience. Doggett, who paid his dues playing piano with Lionel Hampton, Count Basie, and other rhythm and blues greats, was 40 years old when "Honky Tonk" (King, #2, 1956) made the rock charts. He followed the instrumental with other solid hits like "Slow Walk" (King, #26, 1956); "Ram-Bunk-Shush" (King, #67, 1957); "Smokie (Part 2)" (King, #95, 1960); and "Honky Tonk (Part 2)" (King, #57, 1961).

DOMINO, FATS This charter member of the Rock & Roll Hall of Fame got started in the late 1940s, singing and playing rhythm and blues in various clubs throughout the South. His New Orleans twang and plunky piano playing became his trademark on numerous hits such as "Blueberry Hill," "I'm Walkin'," "I Want to Walk You Home," and "Walkin' To New Orleans." Known affectionately to his fans as "The Fat Man" (because of his size, as well as the name of his first rhythm and blues hit), Fats Domino was indeed a giant of early rock & roll. His good-time music was the perfect blend of rhythm and blues and teen-oriented lyrics. His songs were covered by numerous other rock performers, such as Buddy Holly, Pat Boone, the Lettermen, and Ricky Nelson. Fats Domino's greatest hits included:

"Ain't It a Shame"	Imperial	#86	1955
"I'm in Love Again"	Imperial	#5	1956
"Blueberry Hill"	Imperial	#4	1956+
"Blue Monday"	Imperial	#9	1957
"I'm Walkin'"	Imperial	#5	1957
"Valley of Tears"	Imperial	#13	1957
"Wait and See"	Imperial	#27	1957
"Whole Lotta Loving"	Imperial	#6	1958+
"I'm Ready"	Imperial	#16	1959
"I'm Gonna Be a Wheel Someday"	Imperial	#17	1959

"I Want to Walk You Home"	Imperial	#8	1959
"Be My Guest"	Imperial	#8	1959
"Walking to New Orleans"	Imperial	#6	1960
"Three Nights a Week"	Imperial	#15	1960
"My Girl Josephine"	Imperial	#14	1960
"Let the Four Winds Blow"	Imperial	#15	1961
"What a Party"	Imperial	#22	1961
"Jambalaya (On the Bayou)"	Imperial	#30	1961+
"You Win Again"	Imperial	#22	1962
"Red Sails in the Sunset"	Imperial	#35	1963

DON AND JUAN   Their only big hit was "What's Your Name" (Big Top, #7, 1962), a slickly produced R & B rock ballad. The song attracted listeners with its catchy doo wop ending, which had the duo singing, "Shooby doop doop wha da da."

DONEGAN, LONNIE   This English pop singer hit the American charts twice, first with "Rock Island Line" (London, #10, 1956), and later with the novelty song, "Does Your Chewing Gum Lose Its Flavor on the Bed Post Overnight?" (Dot, #5, 1961). The latter song, with its teen-oriented lyrics and hint of rebellion against parents, became a big favorite on "American Bandstand." Donegan's music, which often used the skiffle, an English banjo, shows the variety of styles that appealed to the rock audience.

DONNER, RAL   This Elvis Presley soundalike had three interesting hits in 1961: "Girl of My Best Friend" (Gone, #19, 1961); "You Don't Know What You've Got" (Gone, #4, 1961); and "She's Everything" (Gone, #18, 1961). Though they all had teen-oriented lyrics and a polished sound, the records had an authentic folk quality which distinguished them from most other pop rock of the period.

DOO, DICKEY, AND THE DON'TS   This pop rock group with the too-cute name had several hits in the 1950s, including "Click-Clack" (Swan, #28, 1958); "Nee Nee Na Na Na Na Nu Nu" (Swan, #40, 1958); "Flip Top Box" (Swan, #61, 1958); and "Teardrops Will Fall" (Swan, #61, 1959). Their pleasant harmonies, pop-style songs, and numerous appearances on Dick Clark's "American Bandstand" contributed to their success. Ironically, their recording that sounded the most like real rock & roll, "Did You Cry?" (which was the flip side of "Click Clack"), never became a hit. *See also* Gerry Granahan.

DORMAN, HAROLD This pop rock performer had a Top 30 hit with "Mountain of Love" (Rita, #21, 1960). Later, Johnny Rivers had an even bigger hit with the same song, peaking at number nine on the charts in 1964.

DORSEY, JIMMY Anybody who thinks that the 1950s rock & roll audience wanted nothing to do with the old sounds of their parents would be hard pressed to explain the success of Dorsey's "So Rare" (Fraternity, #2, 1957). The instrumental received air play on numerous rock & roll stations, and sold well among teenagers, proving that the Big Band sound from the 1930s still appealed to American youths in the 1950s.

DORSEY, LEE This R & B rock artist from New Orleans had several hits in the early and mid-1960s, including "Ya Ya" (Fury, #7, 1961); "Do-Re-Mi" (Fury, #27, 1961+); "Ride Your Pony" (Amy, #28, 1965); and "Working in the Coal Mine" (Amy, #8, 1966).

DORSEY, TOMMY Like his brother Jimmy, he kept the Big Band sound in front of the rock & roll audience throughout the 1950s. Teenagers actually danced to his "Tea for Two Cha Cha" (Decca, #7, 1958). The song reflected the continuing popularity of the Dorsey sound, as well as the cha-cha dance craze that swept the nation in the late 1950s (though when teenagers did it, they called it the "Cha-Lypso," just to be different from their parents).

THE DOVELLS Like many pop rockers, this group hailed from Philadelphia, which gave them easy access to important local labels and to Dick Clark's "American Bandstand." Their first hit, a well-done pop rock song called the "Bristol Stomp" (Parkway, #2, 1961), started a new dance craze. They followed up with several weak records based on other dances, e.g., "Do the New Continental" (Parkway, #37, 1962); "Bristol Twistin' Annie" (Parkway, #27, 1962); and "Hully Gully Baby" (Parkway, #25, 1962). They then hit their stride in 1963 with two uptempo songs which captured the lively spirit of rock & roll: "You Can't Sit Down" (Parkway, #3, 1963) and "Betty in Bermudas" (Parkway, #50, 1963). Their lead singer, Len Barry, later had several solo hits, including "1–2–3" (Decca, #2, 1965); "Like a Baby" (Decca, #27, 1966); and "Somewhere" (Decca, #26, 1966).

DOWELL, JOE He made it to the top of the record charts with "Wooden Heart" (Smash, #1, 1961), originally sung by Elvis

Presley in the movie *G.I. Blues*. Dowell's version typifies the middle-of-the-road pop rock records that were so popular in the early 1960s. The song, partly in German, also reflects America's preoccupation with Cold War events in Germany. Although Joe Dowell never duplicated his initial success, he made the Top 30 charts one more time with "Little Red Rented Rowboat" (Smash, #23, 1962).

DRAKE, CHARLIE   This Britisher had a novelty hit with "My Boomerang Won't Come Back" (United Artists, #21, 1962).

THE DREAMLOVERS   The back-up singers on Chubby Checker's "The Twist." Their only big hit was "When We Get Married" (Heritage, #10, 1961), a record that appealed to love-sick teenagers and reflected the traditional values held by most teens in the early 1960s.

THE DRIFTERS   One of the most significant R & B rock groups of the 1950s and 1960s. At various times, their lead singers included R & B rock greats Clyde McPhatter and Ben E. King. Their songs, blending rhythm and blues and white pop, were well-crafted recordings which captured the folk essence of authentic R & B rock. One of their hits, "There Goes My Baby," is a stunning example of how R & B rock could express feelings of lost love. Other records like "Up on the Roof," "On Broadway," and "Under the Boardwalk" provide accurate glimpses of life in urban settings. The Drifters were inducted into the Rock & Roll Hall of Fame in 1987. Their greatest hits included:

"Fools Fall in Love"	Atlantic	#69	1957
"There Goes My Baby"	Atlantic	#2	1959
"Dance with Me"	Atlantic	#15	1959
"This Magic Moment"	Atlantic	#16	1960
"Save the Last Dance for Me"	Atlantic	#1	1960
"I Count the Tears"	Atlantic	#17	1960
"Some Kind of Wonderful"	Atlantic	#32	1961
"Please Stay"	Atlantic	#14	1961
"Sweets for my Sweet"	Atlantic	#16	1961
"When My Little Girl Is Smiling"	Atlantic	#28	1962
"Up on the Roof"	Atlantic	#5	1962
"On Broadway"	Atlantic	#9	1963
"I'll Take You Home"	Atlantic	#25	1963
"Under the Boardwalk"	Atlantic	#4	1964
"Saturday Night at the Movies"	Atlantic	#18	1964

THE DUALS These two guitarists had one hit, an instrumental called "Stick Shift" (Sue, #25, 1961), which reflected teen interest in automobiles.

THE DUBS This group enjoyed their biggest success with "Could This Be Magic?" (Gone, #24, 1957), now considered a doo wop classic.

DUDLEY, DAVE He had a hit with "Six Days On the Road" (Golden Wing, #32, 1963). The country and western–influenced song dealt with cars, trucks, speeding on the highway, and romance—subjects to which many teens could relate.

THE DUPREES Their biggest hit was a romantic ballad called "You Belong to Me" (Coed, #7, 1962). Their smooth pop rock harmonies led to additional hits such as "My Own True Love" (Coed, #13, 1962), with lyrics added to the melody of "Tara's Theme" from *Gone With the Wind*; "Why Don't You Believe Me?" (Coed, #37, 1963); and "Have You Heard?" (Coed, #18, 1963). Their formula for success was simple: they blended traditional white pop with a dash of doo wop, and then added lyrics geared toward teen romance.

DYLAN, BOB Although he would become a major force in rock music by the end of the 1960s and would be enshrined in the Rock & Roll Hall of Fame in 1987, he was relatively unknown during rock & roll's first decade. His greatest contribution in the early 1960s came as a song writer. Peter, Paul, and Mary recorded several Dylan songs, including "Blowing In the Wind," which reached number two on the charts in 1963 and became an anthem for the Civil Rights Movement, and "Don't Think Twice It's All Right" (1963). Dylan's later hits included:

"Subterranean Homesick Blues"	Columbia	#39	1965
"Like a Rolling Stone"	Columbia	#2	1965
"Positively 4th Street"	Columbia	#7	1965
"Rainy Day Women #12 and 35"	Columbia	#2	1966
"I Want You"	Columbia	#20	1966
"Just Like a Woman"	Columbia	#33	1966
"Lay Lady Lay"	Columbia	#7	1969
"Watching the River Flow"	Columbia	#41	1971
"George Jackson"	Columbia	#33	1971 +
"Knockin' on Heaven's Door"	Columbia	#12	1973

"Tangled Up in Blue"	Columbia	#31	1975
"Hurricane (Part I)"	Columbia	#33	1975+
"Gotta Serve Somebody"	Columbia	#24	1979

THE EARLS This pop rock quartet had one hit, "Remember Then" (Old Town, #24, 1962+), a song that reminisced about the doo wop sound.

THE ECHOES They made the Top 20 with "Baby Blue" (Seg-Way, #12, 1961), an excellent pop rock song which featured doo wop style harmonies and plaintive vocals about young love.

EDDY, DUANE Excellent example of instrumental country rock during the late 1950s and early 1960s. Good looks, an inimitable twangy guitar style, and uptempo country and western–influenced songs perfect for fast dancing made Duane Eddy a favorite on "American Bandstand." Some of his recordings like "Rebel Rouser" and the album *The Twang's the Thang* are now classic examples of rock & roll instrumentals. Eddy's greatest hits include:

"Rebel Rouser"	Jamie	#6	1958
"Ram Rod"	Jamie	#28	1958
"Cannonball"	Jamie	#15	1958
"The Lonely One"	Jamie	#23	1959
"Yep!"	Jamie	#30	1959
"Forty Miles of Bad Road"	Jamie	#9	1959
"Some Kind-a Earthquake"	Jamie	#37	1959
"Bonnie Came Back"	Jamie	#26	1960+
"Shazam!"	Jamie	#45	1960
"Because They're Young"	Jamie	#4	1960
"Peter Gunn"	Jamie	#27	1960
"Pepe"	Jamie	#18	1960+
"The Ballad of Paladin"	RCA	#33	1962
"Dance with the Guitar Man"	RCA	#12	1962
"Boss Guitar"	RCA	#28	1963

THE EDSELS This R & B rock group's only hit was "Rama Lama Ding Dong" (Twin, #21, 1961), an excellent example of the doo wop sound of the 1950s and 1960s. When the song was first re-released in 1958 it went nowhere. But after it was released in 1961, it became a Top 30 hit.

EDWARDS, BOBBY His biggest hit came in 1961 with "You're the Reason" (Crest, #11, 1961), a country and western influenced ballad.

EDWARDS, TOMMY   A pop singer in the mold of Nat "King" Cole. His smooth, romantic ballads appealed to teenagers and were perfect for "Lady's Choices," i.e., slow songs at dances where girls got to ask guys to dance. Among his biggest hits were: "It's All in the Game" (MGM, #1, 1958); "Love Is All We Need" (MGM, #15, 1958); "Please Mr. Sun" (MGM, #11, 1959); "The Morning Side of the Mountain" (MGM, #27, 1959); "My Melancholy Baby" (MGM, #26, 1959); and "I Really Don't Want to Know" (MGM, #18, 1960).

THE EL DORADOS   This R & B rock group from Chicago specialized in the doo wop sound. Their biggest hit was "At My Front Door" (Vee Jay, #35, 1955). But they also had several hits on the rhythm and blues charts, including "My Lovin' Baby" (Vee Jay, 1954); "I'll Be Forever Loving You" (Vee Jay, 1955); and "Bim Bam Boom" (Vee Jay, 1956). The group's name was in keeping with the trend of naming groups after popular 1950s cars.

THE ELEGANTS   This quintet from Staten Island had only one hit, "Little Star" (Apt, #1, 1958), but it became a million-seller. The song was an excellent pop rocker, blending adolescent lyrics and doo wop harmonies. Its phenomenal success earned the Elegants the dubious distinction of being one of only four acts during the first decade of rock & roll that reached the number one spot on the charts with their first record, but were never heard from again. (The others were the Silhouettes with "Get a Job," the Hollywood Argyles with "Alley Oop," and the Singing Nun with "Dominique.")

ELLEDGE, JIMMY   His only hit record was "Funny How Time Slips Away" (RCA, #22, 1961+), a country ballad written by Willie Nelson.

ELLIS, SHIRLEY   In the mid 1960s, she had a string of hits with R & B influenced novelty songs like "The Nitty Gritty" (Congress, #8, 1963+); "The Name Game" (Congress, #3, 1964+); and "The Clapping Song" (Congress, #8, 1965).

EPPS, PRESTON   His biggest hit was "Bongo Rock" (Original Sound #14, 1959), followed by the less popular "Bongo Bongo Bongo" (Original Sound, #78, 1960). The two records reflected the public's increasing awareness of the Beat Generation, coffee houses, and bongo drums.

THE ESSEX This group had one of 1963's biggest hits with "Easier Said Than Done" (Roulette, #1, 1963), a bouncy tune with traditional pop lyrics. Their follow-up, "A Walkin' Miracle" (Roulette, #12, 1963), followed the same formula. Their sound, closer to traditional white pop than black rhythm and blues, is a good example of how some R & B rock was being homogenized into pop music by the mid 1960s.

THE ETERNALS These pop rockers never quite made it nationally. Their only record to hit *Billboard*'s Top 100 was "Rockin' in the Jungle" (Hollywood, #78, 1959), backed with "Rock & Roll Cha-Cha-Cha." Both were novelty doo wop songs.

EVANS, PAUL All but forgotten by most members of the rock & roll audience, this pop rocker wrote and recorded some excellent songs during the late 1950s and early 1960s. His biggest hits included the novelty record, "Seven Little Girls Sitting in the Back Seat (Hugging and Kissing With Fred)" (Guaranteed, #9, 1959); "Midnight Special" (Guaranteed, #16, 1960), which later became the theme song of the 1970s TV rock show of the same name; and "Happy Go Lucky Me" (Guaranteed, #10, 1960). In addition, Evans wrote "When," a hit for the Kalin Twins in 1958, and "Roses Are Red, My Love," a number one song for Bobby Vinton in 1962.

EVERETT, BETTY This R & B rock singer did the original version of "You're No Good" (Vee Jay, #51, 1963 +), which later became an even bigger hit for the Swingin' Blue Jeans in 1964 and Linda Ronstadt in 1975. Her other hits included "The Shoop Shoop Song (It's in His Kiss)" (Vee-Jay, #6, 1964) and, with Jerry Butler, "Let It Be Me" (Vee-Jay, #5, 1964).

THE EVERLY BROTHERS One of the super groups of early rock & roll. They mixed country and western music with teen-oriented lyrics to produce a soft, harmonic blend of country rock. Several of their songs, including "Bye Bye Love," "Wake Up Little Susie," "All I Have to Do Is Dream," "Cathy's Clown," and "Crying in the Rain" are among rock & roll's greatest hits. Their records reflected the traditional romantic values and interests of teenagers during the late 1950s and early 1960s. The Everly Brothers' career waned during the mid-1960s, but picked up again in the late 1960s and early 1970s when they made frequent television appearances (including their own summer television series in the early 1970s). Don and Phil split up in 1973 to pursue their individual careers, and then reunited in 1983. Two years later, they were inducted into Rock & Roll's Hall of Fame. Today they stand as a living legacy of 1950s country rock. Their biggest hits include:

"Bye Bye Love"	Cadence	#2	1957
"Wake Up Little Susie"	Cadence	#1	1957
"This Little Girl of Mine"	Cadence	#28	1958
"All I Have to Do Is Dream"	Cadence	#1	1958
"Claudette"	Cadence	#30	1958
"Bird Dog"	Cadence	#2	1958
"Devoted to You"	Cadence	#10	1958
"Problems"	Cadence	#2	1958
"Take a Message to Mary"	Cadence	#16	1959
"Poor Jenny"	Cadence	#22	1959
" 'Til I Kissed You"	Cadence	#4	1959
"Let It Be Me"	Cadence	#7	1960
"When Will I Be Loved"	Cadence	#8	1960
"Like Strangers"	Cadence	#22	1960
"Cathy's Clown"	Warner Bros.	#1	1960
"So Sad"	Warner Bros.	#7	1960
"Lucille"	Warner Bros.	#21	1960
"Ebony Eyes"	Warner Bros.	#8	1961
"Walk Right Back"	Warner Bros.	#7	1961
"Temptation"	Warner Bros.	#27	1961
"Don't Blame Me"	Warner Bros.	#20	1961
"Crying in the Rain"	Warner Bros.	#6	1962
"That's Old Fashioned"	Warner Bros.	#9	1962
"Gone Gone Gone"	Warner Bros.	#31	1964
"Bowling Green"	Warner Bros.	#40	1967
"On the Wings of a Nightingale"	Mercury	#50	1984

THE EXCITERS They had one smash hit in 1962 with "Tell Him" (United Artists, #4, 1962), a pop rock song with teen-oriented lyrics.

FABARES, SHELLEY Nanette Fabray's niece first gained popularity as the teenage daughter on television's "The Donna Reed Show." She hit the top of the record charts with "Johnny Angel" (Colpix, #1, 1962), and followed up with "Johnny Loves Me" (Colpix, #21, 1962). Both records are perfect examples of the mass-produced pop rock of the era. They dealt with teenage romance and reflected stereotypical boy-girl relationships, with the male as the dominant figure.

FABIAN   A prime example of the manufactured pop rock star of the late 1950s and early 1960s. Legend has it that Frankie Avalon's manager, Bob Marcucci, discovered Fabian in South Philadelphia and signed the 15-year-old to a recording contract, simply because he looked like a cross between Elvis Presley and Ricky Nelson. Despite his appearance, according to many critics, Fabian had one major flaw—he couldn't sing! But that didn't stop Marcucci, who marketed Fabian into a successful teen idol, complete with fan clubs, hit records, numerous appearances on "American Bandstand," and even movies (e.g., *Hound Dog Man* in 1959). Among Fabian's best-selling records were: "I'm a Man" (Chancellor, #31, 1959); "Turn Me Loose" (Chancellor, #9, 1959); "Tiger" (Chancellor, #3, 1959); "Come On and Get Me" (Chancellor, #29, 1959); and "Hound Dog Man" (Chancellor, #9, 1959). All these songs tried to cash in on Fabian's good looks, and reflect the era's stereotype of the macho male.

FABRIC, BENT   This Danish musician had one hit in the summer of 1962, an instrumental pop song called "Alley Cat" (Atco, #7, 1962).

FACENDA, TOMMY   This pop rocker made the national charts with a novelty hit, "High School U.S.A." (Atlantic, #28, 1959). There were actually 27 different versions of the song, released in different cities across the United States. Each version referred to specific high schools in the particular city where it was released. The record picked up grass roots appeal, as kids in all the major markets listened to Tommy Facenda singing about their schools.

FAITH, PERCY   This Canadian-born pop musician and his orchestra had a number one record in 1960 with "The Theme from *A Summer Place*" (Columbia, #1, 1960), from the movie of the same name. The record's great success reflects the tremendous popularity of the movie, and shows how success in one medium often spilled over into another. It also indicates that well-done pop music still appealed to many members of the rock & roll audience.

THE FALCONS   A Detroit-based R & B rock group, the Falcons' biggest hit was "You're So Fine" (Unart, #17, 1959). Their only other song to make the pop charts was "I Found a Love" (LuPine, #75, 1962), written by Wilson Pickett, who had just signed on as the group's new lead singer. Pickett later went on to a fabulously successful solo career as a soul singer in the mid and late 1960s, as did another member of the group, Eddie Floyd.

THE FENDERMEN   They exploded onto the national charts in 1960 with a wild rock & roll version of Jimmie Rodgers' country and western classic, "Mule Skinner Blues" (Soma, #5, 1960). Their version combined hip, rockabilly-influenced vocals with frenzied riffs from electric Fender guitars. The resulting hybrid became one of the year's best songs, and one of the true classics in rock & roll history.

FERGUSON, JOHNNY   His only hit came in 1960 with "Angela Jones" (MGM, #27, 1960), a ballad written by John D. Loudermilk. The song, with its catchy tune, fingersnapping, and references to teen romance and school activities, is a fine example of folk-oriented pop rock of the early 1960s.

FERRANTE AND TEICHER   These two pianists from the Juilliard School of Music had several hit singles and albums during the 1960s. Their best-known hits include "Theme from *The Apartment*" (United Artists, #10, 1960); "Exodus" (United Artists, #2, 1960+); and "Tonight" (United Artists, #8, 1961). The great success of these records reflected the popularity of the movies from which the themes were taken, and the teenagers' continuing appreciation of good, romantic popular music.

FIELDS, ERNIE   This pop musician proved that rock & rollers would still buy the Big Band sound in the late 1950s and early 1960s. He made the charts with "In the Mood" (Rendezvous, #4, 1959); "Chattanooga Choo Choo" (Rendezvous, #54, 1960); and "The Charleston" (Rendezvous, #47, 1961).

THE FIESTAS   They had one big hit with "So Fine" (Old Town, #11, 1959), a throwback to the R & B rock sound of the mid-1950s.

FINNEGAN, LARRY   He only had one hit record, but it was a dandy—"Dear One" (Old Town, #11, 1962). His style copied the sound of teen rocker Del Shannon, while his lyrics appealed to any teenager who had ever received a "Dear John" letter.

THE FIREBALLS   This group hailed from New Mexico and was managed by Norman Petty, the same fellow who managed Buddy

Holly and the Crickets. Their early hits, "Torquay" (Top Rank, #39, 1959); "Bulldog" (Top Rank, #24, 1960); and "Quite a Party" (Top Rank, #27, 1961), were well-done country rock instrumentals. In 1963 they added Jimmy Gilmer as a lead singer and had several additional hits, including "Sugar Shack" (Dot, #1, 1963); "Daisy Petal Pickin'" (Dot, #15, 1963); and "Bottle of Wine" (Atco, #9, 1967). *See also* Jimmy Gilmer and the Fireballs.

THE FIREFLIES   They made the national record charts with a pop rock ballad, "You Were Mine" (Ribbon, #21, 1959). The record, which might be described as pop doo wop, clearly shows there was a huge teen market for music that combined traditional pop styles with the new rock beat.

FISHER, MISS TONI   She recorded two rather interesting songs. Her first record to make the charts was "The Big Hurt" (Signet, #3, 1959). For the most part the song was straight out of the pop tradition. Her voice was powerful, but still pure pop. Her lyrics dealt with romance and broken hearts. Again, pure pop. But what made the song stand out from most pop records was its unique use of guitars and electronic reverberation. (The rock star Del Shannon was so taken by the sound that he did his own hit version of it in 1966.) Her second hit came in 1962 with "West of the Wall" (Big Top, #37, 1962), a song that mirrored Cold War tensions and the Berlin Crisis.

THE FIVE BLOBS   The group had a novelty hit, "The Blob" (Columbia, #33, 1958), which was a take-off on the Steve McQueen movie of the same name. The song, written by Burt Bacharach, reflected the popularity of the movie and the public interest in monsters and outer space during the late 1950s.

THE FIVE KEYS   An R & B rock group from the mid-1950s. Their biggest hits were "Out of Sight, Out of Mind" (Capitol, #27, 1956) and "Wisdom of a Fool" (Capitol, #35, 1956).

THE FIVE SATINS   The sound of this group from New Haven, Connecticut, was as smooth as their name. Their biggest hit was "In the Still of the Night" (Ember, #29, 1956), a perfect example of the doo wop style of 1950s R & B rock. The song became one of rock & roll's greatest hits, and made the national record charts on three separate occasions—in 1956, 1960, and 1961. It featured tight harmonies, soaring falsettos, suggestive imagery, and a throbbing sax solo. Their only other big hit was "To the Aisle" (Ember, #25, 1957).

THE FLAMINGOS Another R & B rock group with an extremely sexy sound. Their forte was romantic ballads like "Lovers Never Say Goodbye" (End, #52, 1959); "I Only Have Eyes for You" (End, #11, 1959); "Nobody Loves Me Like You" (End, #30, 1960); and "Mio Amore" (End, #74, 1960), all of which were done in an intimate doo wop style perfect for slow dancing and romancing.

THE FLARES Their only hit record, "Foot Stomping—Part I" (Felsted, #25, 1961), is a good example of early 1960s pop rock aimed at teen dancing.

FLATT AND SCRUGGS This country and western guitar/banjo duo made the rock charts in 1962 with "The Ballad of Jed Clampett" (Columbia, #44, 1962), the theme from the hit TV series "The Beverly Hillbillies." Its success indicates that many teenagers shared the same tastes and interests as adults in the early 1960s.

THE FLEETWOODS Gretchen Christopher, Barbara Ellis, and Gary Troxel formed this group from Olympia, Washington. Their soft pop rock style combined traditional white pop and teen-oriented lyrics with a touch of doo wop. In 1959 they had two number one records, "Come Softly to Me" and "Mr. Blue." Both songs reflected teen interest in romance, and became two of rock & roll's greatest hits.

"Come Softly to me"	Liberty	#1	1959
"Graduation's Here"	Dolton	#39	1959
"Mr. Blue"	Dolton	#1	1959
"You Mean Everything to Me"	Dolton	#84	1959
"Outside My Window"	Dolton	#28	1960
"Runaround"	Dolton	#23	1960
"Tragedy"	Dolton	#10	1961
"He's the Great Imposter"	Dolton	#30	1961
"Lovers by Night, Strangers by Day"	Dolton	#36	1962
"Goodnight My Love"	Dolton	#32	1963

FLINT, SHELBY She had one big hit, "Angel on My Shoulder" (Valiant, #22, 1960+), a pop rock song that reflected the traditional values held by many teenagers in the early 1960s.

THE FONTANE SISTERS   These pop singers first hit the rock charts in 1954 with "Hearts of Stone" (a cover version of the Charms' R & B original), and then followed with "Seventeen" (Dot, #15, 1955); "Daddy-O" (Dot, #11, 1955); and "Eddie My Love" (Dot, #12, 1956), a cover of the Teen Queens' original. Their records, reflecting teen interests of the day, are good examples of how record companies in the mid-1950s tried to cash in on rock & roll by getting traditional white pop artists to imitate the rhythm and blues sound.

FORD, FRANKIE   His only big hit, "Sea Cruise" (Ace, #14, 1959), became one of rock & roll's greatest hits. It was a bouncy tune written by R & B rock artist Huey "Piano" Smith.

THE FOUR FRESHMEN   This pop vocal group from the 1940s left an imprint on the rock charts with their 1956 hit record, "Graduation Day" (Capitol, #27, 1956), a song to which many high school kids could relate. Their style of harmony also provided a model for many rock & roll groups, including the Beach Boys.

THE FOUR PENNIES   This R & B rock group, also singing under the name the Chiffons, patterned their sound and style after the Shirelles. They had two modest hits in 1963, "My Block" (Rust, #67, 1963) and "When the Boy's Happy (the Girl's Happy Too)" (Rust, #95, 1963), both reflecting traditional teen values, romantic interests, and stereotypes of the early 1960s. *See also* The Chiffons.

THE FOUR PREPS   Their clean-cut, college boy image and 1950s pop harmonies made them rock & roll's answer to the Four Lads or Four Aces. At their best, they produced some solid pop rock. "Big Man," a song about teen love gone wrong, was their finest hit. They also did some excellent parodies of rock & roll, including "More Money for You and Me" and "A Letter to the Beatles." Their biggest hits included:

"26 Miles"	Capitol	#4	1958
"Big Man"	Capitol	#5	1958
"Lazy Summer Night"	Capitol	#21	1958
"Cinderella"	Capitol	#69	1958
"Down by the Station"	Capitol	#13	1959+
"Got a Girl"	Capitol	#24	1960
"More Money for You and Me"	Capitol	#17	1961
"A Letter to the Beatles	Capitol	#85	1964

THE FOUR SEASONS   A pop rock group with a pedigree. Two of its members, Frankie Valli and Tommy DeVito, started with a group called the Four Lovers (who had a minor hit in 1956, "You're the Apple of My Eye"). Another member, Bob Gaudio, sang with the Royal Teens (whose biggest hit was "Short Shorts" [1958]). After the three singers joined with Nick Massi in 1962 to form the Four Seasons, they became one of the greatest vocal groups in rock & roll history. Their first three singles, "Sherry" (1962), "Big Girls Don't Cry" (1962), and "Walk Like a Man" (1963), all made it to the number one spot on the charts. Additional hits came one after another throughout the rest of the decade. The Four Seasons' great success can be attributed to excellent harmonies; a distinctive sound led by Frankie Valli's lead falsetto; well-written, melodic songs with upbeat, teen-oriented lyrics; and excellent production work by Bob Crewe. The end product was a dynamic blend of pop and doo wop, showing how good 1960s pop rock could be. Valli and the Four Seasons continued to record throughout the 1970s and 1980s, separately and as a group. Their greatest hits include:

"Sherry"	Vee Jay	#1	1962
"Big Girls Don't Cry"	Vee Jay	#1	1962
"Santa Claus Is Coming to Town"	Vee Jay	#23	1962
"Walk Like a Man"	Vee Jay	#1	1963
"Ain't That a Shame"	Vee Jay	#22	1963
"Candy Girl"	Vee Jay	#3	1963
"Marlena"	Vee Jay	#36	1963
"Stay"	Vee Jay	#16	1964
"Alone"	Vee Jay	#28	1964
"Dawn"	Philips	#3	1964
"Ronnie"	Philips	#6	1964
"Rag Doll"	Philips	#1	1964
"Save It for Me"	Philips	#10	1964
"Big Man in Town"	Philips	#20	1964
"Bye Bye Baby"	Philips	#12	1965
"Toy Soldier"	Philips	#64	1965
"Girl Come Running"	Philips	#30	1965
"Let's Hang On"	Philips	#3	1965
"Don't Think Twice" (sung under the name "The Wonder Who?")	Philips	#12	1965
"Working My Way Back to You"	Philips	#9	1966
"Opus 17 (Don't You Worry 'Bout Me)"	Philips	#13	1966
"I've Got You Under My Skin"	Philips	#9	1966
"Tell It to the Rain"	Philips	#10	1966

"Beggin'"	Philips	#16	1967
"C'Mon Marianne"	Philips	#9	1967
"Watch the Flowers Grow"	Philips	#30	1967
"Will You Love Me Tomorrow"	Philips	#24	1968
"Who Loves You?"	Warner	#3	1975
"December, 1963 (Oh, What a Night)"	Warner	#1	1975+

See also Frankie Valli.

FOXX, INEZ She had a big hit with an R & B rock version of the children's song, "Mockingbird" (Symbol, #7, 1963). The song would later become a hit for Aretha Franklin in 1967 and then for Carly Simon and James Taylor in 1974.

FRANCIS, CONNIE A rock & roll performer who was non-threatening to parents and kids alike. Connie Francis was always much closer to pop than rock. Her middle-of-the-road style and appearance made her appealing to adults and pop-oriented teens, leading to numerous bookings on "American Bandstand." Her biggest hits included pop rock versions of standard pop songs, with an occasional new pop rock song thrown in. Her phenomenal success reflected the more traditional tastes and conservative values of many members of the rock audience in the late 1950s and early 1960s. Connie Francis' biggest hits included:

"Who's Sorry Now"	MGM	#4	1958
"I'm Sorry I Made You Cry"	MGM	#36	1958
"Stupid Cupid"	MGM	#17	1958
"Fallin'"	MGM	#30	1958
"My Happiness"	MGM	#2	1958+
"If I Didn't Care"	MGM	#22	1959
"Lipstick on Your Collar"	MGM	#5	1959
"Frankie"	MGM	#9	1959
"You're Gonna Miss Me"	MGM	#34	1959
"God Bless America"	MGM	#36	1959
"Among My Souvenirs"	MGM	#7	1959
"Mama"	MGM	#8	1960
"Teddy"	MGM	#17	1960
"Everybody's Somebody's Fool"	MGM	#1	1960
"Jealous of You"	MGM	#19	1960
"My Heart Has a Mind of Its Own"	MGM	#1	1960
"Many Tears Ago"	MGM	#7	1960
"Where the Boys Are"	MGM	#4	1961
"Breakin' in a Brand New Broken Heart"	MGM	#7	1961

"Together"	MGM	#6	1961
"He's My Dreamboat"	MGM	#14	1961
"When the Boy in Your Arms"	MGM	#10	1961 +
"Don't Break the Heart That Loves You"	MGM	#1	1962
"Second Hand Love"	MGM	#7	1962
"Vacation"	MGM	#9	1962
"I Was Such a Fool"	MGM	#24	1962
"I'm Gonna Be Warm This Winter"	MGM	#18	1962 +
"Follow the Boys"	MGM	#17	1963
"If My Pillow Could Talk"	MGM	#23	1963
"In the Summer of His Years"	MGM	#46	1963 +

FRANKLIN, ARETHA She came out of the gospel tradition to become the "First Lady of Soul" by the late 1960s. Her only hit on the Top 40 record charts in the early 1960s was "Rock-a-Bye Your Baby with a Dixie Melody" (1961). After switching to Atlantic Records and producer Jerry Wexler, Aretha hit her stride in mid-1967, beginning a phenomenal string of hits that would take her into the late 1980s. Her first number one record, "Respect" in 1967, reflected the civil rights movement and the growing awareness of black pride during the late 1960s. She offered authentic rhythm and blues and gospel at a time when the audience craved it. Aretha Franklin was elected to the Rock & Roll Hall of Fame in 1986. Her greatest hits include:

"Rock-A-Bye Your Baby with a Dixie Melody"	Columbia	#37	1961
"I Never Loved a Man (The Way I Love You)"	Atlantic	#9	1967
"Respect"	Atlantic	#1	1967
"Baby I Love You"	Atlantic	#4	1967
"A Natural Woman (You Make Me Feel Like)"	Atlantic	#8	1967
"Chain of Fools"	Atlantic	#2	1967 +
"(Sweet Sweet Baby) Since You've Been Gone"	Atlantic	#5	1968
"Ain't No Way"	Atlantic	#16	1968
"Think"	Atlantic	#7	1968
"The House That Jack Built"	Atlantic	#6	1968
"I Say a Little Prayer"	Atlantic	#10	1968
"See Saw"	Atlantic	#14	1968
"The Weight"	Atlantic	#19	1969
"I Can't See Myself Leaving You"	Atlantic	#28	1969
"Share Your Love with Me"	Atlantic	#13	1969

"Eleanor Rigby"	Atlantic	#17	1969
"Call Me"	Atlantic	#13	1970
"Spirit in the Dark"	Atlantic	#23	1970
"Don't Play That Song"	Atlantic	#11	1970
"You're All I Need to Get By"	Atlantic	#19	1971
"Bridge Over Troubled Water"	Atlantic	#6	1971
"Spanish Harlem"	Atlantic	#2	1971
"Rock Steady"	Atlantic	#9	1971
"Day Dreaming"	Atlantic	#5	1972
"Angel"	Atlantic	#20	1973
"Until You Come Back to Me"	Atlantic	#3	1973 +
"I'm in Love"	Atlantic	#19	1974
"Something He Can Feel"	Atlantic	#28	1976
"Jump to It"	Arista	#24	1982
"Freeway of Love"	Arista	#3	1985
"Who's Zoomin' Who"	Arista	#7	1985
"Sisters Are Doin' It for Themselves" (with Eurythmics)	RCA	#18	1985
"Another Night"	Arista	#22	1986
"Jumpin' Jack Flash"	Arista	#21	1986
"Jimmy Lee"	Arista	#28	1986 +

FREBERG, STAN   He got his start in the early 1950s doing impersonations, cartoon voices, and radio and TV comedy. He crossed into the history of rock & roll with several parodies of rock songs such as "Heartbreak Hotel" (Capitol, #79, 1956) and "The Old Payola Roll Blues" (Capitol, #99, 1960). His satirical records reflected adult hostilities toward the new youth music.

FREEMAN, BOBBY   This R & B rock performer exploded onto the rock & roll scene in 1958 with his joyfully infectious song, "Do You Wanna Dance?" (Josie, #5, 1958). The song, featuring a distinctive drum beat and pure R & B vocal, showed teen interest in romance and dancing. It quickly became one of rock's all-time greatest hits, and later versions were released by many other artists, including Johnny Rivers, Del Shannon, the Beach Boys, and Bette Midler. Bobby Freeman later went on to record several other outstanding, high-energy R & B rockers, including "Betty Lou Got a New Pair of Shoes" (Josie, #37, 1958); "(I Do) the Shimmy Shimmy" (King, #37, 1960); "C'Mon and Swim" (Autumn, #5, 1964); and "S-W-I-M" (Autumn, #56, 1964).

FREEMAN, ERNIE   This pop producer-arranger made the Top 20 with his cover version of Bill Justice's "Raunchy" (Imperial, #12,

1957). He also worked as an arranger for pop artists like Dean Martin and Frank Sinatra, as well as teen rockers like Paul Anka and Bobby Vee.

THE FROGMEN This instrumental group had one hit called "Underwater" (Candix, #44, 1961), a novelty song that used the croaking noise of a frog to accent the beat.

FULLER, JERRY Although his own recording career wasn't very successful—his biggest hit was "Tennessee Waltz" (Challenge, #63, 1959)—Fuller made a name for himself writing and producing songs for other people. He wrote "Travelin' Man," a number one record for Ricky Nelson in 1961, and the Union Gap's "Over You" (1968) and "Young Girl" (1968).

GABRIEL AND THE ANGELS They only had one minor hit, "That's Life (That's Tough)" (Swan, #51, 1962), but it is one of the most underrated and overlooked, not to mention unsung, records in rock & roll history. The song features Gabriel talking about life gone wrong, while the Angels lament, "That's life." The refrain used the call and response pattern typically found in early rhythm and blues: Gabriel asks, "What's life?" (The Angels respond, "A magazine.") "What's it cost?" ("20 cents.") "But I only got a nickel." ("That's rough.") The song is interesting because it bridges 1950s rock & roll and mid-1960s rock. Its primitive sound and style were a throwback to 1950s R & B rock, while its lyrics contained social commentary, foreshadowing the coming of 1960s folk rock.

GARDNER, DON, & DEE DEE FORD Their biggest hit was "I Need Your Loving" (Fire, #20, 1962), an R & B rocker that was one of the best songs of 1962.

GARI, FRANK He had three hits: "Utopia" (Crusade, #27, 1960); "Lullaby of Love" (Crusade, #23, 1961); and "Princess" (Crusade, #30, 1961). All three, with sophomoric lyrics about adolescent love, are perfect examples of the mass-produced pop rock that was hitting the charts by the early 1960s.

GAYE, MARVIN During the 1960s, his soul and gospel sound earned him numerous hits, including classics like "Hitch Hike" (1963); "Ain't that Peculiar" (1965); and "I Heard It Through the Grapevine" (1968). His success reflected the rise of soul music in the 1960s, which was related to America's growing awareness of the civil rights movement and black pride. By the 1970s, Gaye had established himself as a rock superstar. He had a series of hits with other singers on the Motown label: Gaye and Tammi Terrell found success with "Ain't No Mountain High Enough" (1967), "Your Precious Love" (1967), "Ain't Nothing Like the Real Thing" (1968), and "You're All I Need to Get By" (1968). Gaye and Mary Wells did "Once Upon a Time" (1964) and "What's the Matter With You Baby" (1964). Gaye and Kim Weston had "It Takes Two" (1967). Gaye and Diana Ross combined for "You're a Special Part of Me" (1973) and "My Mistake Was to Love You" (1974). Gaye also continued his solo career with message songs such as "What's Going On," "Mercy Mercy Me (The Ecology Song)," and "Inner City Blues (Make Me Wanna Holler)" in 1971, "Let's Get It On" in 1973, "Got to Give It Up" in 1977, and "Sexual Healing" in 1983. He was inducted posthumously into the Rock & Roll Hall of Fame in 1986. His biggest hits include:

"Stubborn Kind of Fellow"	Tamla	#46	1962
"Hitch Hike"	Tamla	#30	1962
"Pride and Joy"	Tamla	#10	1963
"Can I Get a Witness"	Tamla	#22	1963
"You're a Wonderful One"	Tamla	#15	1964
"Try It Baby"	Tamla	#15	1964
"How Sweet It Is to Be Loved by You"	Tamla	#6	1964
"I'll Be Doggone"	Tamla	#8	1965
"Ain't that Peculiar"	Tamla	#8	1965
"I Heard It Through the Grapevine"	Tamla	#1	1968
"Too Busy Thinking About My Baby"	Tamla	#4	1969
"That's the Way Love Is"	Tamla	#7	1969
"What's Going On"	Tamla	#2	1971
"Mercy Mercy Me (The Ecology Song)"	Tamla	#4	1971
"Inner City Blues (Make Me Wanna Holler)"	Tamla	#9	1971
"Trouble Man"	Tamla	#7	1972
"Let's Get It On"	Tamla	#1	1973
"Come Get to This"	Tamla	#21	1973
"You Sure Love to Ball"	Tamla	#50	1974
"Distant Lover"	Tamla	#28	1974
"I Want You"	Tamla	#15	1976
"Got to Give It Up (Pt.1)"	Tamla	#1	1977
"Sexual Healing"	Columbia	#3	1982 +

THE G-CLEFS Their only big hit was "I Understand (Just How You Feel)" (Terrace, #9, 1961), a pop rock song with just a trace of doo wop. The slow syrupy ballad appealed to romantically inclined teenagers. There were many by the early 1960s, since the Baby Boom generation had finally reached high school and dating age.

GENE AND EUNICE This duo started out in the rhythm and blues field with hits like "Ko Ko Mo" (1955) and "This Is My Story" (1955). Their only record to make the *Billboard* pop charts was "Poco-Loco" (Case, #48, 1959).

GEORGE, BARBARA Her only big hit came in late 1961 with a bouncy, gospel-influenced R & B rocker called "I Know" (AFO, #3, 1961).

GETZ, STAN, AND CHARLIE BYRD These two jazz musicians had a hit with "Desafinado" (Verve, #15, 1962), which reflected the bossa nova dance fad popular in 1962. Getz later paired off with vocalist Astrid Gilberto and reached number five on the national charts in 1964 with the Latin-influenced "The Girl from Ipanema" (Verve, #5, 1964). Both songs show that many members of the rock audience had eclectic tastes.

GIBBS, GEORGIA Her first big hit was "if I Knew You Were Comin' I'd've Baked a Cake" (1950). But by the mid-1950s, Gibbs, like many traditional pop performers, was trying to make records that appealed to the growing rock & roll audience. In 1955 she achieved some commercial, if not artistic, success with "Rock Right" (Mercury, #36, 1955) and covers of LaVerne Baker's "Tweedle Dee" (Mercury, 1955) and Etta James' "Dance with Me, Henry" (Mercury, 1955). Another of her hits, "Hula Hoop Song" (Roulette, #32, 1958), describes the fad that swept the country in the late 1950s.

GIBSON, DON Coming out of a country and western background, he crossed onto the rock charts with such hits as "I Can't Stop Loving You" (RCA, #81, 1958), which became a giant hit for Ray Charles in 1962; "Oh Lonesome Me" (RCA, #8, 1958); "Blue Blue Day" (RCA, #32, 1958); "Just One Time" (RCA, #29, 1960); and "Sea of Heartbreak" (RCA, #21, 1961). His success shows the continuing appeal of country and western music throughout the late 1950s and early 1960s.

GILKYSON, TERRY, AND THE EASYRIDERS This trio mixed pop and folk to produce their big hit, "Marianne" (Columbia, #5,

1957). The song reflects calypso music's growing popularity in the late 1950s.

GILMER, JIMMY, AND THE FIREBALLS   With Gilmer singing lead, they had two big pop rock hits in 1963: "Sugar Shack" (Dot, #1, 1963) and "Daisy Petal Pickin'" (Dot, #15, 1963). Unlike many pop rockers who were hitting the charts in the early 1960s, this group had the potential to record authentic-sounding rock & roll: They were produced by Norman Petty (who helped record some of Buddy Holly and the Crickets' early hits); Jimmy Gilmer had a style and feel for the music that was similar to Holly's; and the Fireballs had some earlier success with instrumental rockers like "Torquay" (1959) and "Quite a Party" (1961). Unfortunately, the whole never equalled its parts. They made some attempts at rockabilly. Jimmy Gilmer recorded an entire album of Holly songs, *Buddy's Buddy*, and the Fireballs provided instrumental accompaniment for original Holly tapes released in the late 1960s and early 1970s. Jimmy Gilmer and the Fireballs also had a hit in 1967 with the folk-influenced "Bottle of Wine." But overall, the group never fulfilled its promise of producing top-notch country rock. Instead, they are best remembered for "Sugar Shack," a number one record that epitomizes the mass-produced pop rock sound that was so common on the charts by the early 1960s. *See also* The Fireballs.

GINO AND GINA   They had one pop rock hit, "(It's Been a Long Time) Pretty Baby" (Mercury, #34, 1958).

THE GIRLFRIENDS   Their only hit came in 1963 with "My One and Only Jimmy Boy" (Colpix, #49, 1963 +). The group's name and song both reflect teen interest in going steady.

THE GLADIOLAS   This R & B rock group suffered the fate of many black artists during the 1950s. The pattern was common: Black rhythm and blues performers would record a song on a small, independent label. Then white pop singers would release their version on a major label (with majors very seldom recording black acts). The large company, with greater marketing capabilities, could distribute the record more easily and quickly to radio stations and to the white public, which often shied away from the R & B originals because of traditional preferences and prejudice. The major label could also guarantee air play on important radio stations in large markets. As a result, the white cover version usually wound up eclipsing the black original in record sales. The Gladiolas are a perfect example. In 1957 they wrote and recorded "Little Darlin'" (Excello, #41, 1957) for a small independent label. The Diamonds, a white pop rock group, then covered the song for Mercury Records, a major company. And it was the Diamonds' version, not the Gladiolas', that became the big hit. It peaked at number two on the charts, as compared to the Gladiolas' number 41. Several years later, the Gladiolas finally achieved success. After changing their name to Maurice Williams and the Zodiacs, they had a number one record in 1960 with "Stay." *See also* Maurice Williams and the Zodiacs.

GLAZER, TOM, & THE CHILDREN'S CHORUS They had a hit in 1963 with "On Top of Spaghetti" (Kapp, #14, 1963). The song, done in a folk style, was a sophomoric parody of the Weavers' "On Top of Old Smokey" (1951). The record's success indicated the continuing appeal of novelty songs, and the rising popularity of folk music.

THE GLENCOVES This pop folk group had one hit, "Hootenanny" (Select, #38, 1963). The song reflected the growing popularity of folk music in the early 1960s, and dealt with group sing-a-long concerts, which were becoming increasingly popular on high school and college campuses.

GOLDSBORO, BOBBY He specialized in the maudlin, glossy pop rock that was reaching the charts by the early 1960s. His first release, "Molly," was a typical "name" song geared to young listeners. His follow-up, "See the Funny Little Clown," was a tearjerker about a heartbroken fellow laughing on the outside while crying on the inside. His numerous hits after 1963, the best of which were probably "Broomstick Cowboy" and "The Straight Life," tended to feature a bland pop philosophy aimed at a rock audience accustomed to meaningful lyrics. His songs reflected the traditional values and interests of the Baby Boom generation. His biggest hits included:

"Molly"	Laurie	#70	1962+
"See the Funny Little Clown"	United Artists	#9	1964
"Me Japanese Boy"	United Artists	#74	1964
"Little Things"	United Artists	#13	1965
"Voodoo Woman"	United Artists	#27	1965
"Broomstick Cowboy"	United Artists	#53	1965+

"It's Too Late"	United Artists	#23	1966
"Honey"	United Artists	#1	1968
"Autumn of My Life"	United Artists	#19	1968
"The Straight Life"	United Artists	#36	1968
"Watching Scotty Grow"	United Artists	#11	1970+
"Summer (The First Time)"	United Artists	#21	1973

GOODMAN, DICKIE This comedy performer first achieved success as part of the Buchanan & Goodman team which had a hit with "The Flying Saucer" in 1956. He then went on his own, and had several novelty hits such as "The Touchables" (Mark-X, #60, 1961) and "Ben Crazy" (Diamond, #44, 1962), which parodied top TV shows.

GORE, LESLEY By the early 1960s, pop rock was being mass-produced specifically for white teenagers living in affluent suburbs. Lesley Gore's records epitomized the sound record companies were after. Her first release, "It's My Party" (1963), was the story of love gone wrong at a teenage birthday party. It had all the right ingredients: a pretty young girl with a bouncy, teenage-sounding voice, singing out in adolescent angst, "It's my party, and I'll cry if I want to." Middle-class teens loved it, and the record shot up to the number one spot on the charts. Additional hits, all done in Lesley Gore's "suburban" pop rock style, soon followed. The girls usually portrayed in Gore's songs reflected traditional values, but they also knew exactly what they wanted. They could gloat over defeating their rivals, as on "Judy's Turn To Cry." They could dig in their heels to get their own way, e.g., "You Don't Own Me." Or they could voice the era's acceptance of sexual double standards, e.g., "That's the Way Boys Are." Gore's great success reflects the suburban teen culture of the early 1960s, and the traditional interests of white, middle-class youths. Her biggest hits were:

"It's My Party"	Mercury	#1	1963
"Judy's Turn to Cry"	Mercury	#5	1963
"She's a Fool"	Mercury	#5	1963
"You Don't Own Me"	Mercury	#2	1963+
"That's the Way Boys Are"	Mercury	#12	1964
"Maybe I Know"	Mercury	#14	1964
"Look of Love"	Mercury	#27	1964+
"Sunshine, Lollipops, and Rainbows"	Mercury	#13	1965
"California Nights"	Mercury	#16	1967

GORME, EYDIE This pop singer had a big hit in 1963 with "Blame It on the Bossa Nova" (Columbia, #7, 1963), based on a popular dance fad of the day. She later had additional success singing two duets with her husband, Steve Lawrence. Both songs, "I Want to Stay Here" (Columbia, #28, 1963) and "I Can't Stop Talking About You" (Columbia, #35, 1963+), reflected traditional values and interests.

GRACIE, CHARLIE This pop rock singer from Philadelphia had two hits in 1957, "Butterfly" (Cameo, #7, 1957) and "Fabulous" (Cameo, #26, 1957).

THE GRADUATES They only had one minor hit, "Ballad of a Girl and Boy" (Shan-Todd, #74, 1959), but it proved to be one of the most interesting songs of the year. The slow, pop rock ballad shows how white teens copied the doo wop style of 1950s R & B rock groups, and reflects teen interest in romance and going steady. The song was co-written by Tom Shannon, the Buffalo, New York, dee jay who wrote "Wild Weekend" for the Rebels.

GRAMMER, BILLY This country and western performer had a major hit on the rock charts in early 1959 with "Gotta Travel On" (Monument, #4, 1958+). His follow-up, "Bonaparte's Retreat" (Monument, #50, 1959), was an unsuccessful attempt to capitalize on other historical records, such as Johnny Horton's "Battle of New Orleans" and Stonewall Jackson's "Waterloo," that were making the charts in 1959.

GRANAHAN, GERRY Although most of his success came as a member of Dickey Doo and the Don'ts, Granahan did have an interesting solo hit in 1958 with "No Chemise, Please" (Sunbeam, #23, 1958). The pop rock record condemned both chemise and sack dresses, popular fashions of the day. *See also* Dickey Doo and the Don'ts.

GRANT, EARL This pianist/organist's unique blend of pop and rhythm and blues earned him several hits in the late 1950s and early 1960s, including "The End" (Decca, #7, 1958); "House of Bamboo" (Decca, #88, 1960); and "Swingin' Gently" (Decca, #44, 1962).

GRANT, JANIE   Like Leslie Gore, Sue Thompson, and Kathy Young, Janie Grant typified the "young teenage girl" pop rock sound of the early 1960s. Her biggest hit was "Triangle" (Caprice, #29, 1961), a song about teen romance. The subject and the way it was presented by Janie with her clean-cut, teenage voice gave white teenagers living in middle-class suburbs something with which they could identify. Her other hits were "Romeo" (Caprice, #75, 1961) and "That Greasy Kid Stuff" (Caprice, #74, 1962).

GREGG, BOBBY, & HIS FRIENDS   The group had two hits reflecting dance crazes of 1962: "The Jam" (Cotton, #29, 1962) and "Potato Peeler" (Cotton, #89, 1962).

GUARALDI, VINCE, TRIO   This jazz group reached the rock charts in 1962 with a pop instrumental called "Cast Your Fate to the Wind" (Fantasy, #22, 1962 +). A later version by Sounds Orchestral became an even bigger hit in 1965.

GUITAR, BONNIE   Her only big hit was "Dark Moon" (Dot, #6, 1957). She also appeared as a guitarist on several records she produced for the Fleetwoods.

HALEY, BILL, AND HIS COMETS   Bill Haley was one of the founding fathers of rock & roll. By the mid-1950s, he and his group were blending country and western, rhythm and blues, and teen-oriented lyrics to produce a sound teens could dance to. Though his music now sounds dated, in the mid-1950s it was revolutionary. Kids went wild over his early hits like "Crazy, Man, Crazy" (1953) and "Shake, Rattle, and Roll" (1954). And when "Rock Around the Clock" (which originally had been recorded in 1954) appeared as the theme in the movie *Blackboard Jungle*, it zoomed to the top of the rock charts in 1955. Haley, with a spit-curl in the middle of his forehead, and the Comets, dressed in sharkskin suits, followed up with hit after hit throughout the rest of the decade. The enthusiastic response of many teenagers shows that the Baby Boom generation was hungering for a new sound that would set them apart from their elders, while the negative reaction of many adults to Haley's music reflects the conservatism of the decade. Haley's contribution to early rock was recognized in 1986 when he was inducted posthumously into the Rock & Roll Hall of Fame. Their greatest hits include:

A. *Hits that made* **Billboard's** *"Best Sellers" charts*

"Crazy, Man, Crazy"	Essex	-	1953
"Shake, Rattle, and Roll"	Decca	-	1954
"Dim Dim the Lights"	Decca	#11	1954+
"Mambo Rock"	Decca	#18	1955
"Birth of the Boogie"	Decca	#26	1955
"Rock Around the Clock"	Decca	#1	1955

B. *Hits charted on* **Billboard** *"Top 100 or "Hot 100" charts*

"Burn that Candle"	Decca	#20	1955
"See You Later, Alligator"	Decca	#6	1956
"R-O-C-K"	Decca	#29	1956
"Rip It Up"	Decca	#30	1956
"Skinnie Minnie"	Decca	#22	1958
"Lean Jean"	Decca	#67	1958

HALL, LARRY His only hit record was "Sandy" (Strand, #15, 1959+). The song was typical of many pop rock songs of the era. It dealt with teen romance, and focused on a girl's name that was commonly found among Baby Boomers.

THE HALOS Their 1961 hit "Nag" (7 Arts, #25, 1961) was a throwback to the R & B rock sound of the late 1950s. The song reinforced a stereotype of the era that portrayed wives, and women in general, as nags interfering with males' pursuit of happiness. The Halos also provided the doo wop backup sound on Curtis Lee's 1961 hit, "Pretty Little Angel Eyes."

HAMILTON IV, GEORGE His youthful, innocent voice and soft, country-influenced sound helped earn him hits with "A Rose and a Baby Ruth" (ABC/Paramount, #6, 1956); "Why Don't They Understand" (ABC/Paramount, #17, 1957+); "I Know Where I'm Goin'" (ABC/Paramount, #43, 1958); "Gee" (ABC/Paramount, #73, 1959); and "Abilene" (RCA, #15, 1963). His records, mixing country and pop, usually dealt with teen romance.

HAMILTON, ROY His background as a gospel singer is evident in his two high-energy hits, "Don't Let Go" (Epic, #13, 1958) and "You Can Have Her" (Epic, #12, 1961). His music shows the continuing influence of rhythm and blues and gospel on rock & roll during the late 1950s and early 1960s.

HARNELL, JOE In 1962 he had a hit with the instrumental, "Fly Me to the Moon–Bossa Nova" (Kapp, #14, 1962+). The song reflected the public's continuing fascination with the space program, and interest in a new dance fad.

HARPO, SLIM He came out of the rhythm and blues tradition and had a medium-sized hit with "Rainin' in My Heart" (Excello, #34, 1961), not to be confused with the Buddy Holly song of the same name. The Harpo song had an authentic folk quality lacking in most rock hits of the early 1960s. Later, he would have an even bigger hit with "Baby Scratch My Back"(Excello, #16, 1966).

THE HARPTONES An early R & B rock group whose rhythm and blues hits included doo wop classics such as "A Sunday Kind of Love" (Bruce, 1953) and "Life Is But a Dream" (Paradise, 1954). They also briefly hit the rock charts with "What Will I Tell My Heart" (Companion, #96, 1961).

HARRIS, EDDIE The success of this saxophonist's jazz version of "Exodus" (Vee Jay, #36, 1961) shows that various musical styles appealed to the rock & roll audience in the early 1960s.

HARRIS, ROLF This Australian was one of the few non-Americans to make the rock charts prior to the coming of the Beatles. He achieved success with three novelty pop songs. His first hit was "Sun Arise" (Epic, #61, 1963), followed by "Tie Me Kangaroo Down Sport" (Epic, #3, 1963). His last song on the charts, "Nick Teen and Al K. Hall" (Epic, #95, 1963), poked fun at two subjects teens could relate to: cigarettes and booze.

HARRIS, THURSTON His biggest hit record was the R & B rock classic, "Little Bitty Pretty One" (Aladdin, #6, 1957), written and also recorded by Bobby Day of "Rockin' Robin" fame.

HARRISON, WILBERT In 1959, two versions of "Kansas City"—one by Harrison and one by Rocky Olson—hit the airwaves. Harrison's record (Fury, #1, 1959), with its authentic R & B rock sound, eventually won out, reaching number one on the charts and becoming one of rock & roll's greatest hits. But Harrison was unable to duplicate his initial success. He dropped out of sight for 10 years, only to come back briefly with "Let's Work Together" (Sue, #32, 1969+).

HAWKINS, DALE This country rocker from Louisiana is perhaps the most overlooked artist in 1950s rock & roll. His biggest hit, "Susie-Q" (Checker, #29, 1957), was one of the best songs of 1957. It was later recorded by numerous other rock performers, including Creedence Clearwater Revival, who had a hit with it in 1968. His second-biggest seller was "La-Do-Dada" (Checker, #32, 1958), a rousing rockabilly song that ranks among the finest rock & roll records from the 1950s. Other hits included two songs that reflected teen interests: "A House, a Car, and a Wedding Ring" (Checker, #88, 1958) and "Class Cutter (Yeah, Yeah, Yeah)" (Checker, #52, 1959).

HAWKINS, RONNIE His hit "Mary Lou" (Roulette, #26, 1959) is proof that country rock was still very much alive in the late 1950s. Although Hawkins' career faded quickly, two members of his backup group, Levon Helm and Robbie Robertson, later achieved superstar status as members of The Band, one of rock's premier groups of the late 1960s and early 1970s.

HAWKINS, SCREAMIN' JAY His claim to fame rests on one rhythm and blues hit, "I Put a Spell on You" (Okeh, 1956), allegedly recorded while he was drunk. The end result was an absolutely wild sound which appealed to the many teenagers sick of the conservatism and strait-laced behavior of the 1950s. Creedence Clearwater Revival later did a cover version of the song, with lead singer John Fogerty turning in a solid performance greatly influenced by Hawkins' original.

HAWLEY, DEAN His only hit was "Look for a Star" (Dore, #29, 1960), from the movie *Circus of Horrors*.

HAYES, BILL This pop vocalist had a number one record in 1955 with "The Ballad of Davy Crockett" (Cadence, #1, 1955). The song, from Walt Disney's *Davy Crockett*, reflected the rise of Crockettmania, appealing to Baby Boomers not yet in their teens. Its popularity showed the stage of development the Baby Boomers had reached in 1955, and foreshadowed things to come. As the Baby Boomers grew older and more sophisticated, songs about dating, then Civil Rights, and then politics would become increasingly popular.

THE HEARTBEATS This R & B rock group had only one big hit, "A Thousand Miles Away" (Rama, #53, 1956+), but the song became one of the more memorable doo wop ballads from the early days of rock & roll. Their lead singer, James Sheppard, later went on to record "Daddy's Home" (1961) with Shep and the Limelites. Both records dealt with teen romance and separation.

HELMS, BOBBY His big year was 1957, when he had two smash hits, "My Special Angel" (Decca, #7, 1957) and "Jingle Bell Rock" (Decca, #6, 1957). Both songs blended country rock and pop rock and became classics of rock & roll. "Jingle Bell Rock" became as important to the rock & roll audience as "White Christmas" was for adults. For five years, from 1957 until 1962, the song was released around Christmas time and became an annual hit on rock charts. It was a great favorite on "American Bandstand," showing that teenagers enjoyed the same type of holiday pop tunes and shared the same old-fashioned values as the older generation. "Jingle Bell Rock" was eventually recorded by many other performers, including Bobby Vee, Chubby Checker, and Bobby Rydell.

HENDERSON, JOE He had his only big hit with a gospel-influenced R & B rock ballad, "Snap Your Fingers" (Todd, #8, 1962). The song used a popular expression of the day and reinforced a stereotype that women were manipulative.

HENDRICKS, BOBBY Reached the charts with an R & B rocker called "Itchy Twitchy Feeling" (Sue, #25, 1958). The song was fast-paced and perfect for teen dance styles of the late 1950s.

HENRY, CLARENCE "FROGMAN" An R & B rock artist of the late 1950s and early 1960s. Perhaps his most interesting record was "Ain't Got No Home" (Argo, #20, 1956+), on which he sang in three different voices, one of which was so low that it earned him the nickname "Frogman." Buddy Holly later did a version of the song, which was almost a carbon-copy of Henry's. His biggest-selling records were "I Don't Know Why I Love You (But I Do)" (Argo, #4, 1961) and "You Always Hurt the One You Love" (Argo, #12, 1961).

HICKEY, ERSEL Tried to capitalize on the success of Elvis Presley, Conway Twitty, and other rock & rollers with unusual-sounding names. His only hit was a solid pop rocker called "Bluebirds Over the Mountain" (Epic, #75, 1958). The song, one of the more interesting of the year, was later recorded by various other performers, including Ritchie Valens and the Beach Boys.

THE HIGHWAYMEN   One of the first pop folk groups to gain popularity in the early 1960s. Their first release, "Michael (Row the Boat Ashore)" (United Artists, #1, 1961), made it to number one on the charts in 1961. They followed up with hits such as "Cotton Fields" (United Artists, #13, 1961 +) and "The Bird Man" (United Artists, #64, 1962), from the popular film *Birdman of Alcatraz*. Their success reflected the maturing of the Baby Boomers. By the early 1960s, many of them had reached college age and were switching to folk music, a more pure and sophisticated sound than rock & roll, which commonly dealt with sophomoric teenage interests.

HILL, JESSIE   A New Orleans piano player, he began as part of Huey Smith & the Clowns, an R & B rock group from the 1950s. He had a solo hit with "Ooh Poo Pah Doo—Part II" (Minit, #28, 1960).

THE HILLTOPPERS   This pop vocal group appealed to some members of the teen audience in the mid-1950s. They were of college age, wore preppie sweaters, and sang slow, romantic ballads such as "P.S. I Love You" (Dot, 1953) and "Only You" (Dot, #9, 1955), and songs aimed at the rock & roll audience like "Ka-Ding-Dong" (Dot, #38, 1956). One of their members, Billy Vaughn, later became quite successful as a musical arranger and pop musician.

HODGES, EDDIE   Began his career in the Broadway show *The Music Man*. After playing Frank Sinatra's son in the movie *A Hole in the Head*, he launched his career as a pop rock singer. His biggest hits were "I'm Gonna Knock on Your Door" (Cadence, #12, 1961); "Bandit of My Dreams" (Cadence, #65, 1962); and "Girls, Girls, Girls (Were Made To Love)" (Cadence, #14, 1962). His adolescent voice, teen-oriented lyrics, and well-crafted pop rock records made him popular among teenagers.

HOLDEN, RON   His only hit record was "Love You So" (Donna, #7, 1960). An interesting beat (reminiscent of the Diamonds' 1957 hit, "Little Darlin' ") and lyrics about young love helped the record make the Top 10.

HOLIDAY, CHICO   Although RCA Records tried to push Holiday as a pop rock star in the late 1950s and early 1960s, he never really caught on with the teen audience. He did manage one minor hit, "Young Ideas" (RCA, #74, 1959).

HOLLAND, EDDIE   This R & B rock artist had a hit with an offbeat song called "Jamie" (Motown, #30, 1962). However, his biggest contribution to rock & roll came as part of the songwriting team of Holland-Dozier-Holland. Together they wrote many rock classics for the Four Tops, the Supremes, and other singers on the Motown label, including "Baby, I Need Your Loving," "Reach Out," and "Baby Love."

HOLLY, BUDDY, AND THE CRICKETS   The best country rock group of the late 1950s. The original members were Buddy Holly, Jerry Allison, Joe B. Mauldin, and Niki Sullivan. Their first single, "That'll Be the Day" (based on an expression used by John Wayne in *The Searchers*), became a number one hit in 1957. Other rockabilly hits followed throughout 1957 and 1958. Buddy Holly, their lead singer and driving force, also recorded as a solo act (his biggest hit was "Peggy Sue" in 1957). Holly died in a 1959 plane crash with rock stars Ritchie Valens and the Big Bopper. Posthumous releases added to his reputation and fueled the cult following that developed in the 1960s and 1970s. In the late 1970s, Holly fans were rewarded with a full-length film biography, *The Buddy Holly Story*, which earned actor Gary Busey an Oscar nomination in the starring role. After Holly's death, the Crickets underwent a series of personnel changes and recorded some excellent music, including early 1960s albums like *Bobby Vee Meets the Crickets* and the Crickets' *Something Old, Something New, Something Blue, Something Else*.

The music of Buddy Holly and the Crickets accurately reflected teen interests, and their records mark the emergence of rock & roll as the new folk music of the young generation. Their songs and style also influenced later rock & rollers. Even a partial list of performers who have recorded Holly songs reads like an encyclopedia of pop stars. It includes pop rock stars like Ricky Nelson, Linda Ronstadt, John Denver, Bobby Vee, Tommy Roe, and the Beach Boys; British rockers like the Beatles, Rolling Stones, Blind Faith, the Searchers, the Dave Clark Five, Herman's Hermits, Peter and Gordon, and the Hollies (who took their name from Buddy Holly); country singers such as Waylon Jennings, Carl Perkins, Skeeter Davis, Susie Allanson, and Billy Crash Craddock; and folk singers like Don McLean, Phil Ochs, Tom Rush, and Jesse Colin Young. Their numerous cover versions of Buddy Holly and the Crickets' songs provide evidence of the lasting impact Holly and his group had on American music. Buddy Holly became a charter member of Rock & Roll's Hall of Fame in 1985. Holly and the Crickets' best-selling hits include:

A. *The Crickets (with Buddy Holly singing lead)*

"That'll Be the Day"	Brunswick	#1	1957
"Oh Boy!"	Brunswick	#10	1957+
"Maybe Baby"	Brunswick	#17	1958
"Think It Over"	Brunswick	#27	1958
"Fool's Paradise"	Brunswick	#58	1958

B. *Buddy Holly (singing as a solo artist)*

"Peggy Sue"	Coral	#3	1957
"Rave On"	Coral	#37	1958
"Early in the Morning"	Coral	#32	1958
"Heartbeat"	Coral	#82	1958+
"It Doesn't Matter Anymore"	Coral	#13	1959

C. *Ivan (Jerry Allison, backed by Holly and Mauldin)*

"Real Wild Child"	Coral	#68	1958

THE HOLLYWOOD ARGYLES   They had one hit, "Alley-Oop" (Lute, #1, 1960), a pop rock novelty song mirroring the great popularity of the Alley-Oop cartoon strip. One of their lead singers, Gary Paxton, previously recorded as one-half of the Skip and Flip duo.

THE HOLLYWOOD FLAMES   Formerly Bobby Day's backup group, they made the charts in 1957 with a solid R & B rocker called "Buzz-Buzz-Buzz" (Ebb, #11, 1957+). The song featured a blasting sax, a driving up-tempo dance beat, and catchy lyrics about the birds and the bees. It was the perfect blend of rhythm and blues and pop, and remains one of the greatest R & B rock hits of the 1950s.

HOMER & JETHRO   These country music performers had a novelty hit in 1959, "The Battle of Kookamonga" (RCA, #14, 1959). The song, which dealt with teenage escapades at summer camp, parodied Johnny Horton's country rock hit, "The Battle of New Orleans."

HORTON, JOHNNY   His biggest hit was "The Battle of New Orleans" (Columbia, #1, 1959), a rollicking country rock song that hit the top of the rock charts in 1959. He followed up with additional country-influenced hits about historical topics, such as "Johnny Reb" (Columbia, #54, 1959); "Sink the Bismarck" (Columbia, #3, 1960), from the movie of the same name; "Johnny Freedom" (Columbia, #69, 1960); and "North to Alaska" (Columbia, #4, 1960), from the John Wayne movie of the same name. Each of the songs reflected the continuing popularity of country and western music, as well as teenagers' acceptance of the traditional values and pride in America's heritage which permeated American life and thought during the late 50s and early 60s.

THE HOT-TODDYS This pop rock group had a hit with "Rockin' Crickets" (Shan-Todd, #57, 1959), an instrumental which featured guitars mimicking the sound of crickets.

HUNTER, IVORY JOE He came out of the rhythm and blues field and recorded several hits during the 1950s. His most successful was "Since I Met You Baby" (Atlantic, #12, 1956).

HUNTER, TAB He began his career as a heartthrob from movies and TV, then switched over to pop music. "Young Love" (Dot, #1, 1957) was one of the first pop rock songs with lyrics written specifically for teenagers. Hunter also made the rock charts with "Ninety-Nine Ways" (Dot, #11, 1957) and "There's No Fool Like a Young Fool" (Warner, #68, 1959).

HUSKY, FERLIN He enjoyed success with "Gone" (Capitol, #4, 1957) and "Wings of a Dove" (Capitol, #12, 1960+). Both were country influenced songs that reflected traditional values regarding romance or religion.

HYLAND, BRIAN The epitome of teen idols of the early 1960s. He was young (still in high school when he had his first hit), good looking, and well groomed. His promoters packaged and sold him as an amazingly shy and reluctant recording star. And teenage girls bought the image, not to mention his records about teen romance and interests. At his best, he turned out some well-crafted pop rock songs, such as "Sealed with a Kiss" or "The Joker Went Wild." But at his worst, he produced slick, commercial pop rock with sophomoric lyrics, e.g., "Itsy Bitsy Teenie Weenie Yellow Polka Dot Bikini."

| "Itsy Bitsy Teenie Weenie Yellow Polka Dot Bikini" | Leader | #1 | 1960 |

"Let Me Belong to You"	ABC/Paramount	#20	1961
"Ginny Come Lately"	ABC/Paramount	#21	1962
"Sealed with a Kiss"	ABC/Paramount	#3	1962
"Warmed-Over Kisses"	ABC/Paramount	#24	1962
"I'm Afraid to Go Home"	ABC/Paramount	#63	1963
"The Joker Went Wild"	Philips	#20	1966
"Run, Run, Look and See"	Philips	#25	1966
"Gypsy Woman"	Uni	#3	1970

IFIELD, FRANK One of the few Englishmen who reached the borders of America's rock charts before the Beatles. His unusual sound, a combination of country and western and pop, earned him hits with "I Remember You" (Vee Jay, #5, 1962); "Lovesick Blues" (Vee Jay, #44, 1962 +); and "I'm Confessin' (That I Love You)" (Capitol, #58, 1963).

THE IKETTES These three girls were the backup singers for Ike and Tina Turner. They achieved success of their own with an R & B rocker called "I'm Blue" (Atco, #19, 1962).

THE IMPALAS Their only big hit was "Sorry (I Ran All the Way Home)" (Cub, #2, 1959), an interesting doo wop record that dealt with teen romance. Like many groups of the era, they named themselves after a car. But unlike most other groups, the Impalas were integrated, featuring a black lead singer and three white backup singers.

THE IMPRESSIONS One of the super groups of rock & roll's first decade. Two of their original members were Jerry Butler and Curtis Mayfield, both of whom later achieved success as solo artists. The Impressions backed Jerry Butler on his 1958 classic, "For Your Precious Love," and then went on to record hits of their own throughout the 1960s. Their music, a fine blend of rhythm and blues, gospel, and pop, often focused on traditional values or religious themes. Their sound anticipated the rise of soul music and reflected the public's growing interest in the civil rights movement and Afro-American culture. The Impressions' greatest hits include:

"Gypsy Woman"	ABC/Paramount	#20	1961
"It's All Right"	ABC/Paramount	#4	1963
"Talking About My Baby"	ABC/Paramount	#12	1964
"I'm So Proud"	ABC/Paramount	#14	1964
"Keep On Pushing"	ABC/Paramount	#10	1964

"You Must Believe Me"	ABC/Paramount	#15	1964
"Amen"	ABC/Paramount	#7	1964 +
"People Get Ready"	ABC/Paramount	#14	1965
"We're a Winner"	ABC/Paramount	#14	1967 +
"Fool for You"	Curtom	#22	1968
"This Is My Country"	Curtom	#25	1968 +
"Choice of Colors"	Curtom	#21	1969
"Check Out Your Mind"	Curtom	#28	1970
"Finally Got Myself Together"	Curtom	#17	1974

INGMANN, JORGEN This Dane's instrumental, "Apache" (Atco, #2, 1961), became one of the biggest hits of 1961. The song featured guitar riffs that made the sound of arrows whizzing by. It hit the charts at a time when westerns dominated American television, and reflected America's continuing fascination with the West and American Indians.

THE INNOCENTS They had two minor hits: "Honest I Do" (Indigo, #28, 1960) and "Gee Whiz" (Indigo, #28, 1960 +). They also sang backup on Kathy Young's hit single, "A Thousand Stars" (1960). *See also* Kathy Young and the Innocents.

THE ISLANDERS Their only hit was an exotic pop instrumental called "The Enchanted Sea" (Mayflower, #15, 1959).

THE ISLEY BROTHERS They exploded onto the rock scene in 1959 with an excellent R & B rocker called "Shout—Part I" (RCA, #47, 1959). They came back three years later with the equally impressive "Twist and Shout" (Wand, #17, 1962). The songs became two of rock & roll's greatest hits. After a brief spell at Motown Records, where they recorded "This Old Heart of Mine" (Tamla, #12, 1966), the Isleys went on to record many other hits, including "It's Your Thing" (T-Neck, #2, 1969); "I Turned You On" (T-Neck, #23, 1969); "Love the One You're With" (T-Neck, #18, 1971); "That Lady (Part 1)" (T-Neck,#6, 1973); "Fight the Power" (T-Neck, #4, 1975); and "For the Love of You" (T-Neck, #22, 1975).

IVAN He was actually Jerry Allison, drummer for the Crickets. He recorded "Real Wild Child" (Coral, #68, 1958), reflecting a 1950s stereotype of teenage juvenile delinquents. Other members of the Crickets—Buddy Holly and Joe Mauldin—sang and played backup on the record. *See also* Buddy Holly and the Crickets.

IVES, BURL   This folk singer and actor had four hit records in the early 1960s: "A Little Bitty Tear" (Decca, #9, 1961 +); "Funny Way of Laughing" (Decca, #10, 1962); "Call Me Mr. In-Between" (Decca, #19, 1962); and "Mary Ann Regrets" (Decca, #39, 1962). His success evidenced the rising popularity of folk music in the early 1960s.

THE IVY THREE   Their only hit was a novelty song, "Yogi" (Shell, #8, 1960), based on the popular Yogi Bear cartoon character from the "Huckleberry Hound" TV show. The record's success indicates that members of the rock audience were still young enough to relate to cartoons.

THE JACKS   This R & B rock group had a minor hit with "Why Don't You Write Me" (RPM, #82, 1955). *See also* the Cadets.

JACKSON, CHUCK   An R & B rock singer of the early 1960s. His biggest hits were "I Don't Want to Cry" (Wand, #36, 1961) and "Any Day Now" (Wand, #23, 1962). His gospel-influenced sound was a throwback to 1950s rhythm and blues.

JACKSON, STONEWALL   This country and western singer named after the Confederate general made the rock charts in 1959 with a foot-stomper called "Waterloo" (Columbia, #4, 1959). Like Johnny Horton's "Battle of New Orleans" from the same year, this record reflected the rock audience's interest in historical subjects, and showed the continuing influence of country music on rock & roll.

JACKSON, WANDA   Coming out of an Oklahoma country and western background, she first crossed over to the rock charts with "Let's Have a Party" (Capitol, #37, 1960), a wild country rocker that ranks as one of the best rock & roll records of all time. Her later hits, "Right or Wrong" (Capitol, #29, 1961), "In the Middle of a Heartache" (Capitol, #27, 1961), and "If I Cried Every Time You Hurt Me" (Capitol, #58, 1962), were more firmly rooted in country music.

JAMES, ETTA   One of the first rhythm and blues singers to gain an audience among white listeners. Her early R & B hits like "Roll with Me, Henry" (Modern, 1955) and "Good Rockin' Daddy" (Modern, 1955) were rock & roll prototypes. She later achieved some success on the rock charts with "All I Could Do Was Cry" (Argo, #33, 1960); "Trust in Me" (Argo, #30, 1961); "Don't Cry Baby" (Argo, #39, 1961); and "Pushover" (Argo, #25, 1963).

JAMES, JONI This 1950s pop singer made the rock charts in 1960 with "My Last Date with You" (MGM, #38, 1960+), the answer song to Floyd Cramer's "Last Date" (1960).

JAMES, SONNY Another example of a country and western performer who found great success on the rock charts. His biggest hit was "Young Love" (Capitol, #2, 1956+), a song about adolescent romance that had also been recorded by Tab Hunter. He followed up with another hit aimed directly at the teen market, "First Date, First Kiss, First Love" (Capitol, #25, 1957). He later became one of country music's biggest stars.

THE JAMIES Their only hit record was a bouncy pop rocker called "Summertime, Summertime." Fortunately for them, it was a hit twice—first in 1958 (Epic, #26, 1958) and then again in 1962 (Epic, #38, 1962). The song became an anthem for youths looking forward to summer vacation.

JAN & ARNIE This pop rock duo had one of 1958's biggest and best rock & roll hits with "Jennie Lee" (Arwin, #8, 1958), a lively, high-energy doo wop song. Although their next release, "Gas Money" (Arwin, #81, 1958), didn't do as well on the charts, it did strike a responsive chord among teenagers interested in cars. When Arnie quit the group, Jan found himself a new partner and went on to greater success as part of the duo Jan & Dean.

JAN & DEAN Jan Berry and Dean Torrence had a long string of hits in the late 1950s and early 1960s (actually, Jan's success began as part of the group Jan & Arnie). Their early hits like "Baby Talk" and "Heart and Soul" featured Jan & Dean's pop rock version of doo wop. Later they switched to Beach Boys–type harmonies on hits such as "Surf City" (co-written by Jan and Beach Boy Brian Wilson), "Dead Man's Curve," and "Sidewalk Surfin'." Most of their records featured upbeat vocals and reflected teen interest in romance, surfing, and cars. Their biggest hits include:

"Baby Talk"	Dore	#10	1959
"Clementine"	Dore	#65	1960
"Heart and Soul"	Challenge	#25	1961

"A Sunday Kind of Love"	Liberty	#95	1962
"Tennessee"	Liberty	#69	1962
"Linda"	Liberty	#28	1963
"Surf City"	Liberty	#1	1963
"Honolulu Lulu"	Liberty	#11	1963
"Drag City"	Liberty	#10	1963+
"Dead Man's Curve"	Liberty	#8	1964
"The New Girl in School"	Liberty	#37	1964
"Ride the Wild Surf"	Liberty	#16	1964
"The Anaheim, Azusa & Cucamonga Sewing Circle, Book Review, and Timing Association"	Liberty	#77	1964
"Sidewalk Surfin'"	Liberty	#25	1964
"You Really Know How to Hurt a Guy"	Liberty	#27	1965
"I Found a Girl"	Liberty	#30	1965
"Batman"	Liberty	#66	1966
"Popsicle"	Liberty	#21	1966

THE JARMELS They enjoyed brief success with an R & B rock song called "A Little Bit of Soap" (Laurie, #12, 1961).

JAY AND THE AMERICANS A pop rock group that achieved considerable success throughout the 1960s. Their first hit was "She Cried" (1962), a well-done doo wop ballad about teen romance. Their next release, "This Is It" (1962), was also a solid recording, but went nowhere on the charts. After changing lead singers (Jay Black replaced Jay Traynor), they bounced in 1963 with "Only in America," a Broadway-sounding hit that plugged into the patriotic feelings associated with Kennedy's New Frontier. Their polished, operatic pop rock sound earned them numerous other hits throughout the 1960s, such as "Cara Mia" and "Some Enchanted Evening." Their best-selling records include:

"She Cried"	United Artists	#5	1962
"Only in America	United Artists	#25	1963
"Come a Little Bit Closer"	United Artists	#3	1964
"Let's Lock the Door"	United Artists	#11	1964+
"Think of the Good Times"	United Artists	#57	1965
"Cara Mia"	United Artists	#4	1965
"Some Enchanted Evening"	United Artists	#13	1965
"Sunday and Me"	United Artists	#18	1965
"Livin' Above Your Head"	United Artists	#76	1966
"Crying"	United Artists	#25	1966

"This Magic Moment"	United Artists	#6	1968 +
"Walkin' in the Rain	United Artists	#19	1969 +

THE JAYHAWKS Their first hit was a R & B rock novelty song, "Stranded in the Jungle" (Flash, #18, 1956). They later made the charts as the Marathons with "Peanut Butter" (1961), and then as the Vibrations with "The Watusi" (1961) and other hits in the mid-1960s.

THE JAYNETTS This all-girl group had a major hit in 1963 with "Sally Go 'Round the Roses" (Tuff, #2, 1963). The song had an unusual, gospel-influenced folk quality, which helped make it one of the outstanding R & B rock hits of the early 1960s

JENSEN, KRIS He made the Top 20 in 1962 with "Torture" (Hickory, #20, 1962), a well-done pop rock song about the anguish of teenage love.

JIMENEZ, JOSE This was a character created by comedian Bill Dana. In 1961 Dana had a hit single with "The Astronaut" (Kapp, #19, 1961), a record that reflected America's fascination with the space program. It also evidenced the Hispanic stereotypes present in the early 1960s.

THE JIVE BOMBERS An R & B rock group whose only hit was "Bad Boy" (Savoy, #36, 1957).

THE JIVE FIVE This Brooklyn quintet enjoyed its greatest success in 1961 with "My True Story" (Beltone, #3, 1961), a throwback to the R & B rock sound of the 1950s.

JO, DAMITA Her hit record "I'll Save the Last Dance for You" (Mercury, #22, 1960) answered the Drifters' "Save the Last Dance For Me." Her style, a blend of R & B rock and pop rock, also earned her hits with "Keep Your Hands Off of Him" (Mercury, #75, 1961) and "I'll Be There" (Mercury, #12, 1961).

JOHNNIE & JOE This duo recorded one of rock & roll's classics: "Over the Mountain, Across the Sea" (Chess, #8, 1957). The song epitomized R & B rock ballads of the 1950s.

JOHNNY & THE HURRICANES In 1959 and 1960, this instrumental group from Toledo, Ohio, was one of the hottest rock groups around. Their first hit, "Crossfire" (Warwick, #23, 1959), was a fast-paced pop rocker. Their next three hits were rock & roll versions of traditional songs. Their biggest hit, "Red River Rock" (Warwick, #5, 1959), was a take-off on "Red River Valley"; "Reveille Rock" (Warwick, #25, 1959) was a rock version of the army bugle call; and "Beatnik Fly" (Warwick, #15, 1960), which tried to capitalize on the public's growing awareness of the Beat Generation, was a rock version of "Blue Tail Fly."

JOHNSON, MARV   He had several hits in the late 1950s and early 1960s, including three of the finest R & B rock songs of the era: "You Got What It Takes" (United Artists, #10, 1959+); "I Love the Way You Love Me" (United Artists, #9, 1960); and "(You've Got To) Move Two Mountains" (United Artists, #20, 1960).

THE JOINER, ARKANSAS, JUNIOR HIGH SCHOOL BAND   This was a real junior high school marching band! Their recording, "National City" (Liberty, #53, 1960), received a lot of airplay on "American Bandstand" and became a surprise hit in 1960. Not only was it novel, but it gave teenagers something they could identify with, since many of them were in junior or senior high school themselves.

JONES, JACK   This pop singer—the son of singer Allan Jones—first hit the rock charts with such records as "Lollipops and Roses" (Kapp, #66, 1962); "Wives and Lovers" (Kapp, #14, 1963+), based on the movie of the same name; and "Love with the Proper Stranger" (Kapp, #62, 1964), from the movie of the same title. His appearance and style were throwbacks to traditional pop performers like Frank Sinatra, Perry Como, and Andy Williams, and his success throughout the 1960s shows that many teenagers of that decade still shared the tastes and values of their parents' generation.

JONES, JIMMY   His big year was 1960, when he had two Top 10 hits: "Handy Man" (Cub, #2, 1959+), later a hit for James Taylor, and "Good Timin'" (Cub, #3, 1960). Both are excellent examples of the high-energy R & B rock style that was popular in the early 1960s.

JONES, JOE   An R & B rock singer of the late 1950s and early 1960s. His only hit, "You Talk Too Much" (Roulette, #3, 1960), focused on a popular female stereotype of the day.

JUSTIS, BILL He began as a staff producer and session musician for Sun Records in the mid-1950s. His instrumental, country rock style earned him hits with "Raunchy" (Phillips, #2, 1957) and "College Man" (Phillips, #42, 1958). "Raunchy" became a slang expression, meaning disgusting or messy, while "College Man" mirrored adolescent rebellion against school, books, or anything intellectual.

KAEMPFERT, BERT In 1961 this German musician and bandleader made it to the top of the charts with the beautiful "Wonderland by Night" (Decca, #1, 1960 +). The song was perfect for teenagers who liked romantic slow dancing, and showed that many members of the rock audience also appreciated well-done pop songs. Kaempfert found additional success with hits like "Tenderly" (Decca, #31, 1961) and "Red Roses for a Blue Lady" (Decca, #11, 1965).

THE KALIN TWINS These clean-cut pop rockers had a brief but successful career singing about teenage romance. They had two big hits in 1958: "When" (Decca, #5, 1958), which was written by Paul Evans; and "Forget Me Not" (Decca, #12, 1958).

KALLEN, KITTY After starting out as a vocalist with Jimmy Dorsey and Harry James, she later made the rock charts with "My Coloring Book" (RCA, #18, 1962 +), a romantic ballad that revolved around a youth-oriented metaphor.

K-DOE, ERNIE From New Orleans, he had only one big hit, but it became one of the most popular songs in rock & roll history. His R & B rock novelty record, "Mother-in-Law" (Minit, #1, 1961), struck a responsive chord among those dissatisfied with in-laws, and zoomed to the top of the rock charts.

KELLER, JERRY This pop rock singer had a big hit in 1959 called "Here Comes Summer" (Kapp, #14, 1959). The song dealt with teenagers' longing for summer vacation, with lyrics that focused on teen interest in dating, drive-ins, swimming, and flat top haircuts.

KELLUM, MURRAY Although his "Long Tall Texan" (M.O.C., #51, 1963) barely made the rock charts when it was first released, the song eventually developed a strong grassroots following. With its images of the Old West and basic R & B rock beat, "Long Tall Texan" became a favorite of many garage bands throughout the 1960s.

KENNER, CHRIS   His only big hit was "I Like It Like That" (Instant, #2, 1961), a bouncy R & B rocker with a catchy hook. He also wrote and recorded "Land of 1,000 Dances" (Instant, #77, 1963), which later became an even bigger hit for Cannibal and the Headhunters in 1965 and Wilson Pickett in 1966.

KIMBERLY, ADRIAN   Had a surprise hit in 1961 with an instrumental version of the graduation march, "Pomp and Circumstance" (Calliope, #34, 1961). The song became an instant success among high school and college students eager for graduation.

KING, B. B.   This legendary blues singer and guitarist had trouble crossing over to the rock charts in the 1950s and early 1960s. His style, which remained true to the blues tradition, may have been too alien for the middle-class tastes of most white teenagers. Not until the mid and late 1960s—when he was "suddenly" discovered by white listeners after being cited as a major influence by guitar heroes like Eric Clapton and Mike Bloomfield—did King become a success on the rock and pop charts. After touring with the Rolling Stones in 1969, he earned his first Top 10 hit with "The Thrill Is Gone" (Blues Way, #15, 1969 +). His only other big hit on the rock charts was "I Like to Live the Love" (ABC, #28, 1973 +). He was elected to the Rock & Roll Hall of Fame in 1986.

KING, BEN E.   His career took off when he joined the Drifters, one of the most successful R & B rock groups of all time. King's expressive, crystal-clear voice provided the lead vocals on Drifter hits such as "There Goes My Baby" (1959), "Dance with Me" (1959), "This Magic Moment" (1960), and "Save the Last Dance for Me" (1960). After going out on his own, he achieved success with classics like "Spanish Harlem" (Atco, #10, 1960 +); "Stand By Me" (Atco, #4, 1961); "Don't Play That Song" (Atco, #11, 1962); "I (Who Have Nothing)" (Atco, #29, 1963); and "Supernatural Thing—Part I" (Atlantic, #5, 1975). In 1986 "Stand By Me" became a hit again (Atlantic, #9, 1986), after it appeared as the theme in the Rob Reiner film *Stand By Me*, a nostalgic movie about coming of age in the early 1960s. *See also* The Drifters.

KING, CAROLE One of the most successful writers and singers in the history of rock & roll, her career has been intertwined with the history of rock music. She was the subject of Neil Sedaka's 1959 hit, "Oh! Carol." In the early 1960s she teamed with husband Gerry Goffin to write hits like "Will You Love Me Tomorrow?" for the Shirelles; "Go Away Little Girl" for Steve Lawrence; "The Loco-Motion" for Little Eva; "Take Good Care of My Baby," "Walkin' With My Angel," and "Sharing You" for Bobby Vee; "Her Royal Majesty" for Jimmy Darren; "One Fine Day" for the Chiffons; and "Every Breath I Take" for Gene Pitney, to name just a few. She also achieved some success as a recording artist in the early 1960s, with excellent pop rock records like "It Might As Well Rain Until September" and "He's a Bad Boy." During the early 1970s, after touring with James Taylor, Carole King became a superstar in her own right with *Tapestry*, one of the best-selling albums of all time. Her greatest hits include:

"It Might As Well Rain Until September"	Dimension	#22	1962
"He's a Bad Boy"	Dimension	#94	1963
"It's Too Late"	Ode	#1	1971
"So Far Away"	Ode	#14	1971
"Sweet Seasons"	Ode	#9	1972
"Been to Canaan"	Ode	#24	1972 +
"Believe in Humanity"	Ode	#28	1973
"Jazzman"	Ode	#2	1974
"Nightingale"	Ode	#9	1975
"Only Love Is Real"	Ode	#28	1976
"Hard Rock Cafe"	Capitol	#30	1977
"One Fine Day"	Capitol	#12	1980

KING, CLAUDE Country and western influences continued to appear on the rock charts in 1962, as evidenced by King's Top 10 record, "Wolverton Mountain" (Columbia, #6, 1962).

KING, FREDDY This blues-influenced guitarist had a medium-sized hit with the instrumental "Hide Away" (Federal, #29, 1961).

THE KINGSMEN Not to be confused with the Kingsmen of "Louie Louie" fame, these Kingsmen were actually Bill Haley's backup group, the Comets. They had a hit of their own with the instrumental "Week End" (East West, #84, 1958), a song that appealed to teenagers who lived for Fridays and Saturdays.

THE KINGSMEN　This white pop rock group from Portland, Oregon, exploded onto the rock scene in 1963 with a dynamic and wild cover of Richard Berry's R & B song, "Louie Louie." The record—with its R & B–influenced vocal, unintelligible and allegedly obscene lyrics, and electric bass powering a solid rock beat—shot up the record charts, sending ripples across American society. Radio stations, town councils, and state legislatures tried to ban the record. But the garbled lead vocal was just vague enough to avoid legal action. Many insisted that there were actually two sets of lyrics—one "clean," which was presented to the adult establishment, the other "dirty," which circulated among youths in the know. Remarkably, both versions seemed to fit when listening to the record. The commotion surrounding "Louie Louie" reflected conservative sexual attitudes of the day. The song eventually became one of rock & roll's all-time greatest hits, and a favorite of garage bands across the country. The Kingsmen had a hit with it again when it was re-released in 1966. More than 10 years later, John Belushi recorded a version of the song for the movie *Animal House,* and his record also made the charts. Although the Kingsmen's later releases never equalled the success or notoriety of "Louie Louie," they did help establish the band as one of the supergroups of the early 1960s.

"Louie Louie"	Wand	#2	1963
"Money"	Wand	#16	1964
"Little Latin Lupe Lu"	Wand	#46	1964
"Death of an Angel"	Wand	#42	1964
"The Jolly Green Giant"	Wand	#4	1965
"Louie Louie" (re-release)	Wand	#97	1966

THE KINGSTON TRIO　Bob Shane, Nick Reynolds, and Dave Guard (later replaced by John Stewart) had a number one record in 1958 with a folk song called "Tom Dooley." They followed up with other popular folk songs, establishing the group as one of the top performing acts around. Their style mixed traditional folk with pop music, and ushered in the arrival of folk on the pop music scene. In an era when most songs were about romance or dancing, or referred to politics in only subtle ways, the Kingston Trio sang about real people, events, and issues. In 1959, they made the Top 20 charts with "M.T.A.," a song that condemned Boston's Metropolitan Transit Authority for a fare increase. In 1962, they scored again with the hit record, "Where Have All the Flowers Gone," a pointed anti-war song. That same year they also found success with "Scotch and Soda," a simple yet eloquent song about naturally and artificially-induced highs. And the following year, they attacked greed and materialism with their hit, "Greenback Dollar" (which, bowing to the conservative attitudes of the day, deleted the word "damn" from the lyrics).

The Kingston Trio's great popularity in the late 1950s and early 1960s indicated that a large segment of the young audience wanted music that was more sophisticated, and more socially relevant, than rock & roll. The young audience's acceptance of the Kingston Trio's pop folk sound paved the way for Peter, Paul, and Mary, Bob Dylan, and other folk and folk rock artists of the mid and late 1960s. The Kingston Trio's greatest hits include:

"Tom Dooley"	Capitol	#1	1958
"The Tijuana Jail"	Capitol	#12	1959
"M.T.A."	Capitol	#15	1959
"A Worried Man"	Capitol	#20	1959
"El Matador"	Capitol	#32	1960
"Bad Man Blunder"	Capitol	#37	1960
"Where Have All the Flowers Gone"	Capitol	#21	1962
"Scotch and Soda"	Capitol	#81	1962
"Greenback Dollar"	Capitol	#21	1963
"Reverend Mr. Black"	Capitol	#8	1963

THE KIRBY STONE FOUR   Their only hit came in 1958 with "Baubles, Bangles, and Beads" (Columbia, #50, 1958), from the Broadway musical *Kismet*. The fact that this type of song received considerable airplay on many rock & roll stations indicates that at least some members of the rock audience were still enjoying traditional pop music.

KNIGHT, GLADYS, & THE PIPS   This R & B rock group had several hits in the early 1960s, including "Every Beat of My Heart," "Letter Full of Tears," and "Giving Up." Most of their biggest hits came in the late 1960s and early 1970s. Their long-term success shows the continuing influence of gospel and R & B styles on rock music. Their biggest hits include:

"Every Beat of My Heart"	Vee-Jay	#6	1961
"Letter Full of Tears"	Fury	#19	1961+
"Giving Up"	Maxx	#38	1964
"I Heard It Through the Grapevine"	Soul	#2	1967
"The End of Our Road"	Soul	#15	1968
"The Nitty Gritty"	Soul	#19	1969

"Friendship Train"	Soul	#17	1969
"If I Were Your Woman"	Soul	#9	1970+
"Neither One of Us"	Soul	#2	1973
"Daddy Could Swear, I Declare"	Soul	#19	1973
"Midnight Train to Georgia"	Buddah	#1	1973
"I've Got to Use My Imagination"	Buddah	#4	1973+
"Best Thing That Ever Happened to Me"	Buddah	#3	1974
"On and On"	Buddah	#5	1974
"The Way We Were/Try to Remember"	Buddah	#11	1975
"Part Time Love"	Buddah	#22	1975

KNIGHT, SONNY In 1956 he had a Top 20 hit with an R & B rock song called "Confidential" (Dot, #20, 1956).

THE KNOCKOUTS This pop rock group had a hit in 1960 with "Darling Lorraine" (Shad, #46, 1959+), which, like many rock & roll songs of the day, focused on a girl's name.

KNOX, BUDDY He started out as a member of a Texas country rock group called The Rhythm Orchids, which also included Jimmy Bowen. Knox later became one of the most successful rockabilly artists of the late 1950s. His biggest hit, "Party Doll," was condemned by some parents and conservative groups for its allegedly suggestive lyrics. His best-selling hits were:

"Party Doll"	Roulette	#2	1957
"Rock Your Little Baby to Sleep"	Roulette	#23	1957
"Hula Love"	Roulette	#12	1957
"Somebody Touched Me"	Roulette	#22	1958
"Lovey Dovey"	Liberty	#25	1960+

KOFFMAN, MOE, QUARTETTE This group had a hit in 1958 with "The Swingin' Shepherd Blues" (Jubilee, #36, 1958), a jazz-influenced song that showed the eclectic tastes of some members of the rock & roll audience.

KOKOMO In 1961 this group had a big hit with "Asia Minor" (Felsted, #8, 1961), a lively rock & roll version of a Grieg Piano Concerto.

THE KUF-LINX Their only hit was "So Tough" (Challenge, #76, 1958). The record focused on the teen expression "tough," meaning beautiful or good-looking.

THE LAFAYETTES They had one of the more interesting hits of 1962: "Life's Too Short" (RCA, #87, 1962). The song captured the authentic feel of 1950s R & B rock, despite the fact that the Lafayettes were an all-white pop rock group. The lyrics, expressing the singer's desire to remain with only one girl since "life's too short to mess around," reflect the traditional monogamous attitudes of the day.

LANCE, MAJOR His first hit, "The Monkey Time," focused on one of the most popular dance crazes of 1963. Additional hit records followed, making Major Lance one of the hottest R & B rock singers in 1963 and 1964. All of his biggest hits (with the exception of "The Matador") were written by Curtis Mayfield and are good examples of early 1960s soul music. His best-sellers include:

"The Monkey Time"	Okeh	#8	1963
"Hey Little Girl"	Okeh	#13	1963
"Um, Um, Um, Um, Um, Um"	Okeh	#5	1964
"The Matador"	Okeh	#20	1964
"Rhythm"	Okeh	#24	1964

LAUREN, ROD A good example of the slick, commercial pop rock that was being mass-produced for teenagers by the early 1960s. Despite RCA's attempts to market Lauren as a hot new teen idol, only one of Lauren's records became a hit. In 1960 he made the Top 40 charts with "If I Had a Girl"(RCA, #31, 1959 +), a sophomoric ballad about teenage romance.

LAURIE, LINDA She had a hit in 1959 with a rather bizarre song, "Ambrose (Part 5)" (Glory, #52, 1959). The novelty record consisted of Laurie speaking to her boyfriend Ambrose, who every once in awhile would reply, "Just keep walkin'." His tough-sounding voice echoed teen rebellion of the 1950s, while her constant chatting reflected a 1950s stereotype of teenage girls.

LAWRENCE, STEVE This pop singer got his start as a regular on Steve Allen's "Tonight Show" (where he met his future wife, singer Eydie Gorme). His first appearance on the rock charts came with a cover version of Buddy Knox's "Party Doll" (Coral, #10, 1957). By the early 1960s he was aiming his material at the young audience. In 1960 he had a big hit with a solid pop rock song about teen love called "Pretty Blue Eyes" (ABC/Paramount, #9, 1959 +), which was also recorded by the Crickets. He followed up with the equally well-done "Footsteps" (ABC/Paramount, #7, 1960), an up-tempo number about love gone wrong. Although his next release, "Portrait of My Love" (United Artists, #9, 1961), was more pop than rock, it too did extremely well on the rock charts. In 1963 he earned his biggest hit yet, "Go Away Little Girl" (Columbia, #1, 1962+), an excellent pop rock ballad written by composers Carole King and Gerry Goffin. His follow-ups included "Don't Be Afraid, Little Darlin'" (Columbia, #26, 1963); "Poor Little Rich Girl" (Columbia, #27, 1963); and "Walking Proud" (Columbia, #26, 1963). Lawrence's success on the rock charts shows that many teenagers still enjoyed pop-oriented songs in the early 1960s.

LEE, BRENDA She arrived on the rock & roll scene in 1959 with a dynamite country rocker called "Sweet Nothins'." The song, featuring a catchy melody, suggestive lyrics, and Lee's powerful R & B–sounding vocal, zoomed into the Top 5 on the record charts. Brenda Lee quickly proved she was no one-hit wonder, as she rang up 12 Top 10 records over the next three years. Her tremendous popularity resulted from her unique voice, her well-crafted blend of country rock and pop, and excellent records that dealt with teen interests. Brenda Lee's greatest hits include:

"Sweet Nothins'"	Decca	#4	1959+
"I'm Sorry"	Decca	#1	1960
"That's All You Gotta Do"	Decca	#6	1960
"I Want to Be Wanted"	Decca	#1	1960
"Rockin' Around the Christmas Tree"	Decca	#14	1960
"Emotions"	Decca	#7	1960+
"You Can Depend on Me"	Decca	#6	1961
"Dum Dum"	Decca	#4	1961
"Fool #1"	Decca	#3	1961
"Break It to Me Gently"	Decca	#4	1962
"Everybody Loves Me But You"	Decca	#6	1962
"Heart in Hand"	Decca	#15	1962
"All Alone Am I"	Decca	#3	1962
"Losing You"	Decca	#6	1963
"Grass Is Greener"	Decca	#17	1963
"As Usual"	Decca	#12	1963+
"Too Many Rivers"	Decca	#13	1965
"Coming On Strong"	Decca	#11	1966

LEE, CURTIS This pop rocker (who was discovered by Ray Peterson) had one of the outstanding hits of 1961 with "Pretty Little Angel

Eyes" (Dunes, #7, 1961). Produced by Phil Spector and powered by high-energy vocals and soaring falsettos, the record featured backup vocals by the Halos, the R & B rock group who had a hit with "Nag." The song is an excellent example of early 1960s' doo wop.

LEE, DICKEY His 1962 hit, the tearjerker "Patches" (Smash, #6, 1962), is a good example of the "Death Rock" popular in the early 1960s. The song told a maudlin tale of tragic love between an upper-class boy and lower-class girl. When his parents refuse to allow the romance, Patches is found "face down" in the local river, and the boy promises to join her that night. The song reflected teenagers' interest in tragic romance and showed the continuing appeal of the Romeo and Juliet theme. Like other rock & roll songs about death, "Patches" might also be an indication of teenage anxieties. Dickey Lee's later hits also focused on girls' names: "I Saw Linda Yesterday" (Smash, #14, 1962 +); "Don't Wanna Think About Paula" (Smash, #68, 1963); and "Laurie (Strange Things Happen)" (TCV Hall, #14, 1965).

LEE, PEGGY One of the best pop music stylists of all time, she made the rock charts in 1958 with "Fever" (Capitol, #8, 1958), a stunning interpretation of Little Willie John's R & B song.

LEIBER, JERRY, AND MIKE STOLLER One of the most prolific and accomplished songwriting teams in the history of rock & roll. They skillfully mixed rhythm and blues and pop to produce hit records for Elvis Presley, the Coasters, and many other rock performers. Their immense songwriting talent was officially recognized in 1986 when they were inducted into the Rock & Roll Hall of Fame. Some of their most successful songs (and the performers who recorded them) include:

"Love Potion #9" (Clovers)
"Kansas City" (Wilbert Harrison)
"Hound Dog" (Elvis Presley)
"Love Me" (Elvis Presley)
"Jailhouse Rock" (Elvis Presley)
"Don't" (Elvis Presley)
"You're So Square" (Elvis Presley)
"Loving You" (Elvis Presley)
"She's Not You" (Elvis Presley)
"Bossa Nova Baby" (Elvis Presley)

"Searchin' " (the Coasters)
"Charlie Brown" (Coasters)
"Yakety Yak" (Coasters)
"Young Blood" (Coasters)
"Along Came Jones (Coasters)
"Poison Ivy" (Coasters)
"Dance with Me" (Drifters)
"Stand By Me" (Ben E. King)

LESTER, KETTY Another example of a pop vocalist who could sell records to the teen audience. She reached the rock charts with "Love Letters" (Era, #5, 1962), a topic many teenagers could relate to. The song became a hit for Elvis Presley in 1966.

THE LETTERMEN These three handsome guys, who wore high school letter sweaters during stage performances, had a clean-cut, youthful look that appealed to many teens. Their soft pop rock style earned them hits with pop standards like "The Way You Look Tonight" (Capitol, #13, 1961) and "When I Fall in Love" (Capitol, #7, 1961+), as well as teen-oriented songs such as "Come Back Silly Girl" (Capitol, #17, 1962); "How Is Julie" (Capitol, #17, 1962); and "Silly Boy" (Capitol, #81, 1962). In an era when slow dancing and making out were favorite teen pastimes, Lettermen records—featuring smooth, romantic harmonies—became a fixture at high school record hops. Their success continued throughout the 1960s and 1970s with hits like "Theme From *A Summer Place*" (Capitol, #16, 1965); "Goin' Out of My Head/ Can't Take My Eyes Off You" (Capitol, #7, 1967+); and "Hurt So Bad" (Capitol, #12, 1969).

LEWIS, BARBARA She made the Top 20 charts with three R & B rock ballads: "Hello Stranger" (Atlantic, #3, 1963); "Baby, I'm Yours" (Atlantic, #11, 1965); and "Make Me Your Baby" (Atlantic, #11, 1965).

LEWIS, BOBBY His first record, an R & B rocker called "Tossin and Turnin' " (Beltone, #1, 1961), hit the top of the charts in 1961. The novelty song seemed like an insomniac's version of Bobby Darin's 1958 classic about taking a bath, "Splish Splash." Both hits featured an upbeat tempo and a frantic delivery. Like many rock & roll singers, Lewis found it hard to duplicate his initial success. His only other big hit was "One Track Mind" (Beltone, #9, 1961).

LEWIS, JERRY LEE From the start, he was the wild man of rock & roll. His long blond hair cascaded down his forehead as he banged out notes on the piano, sometimes with his elbows. His seemingly lascivious, raucous, and rebellious brand of country rock exploded onto the charts in 1957 with a dynamite, rockabilly song called "Whole Lot of Shakin' Going On" (Sun, #3, 1957). He followed up with equally sensational rockers like "Great Balls of Fire" (Sun, #2, 1957+); "Breathless" (Sun, #7, 1958); and "High School Confidential" (Sun, #21, 1958). But then it ended as suddenly as it had begun. When news leaked out that Lewis had married his 13-year-old third cousin, his popularity plummeted. Radio and TV stations were reluctant to play his songs, while many adults shook their heads in an "I told you so" manner at "the bad boy" of rock & roll. In the end, Lewis was a magnificent shooting star in the rock & roll universe. His high-energy rockabilly provided some of the finest rock of the decade. And public reaction to his style sheds light on 1950s values and tastes. For many teens, Lewis represented rebellion and sexuality. For many conservative adults he epitomized the licentiousness and degradation which they associated with rock & roll. Ironically, Jerry Lee Lewis outlived most of his musical contemporaries. By the late 1970s he had resurfaced as a bona fide country star with hits like "What's Made Milwaukee Famous (Has Made a Loser Out of Me)" (Smash, #94, 1968) and "Me and Bobby McGee" (Mercury, #40, 1971+). He made the rock charts with "Drinking Wine Spo-Dee O Dee" (Mercury, #41, 1973). And in 1985, he was inducted into the Rock & Roll Hall of Fame.

LEWIS, SMILEY Another example of an early R & B rock artist who lost out to a white pop artist covering his song. In 1955 Lewis made the R & B charts with "I Hear You Knockin'" (Imperial, 1955), but it was Gale Storm's cover version that became the big national hit on the pop charts.

THE LIMELITERS This pop folk group featured Glen Yarborough as one of its three members. Their only hit came with "A Dollar Down" (RCA, #60, 1961). The song reflected the materialism of early 1960s America, and the group's success foreshadowed folk music's rise in popularity.

LINDEN, KATHY Many rock & roll songs of the 1950s, like traditional pop songs, used popular boys' or girls' names in their titles.

Linden used this formula to achieve success with two pop rock ballads: "Billy" (Felsted, #7, 1958) and "Goodbye, Jimmy, Goodbye" (Felsted, #11, 1959).

LITTLE ANTHONY AND THE IMPERIALS This group had one of the biggest hits of 1958 with "Tears on My Pillow" (End, #4, 1958). The record epitomized the 1950s doo wop ballad style, and reflected teenage concerns with love and romance. They followed up with two minor hits, "Wishful Thinking" (End, #79, 1959) and "A Prayer and a Juke Box" (End, #81, 1959), before scoring big with "Shimmy Shimmy Ko Ko Bop" (End, #24, 1959 +), a song about sensuous teenage dancing. Later in the 1960s they found even greater success with pop-oriented records like "I'm on the Outside Lookin' In" (DCP, #15, 1964); "Goin' Out of My Head" (DCP, #6, 1964); "Hurt So Bad" (DCP, #10, 1965); and "Take Me Back" (DCP, #16, 1965).

LITTLE CAESAR AND THE ROMANS Their biggest hit was "Those Oldies But Goodies (Remind Me of You)" (Del-Fi, #9, 1961). The record's success shows that the Baby Boomers were getting old enough by the early 1960s to have nostalgic rock & roll favorites. The song later became a natural for rock & roll nostalgia groups of the 1970s like Sha Na Na and Big Wheelie and the Hubcaps. It was also performed by John Cafferty and the Beaver Brown Band as part of an "oldies" nightclub act in the 1980s movie, *Eddie and the Cruisers*. Although Little Caesar and the Romans never had another major hit, they did achieve some success with "Hully Gully Again" (Del-Fi, #54, 1961), a song about an early 1960s dance fad.

THE LITTLE DIPPERS They had a hit with a romantic pop rock ballad called "Forever" (University, #9, 1960).

LITTLE EVA Legend has it that she was discovered while babysitting for songwriters Carole King and Gerry Goffin. They liked her R & B rock style and gave her one of their compositions to record. That record, "The Locomotion" (Dimension, #1, 1962), proved to be the biggest hit of Little Eva's brief career. The song helped popularize a new dance fad in a year when teenagers were going crazy over the Twist and other types of dances. Little Eva's later hits included "Keep Your Hands Off My Baby" (Dimension, #12, 1962) and another dance song, "Let's Turkey Trot" (Dimension, #20, 1963).

LITTLE JO ANN   This seven-year-old girl enjoyed some success in 1962 with "My Daddy Is President" (Kapp, #67, 1962), a novelty record that reflected America's fascination with the youthful, vigorous John F. Kennedy.

LITTLE JOE & THE THRILLERS   Their only hit came in 1957 with a song called "Peanuts" (Okeh, #22, 1957). The record was one of the best of the year, and typifies the R & B rock sound of the 1950s.

LITTLE JOEY AND THE FLIPS   Another one-hit group. Their record, "Bongo Stomp" (Joy, #33, 1962), reflected the bongo fad of the early 1960s, a result of public interest in the Beat Generation.

LITTLE RICHARD   For many members of the rock & roll audience, this wild R & B rocker epitomized what earlier rock music was all about. He screamed out his vocals, pounded his piano, and spewed forth sexually suggestive lyrics as he racked up hit after hit during the 1950s. Before he was done, Little Richard left his imprint on the new music. His style and songs became rock & roll archetypes, influencing contemporaries like Elvis Presley and Buddy Holly, as well as later rockers such as the Beatles, Creedence Clearwater Revival, and Mitch Ryder and the Detroit Wheels. Little Richard was one of the most significant artists of rock & roll's first decade, and his greatest hits are among the greatest in rock music history. He retired from rock & roll to become a minister in the early 1960s, but later returned to record new material in the late 1960s and 1970s. A year after being inducted into the Rock & Roll Hall of Fame, he turned in a fine acting performance in the 1986 comedy film, *Down and Out in Beverly Hills*. He also had a hit with "Great Gosh A'Mighty!" (MCA, #42, 1986), the theme from the movie. Little Richard's biggest hits from the 1950s include:

"Tutti-Frutti"	Specialty	#21	1956
"Long Tall Sally"	Specialty	#13	1956
"Slippin' and Slidin'"	Specialty	#33	1956
"Rip It Up"	Specialty	#27	1956
"Ready Teddy"	Specialty	#44	1956
"The Girl Can't Help It"	Specialty	#49	1957
"Lucille"	Specialty	#21	1957
"Send Me Some Lovin'"	Specialty	#54	1957
"Jenny Jenny"	Specialty	#14	1957

"Keep a Knockin' "	Specialty	#8	1957
"Good Golly, Miss Molly"	Specialty	#10	1958
"Ooh! My Soul!	Specialty	#35	1958
"Baby Face"	Specialty	#41	1958

LITTLE WILLIE JOHN   Coming out of the rhythm and blues tradition, he made the rock charts with R & B rock hits like "Fever" (King, #27, 1956), which was later done by Peggy Lee in 1958; "Talk to Me, Talk to Me" (King, #20, 1958), which was redone by Sunny and the Sunglows in 1963; and "Sleep" (King, #13, 1960).

LOCKLIN, HANK   This country and western performer reached the rock charts with "Please Help Me, I'm Falling" (RCA, #8, 1960), a song that stressed the traditional value of marital fidelity. The record's success showed the continuing influence of country music on the rock audience in the early 1960s.

LOLITA   By 1960 Germany was back in the news. Soviet Premier Khrushchev had recently proclaimed that the four-power occupation of Berlin must end. The Berlin Crisis and the building of the Berlin Wall were about to occur, while on a lighter note, soldier Elvis Presley was stationed in West Germany. In the midst of these events, Austrian pop singer Lolita released her record, "Sailor" (Kapp, #5, 1960). The song, entirely in German, rode the wave of public interest toward the top of the rock charts.

LONDON, LAURIE   This 13-year-old from England had a smash hit in the United States with "He's Got the Whole World (In His Hands)" (Capitol, #2, 1958). The immense popularity of the song reflected America's great interest in religion during the 1950s, and showed that many members of the rock & roll audience still had traditional values.

LOPEZ, TRINI   His success on the rock charts occurred at a time when Hispanic influence was on the rise in the United States. The 1950s and early 1960s witnessed the cha cha, the great popularity of *West Side Story*, the rapid growth of the Hispanic-American population, and the emergence of Fidel Castro and other Latin American leaders in international affairs. Lopez arrived on the pop music scene in 1963, powered by good looks and a high-energy performing style. He grafted Hispanic rhythms and vocals onto R & B, folk, and pop to earn hits like "If I Had a Hammer" (Reprise, #3, 1963); "Kansas City" (Reprise, #23, 1963 +); "Jailer, Bring Me Water" (Reprise, #94, 1964); and "Lemon Tree" (Reprise, #20, 1965). His live performances and prototypical folk rock style set him apart from many of the other less talented pop rock singers of the era.

LOS INDIOS TABAJARAS Another example of Hispanic influence on the rock charts in the early 1960s. These two Brazilian brothers found success with two simple, yet hauntingly beautiful, guitar instrumentals: "Maria Elena" (RCA, #6, 1963) and "Always in My Heart" (RCA, #82, 1964).

LOU, BONNIE She had a hit in 1955 with "Daddy-O" (King, #14, 1955), a song that made use of a popular teenage expression. The term also appeared in other successful pop culture ventures. In the movie *Blackboard Jungle*, kids referred to Glenn Ford's teacher character as "Daddy-O." The term was used again in the Sparkletones' 1957 hit, "Black Slacks" (i.e., "Black slacks make you cool, Daddy-O").

LOUDERMILK, JOHN D. Although he achieved some success in 1961 as a singer with "Language of Love" (RCA, #32, 1961), he is best known for the top-quality country rock hits he wrote for others. Among his best-known compositions are "A Rose and a Baby Ruth" and "Abilene" (recorded by George Hamilton IV); "Norman" (Sue Thompson); "Angela Jones" (Johnny Ferguson); "Ebony Eyes" (the Everly Brothers); "Stayin' In" (Bobby Vee); "Waterloo" (Stonewall Jackson); and "Tobacco Road" (the Nashville Teens). Loudermilk also had a hit, "Sittin' in the Balcony" (Colonial, #38, 1957), recorded under the name Johnny Dee.

LOVE, DARLENE Her career is linked with record producer Phil Spector. After signing with his record company to sing on various recordings, she wound up singing lead on the Crystals' "He's a Rebel," a Spector-produced single that hit number one in 1962. At Spector's request she joined Bob B. Soxx and the Blue Jeans and sang lead on their hit, "Zip-a-Dee-Doo-Dah," also in 1962. The following year, Darlene Love achieved success on her own with three R & B rock hits produced by Phil Spector: "Today I Met the Boy I'm Gonna Marry" (Philles, #39, 1963); "Wait 'Til My Bobby Gets Home" (Philles, #26, 1963); and "A Fine, Fine Boy" (Philles, #53, 1963).

LOWE, JIM This disc jockey turned pop singer had three big hits on the rock charts in 1956 and 1957: "The Green Door" (Dot, #1, 1956); "Four Walls" (Dot, #15, 1957); and "Talkin' to the Blues" (Dot, #20, 1957).

LUCAS, MATT He had a minor hit in 1963 with a country-influenced pop rock song called "I'm Movin' On" (Smash, #56, 1963).

LUKE, ROBIN His composition "Susie Darlin'" (Dot, #5, 1958) was one of the most interesting hits of 1958. Unlike many pop rock songs that dealt with girls' names, this one had an authentic folk quality. The record was a dynamic pop rocker that featured use of an echo chamber, amplified guitar riffs, and Luke's excellent lead vocal, which was reminiscent of Buddy Holly's rockabilly style.

LUMAN, BOB Another one-hit artist. He had a Top 10 single with "Let's Think About Living" (Warner, #7, 1960). Done in a country and western style, the record urged the listener to forget social problems and to concentrate on love and living, a belief shared by many during the socially and politically apathetic 1950s.

LYMAN, ARTHUR This Hawaiian musician's biggest hit was "Yellow Bird" (Hi Fi, #4, 1961), an exotic-sounding pop instrumental with a Caribbean flavor along the lines of Martin Denny's earlier hit, "Quiet Village."

LYMON, FRANKIE, AND THE TEENAGERS Featuring 12-year-old Frankie Lymon as the lead singer, they were the prototypes for later groups like the Osmonds and the Jackson Five. Their first hit was the 1956 R & B rock classic, "Why Do Fools Fall in Love?" (Gee, #7, 1956). Other hits included "I Want You to Be My Girl" (Gee, #13, 1956); "The ABC's of Love" (Gee, #77, 1956); "Goody Goody" (Gee, #20, 1957); and "Little Bitty Pretty One" (Roulette, #58, 1960). Their songs, a blend of R & B rock and pop rock, were aimed directly at the young teen audience.

LYNN, BARBARA Her only hit came in 1962 with the R & B–influenced "You'll Lose a Good Thing" (Jamie, #8, 1962).

McCRACKLIN, JIMMY A rhythm and blues artist from the 1950s whose biggest hit was "The Walk" (Checker, #7, 1958). The song became a dance craze after it was performed by teenagers on "American Bandstand."

McDANIELS, GENE Although he came out of a gospel background, his sound in the early 1960s was closer to pop rock. His first hit, "A Hundred Pounds of Clay" (Liberty, #3, 1961), maintained that God had created woman out of clay to provide "lots of lovin' for a man." The lyrics offer an interesting look at contemporary beliefs regarding religion, romance, and the role of women in society. He followed up with other hits such as "A Tear" (Liberty, #31, 1961); "Tower of Strength" (Liberty, #5, 1961); "Chip Chip" (Liberty, #10, 1962); and "Point of No Return" (Liberty, #21, 1962). McDaniels' records were produced by Snuff Garrett, who also was responsible for hits by many other pop rock artists, including Bobby Vee and Gary Lewis and the Playboys.

McFADDEN, BOB, AND DOR They had some success in 1959 with a novelty record called "The Mummy" (Brunswick, #39, 1959).

THE McGUIRE SISTERS These pop singers gained fame as regulars on Arthur Godfrey's TV show in the mid-1950s. They had their first hit record with a cover version of the Spaniels' "Goodnight, Sweetheart, Goodnight" (Coral, 1954). The following year they earned the biggest hit of their career with a cover of the Moonglows's "Sincerely" (Coral, #1, 1955). They later made the rock charts with "He" (Coral, #12, 1955); "Goodnight, My Love" (Coral, #32, 1956 +); "Sugartime" (Coral, #1, 1957 +); "May You Always" (Coral, #11, 1959); and "Just for Old Time's Sake" (Coral, #20, 1961). Their great success reflected the continuing popularity of traditional pop throughout the early years of rock & roll.

MACK, LONNIE: In 1963 this country and western guitarist had a big hit with an instrumental version of Chuck Berry's "Memphis" (Fraternity, #5, 1963).

McKUEN, ROD He is best known as a pop poet from the late 1960s and 1970s, but he did try his hand at rock & roll in the early 1960s. He had a minor hit with "Oliver Twist" (Spiral, #76, 1962), a pop rock song that tried to capitalize on the Twist dance craze.

McLEAN, PHIL His only hit record was "Small Sad Sam" (Versatile, #21, 1961 +), a parody of Jimmy Dean's "Big Bad John."

McPHATTER, CLYDE He started his career singing rhythm and blues with Billy Ward and the Dominoes. In 1953 he helped form the Drifters (who, after splitting with McPhatter, enjoyed considerable success with songs like "There Goes My Baby" and "Under the Boardwalk"). McPhatter launched his solo career in 1954, and went on to record rock & roll classics like "A Lover's Question" and "Lover Please." His contribution to early rock earned him induction into the Rock & Roll Hall of Fame in 1986. His biggest hits include:

"Treasure of Love"	Atlantic	#22	1956
"Just to Hold My Hand"	Atlantic	#30	1957
"A Lover's Question"	Atlantic	#6	1958 +
"Lovey Dovey"	Atlantic	#49	1959
"Ta Ta"	Mercury	#23	1960
"Lover Please"	Mercury	#7	1962
"Little Bitty Pretty One"	Mercury	#25	1962

MAESTRO, JOHNNY Former lead singer of the Crests, also known as Johnny Mastro. He had two pop rock hits in 1961: "Model Girl" (Coed, #20, 1961), which reflected contemporary stereotypes of women; and "What a Surprise" (Coed, #33, 1961).

MAHARIS, GEORGE He rode to fame as the handsome Buz Murdock character on TV's "Route 66." Like many other TV idols of the period (e.g., Ricky Nelson, Edd Byrnes, Paul Petersen), he tried to transfer his popularity to pop music. Maharis found the new road too rough to handle, although he did reach the Top 30 with "Teach Me Tonight" (Epic, #25, 1962).

THE MAJORS This R & B rock group had one big hit, "A Wonderful Dream" (Imperial, #22, 1962).

MANCINI, HENRY The long-term success of this musician/composer/arranger/conductor provides ample evidence that not all teenagers were rebellious in the 1960s or years thereafter. Many members of the rock & roll audience enjoyed listening to the soft pop music of their parents' generation. Mancini's early hits included "Mr. Lucky" (RCA, #21, 1960), the theme from the TV show of the same name, and "Moon River" (RCA, #11, 1961), from the movie *Breakfast at Tiffany's*. Most of his later hits were title themes from movies, e.g., "Days of Wine and Roses" (RCA, #33, 1963); "Charade" (RCA, #36, 1963+); *"The Pink Panther Theme"* (RCA, #31, 1964); "Love Theme from *Romeo and Juliet*" (RCA, #1, 1969); and "Theme from *Love Story*" (RCA, #13, 1971).

MANN, BARRY In 1961 he had a hit with "Who Put the Bomp (In the Bomp, Bomp, Bomp)?" (ABC/Paramount, #7, 1961), a well-crafted novelty record that parodied doo wop. Mann was also one of the most talented songwriters of the early 1960s. He wrote or co-wrote (mostly with his wife Cynthia Weil) numerous pop rock hits, including rock & roll classics such as "The Bristol Stomp" for the Dovells; "I'm Gonna Be Strong" and "Looking Through the Eyes of Love" for Gene Pitney; "Swingin' School" and "Wild One" for Bobby Rydell; "Come Back Silly Girl" for the Lettermen; "You've Lost That Lovin' Feeling" and "Soul and Inspiration" for the Righteous Brothers; "Kicks" and "Hungry" for Paul Revere and the Raiders; and "Footsteps" for Steve Lawrence.

MANN, CARL His biggest hit came in 1959 with a country rock version of the Nat King Cole song, "Mona Lisa" (Phillips, #25, 1959).

MANN, GLORIA In 1955 this pop singer reached the number 24 position on the best-seller charts with a cover of the Penguins' R & B rock ballad, "Earth Angel" (Sound, 1955). The next year she scored again with "Teen-Age Prayer" (Sound, #21, 1955+), another youth-oriented song.

MANTOVANI Known for lush orchestral arrangements, Mantovani and his orchestra had several hits on the rock charts during the late 1950s and early 1960s. All themes from popular movies of the day, the hits included "Around the World" (London, #12, 1957); "Theme from *The Sundowners*" (London, #93, 1960); and "Main Theme from *Exodus*" (London, #31, 1960+).

THE MARATHONS This R & B rock group also recorded as the Vibrations and the Jayhawks. They started out as the Jayhawks with the hit, "Stranded in the Jungle" (1956). After changing their name to the Marathons, they made the rock charts again with "Peanut Butter" (Arvee, #20, 1961), a catchy R & B rock song about a popular food. Then, singing as the Vibrations, they

43. The Fleetwoods (Ball State University Photo Service)

44. The Four Seasons (Courtesy of Vee Jay Records)

45. Jerry Lee Lewis (Courtesy of Sun Records)

46. The Moonglows, from the movie *Mister Rock and Roll,* which also starred disc jockey Alan Freed (Courtesy of MCA Records)

47. "Million Dollar Quartet": Jerry Lee Lewis, Carl Perkins, Elvis Presley, and Johnny Cash (Courtesy of Sun Records)

48. The Righteous Brothers (Courtesy of Vee Jay Records)

49. Del Shannon (Ball State University Photo Service)

50. Bobby Vee (Ball State University Photo Service)

added two more hits: "The Watusi" (Checker, #25, 1961) and "My Girl Sloopy" (Atlantic, #26, 1964).

THE MARCELS   They had two smash hits in 1961. Their first was an enormously popular doo wop version of the Rodgers and Hart classic, "Blue Moon" (Colpix, #1, 1961). They applied the same treatment to "Heartaches" (Colpix, #7, 1961), a Guy Lombardo hit from the 1930s, and the result was another big hit. Both records were outrageous blends of R & B rock and traditional pop, and appealed to teens who liked pop but still wanted music that sounded like rock & roll.

MARCH, LITTLE PEGGY   Her records are good examples of the slick, formula pop rock that was mass produced for the teen market by the early 1960s. Her first record, "I Will Follow Him" (RCA, #1, 1963), reflected the traditional belief that males should dominate females. Her follow-up hit, "I Wish I Were a Princess" (RCA, #32, 1963), also reflected the sexual stereotypes and fantasies of the day. Her last big hit, "Hello Heartache, Goodbye Love" (RCA, #26, 1963), dealt with typical teen interests in love and romance.

MARCHAN, BOBBY   An R & B rock singer of the late 1950s and early 1960s. His initial success came as part of the group Huey Smith and the Clowns, with songs such as "Don't You Just Know It?" (1958) and "Don't You Know Yockomo" (1958). Later as a solo artist, he had a Top 40 hit with "There's Something on Your Mind" (Fire, #31, 1960).

MARESCA, ERNIE   His big hit of 1962, "Shout! Shout! (Knock Yourself Out)" (Seville, #6, 1962), is an excellent example of the authentic, folk-quality pop rock that was still being produced in the early 1960s. This high-energy song reflected teen interest in dancing, parties, and rock & roll. Maresca was also a successful song writer and helped write many hits for Dion and Dion and the Belmonts. His credits include Dion's "Runaround Sue" and "The Wanderer."

THE MARK IV   This Chicago quartet's biggest hit was the novelty record "I Got a Wife" (Mercury, #24, 1959), a pop rock song that reflected contemporary humor about marriage.

THE MARKETTS This West Coast instrumental group had several pop rock hits in the early and mid 1960s. Their first two "Surfer's Stomp" (Liberty, #31, 1962) and "Balboa Blue" (Liberty, #48, 1962), reflected the popularity of the surfing craze. Their last two, "Out of Limits" (Warner, #3, 1963+) and "Batman Theme" (Warner, #17, 1966), were themes from two popular TV shows of the era.

THE MAR-KEYS Their biggest hit was "Last Night" (Satellite, #3, 1961), an R & B rock instrumental that sounded like backup music for bump and grind dancers at the local strip-tease joint. The record featured a wicked sax riff that oozed sexuality, and was punctuated every once in a while by a lusty voice that groaned, "Aah, last night." The song quickly became a favorite with teens and garage bands across the country. Other hits by the Mar-Keys included "Morning After" (Stax, #60, 1961) and dance-related songs like "Pop-Eye Strut" (Stax, #94, 1962) and "Philly Dog" (Stax, #89, 1966). The Mar-Keys doubled as the early house band for the fledgling Stax Records in Memphis, and two members of the group, Steve Cropper and Donald Dunn, later joined Booker T. and the MG's.

MARTERIE, RALPH This pop musician got his start playing trumpet with Paul Whiteman and Percy Faith. By the 1950s he was enjoying considerable success with his own band. He first crossed paths with rock & roll in 1953 when he did a cover version of Bill Haley's "Crazy, Man, Crazy" (Mercury, 1953). Listening to it now, one is struck by the incongruity of the record. Like water and oil, Marterie's 1940s Big Band sound and Haley's rock & roll song just don't mix. Yet, at the time, many teenagers bought the record, thinking it was "cool" rock & roll. Marterie's later hits included "Tricky" (Mercury, #25, 1957) and "Shish-Kebab" (Mercury, #10, 1957).

MARTHA & THE VANDELLAS One of the better girl groups of the early and mid 1960s, they came out of the Motown stable to record some of the finest R & B rock of the era. Their style epitomized the "Motown Sound"—a slickly produced, commercial blend of R & B rock and pop—which became extremely popular among whites in an era when the civil rights movement was drawing attention to black music and culture. Their biggest hits included:

"Come and Get These Memories"	Gordy	#29	1963
"Heat Wave"	Gordy	#4	1963
"Quicksand"	Gordy	#8	1963 +
"Live Wire"	Gordy	#42	1964
"Dancing in the Street"	Gordy	#2	1964
"Wild One"	Gordy	#34	1964 +
"Nowhere to Run"	Gordy	#8	1965
"My Baby Loves Me"	Gordy	#22	1966
"I'm Ready for Love"	Gordy	#9	1966
"Jimmy Mack"	Gordy	#10	1967
"Honey Chile"	Gordy	#11	1967

MARTIN, DEAN   Starting out as half of the Dean Martin and Jerry Lewis comedy act, Martin later enjoyed success as a pop singer. Unlike most pop singers of the 1950s, Martin continued to make hit records even after the arrival of rock & roll. His long-term success shows that many members of the rock audience continued to appreciate traditional pop songs, and may indicate that many of the kids who grew up on Martin and Lewis retained a warm place in their hearts for the performer when they became teenagers and adults. After Martin moved to Frank Sinatra's Reprise label, most of his hit records were produced by former country rock star Jimmy Bowen. Some of his best-selling records were:

"Memories Are Made of This"	Capitol	#1	1955 +
"Return to Me"	Capitol	#4	1958
"Angel Baby"	Capitol	#30	1958
"Volare"	Capitol	#12	1958
"On An Evening in Roma"	Capitol	#59	1959
"Everybody Loves Somebody"	Reprise	#1	1964
"The Door Is Still Open to My Heart"	Reprise	#6	1964
"You're Nobody Till Somebody Loves You"	Reprise	#25	1964 +
"Send Me the Pillow You Dream On"	Reprise	#22	1965
"Houston"	Reprise	#21	1965
"I Will"	Reprise	#10	1965

MARTIN, TRADE   He had a hit record with "That Stranger Used to Be My Girl" (Coed, #28, 1962), a pop rock song dealing with teen romance and broken hearts.

MARTIN, VINCE, AND THE TARRIERS   Their blend of pop and folk earned them a hit with "Cindy, Oh Cindy" (Glory, #12, 1956), which reflected the public's interest in Calypso music in 1956. Two of the Tarriers later graduated to bigger things. Alan Arkin became a popular movie actor, while Erik Darling joined the Rooftop Singers and had a number one record in 1962, "Walk Right In."

MARTINDALE, WINK   In 1959 his record "Deck of Cards" (Dot, #7, 1959) broke into the Top 10 charts on rock stations across the country. The song dealt with gambling and God, and reflected contemporary interest in religion. Martindale later went on to become a popular TV game show host.

MARTINO, AL   This pop singer's career began in the early 1950s. His biggest hits on the rock charts were "I Love You Because" (Capitol, #3, 1963); "Painted, Tainted Rose" (Capitol, #15, 1963); "I Love You More and More Every Day" (Capitol, #9, 1964); "Tears and Roses" (Capitol, #20, 1964); "Spanish Eyes" (Capitol, #15, 1965 +); "Mary in the Morning" (Capitol, #27, 1967); and "To the Door of the Sun" (Capitol, #17, 1974). His success, like that of other pop singers from the era, shows that many teenagers in the 1960s and 1970s still retained traditional values and musical tastes.

THE MARVELETTES   Like other top girl groups from the early 1960s, their sound and style had an implicit sexuality. Their biggest hit, "Please Mr. Postman" (Tamla, #1, 1961), was Motown's first number one record. They followed up with "Twistin' Postman" (Tamla, #34, 1962), which reflected the popularity of the Twist dance craze. Next came two hits that employed traditional sexual stereotypes: "Playboy" (Tamla, #7, 1962) and "Beechwood 4-5789" (Tamla, #17, 1962). Their other best sellers included solid R & B rock songs like "Too Many Fish in the Sea" (Tamla, #25, 1964 +); "Don't Mess with Bill" (Tamla, #7, 1966); "The Hunter Gets Captured By the Game" (Tamla, #13, 1967); and "My Baby Must Be a Magician" (Tamla, #17, 1967 +).

MARVIN AND JOHNNY   This R & B rock duo had minor success with "Cherry Pie" (Modern, 1954) and "Tick Tock" (Modern, 1954). In 1960 "Cherry Pie" became an even bigger hit for Skip and Flip.

MASTRO, JOHNNY *See* Maestro, Johnny.

MATHIS, JOHNNY He was the king of mood music during rock & roll's first decade. His hit singles and albums were perfect for slow dancing and making out, two favorite teen pastimes. They also reflected the continuing popularity of traditional pop on the rock charts. Among his most popular hits were:

"Wonderful! Wonderful!"	Columbia	#17	1957
"It's Not for Me to Say"	Columbia	#5	1957
"Chances Are"	Columbia	#5	1957
"The Twelfth of Never"	Columbia	#51	1957
"No Love But Your Love"	Columbia	#48	1957+
"Teacher Teacher"	Columbia	#43	1958
"A Certain Smile"	Columbia	#19	1958
"Call Me"	Columbia	#21	1958
"Small World"	Columbia	#20	1959
"Misty"	Columbia	#12	1959
"Starbright"	Columbia	#25	1960
"Maria"	Columbia	#78	1960
"Gina"	Columbia	#6	1962
"What Will Mary Say"	Columbia	#9	1963
"Too Much, Too Little, Too Late" (duet with Deniece Williams)	Columbia	#1	1978
"Friends In Love" (duet with Dionne Warwick)	Arista	#38	1982

THE MATYS BROTHERS They had a hit with "Who Stole the Keeshka?" (Select, #55, 1963), a novelty song about Polish food. The record sparked teen interest in the polka, coming at a time when teenagers were interested in various dances such as the Twist, the Fly, and the Mashed Potatoes.

MAYER, NATHANIEL This R & B rock artist had a hit in 1962 with "Village of Love" (Fortune, #22, 1962).

MEADER, VAUGHN This comedian and impressionist received a lot of airplay in the early 1960s for his best-selling album, *The First Family*. It satirized the new president, John F. Kennedy, and various members of his family. The great success of his album, and its play on rock & roll stations, reflected the emergence of JFK as a media star and youth hero by the early 1960s.

THE MEGATONS They had one minor hit, "Shimmy, Shimmy Walk, Part I" (Checker, #88, 1962), a song that tried to capitalize on the popularity of new dance crazes in 1962. The name of the group also reflected public awareness of nuclear bombs in an era marked by the Berlin Crisis and Cuban Missile Crisis.

THE MEGATRONS These studio musicians' only hit came in 1959 with "Velvet Waters" (Accousticon, #55, 1959).

THE MELLO-KINGS This pop rock group found success in 1957 with a doo wop song, "Tonight, Tonight" (Herald, #77, 1957). They also had several other regional hits that never made the national charts: "Sassafras" (Herald, 1957); "Baby Tell Me" (Herald, 1958); and "Valerie" (Herald, 1958).

THE MELLO-TONES Their only hit, "Rosie Lee" (Gee, #24, 1957), was typical of early rock & roll songs about girls' names.

THE MELODEERS A pop rock group of the early 1960s. Their doo wop version of "Rudolph the Red Nosed Reindeer" (Studio, #71, 1960) was a minor hit during the 1960 Christmas season.

MICKEY AND SYLVIA This R & B rock duo had a smash hit with "Love Is Strange" (Groove, #13, 1957), featuring fine rhythm and blues guitar riffs and sexually suggestive lyrics. They followed up with "There Oughta Be a Law" (Vik, #47, 1957) and Dearest" (Vik, #85, 1957). In 1973 Sylvia staged a brief comeback with "Pillow Talk" (Vibration, #3, 1973), using the same erotic delivery that gained her notoriety with "Love Is Strange."

MILES, GARRY His hit, "Look for a Star" (Liberty, #16, 1960), was taken from the movie *Circus of Horrors*. The song, and Miles' style, typified formula pop rock of the early 1960s.

MILLER, CLINT He had a minor hit with "Bertha Lou" (ABC/Paramount, #79, 1958). Even when this record first came out, it was difficult to tell whether it was a parody of rock & roll songs about girls' names or simply another formula pop rock song.

MILLER, NED His biggest hit was a country and western–influenced song called "From a Jack to a King" (Fabor, #6, 1962 +).

MILLS, HAYLEY The daughter of British actor John Mills, Hayley first achieved success starring in a series of Walt Disney movies. Her popularity transferred over to the rock charts through hits such as "Let's Get Together" (Vista, #8, 1961), which was from the film *The Parent Trap;* and "Johnny Jingo" (Vista, #21, 1962). Her songs epitomized the pleasant-sounding formula pop rock of the early 1960s.

THE MILLS BROTHERS Even this famous 1940s vocal group tried to capitalize on the growing teen market during the mid-1950s. They had a medium-sized hit with "Queen of the Senior Prom" (Decca, #39, 1957). Their follow-up, a cover of the Silhouettes' number one hit record, "Get a Job", failed to make the national charts.

MIMMS, GARNET, AND THE ENCHANTERS The authentic, gospel-influenced sound of this R & B rock group paved the way for their success in the early 1960s. They first made the rock charts in 1963 with "Cry Baby" (United Artists, #4, 1963), and followed with a two-sided hit: "Baby Don't You Weep" (United Artists, #30, 1963) backed with "For Your Precious Love" (United Artists, #26, 1963 +).

MINEO, SAL His greatest success came as an actor, appearing in Broadway hits such as *The Rose Tatoo* and *The King and I,* as well as in movies like *Rebel Without a Cause, Exodus,* and *Cheyenne Autumn.* But he also enjoyed some success as a recording artist with several hit records aimed at the teen audience, including "Start Movin'" (Epic, #10, 1957); "Lasting Love" (Epic, #35, 1957); and "Party Time" (Epic, #47, 1957).

THE MIRACLES Led by lead singer Smokey Robinson, they became one of the super groups of the 1960s and early 1970s, with hits like "Shop Around," "You've Really Got a Hold on Me," and "Mickey's Monkey." Their music reflected teen interest in dancing and romance and helped establish the Motown sound. Their well-crafted songs, many of which were written by Robinson, featured tight harmonies and soulful lyrics. The records were slickly produced hybrids of R & B rock and pop, and appealed to many whites whose consciousness of black music and culture had been raised by the growing civil rights movement of the early 1960s. The group, recognizing the importance of lead singer and writer

Smokey Robinson, changed its name to Smokey Robinson and the Miracles in 1967. After Robinson retired in 1972, the Miracles went on to record several more big hits, including "Do It Baby" (1974) and "Love Machine (Part I)" (1975+). Robinson later returned as a solo act with many hits in the 1970s and 1980s, including "Cruisin'" (1979+) and "Being With You" (1981). Smokey Robinson was elected to the Rock & Roll Hall of Fame in 1986. The Miracles' greatest hits from the 1960s and early 1970s include:

"Shop Around"	Tamla	#2	1960+
"What's So Good About Good-By"	Tamla	#35	1962
"I'll Try Something New"	Tamla	#39	1962
"You've Really Got a Hold on Me"	Tamla	#8	1962+
"A Love She Can Count On"	Tamla	#31	1963
"Mickey's Monkey"	Tamla	#8	1963
"I Gotta Dance to Keep from Crying"	Tamla	#35	1963+
"I Like It Like That"	Tamla	#27	1964
"That's What Love Is Made Of"	Tamla	#35	1964
"Ooo Baby Baby"	Tamla	#16	1965
"The Tracks of My Tears"	Tamla	#16	1965
"My Girl Has Gone"	Tamla	#14	1965
"Going To a Go-Go"	Tamla	#11	1965+
"I'm the One You Need"	Tamla	#17	1966
"The Love I Saw in You Was Just a Mirage"	Tamla	#20	1967
"I Second That Emotion"	Tamla	#4	1967
"If You Can Want"	Tamla	#11	1968
"Baby, Baby Don't Cry"	Tamla	#8	1969
"The Tears of a Clown"	Tamla	#1	1970

THE CHAD MITCHELL TRIO Another example of the emerging pop folk of the early 1960s. Among their best-known records were "Lizzie Borden" (Kapp, #44, 1962) and "The Marvelous Toy" (Mercury, #43, 1963+).

MITCHELL, GUY He began his career as a pop singer in the 1940s. By the mid-1950s he was recording material aimed at the growing teen market. His hit records were a lively blend of country rock and pop. His top sellers included "Singing the Blues" (Columbia, #1, 1956); "Knee Deep in the Blues" (Columbia, #16, 1957); "Rock-A-Billy" (Columbia, #13, 1957); and "Heartaches By the Number" (Columbia, #1, 1959).

MITCHUM, ROBERT This veteran movie and TV actor made the rock charts in 1958 with "The Ballad of Thunder Road" (Capitol, #62, 1958), taken from his movie of the same name. The song was re-released in 1962, and again became a minor hit.

MODUGNO, DOMENICO In 1958 this Italian pop singer had the biggest hit of the year, "Nel Blu Dipinto Di Blu (Volare)" (Decca, #1, 1958). Although sung entirely in Italian, the song had a memorable melody and a catchy refrain. Soon teenagers, like adults, were enjoying and buying the record—providing evidence that many members of the rock audience and adults shared similar tastes.

THE MONARCHS Their hit, "Look Homeward Angel" (Sound Stage, #47, 1964), is a good example of an early 1960s pop rock ballad.

THE MONOTONES They only had one hit, "Book of Love" (Argo, #5, 1958), but it became one of rock & roll's all-time classics. The song features a fast dance beat and lyrics about romance. Listening to it now, one can almost imagine teenagers standing on a city street corner, singing primitive harmonies while banging out the beat on a garbage can. It was simple, folk-oriented doo wop at its best.

MONRO, MATT A British pop singer who had some success on American rock charts with traditional pop hits like "My Kind of Girl" (Warwick, #18, 1961) and "Walk Away" (Liberty, #23, 1964+).

MONROE, VAUGHN This 1940s vintage pop singer tried his hand at rock & roll in the mid 1950s. His most successful venture into the teen market was "Black Denim Trousers and Motorcycle Boots" (RCA, #38, 1955).

MONTE, LOU He had several novelty hits in the late 1950s and early 1960s, including "Lazy Mary" (RCA, #12, 1958); "The Sheik of Araby" (RCA, #54, 1958); "Pepino the Italian Mouse" (Reprise, #5, 1962+); and "Pepino's Friend Pasqual (The Italian Pussy Cat)" (Reprise, #78, 1963). The songs, all reflecting contemporary stereotypes of Italians, received a lot of air play on "American Bandstand" and became teenage favorites.

MONTEZ, CHRIS He first arrived on the rock scene in 1962 with a fast-paced rocker called "Let's Dance" (Monogram, #4, 1962), which celebrated the Twist, the Stomp, the Mashed Potato, and other teen dances. Although the ballad on the flip side, "You're the One," did not become a hit, it, too, was an example of excellent pop rock in the early 1960s. Later, Montez came under the influence of Herb Alpert, and began recording more middle-of-the-road pop songs, such as "Call Me" (A&M, #22, 1966); "The More I See You" (A&M, #16, 1966); "There Will Never Be Another You" (A&M, #33, 1966); and "Time After Time" (A&M, #36, 1966).

THE MOONGLOWS This early R & B rock group had several hits, including "Sincerely" (Chess, #20 on the Jukebox Charts, 1955); "See Saw" (Chess, #28, 1956); and "Ten Commandments of Love" (Chess, #22, 1958). The latter song, which reflected the traditional values of many teenagers, remains a classic example of 1950s doo wop.

MOORE, BOB He began as a studio musician, working on records by Elvis Presley, Roy Orbison, and other country rockers. In 1961 he had an instrumental hit with "Mexico" (Monument, #7, 1961).

MORISETTE, JOHNNY This R & B rock singer had a minor hit, "Meet Me at the Twistin' Place" (Sar, #63, 1962), which reflected the popularity of that dance craze in 1962.

THE MORMON TABERNACLE CHOIR They actually made it to the rock charts in 1959 with a stirring version of "The Battle Hymn of the Republic" (Columbia, #13, 1959), backed by the Philadelphia Orchestra. The song's tremendous popularity was an indication of public interest in God and country in the late 1950s.

MOZART QUINTET, MICKEY Their only hit came in 1959 with a jazz-influenced song, "Little Dipper" (Roulette, #30, 1959).

MURAD'S HARMONICATS, JERRY These pop performers reached the rock charts with a harmonica version of "Cherry Pink and Apple Blossom White" (Columbia, #56, 1960+).

THE MURMAIDS This all-girl trio almost made it to the top of the rock charts with "Popsicles and Icicles" (Chattahoochee, #3,

1963 +), a pleasant pop rock song that plugged into teen interests and childhood memories. The song was composed by David Gates, who later became the driving force behind the rock group, Bread.

MYLES, BILLY He made the Top 30 with "The Joker" (Ember, #30, 1957), an R & B rock song.

THE MYSTICS Their only big hit was "Hushabye" (Laurie, #20, 1959), an excellent pop rock record that combined doo wop harmonies with a pop sound. The song, ostensibly about teen romance, is just one of many rock & roll records that employed childhood imagery or themes.

NELSON, RICKY One of rock & roll's early superstars and original teen idols. He first gained national attention as the young, wisecracking son on "Ozzie and Harriet," a popular TV show of the 1950s and early 1960s. After Ricky sang a cover version of Fats Domino's "I'm Walkin'" on the show in 1957, the song zoomed onto the Top 20 rock charts. That marked the beginning of Nelson's extremely successful rock & roll career. Over the next six years, he racked up 30 hits on the Top 30 charts. No doubt his success was aided by weekly TV exposure and a clean-cut image that appealed to many white, middle-class teens. Yet Nelson was not simply a media creation. He could rock with the best of them, as evidenced by such hits as "Believe What You Say," "My Bucket's Got a hole in It," or "Hello Mary Lou" (which was written by Gene Pitney), and then turn right around and croon out excellent ballads like "Poor Little Fool," "Lonesome Town," or "Travelin' Man." Many of his top hits are now considered rock & roll classics. His music had an authentic folk quality—it was rockabilly with a suburban touch. Nelson's records, which featured top rock musicians such as James Burton on lead guitar, Joe Osborne on bass, and Richie Frost on drums, generally reflected teen interest in dating and romance.

Although Ricky Nelson's career faded after he switched to the Decca label and began making more pop-oriented records, he did make a comeback in the late 1960s and 1970s with several excellent hit singles (e.g., "She Belongs to Me," "Garden Party," "Easy to Be Free") and albums that blended rock, country, and folk. He and his backup group, the Stone Canyon Band, died in a 1985 plane crash on New Year's Eve near DeKalb, Texas. The following year Ricky Nelson was inducted posthumously into the Rock & Roll Hall of Fame. His greatest hits include:

"I'm Walkin'"	Verve	#17	1957
"A Teenager's Romance"	Verve	#8	1957
"You're My One and Only One"	Verve	#14	1957
"Be-Bop Baby"	Imperial	#5	1957
"Have I Told You Lately That I Love You"	Imperial	#29	1957
"Stood Up"	Imperial	#5	1957+
"Waitin' in School"	Imperial	#18	1957+
"Believe What You Say"	Imperial	#4	1958
"My Bucket's Got a Hole in It"	Imperial	#18	1958
"Poor Little Fool"	Imperial	#1	1958
"Lonesome Town"	Imperial	#7	1958
"I Got a Feeling"	Imperial	#10	1958
"Never Be Anyone Else But You"	Imperial	#6	1959
"It's Late"	Imperial	#9	1959
"Just a Little Too Much"	Imperial	#9	1959
"Sweeter Than You"	Imperial	#9	1959
"I Wanna Be Loved"	Imperial	#20	1959
"Mighty Good"	Imperial	#38	1959
"Young Emotions	Imperial	#12	1960
"I'm Not Afraid"	Imperial	#27	1960
"Yes Sir, That's My Baby"	Imperial	#34	1960
"You Are the Only One"	Imperial	#25	1960+
"Travelin' Man"	Imperial	#1	1961
"Hello Mary Lou"	Imperial	#9	1961
"A Wonder Like You"	Imperial	#11	1961
"Everlovin'"	Imperial	#16	1961
"Young World"	Imperial	#5	1962
"Teenage Idol"	Imperial	#5	1962
"It's Up to You"	Imperial	#6	1962+
"That's All"	Imperial	#48	1963
"String Along"	Decca	#25	1963
"Fools Rush In"	Decca	#12	1963
"For You"	Decca	#6	1963+
"The Very Thought of You"	Decca	#26	1964
"There's Nothing I Can Say"	Decca	#47	1964
"She Belongs to Me"	Decca	#33	1969+
"Easy to Be Free"	Decca	#48	1970
"Garden Party"	Decca	#6	1972
"Palace Guard"	MCA	#65	1973

NELSON, SANDY This drummer had several outstanding instrumental pop rock hits, including "Teen Beat" (Original Sound, #4, 1959); "Let There Be Drums" (Imperial, #7, 1961); and "Drums Are My Beat" (Imperial, #29, 1962).

THE NEW CHRISTY MINSTRELS Named after Edwin P. Christy's Minstrels of the late nineteenth century, they were formed in 1962 by folk singer Randy Sparks. Their biggest hits were "Green Green" (Columbia, #14, 1963); "Saturday Night" (Columbia, #29 1963); and "Today" (Columbia, #17, 1964). Their success occurred at a time when folk music was on the rise, and foreshadowed the popular folk movement of the mid to late 1960s. One of the group's members, Barry McGuire (whose raspy lead vocal was featured on "Green, Green"), later had a number one hit with "Eve of Destruction" (1965).

NEWTON, WAYNE Bobby Darin produced Newton's first hit, "Heart" (Capitol, #82, 1963), a well-done pop rock song aimed at teen romance. His follow-up, "Danke Schoen" (Capitol, #13, 1963), was closer to the pop mainstream and launched his career as a traditional pop artist. Many other hits followed, including "Red Roses for a Blue Lady" (Capitol, #23, 1965) and "Daddy Don't You Walk So Fast" (Chelsea, #4, 1972), as Wayne Newton established himself as one of the top acts in Las Vegas.

NINO & THE EBB TIDES They had some success in the early 1960s with pop rock hits like "Those Oldies But Goodies" (Madison, 1961) and "Juke Box Saturday Night" (Madison, #57, 1961). Both reflected teen interest in collecting and remembering old rock & roll records.

NITZSCHE, JACK He earned his rock & roll stripes as a musical arranger for Phil Spector. In 1963 he had an instrumental hit of his own, "The Lonely Surfer" (Reprise, #39, 1963), which reflected the surf fad of the day. He later did production work for Neil Young and other rock artists on the West coast.

NOGUEZ, JACKY His recording "Ciao, Ciao Bambino" (Jamie, #24, 1959) rode up the rock charts on the coattails of Domenico Modugno's smash hit of 1958, "Nel Blu Dipinto Di Blu (Volare)." Teenagers, like adults, were caught up in the craze for Italian music.

NORMAN, JIMMY Norman's gritty R & B–influenced vocal made "I Don't Love You No More" (Little Star, #47, 1962) one of the more interesting pop rock hits of 1962.

NORVOUS, NERVOUS: In 1956 Nervous (Jimmy Drake) had a big hit with "Transfusion" (Dot, #13, 1956), a novelty record about a car crash. The song, with its automobile subject and black humor about transfusions and victims (e.g., "shoot the juice to me, Bruce"), became quite popular among teenagers and adults. His follow-up hit was another novelty record, "Ape Call" (Dot, #28, 1956).

THE NUTMEGS Their doo wop style brought them success with "Story Untold" (Herald, 1955) and "Ship of Love" (Herald, 1955), two songs focusing on dating and romance.

THE NU TORNADOS Their only hit record, "Philadelphia, U.S.A." (Carlton, #26, 1958), reflected teen interests in dancing, as well as Philadelphia's reputation as a rock & roll mecca, since "American Bandstand" originated there.

THE NUTTY SQUIRRELS Capitalizing on David Seville's "Chipmunk Song," they speeded up their voices, like the Chipmunks, and found success with a novelty pop rock record called "Uh! Oh! Part 2" (Hanover, #14, 1959).

OLSON, ROCKY His recording of "Kansas City" (Chess, #60, 1959), which featured a gravelly lead vocal, was released at the same time as Wilbert Harrison's version. But the Harrison record became the bigger hit, climbing all the way to number one.

THE OLYMPICS Their novelty hit, "Western Movies" (Demon, #8, 1958), reflected the great popularity of westerns in the mid and late 1950s. Although this Los Angeles R & B rock group never had another Top 40 hit, they did achieve some success with "Big Boy Pete" (Arvee, #50, 1960); "Shimmy Like Kate" (Arvee, #42, 1960); and "The Bounce" (Tri Disc, #40, 1963).

ORBISON, ROY In the mid-1950s he was one of several country rock artists performing on the Sun record label (others included Elvis Presley, Jerry Lee Lewis, Carl Perkins, and Johnny Cash). Although his only hit for Sun was "Ooby Dooby" (Sun, #59,

1956), he did write "Claudette" for the Everly Brothers and co-wrote "You've Got Love" for Buddy Holly and the Crickets.

His greatest success came on Monument Records, where he wrote and recorded many country rockers that became some of rock & roll's greatest hits. His first major hit, "Only the Lonely," found Orbison sounding much like a young Elvis Presley. But in the hits that followed, a distinct "Orbison sound" emerged, characterized by an astounding vocal range, well-crafted compositions about teen romance and emotions, and production work that often built a powerful crescendo into the music. Roy Orbison represented country rock at its finest.

He came back in 1980 with a duet with Emmy Lou Harris called "That Lovin' You Feelin' Again." Orbison's induction into the Rock & Roll Hall of Fame in 1986 sparked a revival of his career. After a successful concert on cable TV (that featured superstars like Bruce Springsteen, Jackson Browne, and Elvis Costello in his backup band), Orbison teamed with K. D. Lang for a new hit version of "Crying" (1988). He then joined forces with Bob Dylan, George Harrison, Tom Petty, and Jeff Lynne to record one of 1988's finest albums, *The Traveling Wilburys, Volume 1*. In the midst of his comeback, Orbison died in 1988. Shortly thereafter, his final album, *Mystery Girl*, was released and became a major success. Roy Orbison's greatest hits from the 1950s and 1960s include:

"Ooby Dooby"	Sun	#56	1956
"Up Town"	Monument	#72	1960
"Only the Lonely"	Monument	#2	1960
"Blue Angel"	Monument	#9	1960
"I'm Hurtin'"	Monument	#27	1960+
"Running Scared"	Monument	#1	1961
"Crying"	Monument	#2	1961
"Candy Man"	Monument	#25	1961
"Dream Baby"	Monument	#4	1962
"The Crowd"	Monument	#26	1962
"Leah"	Monument	#25	1962
"Workin' for the Man"	Monument	#33	1962
"In Dreams"	Monument	#7	1963
"Falling"	Monument	#22	1963
"Mean Woman Blues"	Monument	#5	1963
"Blue Bayou"	Monument	#29	1963
"Pretty Paper"	Monument	#15	1963+
"It's Over"	Monument	#9	1964

"Oh, Pretty Woman"	Monument	#1	1964
"Good Night"	Monument	#21	1965
"Ride Away"	Monument	#25	1965

THE ORIOLES   They were one of the first rhythm and blues groups to cross over to the predominately white pop charts in the early 1950s. Some of their biggest hits were "What Are You Doing New Year's Eve" (Jubilee, 1949); "Baby, Please Don't Go" (Jubilee, 1952); and their classic, "Crying in the Chapel" (Jubilee, 1953).

ORLANDO, TONY   He found success in 1961 with two very good pop-rock records, "Halfway to Paradise" (Epic, #39, 1961) and "Bless You" (Epic, #15, 1961), both geared toward teenage romance. More than a decade later he returned to the pop charts as a member of Dawn (later changed to Tony Orlando and Dawn), and achieved phenomenal success with hits such as "Candida" (Bell, #3, 1970); "Knock Three Times" (Bell, #1, 1971 +); "Tie a Yellow Ribbon Round the Ole Oak Tree" (Bell, #1, 1973); "Say, Has Anybody Seen My Sweet Gypsy Rose" (Bell, #3, 1973); and "He Don't Love You (Like I Love You)" (Elektra, #1, 1975).

THE ORLONS   Their brand of R & B rock was in some ways closer to pop than rhythm and blues. Their first hit was about a new dance craze, "The Wah Watusi" (Cameo, #2, 1962). They followed with other pop-influenced records like "Don't Hang Up" (Cameo, #4, 1962); "South Street" (Cameo, #3, 1963); "Not Me" (Cameo, #12, 1963); and "Cross Fire" (Cameo, #19, 1963).

OTIS, JOHNNY   Although he was of Greek descent, he became one of the legendary figures in 1950s rhythm and blues. Otis influenced numerous R & B artists and became a shaper of early R & B rock as a bandleader, composer, arranger, and talent scout (he organized Johnny Otis' R & B Caravan, a traveling review in the 1950s). He also recorded one of the greatest hits in rock & roll history, "Willie and the Hand Jive" (Capitol, #9, 1958), which touched off a new dance craze on "American Bandstand."

OWEN, REG   This European bandleader had a big hit in 1959 with "Manhattan Spiritual" (Palette, #10, 1958 +).

OWENS, DONNIE   His only hit was a country rock song called "Need You" (Guyden, #25, 1958).

PAGE, PATTI: This pop vocalist from Oklahoma began her career in the late 1940s, and continued to enjoy success throughout the 1950s and 1960s. She hit the rock charts with songs like "Old Cape Cod" (Mercury, #7, 1957); "Left Right Out of Your Heart" (Mercury, #13, 1958); "One of Us (Will Weep Tonight)" (Mercury, #31, 1960); and "Hush, Hush, Sweet Charlotte" (Columbia, #8, 1965). Her long-term success shows that old-fashioned pop music, with its traditional sound and values, continued to sell well to teenagers, even after the advent of allegedly rebellious rock & roll.

PAONE, NICK He had a minor hit with a novelty record called "Blah, Blah, Blah" (ABC/Paramount, #57, 1959).

THE PARADONS Another one-hit group. Their brief shining moment came in 1960 with an R & B rock song called "Diamonds and Pearls" (Milestone, #18, 1960).

THE PARAGONS Their doo wop style earned them a regional hit in 1957 with "Florence" (Winley, 1957), and then later a national hit, "If" (Tap, #82, 1961).

THE PARIS SISTERS They hit the rock charts in the early 1960s with three exciting records, "Be My Boy" (Gregmark, #56, 1961); "I Love How You Love Me" (Gregmark, #5, 1961); and "He Knows I Love Him Too Much" (Gregmark, #34, 1962). All three were produced by Phil Spector and featured soft, intimate, and erotic vocals. The songs captured the implicit sexuality of early rock & roll, while reflecting teen interest in love and dating.

PARKER, FESS He will always be remembered for his television portrayal of Davy Crockett. The character touched off Crockett-mania among young Baby Boomers in the 1950s, making advertisers realize the economic potential of the new youth market. Fess tried to capitalize on his character's popularity by recording "The Ballad of Davy Crockett" (Columbia, 1955), but his version was overshadowed by Bill Hayes' earlier one on the Cadence label. In 1957 Parker had better luck with "Wringle Wrangle" (Disneyland, #21, 1957), from the Disney movie, *Westward Ho, the Wagons.*

PARSONS, BILL His name is on the label as the singer of "The All-

American Boy" (Fraternity, #2, 1958 +), which told the story of Elvis Presley's rise to fame and induction into the army. But Parsons, who wrote the song, did not sing the lyrics—Bobby Bare did. Fraternity Records apparently liked Bare's record, but released it under Parson's name because Bare was in the army and unavailable for a promotional tour. The record company sent Parsons out to lip sync Bare's vocal. To this day Bill Parsons, and not Bobby Bare, is listed as the artist performing "The All-American Boy."

THE PASSIONS This pop rock group had some success with a doo wop ballad, "Just to Be With You" (Audicon, #69, 1959).

THE PASTEL SIX They reached the rock charts in 1962, a year when songs about the Twist and other types of dances were popular. Their dance record urged teens to do "The Cinnamon Cinder (It's a Very Nice Dance)" (Zen, #25, 1962 +).

THE PASTELS They had only one hit, an R & B rock song entitled "Been So Long" (Argo, #24, 1958).

PAT AND THE SATELLITES The year was 1959, and Americans were still talking about the Soviet/American race for space. Pat and the Satellites reflected this interest not only with their group's name, but also with the title of their only hit record, "Jupiter-C" (Atco, #81, 1959), a lively pop rock instrumental.

PATIENCE AND PRUDENCE These sisters, ages 11 and 14, had two big hits in 1956: "Tonight You Belong to Me" (Liberty, #6, 1956) and "Gonna Get Along Without Ya Now" (Liberty, #12, 1956). Their adolescent-sounding vocals appealed to teenagers, as did the lyrics about love and romance. The records are excellent examples of early pop rock geared to the young audience.

PAUL, LES, AND MARY FORD This husband-and-wife team enjoyed extraordinary success in the early 1950s with pop hits like "Nola" (1950); "The World Is Waiting for the Sunrise" (1951); "I'm Confessin'" (1952); and "Vaya Con Dios" (1953). Their tight harmonies, sophisticated production work, and Paul's innovative electric guitar pointed the way for later rock & roll artists. Les Paul was inducted into the Rock & Roll Hall of Fame in 1987.

PAUL AND PAULA Their real names were Ray Hildebrand and Jill Jackson. Their first record, "Hey Paula" (Philips, #1, 1962+), featured a saccharine dialogue between Paul and Paula, explaining how they desperately wanted to marry each other. Reflecting teen interest in romance, and traditional values about marriage, the song shot up to the number one spot on the charts. The formula worked again with "Young Lovers" (Philips, #6, 1963), and again, this time with a twist, on "First Quarrel" (Philips, #27, 1963). But then they faded fast. Paul and Paula never had another big hit and, to the dismay of their fans, broke up their act in 1963. Paul and Paula's records epitomized the slick, mass-produced pop rock of the early 1960s, which catered to teen interest in dating, going steady, and getting married.

THE PEARLETTES They recorded "Duchess of Earl" (Vee-Jay, #96, 1962), the answer to Gene Chandler's "Duke of Earl."

PEDICIN, MIKE He enjoyed some success in 1958 with "Shake A Hand" (Cameo, #71, 1958), a cover version of Faye Adams' rhythm and blues classic.

PEDRICK, BOBBY, JR. In 1958 he had a hit with "White Bucks and Saddle Shoes" (Big Top, #74, 1958), a pop rock song reflecting fashions of the day. Years later, singing under the name Robert John, he had several more hits, including "If You Don't Want My Love" (Columbia, #49, 1968); "The Lion Sleeps Tonight" (Atlantic, #3, 1972); "Sad Eyes" (EMI America, #1, 1979); and "Hey There Lonely Girl" (EMI America, #31, 1980).

THE PENGUINS This R & B rock group, named after the Kool cigarettes' penguin trademark, recorded the original version of "Earth Angel" (Doo Tone, 1954+). The song is now regarded as one of the all-time classics in rock & roll history. Although their version made it to number eight on the *Billboard* Best Sellers Chart, it had to share the limelight with the Crew Cuts' inferior cover version, an irony reflecting social and economic realities of the day.

THE PENTAGONS They had a medium-size hit in 1961 with "To Be Loved (Forever)" (Donna, #48, 1961), an R & B rock song about love and romance.

THE PERCELLS Their only hit came in 1963 with a pop rock ballad called "What Are Boys Made Of" (ABC/Paramount, #53, 1963).

PERICOLI, EMILIO This Italian recording star hit it big on U.S. charts in 1962 with "Al Di La" (Warner, #6, 1962), from the movie *Rome Adventure*. The success of the lush, romantic ballad, sung entirely in Italian, is evidence of the continuing popularity of traditional pop among many teenagers.

PERKINS, CARL Another early country rocker who got his start on Sam Phillips' Sun label. In 1956 his "Blue Suede Shoes" (Sun, #4, 1956), a song written by Perkins, climbed to the number four spot on the *Billboard* charts, beating Elvis Presley's version, which peaked at number 24. The song, one of rock & roll's all-time greatest hits, is an excellent example of early rockabilly, and reflects a fashion craze. Perkins later reworked the formula with minor hits such as "Pink Pedal Pushers" (Columbia, #91, 1958) and "Pointed Toe Shoes" (Columbia, #93, 1959). He was inducted into the Rock & Roll Hall of Fame in 1986.

PETER, PAUL, AND MARY The top folk group of the early 1960s. Their first hit, "Lemon Tree" (1962), mixed folk music with fairly traditional pop lyrics about love. Their next record, "If I Had a Hammer" (1962), provided social commentary about American society and more accurately showed the group's direction. Their next hit, "Puff the Magic Dragon" (1963), was a whimsical nursery tale about getting old (many members of the Baby Boom generation saw it as an allegory about smoking marijuana). They followed up with the significant "Blowin' in the Wind" (1963), a folk song written by Bob Dylan. It became an anthem for the growing Civil Rights movement and, in the process, introduced an entire generation to Dylan's music. Many other hits followed, establishing Peter, Paul, and Mary and folk music as major forces on the rock charts. Their initial success reflected the social changes hitting American society and culture by the early 1960s. It also showed that as the Baby Boomers grew older, many of them turned to folk music, which seemed more sophisticated and politically relevant than rock & roll. Peter, Paul, and Mary's greatest hits include:

"Lemon Tree"	Warner Brothers	#35	1962
"If I Had a Hammer"	Warner Brothers	#10	1962
"Puff the Magic Dragon"	Warner Bros.	#2	1963

"Blowin' in the Wind"	Warner Bros.	#2	1963
"Don't Think Twice, It's All Right"	Warner Bros.	#9	1963
"Stewball"	Warner Bros.	#35	1963
"Tell It on the Mountain"	Warner Bros.	#33	1964
"For Lovin' Me"	Warner Bros.	#30	1965
"I Dig Rock and Roll Music"	Warner Bros.	#9	1967
"Too Much of Nothing"	Warner Bros.	#35	1967
"Day Is Done"	Warner Bros.	#21	1969
"Leaving on a Jet Plane"	Warner Bros.	#1	1969

PETERSEN, PAUL By the time he tried his hand at rock & roll in the early 1960s, he was already a veteran TV star. He gained fame first as a "Mickey Mouse Club" Mouseketeer and then as the teenage son on "The Donna Reed Show." In 1962 he had two pop rock hits. His first, "She Can't Find Her Keys" (Colpix, #19, 1962), dealt with teenagers saying goodnight on the doorstep. His other big hit, "My Dad" (Colpix, #6, 1962+), provided teens with a maudlin tribute to their fathers, showing that many members of the rock audience were anything but rebellious. Other teen-oriented hits included "Keep Your Love Locked (Deep in Your Heart)" (Colpix, #58, 1962); "Lollipops and Roses" (Colpix, #54, 1962); "Amy" (Colpix, #65, 1963); and "The Cheer Leader" (Colpix, #78, 1963+).

PETERSON, RAY His greatest successes came with maudlin, pop rock ballads about young love. In 1960 Peterson released "Tell Laura I Love Her," the quintessential "Death Rock" song. The tearjerker dealt with tragedy on the drag-racing strip, and appealed to teenage insecurities and interest in cars, love, marriage, and religion. His biggest hits included:

"The Wonder of You"	RCA	#25	1959
"Goodnight My Love"	RCA	#64	1959
"Tell Laura I Love Her"	RCA	#7	1960
"Corinna, Corinna"	Dunes	#9	1960
"Sweet Little Kathy"	Dunes	#100	1961
"Missing You"	Dunes	#29	1961
"I Could Have Loved You So Well"	Dunes	#57	1961+
"Give Us Your Blessing"	Dunes	#70	1963
"The Wonder of You"	RCA	#70	1964

THE PETS They had one hit in 1958 with a novelty song called "Cha-Hua-Hua" (Arwin, #34, 1958).

PETTY, NORMAN, TRIO Petty, the producer of many of Buddy Holly and the Crickets' early hits, had minor success in 1957 with pop songs like "Almost Paradise" (ABC/Paramount, #56, 1957) and "The First Kiss" (Columbia, #81, 1957).

PHILLIPS, LITTLE ESTHER This R & B singer had two hits on the rhythm and blues charts in the early 1950s with "Cupid's Boogie" (Savoy, 1950) and "Ring-A-Ding-Doo" (Federal, 1952). Her biggest hit on the rock charts was "Release Me" (Lenox, #8, 1962). The song was later a hit for Englebert Humperdinck in 1967.

PHILLIPS, PHIL His only hit, "Sea of Love" (Mercury, #2, 1959), became one of rock's all-time classics. The R & B rock ballad dealt with teen love and was later covered by numerous performers, including the Honeydrippers and Del Shannon.

PICKETT, BOBBY (BORIS) His big year was 1962, when he had two novelty hits in the Top 30. The first, "Monster Mash" (Garpax, #1, 1962), featured Pickett's Boris Karloff–like voice in a parody of Dee Dee Sharp's hit dance record, "Mashed Potato Time." The record shot up to number one on the rock charts, and became a hit again in 1970 and 1973. The follow-up, "Monsters' Holiday" (Garpax, #30, 1962), used the same formula of monsters and goulish talk. Pickett's songs reflected teen interest in horror movies and themes.

PICKETT, WILSON He began his career in 1962 with the Falcons, a Detroit R & B rock group that had a hit in 1959 with "You're So Fine." In 1963 Pickett went off on his own and achieved minor success with "If You Need Me" and "It's Too Late." After signing with Atlantic Records in the mid 1960s, he went on to become a big star with a string of impressive hits, including "Land of 1,000 Dances" and "Funky Broadway." His tremendous popularity marked the emergence of soul music, a 1960s off-shoot of R & B rock, and reflected the public's interest in authentic black music during this era of civil rights. Pickett's greatest hits include:

"If You Need Me"	Double-L	#64	1963
"It's Too Late"	Double-L	#49	1963
"In the Midnight Hour"	Atlantic	#21	1965
"634-5789 (Soulsville, U.S.A.)"	Atlantic	#13	1966
"Land of 1,000 Dances"	Atlantic	#6	1966
"Mustang Sally"	Atlantic	#23	1966

"Everybody Needs Somebody to Love"	Atlantic	#29	1967
"I Found a Love"	Atlantic	#32	1967
"Funky Broadway"	Atlantic	#8	1967
"Stag-O-Lee"	Atlantic	#22	1967
"She's Lookin' Good"	Atlantic	#15	1968
"I'm a Midnight Mover"	Atlantic	#24	1968
"Hey Jude"	Atlantic	#23	1968+
"Sugar Sugar"	Atlantic	#25	1970
"Engine #9"	Atlantic	#14	1970
"Don't Let the Green Grass Fool You"	Atlantic	#17	1971
"Don't Knock My Love"	Atlantic	#13	1971
"Fire and Water"	Atlantic	#24	1971+

PIERCE, WEBB This well-known country and western singer crossed over to the rock charts in 1959 with "I Ain't Never" (Decca, #24, 1959), showing the continuing appeal of country-influenced music among teenagers.

PITNEY, GENE One of rock & roll's most talented stars and teen idols of the early 1960s. Not only did he have the looks of a matinee star, but he was also a dynamic performer with an incredible voice and range. His hit records included solid rock songs like "I Wanna Love My Life Away" (written by Pitney) and "Every Breath I Take" (written by Carole King and Gerry Goffin and produced by Phil Spector), as well as more pop-oriented records such as "Town Without Pity" (from the movie of the same name) and "The Man Who Shot Liberty Valence" (a Bacharach-David composition inspired by the movie of the same name). Unlike most pop rock singers and teen idols of the era, Pitney involved himself in all aspects of his records: he wrote some of his own hits, and often helped produce the records. He also wrote hits for other performers, including "Hello Mary Lou" for Rick Nelson; "Rubber Ball" for Bobby Vee; and "He's a Rebel" for the Crystals. Pitney could do it all. His records, which generally reflected teen interest in romance, stand as some of the finest examples of early 1960s pop rock. His greatest hits include:

"I Wanna Love My Life Away"	Musicor	#39	1961
"Every Breath I Take"	Musicor	#42	1961
"Town Without Pity"	Musicor	#13	1961+
"The Man Who Shot Liberty Valance"	Musicor	#4	1962
"Only Love Can Break a Heart"	Musicor	#2	1962
"Half Heaven—Half Heartache"	Musicor	#12	1962+
"Mecca"	Musicor	#12	1963

"True Love Never Runs Smooth"	Musicor	#21	1963
"Twenty-Four Hours from Tulsa"	Musicor	#17	1963
"That Girl Belongs to Yesterday"	Musicor	#49	1964
"It Hurts to Be in Love"	Musicor	#7	1964
"I'm Gonna Be Strong"	Musicor	#9	1964
"I Must Be Seeing Things"	Musicor	#31	1965
"Last Chance to Turn Around"	Musicor	#13	1965
"Looking Through the Eyes of Love"	Musicor	#28	1965
"Backstage"	Musicor	#25	1966
"She's a Heartbreaker"	Musicor	#16	1968
"She Lets Her Hair Down"	Musicor	#89	1969 +

THE PIXIES THREE   Their sound, featuring adolescent female voices and teen-oriented lyrics, is a good example of early 1960s pop rock geared to the young audience. Their biggest hits were "Birthday Party" (Mercury, #40, 1963) and "442 Glenwood Avenue" (Mercury, #56, 1964).

PLATT, EDDIE   Although this saxophonist's rendition of "Tequila" (ABC/Paramount, #20, 1958), did make the rock charts, it was overshadowed by the Champs' version, which became the number one record across America.

THE PLATTERS   This R & B rock group became one of the most successful acts in rock & roll's first decade. Their greatest hits, such as "The Great Pretender," "My Prayer," "Twilight Time," and "Smoke Gets in Your Eyes," became rock & roll standards perfect for slow dancing at record hops and parties. Although their sound and style were closer to pop than rock, the rock & roll audience embraced them anyway. The Platters' best-selling records include:

"Only You"	Mercury	#5	1955
"The Great Pretender"	Mercury	#1	1955 +
"You've Got the Magic Touch"	Mercury	#4	1956
"My Prayer"	Mercury	#1	1956
"You'll Never Know"	Mercury	#11	1956
"It Isn't Right"	Mercury	#23	1956
"On My Word of Honor"	Mercury	#27	1956 +
"I'm Sorry"	Mercury	#11	1957
"My Dream"	Mercury	#26	1957
"Twilight Time"	Mercury	#1	1958
"Smoke Gets in Your Eyes"	Mercury	#1	1958 +

"Enchanted"	Mercury	#12	1959
"Harbor Lights"	Mercury	#8	1960
"Red Sails in the Sunset"	Mercury	#36	1960
"To Each His Own"	Mercury	#21	1960
"I'll Never Smile Again"	Mercury	#25	1961
"With This Ring"	Musicor	#14	1967

THE PLAYBOYS   Their only hit, "Over the Weekend" (Cameo, #62, 1958), was a pop rock ballad about teen love. It became a favorite on "American Bandstand," where it was often used as a "lady's choice," i.e., a slow dance where the girls asked the boys to dance.

THE PLAYMATES   They had several pop rock hits in the late 1950s. Their first was a cover of the Twintones' "Jo-Ann" (Roulette, #20, 1958), followed by another ballad, "Don't Go Home" (Roulette, #22, 1958). Later in 1958 they almost made the top of the charts with "Beep Beep" (Roulette, #4, 1958), a novelty song about a race between a big car and little car which appealed to teens interested in autos. The following year they had their last Top 20 hit with "What Is Love?" (Roulette, #15, 1959). Their answer, "five feet of heaven in a pony tail," revealed sexual attitudes and fashions of the day.

POMUS, DOC, AND MORT SHUMAN   One of the top songwriting teams of the late 1950s and early 1960s, they wrote literally hundreds of songs, including "Teenager in Love" for Dion and the Belmonts; "Sweets for My Sweet," "This Magic Moment," and "Save the Last Dance for Me" for the Drifters; "Hushabye" for the Mystics; "Surrender," "Little Sister," and "Marie's the Name" for Elvis Presley; "Go Jimmy Go" for Jimmy Clanton; "I'm a Man," "Turn Me Loose," and "Hound Dog Man" for Fabian; and "Suspicion" for Terry Stafford.

THE PONI-TAILS   These three girls scored big with a pop rock ballad called "Born Too Late" (ABC/Paramount, #7, 1958). The song focused on a teenage girl's desire to win the older boy of her dreams—a thought undoubtedly shared by thousands of American girls suffering from crushes on upperclassmen. The group always wore the faddish ponytails from which they took their name, gearing themselves to the teen audience.

POURCEL, FRANK, AND HIS FRENCH FIDDLES   He had a big hit in 1959 with a lush instrumental version of the Platters' "Only You"

(Capitol, #9, 1959). The record's success indicates that many teenagers were still listening to and buying traditional pop records, contrary to the popular belief that members of the rock & roll audience were always rebellious.

POWERS, JOEY His only big hit was "Midnight Mary" (Amy, #10, 1963+), a pop rock ballad about young love and the will to marry someone against parental objection—themes dating back at least to *Romeo and Juliet*.

PRADO, PEREZ This Cuban mambo band leader was able to cross over to the rock charts. He made it all the way to number one and received a considerable amount of exposure on "American Bandstand" with his hit, "Patricia" (RCA, #1, 1958), a pop instrumental about a popular girl's name.

PRESLEY, ELVIS Rock star Buddy Holly once said of Elvis, "Without Elvis Presley, none of us could have made it." Holly was right on the mark. Although Elvis was not the inventor of rock & roll, he certainly did more than any other artist to popularize it. His unique blend of white country and western music and black rhythm and blues helped him land an astonishing 49 hits, including 13 number one records, in the Top 30 between 1956 and 1963. His first big hit, "Heartbreak Hotel," exploded onto the record charts in 1956. The song, featuring Elvis in an echo chamber growling out a bluesy tale of broken love and ruin, sent teenagers scurrying to record stores. As hit followed hit, several main themes emerged in Elvis' music. He sang of teenage love (e.g., "Don't Be Cruel," "Love Me Tender," and "Can't Help Falling in Love"); he sang of teen interests (e.g., "Teddy Bear," "Wear My Ring Around Your Neck," or "Good Luck Charm"); he sang of traditional teen values ("Old Shep," "Money Honey," "Peace in the Valley," and "Follow That Dream"); and, at times, he sang of teenage bravado and defiance (e.g., "Blue Suede Shoes," "Hound Dog," "Jailhouse Rock," and "U.S. Male"). Elvis could rock with the best rhythm and blues shouters, and then croon out a slow ballad that sent chills up girls' spines.

But Elvis Presley was more than just a successful rock star—he was a cultural hero. He symbolized rock & roll, the new generation, and changing values. Taking black songs and making them respectable for whites, Presley helped transform R & B race music into rock & roll. As Little Richard noted, "It took people like Elvis to open the door for this kind of music, and I thank God for Elvis Presley." For many fans Elvis became a conduit into the allegedly sinful and rebellious world of rock & roll and rhythm and blues. He became rock & roll incarnate.

Elvis represented the new way of life on the 1950s horizon. His vocals and physical movements on stage were charged with sexual electricity. Was he deliberately trying to be sexy? "No," he answered emphatically, "when music starts, I [just] gotta move." The image of Elvis—gyrating to the beat, rockin' up a storm—was a potent one. In his wild pink shirts, black slacks, or gold-lamé suits, Elvis showed teens that sex and uninhibited pleasure were what it was all about. Implicit was a questioning of sexual conformity and racial attitudes in America. The "race music" beat, the jive talk, the uninhibited sexuality, and the "cat clothes" (i.e., the name given to loud-colored clothes associated with blacks in the 1950s) were indictments of 1950s segregation policies and consensus behavior.

Elvis was often portrayed as the symbol of alienated youth, rock & roll's answer to James Dean. He copied Dean's sneer and cool persona (supposedly Elvis has seen every Dean film a dozen times), and came across as a nonconformist, singing rock & roll, wearing a D.A. (hair combed in the style of the feathers on a duck's tail) and long sideburns, dressing in wild clothes, and thrusting his pelvis to the beat. Yet Presley was no rebel without a cause. He knew his mission—to propagate the new sound.

Paradoxically, Elvis also symbolized traditional beliefs and values. His career personified the rags-to-riches theme long evident in American life and thought. It was a classic success story: poor country boy strikes it rich in the big city. Elvis dramatically proved that even a southern boy from humble origins could escape from poverty, if he worked hard and had faith in God, country, and motherhood. One of his own songs, "Follow That Dream," summed it up best. Yet Elvis was no mere follower. He relentlessly pursued his dream until he caught it. He then became the dream, basking in the fame, adulation, and fortune America showered upon him. Horatio Alger could not have created a more perfect archetype.

The young Elvis was also the embodiment of Thomas Jefferson's Agrarian Myth—the idealized American with roots in the soil, untainted by the corrupting influences of civilization and cities. He was Mr. Everyman: pious, respectful, modest, yet capable. Elvis was what democracy was all about. No man was better than he. But he was better than no man. When he was first asked about the reason for his success, Elvis replied, "I don't know what it is, I just fell into it, really." Such humility struck a responsive chord. In true American fashion, success had pursued the man, until the man caught it. Like Andrew Jackson, Davy Crockett, Abe Lincoln, and others from the pantheon of American folk heroes, Elvis had made it big. But he remained the "common man."

Presley symbolized other traditional values. His country and religious recordings reflected a continuing adherence to community, family, and God. Like most Americans, Elvis was also materialistic. He bought cars for every day of the week, and was particularly proud of his pink Cadillac. When questioned he would joke, "I was thinking about a Presley used car lot."

Elvis became a glossy symbol of conspicuous consumption in America. He bought clothes, toys, jewelry, sports equipment, TVs, and other consumer goods like most people devour potato chips. Soft goods, durable goods, any goods, they were all the same to him. The more he made the more he spent. And the more he spent, the more Americans loved him. After all, wouldn't they do the same if they could? Elvis was like a little boy in a toy store, with one big difference—this little boy could afford any toys he wanted. It had a fairy tale ring to it. His innocent approach to consumption ("Aw shucks, I'm just havin' some fun") provided a charming naîveté. His ability to fulfill every wish smacked of Aladdin's lamp. And his propensity for lavishing Cadillacs and gifts on friends and strangers alike recalled the Good Samaritan, if not Robin Hood.

Elvis reached the dazzling heights, indeed the pinnacle, of his chosen career. That achievement, in the eyes of Americans who value excellence, also made Presley worthy of adulation. He was clearly tops in his field, the king of rock & roll, a superstar. He was a talented performer and singer, innovative yet traditional. He had it all: charm, looks, charisma, modesty, sex appeal, ambition, luck, and ability. Furthermore, he was colorful and Americans have always liked to be entertained by their heroes. He knew exactly what he wanted to do, and he did it. And he did it like no one before him ever had. His 14 consecutive million-sellers and legions of fans stand as testimony to his greatness. And his shining star lit the way for others who followed. Beatle John Lennon remembered, "I basically became a musician because of Elvis Presley." Folk rock king Bob Dylan said, "Elvis recorded a song of mine. That's the one recording I treasure most." And Bruce Springsteen, the "Boss" of contemporary rock, explained, "That

Elvis, man, he is all there is. There ain't no more. Everything starts and ends with him. He wrote the book."

As a cultural hero, Elvis became all things to all people. Defiant teens saw him as their leader. Middle-aged mothers looked at him as a son. Country and western fans cheered him as a good 'ole boy. Religious music enthusiasts welcomed him as a fellow traveler. He was a rocker, a pop singer, a blues singer, a country artist, a religious artist, a matinee idol, a TV star, a movie star, and a friend everyone thought they knew. He was, as the phrase goes, a legend in his own time.

Elvis' career clearly reflects those times. His music was influenced by the biracial culture of the rural South. And his success was linked to a changing America: a land of media proliferation, mass advertising, and sweeping demographic change. The mass movement of southern blacks and whites to northern cities, and the Baby Boomers' coming of age, set the stage for Elvis' drama. Like rock & roll itself, Presley was a product of the times.

The reaction of some adults to Presley provides insight into the conservative times. Reflecting the anxieties and conformity of the 1950s, some people, self-righteous Puritans and paranoid politicians included, bombarded Presley with "Elvis the Pelvis" jokes and other boorish remarks. Other fearful adults blasted Elvis as a threat to morality, segregation, religion, traditional music, and social order.

While some adults despised Elvis and others were undecided, teenagers understood. They knew he was the symbol of the new sound, the rock & roll prophet who would deliver them from the sins of 1950s conservatism. He was a new culture hero, representing the new youth culture, as well as the old myths involving God, love, and country. He symbolized tradition and innovation, racial harmony, freedom, property, individualism, and the pursuit of happiness. Elvis Presley was, for them, an American icon.

Presley's phenomenal success reveals much about the times. As the king of rock & roll, he personified the myths and beliefs of his subjects. And his songs, sound, and style reflected the dreams, interests, and values of the American people. Even Elvis' death in 1977 did not end his status as a culture hero, as evidenced by the yearly pilgramages his fans make to Graceland, the Presley estate near Memphis, Tennessee. Elvis Presley was enshrined in the Rock & Roll Hall of Fame in 1985. His greatest hits include:

"Heartbreak Hotel"	RCA	#1	1956
"I Was the One"	RCA	#23	1956

"Blue Suede Shoes"	RCA	#24	1956
"Money Honey"	RCA	#76	1956
"I Want You, I Need You, I Love You"	RCA	#3	1956
"My Baby Left Me"	RCA	#31	1956
"Don't Be Cruel"	RCA	#1	1956
"Hound Dog"	RCA	#2	1956
"Blue Moon"	RCA	#55	1956
"Love Me Tender"	RCA	#1	1956
"Love Me"	RCA	#6	1956+
"Too Much"	RCA	#2	1957
"All Shook Up"	RCA	#1	1957
"Peace in the Valley"	RCA	#39	1957
"Teddy Bear"	RCA	#1	1957
"Loving You"	RCA	#28	1957
"Jailhouse Rock"	RCA	#1	1957
"Treat Me Nice"	RCA	#27	1957
"Don't"	RCA	#1	1958
"I Beg of You"	RCA	#8	1958
"Wear My Ring Around Your Neck"	RCA	#3	1958
"Doncha' Think It's Time"	RCA	#21	1958
"Hard-Headed Woman"	RCA	#2	1958
"One Night"	RCA	#4	1958
"I Got Stung"	RCA	#8	1958
"A Fool Such As I"	RCA	#2	1959
"I Need Your Love Tonight"	RCA	#4	1959
"A Big Hunk O' Love"	RCA	#1	1959
"My Wish Came True"	RCA	#12	1959
"Stuck On You"	RCA	#1	1960
"Fame and Fortune"	RCA	#17	1960
"It's Now or Never"	RCA	#1	1960
"Are You Lonesome Tonight?"	RCA	#1	1960
"I Gotta Know"	RCA	#20	1960
"Surrender"	RCA	#1	1961
"Flaming Star"	RCA	#14	1961
"I Feel So Bad"	RCA	#5	1961
"Little Sister"	RCA	#5	1961
"(Marie's the Name) His Latest Flame"	RCA	#4	1961
"Can't Help Falling in Love"	RCA	#2	1961+
"Rock-A-Hula Baby"	RCA	#23	1961+
"Good Luck Charm"	RCA	#1	1962
"Follow That Dream"	RCA	#15	1962
"She's Not You"	RCA	#5	1962
"Return to Sender"	RCA	#2	1962

"One Broken Heart for Sale"	RCA	#11	1963
"(You're the Devil) In Disguise"	RCA	#3	1963
"Bossa Nova Baby"	RCA	#8	1963
"Witchcraft"	RCA	#32	1963
"Kissin' Cousins"	RCA	#12	1964
"Viva Las Vegas"	RCA	#29	1964
"Such a Night"	RCA	#16	1964
"Ask Me"	RCA	#12	1964
"Crying in the Chapel"	RCA	#3	1965
"(Such an) Easy Question"	RCA	#11	1965
"I'm Yours"	RCA	#11	1965
"Puppet on a String"	RCA	#14	1965
"Frankie and Johnny"	RCA	#25	1966
"Love Letters"	RCA	#19	1966
"Big Boss Man"	RCA	#38	1967
"U.S. Male"	RCA	#28	1968
"If I Can Dream"	RCA	#12	1968 +
"Memories"	RCA	#35	1969
"In the Ghetto"	RCA	#3	1969
"Suspicious Minds"	RCA	#1	1969
"Don't Cry Daddy"	RCA	#6	1969 +
"Kentucky Rain"	RCA	#16	1970
"The Wonder of You"	RCA	#9	1970
"You Don't Have to Say You Love Me"	RCA	#11	1970
"I Really Don't Want to Know"	RCA	#21	1970 +
"An American Trilogy"	RCA	#66	1972
"Burning Love"	RCA	#2	1972
"Separate Ways"	RCA	#20	1972 +
"Steamroller Blues"	RCA	#17	1973
"If You Talk in Your Sleep"	RCA	#17	1974
"Promised Land"	RCA	#14	1974
"My Boy"	RCA	#20	1975
"T-R-O-U-B-L-E"	RCA	#35	1975
"Way Down"	RCA	#18	1977
"My Way"	RCA	#22	1977
"Guitar Man"	RCA	#28	1981

PRESTON, JOHNNY His brand of country-influenced pop rock earned him three big hits. His first record, "Running Bear" (Mercury, #1, 1959 +), was written by his friend and mentor, J.P. Richardson (better known as the Big Bopper). "Running Bear" told the tragic tale of a young Indian warrior and his lovesick Indian maid, Little White Dove. The story, complete with oom-pah-pah war cries in the background (sung by the Big Bopper), was an odd mixture of contemporary stereotypes of American Indians, a Dove Soap commercial, and the Romeo and Juliet theme. His next hit, "Cradle of Love" (Mercury, #7, 1960), was a reworking of the "rock-a-bye baby on the tree top" nursery rhyme. The lyrics were altered to deal with teen romance, and then arranged to a rock & roll beat. Preston's last big hit was an R & B rock-influenced song, "Feel So Fine" (Mercury, #14, 1960).

PREVIN, ANDRE, AND DAVID ROSE   These two pop musicians and orchestra leaders pooled their talents in 1959 to produce an instrumental hit, "Like Young" (MGM, #46, 1959). The title, following the jive talk pattern of using the word "like" as an adjective, obviously was geared to the teenage audience.

PRICE, LLOYD   One of the outstanding R & B rock artists of the 1950s and early 1960s. His 1952 rhythm and blues classic, "Lawdy Miss Clawdy," is generally regarded as a prototype of rock & roll. Several of his later hits, "Just Because" (1957), "Stagger Lee" (1958 +), and "Personality" (1959), are now recognized as three of rock & roll's greatest hits. His biggest hits include:

"Lawdy Miss Clawdy"	Specialty	-	1952
"Just Because"	ABC/Paramount	#29	1957
"Stagger Lee"	ABC/Paramont	#1	1958 +
"Where Were You on Our Wedding Day?"	ABC/Paramount	#23	1959
"Personality"	ABC/Paramount	#2	1959
"I'm Gonna Get Married"	ABC/Paramount	#3	1959
"Come Into My Heart"	ABC/Paramount	#20	1959
"Lady Luck"	ABC/Paramount	#14	1960
"Question"	ABC/Paramount	#19	1960
"Misty"	Double-L	#21	1963

PRYSOCK, RED   This rhythm and blues saxophonist had some success in the mid-1950s recording lively songs, such as "Hand Clappin'" (Mercury, 1955) and "Rock n' Roll Party" (Mercury, 1956).

PURSELL, BILL   He made the rock charts in 1963 with a romantic piano instrumental called "Our Winter Love" (Columbia, #9, 1963). The record's success reflected the traditional tastes of many members of the rock & roll audience.

THE QUAKER CITY BOYS Their name played on the fact that they were from Philadelphia, the home of "American Bandstand." They had one minor hit, "Teasin' " (Swan, #39, 1958+).

THE QUARTER NOTES They had a hit with "Record Hop Blues" (Wizz, #82, 1959), a pop rock song reflecting the popularity of record hops where teenagers would dance to hit records.

THE QUIN-TONES They had a Top 20 hit with "Down the Aisle of Love" (Hunt, #20, 1958), showing that many teenagers held rather traditional values concerning love and marriage.

THE RAINDROPS This duo was composed of the husband/wife team Jeff Barry and Ellie Greenwich, who wrote or co-wrote many pop rock hits, including "Be My Baby" and "Baby I Love You" for the Ronettes; "Then He Kissed Me" and "Da Doo Ron Ron" for the Crystals; "Leader of the Pack" and "Give Us Your Blessings" for the Shangri-Las; "Chapel of Love" for the Dixie Cups; "Maybe I Know" for Leslie Gore; "Do Wah Diddy Diddy" for Manfred Mann; and "Hanky Panky" for Tommy James and the Shondells. In 1963 they had some hits of their own with three pop rock songs that dealt with teenage romance: "What a Guy" (Jubilee, #41, 1963); "The Kind of Boy You Can't Forget" (Jubilee, #17, 1963); and "That Boy John" (Jubilee, #64, 1963+).

RAINWATER, MARVIN One of the few American Indians ever to make the rock charts. His biggest hit was "Gonna Find Me a Bluebird" (MGM, #18, 1957).

RALKE, DON This pop musician had some success in 1959 with "77 Sunset Strip" (Warner, #69, 1959), the theme from a popular TV show about private eyes. Teenagers in particular were attracted to one character on the show, "Kookie," a jive-talking parking lot attendant who in some ways was a prototype for the "Fonzie" character on the 1970s sitcom, "Happy Days." *See* Edd Byrnes.

THE RAMRODS They made the Top 30 with an instrumental pop rock version of "Ghost Riders in the Sky" (Amy, #30, 1961). The song featured the sound of horses and cattle, and reflected teen interest in westerns, which were extremely popular on TV in the early 1960s.

RANDAZZO, TEDDY This pop rock singer never quite made it as a teen idol in the early 1960s. His biggest hits included "Little Serenade" (Vik, #66, 1958); "The Way of a Clown" (ABC/Paramount, #44, 1960); and "Big Wide World" (Colpix, #51, 1963). He also co-starred with Alan Freed in the movie *Mr. Rock & Roll*, and wrote several songs for other artists, including "Goin' Out of My Head," which became a big hit in the late 1960s for both Anthony and the Imperials and the Lettermen.

THE RAN-DELLS Their only hit, "Martian-Hop" (Chairman, #16, 1963), was a novelty pop rock song that reflected teen interest in dancing and public interest in the space program in the early 1960s.

RANDOLPH, BOOTS This Nashville studio musician and saxophonist made the rock charts with a lively instrumental, "Yakety Sax" (Monument, #35, 1963), which was a take-off on the Coasters' earlier hit, "Yakety Yak."

RANDY AND THE RAINBOWS They had one of the biggest hits of 1963 with "Denise" (Rust, #10, 1963). Like many pop rock songs of this era, it dealt with a girl's name. The joyful song, with its upbeat melody and pop rock harmonies reminiscent of 1950s doo wop, reflected the buoyant spirits and optimism that prevailed among many teenagers in the early 1960s.

RAY, DIANE In 1963, she had a hit with "Please Don't Talk to the Lifeguard" (Mercury, #31, 1963), a pop rock song that reflected sexual stereotypes of the early 1960s. It was released at a time when surfing and beaches were quite popular among teens.

RAY, JAMES His "If You Gotta Make a Fool of Somebody" (Caprice, #22, 1961 +) was one of the finest R & B–influenced hits of 1962.

RAY, JOHNNY This white pop vocalist from the 1950s developed a style that was a prototype for early rock & roll. His emotional delivery (which sometimes had him crying on stage) and rhythm and blues–influenced vocals earned him several big hits, including "Cry" (Okeh, 1951); "The Little White Cloud That Cried" (Okeh, 1951); "Just Walkin' in the Rain" (Columbia, #2, 1956); and "You Don't Owe Me a Thing" (Columbia, #10, 1957).

RAYBURN, MARGIE This pop vocalist crossed over to the rock charts with "I'm Available" (Liberty, #16, 1957), which appealed to teens interested in romance and dating.

THE RAYS This R & B rock group from New York had only one big hit, "Silhouettes" (Cameo, #3, 1957), but it became one of rock & roll's all-time greats. The doo wop ballad, written by Bob Crewe, told a tale about a guy going to visit his girl friend. As he approached her doorstep, he was shocked to see two silhouettes on the shade hugging and kissing. He pounded on the door, and as it swung open he received his second shock—he was on the wrong block. The ironic lyrics played on teen interest in romance, and the identical design of 1950s tract homes.

THE REBELS This garage band from Buffalo, New York, had a smash hit in 1963 with an excellent instrumental called "Wild Weekend" (Swan, #8, 1962 +). The song had been written by Tommy Shannon, a young disc jockey on WKBW radio in Buffalo, as the theme of his show. Soon, teens were tuning in just to hear the theme: "Listen to the Tommy Shannon Show/ 'KB radio/ Top tunes, news, and weather/ In Buffalo, we'll get together/ on the Tom Shannon Show." When Shannon had a local group, the Rebels, record it as an instrumental, it shot up the national record charts. The Rebels later changed their name to the Rockin' Rebels (partly to avoid confusion with Duane Eddy's group, already named the Rebels). Their next release, "Rockin' Crickets" (Swan, #87, 1963), was another well-done pop rock instrumental, but it barely made the charts.

REDDING, OTIS A pioneer of soul music, this R & B rock great had one minor hit during rock & roll's first decade, "These Arms of Mine" (Volt, #85, 1963). Most of his success came later with soul hits like "I've Been Loving You Too Long" (Volt, #21, 1965); "Respect" (Volt, #35, 1965); "Satisfaction" (Volt, #31, 1966); "Try a Little Tenderness" (Volt, #25, 1966 +); "Shake" (Volt, #47, 1967); "Knock on Wood" (a duet with Carla Thomas) (Stax, #30, 1967); "Sittin' on the Dock of the Bay" (Volt, #1, 1968); "The Happy Song (Dum Dum)" (Volt, #25, 1968); and "Papa's Got a Brand New Bag" (Atco, #21, 1968 +). Redding's career was cut short by his death in a plane crash in 1967.

RED RIVER DAVE This country and western singer struck a responsive chord among patriotic Americans in 1960 with his hit,

"There's a Star Spangled Banner Waving Somewhere, No. 2 (The Ballad of Francis Powers)" (Savoy, #64, 1960). The record dealt with the U-2 incident (i.e., the downing of Francis Powers' American spy plane over the Soviet Union), and reflected Cold War tensions of the early 1960s.

REED, DENNY His "A Teenager Feels It Too" (3 Trey, #94, 1960) was a minor pop rock hit aimed directly at the young audience.

REED, JIMMY An R & B rock performer of the late 1950s and early 1960s. Some of his more memorable blues-influenced hits were "Honest I Do" (Vee-Jay, #32, 1957); "Baby What You Want Me to Do" (Vee-Jay, #37, 1960); and "Aw Shucks, Hush Your Mouth" (Vee-Jay, #93, 1962).

REESE, DELLA She came out of a gospel background to record R & B rock hits like "And That Reminds Me" (Jubilee, #29, 1957); "Don't You Know?" (RCA, #2, 1959); and "Not One Minute More" (RCA, #16, 1959+).

REEVES, JIM This country and western star had several big hits on the rock charts, including "Four Walls" (RCA, #12, 1957); "He'll Have to Go" (RCA, #2, 1959+); "I'm Getting Better" (RCA, #37, 1960); and "Am I Losing You" (RCA, #31, 1960), all of which were produced by Chet Atkins. Reeves died in a plane crash in 1964.

THE REGENTS They first made the rock charts with "Barbara Ann" (Gee, #13, 1961), an interesting blend of pop rock and doo wop. The song later became an even bigger hit for the Beach Boys. The Regents' only other hit was "Runaround" (Gee, #28, 1961).

RENAY, DIANE Her biggest hit, "Navy Blue" (20th Century, #6, 1964), dealt with enlisting in the navy and sounded similar to the Murmaids' 1963 hit, "Popsicles and Icicles." Her second release, "Kiss Me Sailor" (20th Century, #29, 1964), followed the same formula, i.e., high school girl falls for patriotic sailor boy. Renay's records epitomize the teen-oriented pop rock of the early 1960s, and reflect patriotic sentiments of the day.

RESTIVO, JOHNNY This pop rock singer and weight lifter had minor success with "The Shape I'm In" (RCA, #80, 1959).

THE REVELS   Their "Midnight Stroll" (Norgolde, #35, 1959) was released just before Halloween. It had a spooky sound, replete with midnight tolls and wailing ghosts. Teens loved it. Not only was it a great novelty record, but it also plugged into a popular dance and teen interest in horror stories.

REVERE, PAUL, AND THE RAIDERS   Their gimmick was dressing up like Revolutionary War soldiers. They had some success in the early 1960s with "Like Long Hair" (1961) and a cover of the Kingsmen's "Louie Louie," which never made the national charts. Most of their hit records, however, came in the mid and late 1960s, after they became regulars on Dick Clark's TV show, "Where the Action Is." Their greatest hits include:

"Like Long Hair"	Gardena	#38	1961
"Steppin' Out"	Columbia	#46	1965
"Just Like Me"	Columbia	#11	1965 +
"Kicks"	Columbia	#4	1966
"Hungry"	Columbia	#6	1966
"The Great Airplane Strike"	Columbia	#20	1966
"Good Thing"	Columbia	#4	1966 +
"Ups and Downs"	Columbia	#22	1967
"Him or Me, What's It Gonna Be?"	Columbia	#5	1967
"I Had a Dream"	Columbia	#17	1967
"Too Much Talk"	Columbia	#19	1968
"Mr. Sun, Mr. Moon"	Columbia	#18	1969
"Let Me"	Columbia	#20	1969
"Indian Reservation"	Columbia	#1	1971
"Birds of a Feather"	Columbia	#23	1971

REYNOLDS, DEBBIE   This actress reached the top of the rock charts with "Tammy" (Coral, #1, 1957), the title song from her movie, *Tammy and the Bachelor*. The movie and pop song had tremendous appeal for the millions of teenage girls in love with love.

REYNOLDS, JODY   His "Endless Sleep" (Demon, #5, 1958) was a prototype for what came to be known as "Death Rock." The song told the story of a girl's supposed drowning, and how her boyfriend was beckoned to join in her "endless sleep." The tragic and eerie lyrics, like those found in other Death Rock songs such as "Teen Angel" or "Tell Laura I Love Her", may have provided psychological release for teens frustrated by love and growing pains.

RICH, CHARLIE Signed to the Sun label as a rockabilly artist, he began his career with "Lonely Weekends" (Phillips, #22, 1960). Then came a five-year draught, which ended in 1965 with the hit "Mohair Sam" (Smash, #21, 1965). More hard times followed, and the next time Rich made the Top 40, he was a full-fledged country and western singer. He recorded songs like "Behind Closed Doors" (Epic, #15, 1973); "The Most Beautiful Girl" (Epic, #1, 1973); "There Won't Be Anymore" (RCA, #18, 1974); "A Very Special Love Song" (Epic, #11, 1974); "I Love My Friend" (Epic, #24, 1974); and "Every Time You Touch Me" (Epic, #19, 1975).

RICHARD, CLIFF He was one of the few English performers to make the American rock charts prior to the Beatles' arrival in 1964. Billed as England's answer to Elvis Presley, Richard earned minor hits with pop rock songs like "Living Doll" (ABC/Paramount, #30, 1959); "Lucky Lips" (Epic, #62, 1963); and "It's All in the Game" (Epic, #25, 1963+). Actually, his best record from the early 1960s—a Buddy Holly–sounding song called "Please Don't Tease"—never even made the national charts. Richard's career in the United States didn't really take off until the late 1970s with hits like "Devil Woman" (Rocket, #6, 1976); "We Don't Talk Anymore" (EMI-America, #7, 1979+); "Dreaming" (EMI-America, #10, 1980); and "A Little in Love" (EMI America, #17, 1980+).

RICK AND THE KEENS They had a minor hit in 1961 with "Peanuts" (Smash, #60, 1961), a song that had been a hit for Little Joe and the Thrillers back in 1957.

RIDDLE, NELSON This orchestra leader and arranger for top pop artists like Frank Sinatra and Nat King Cole had several pop hits in the 1950s and early 1960s. One in particular, "Route 66 Theme" (Capitol, #30, 1962), received airplay on many rock & roll stations, since it was inspired by a TV show that was quite popular among teens. "Route 66" was the story of two young men who found romance and adventure while driving across America in their Corvette. It wasn't Jack Kerouac, but it still struck a responsive chord among many teens interested in cars, traveling, romance, and excitement.

THE RIGHTEOUS BROTHERS Bill Medley and Bobby Hatfield formed this pop rock duo in the early 1960s, taking their name from the black slang term "righteous," meaning authentic or soulful. In 1963 they had their first hit with "Little Latin Lupe Lu," which later became an even bigger hit for the Kingsmen. But it wasn't until the following year that the Righteous Brothers became an enormous success. Two events dramatically changed the direction of their career: They became regulars on the television show "Shindig," giving them weekly exposure to millions of viewers; and they signed with Phil Spector's Philles record company. Spector threw all his energy and talent into producing their records, resulting in the stunning "You've Lost That Lovin' Feelin'" (written by Spector, Barry Mann, and Cynthia Weil). The Righteous Brothers' sound was soon christened "blue-eyed soul," and many other hits followed.

In 1968 Hatfield and Medley split up, but after their solo careers went nowhere, they reunited again in the mid 1970s and found success with a nostalgic song, "Rock and Roll Heaven." After a few more years together, they again went their separate ways. Bill Medley went on to sing a duet with Jennifer Warnes, "The Time of My Life" (1987), the Oscar-winning theme from the movie *Dirty Dancing*. The Righteous Brothers' greatest hits include:

"Little Latin Lupe Lu"	Moonglow	#49	1963
"You've Lost That Lovin' Feelin'"	Philles	#1	1964+
"Just Once in My Life"	Philles	#9	1965
"Unchained Melody"	Philles	#4	1965
"Ebb Tide"	Philles	#5	1965+
"(You're My) Soul and Inspiration"	Verve	#1	1966
"He"	Verve	#18	1966
"Go Ahead and Cry"	Verve	#30	1966
"Rock and Roll Heaven"	Haven	#3	1974
"Give It to the People"	Haven	#20	1974
"Dream On"	Haven	#32	1974

RILEY, BILLY LEE   Although this rockabilly artist never made *Billboard's* national charts, he did have several regional hits on the Sun label. His "Flyin' Saucers Rock & Roll" (Sun, 1957) reflected public interest in UFOs, while "Red Hot" (Sun, 1957) featured Jerry Lee Lewis, another Sun artist, on piano.

THE RINKY-DINKS   *See* Bobby Darin.

RIOS, AUGIE   This lad, while still in his early teens, had a hit during the Christmas season of 1958 with "Donde Está Santa Claus"

(Metro, #47, 1958). The song, mostly in Spanish, had a boy asking his mama, "Where is Santa Claus?" The novelty record became a favorite on "American Bandstand" and among teenagers still young enough to remember believing in Santa Claus.

THE RIP CHORDS   These pop rockers from Southern California had minor success in 1963 with "Here I Stand" (Columbia, #51, 1963) and "Gone" (Columbia, #88, 1963). Both featured harmonies and falsettos reminiscent of the Four Seasons. They found even greater success copying the Beach Boys' style, and drove toward the top of the rock charts with "Hey Little Cobra" (Columbia, #4, 1963 +) and "Three Window Coupe" (Columbia, #28, 1964), two songs that reflected teen interest in cars and hot-rodding.

RITTER, TEX   Country singer and grade "B" western movie cowboy (also the father of TV star John Ritter). He hit the rock charts in 1961 with "I Dreamed of a Hill-Billy Heaven" (Capitol, #20, 1961). The song was a nostalgic look at many of the top country and western performers who had passed away. Its success not only showed that many members of the rock & roll audience had an interest in country and western music, but it reflected the nostalgic feelings that many Baby Boomers had for Tex, whom they had watched on Saturday morning TV westerns when they were growing up.

THE RIVIERAS   This pop rock group had a big hit with "California Sun" (Riviera, #5, 1964). The song reflected teenagers' fascination with surfing, beaches, and California in the early 1960s, and also mentioned popular dance fads of the era.

THE RIVINGTONS   Perhaps a better name for them would have been the Riveters, since their staccato vocals sounded like pneumatic hammers driving rivets into sheet metal. They made the rock charts with two R & B rock novelty songs, "Papa-Oom-Mow-Mow" (Liberty, #48, 1962) and "The Bird's the Word" (Liberty, #52, 1963). A later hit, "Surfin' Bird" done by the Trashmen in 1963, was a composite of the Rivingtons' two songs.

ROBBINS, MARTY   One of the few country and western stars to cross over consistently to the rock charts in the 1950s and early 1960s—perhaps because teenagers could relate to his songs. Robbins sang about about senior proms and high school on "A White

Sport Coat (and a Pink Carnation)" and "Cap and Gown." He dealt with teen romance and marriage on songs like "She Was Only Seventeen" and "Just Married." And he focused on Western themes (which many teenagers found interesting in a period dominated by TV westerns) on records such as "El Paso," "Big Iron," and "Ballad of the Alamo." His biggest hits include:

"Singin' the Blues"	Columbia	#26	1956
"A White Sport Coat (and a Pink Carnation)"	Columbia	#3	1957
"Just Married"	Columbia	#35	1958
"She Was Only Seventeen"	Columbia	#27	1958
"Cap and Gown"	Columbia	#45	1959
"El Paso"	Columbia	#1	1959
"Big Iron"	Columbia	#26	1960
"Is There Any Chance"	Columbia	#31	1960
"Ballad of the Alamo"	Columbia	#34	1960
"Don't Worry"	Columbia	#3	1961
"Devil Woman"	Columbia	#16	1962
"Ruby Ann"	Columbia	#18	1962

ROBERT AND JOHNNY They only had one hit, "We Belong Together" (Old Town, #33, 1958), but the romantic doo wop ballad became one of rock & roll's all-time classics.

ROBERTSON, DON This pop artist had a big hit in 1956 with an upbeat instrumental, "The Happy Whistler" (Capitol, #6, 1956).

ROBIC, IVO In 1959 Germany was back in the news. Only months before Soviet Premier Khrushchev had demanded that Berlin, and perhaps all of Germany, be reunified. With public attention focused on that Cold War target, a Yugoslavian pop singer, Ivo Robic, released "Morgen" (Laurie, #13, 1959). The pleasant-sounding song, recorded in German, caught the public mood and became a Top 20 record.

ROBIN, TINA This pop rock singer recorded "Dear Mr. D.J. Play It Again" (Mercury, #95, 1961), reflecting the rock & roll audience's interest in music, romance, and Top 40 radio.

THE ROBINS They had an R & B rock hit with "Smokey Joe's Cafe" (Atco, #79, 1955), written by Jerry Leiber and Mike Stoller. Two members of the group later formed the Coasters and recorded numerous other Leiber and Stoller hits like "Yakety Yak."

ROBINSON, FLOYD   During the summer of 1959 he had a Top 20 hit with a pop rock song called "Makin' Love" (RCA, #20, 1959). It dealt with teen interest in skipping school, romance, and kissing. The flip side, "My Girl," although never a hit, was a crazy novelty song about a guy's weird girlfriend.

ROBINSON, SMOKEY, AND THE MIRACLES   *See* the Miracles.

ROCHELL AND THE CANDLES   Their only hit came in 1961 with "Once Upon a Time" (Swingin', #26, 1961), an R & B rock ballad.

THE ROCK-A-TEENS   They made it into the Top 20 with a lively instrumental called "Woo-Hoo" (Roulette, #16, 1959). The record, a garage band mixture of doo wop and pop rock, featured fast-paced guitars and drums, with a group member singing "Woo-Hoo" over and over again as the melody.

THE ROCKIN' REBELS   *See* the Rebels.

THE ROCKY FELLERS   This pop rock act from the Phillipines, four brothers (aged 8 to 18) and their father, made the rock charts with "Killer Joe" (Scepter, #16, 1963) and "Like the Big Guys Do" (Scepter, #55, 1963). Both were upbeat, cheery songs about young teenagers in love.

RODGERS, EILEEN   A veteran pop singer who crossed over to the rock charts in 1958 with a romantic ballad called "Treasure of Your Love" (Columbia, #26, 1958).

RODGERS, JIMMIE   His unique blend of folk and rock earned him a string of hits in the late 1950s, beginning with "Honeycomb," a number one record in 1957. He made a brief comeback in the mid-1960s, and even got his own television variety show on CBS, as a summer replacement for Carol Burnett. His great success showed that the rock & roll audience had eclectic tastes, and foreshadowed the coming of 1960s folk rock. Jimmie Rodgers' greatest hits include:

"Honeycomb"   Roulette   #1   1957

"Kisses Sweeter Than Wine"	Roulette	#7	1957
"Oh-Oh, I'm Falling in Love Again"	Roulette	#22	1958
"Secretly"	Roulette	#4	1958
"Make Me a Miracle"	Roulette	#54	1958
"Are You Really Mine"	Roulette	#10	1958
"Bimbombey"	Roulette	#11	1958
"I'm Never Gonna Tell"	Roulette	#36	1959
"Ring-A-Ling-A-Lario"	Roulette	#32	1959
"Tucumcari"	Roulette	#32	1959
"T.L.C. Tender Love and Care"	Roulette	#24	1960
"It's Over"	Dot	#37	1966
"Child of Clay"	A&M	#31	1967

ROE, TOMMY He charged onto the rock charts in 1962 with "Sheila," a number one record that featured a Buddy Holly–like lead vocal and a galloping drum beat patterned after the one found on Holly's 1957 hit, "Peggy Sue." The flip side, "Save Your Kisses," was another excellent pop rock song influenced by Buddy Holly's rockabilly style. Roe admitted that Holly was his idol, and that he was indeed copying his sound. Throughout the rest of the 1960s and into the 1970s, Roe racked up hit after hit. At his best, on songs like "Sheila," "Everybody," and "Come On," Tommy Roe exhibited an authentic rockabilly sound. But at his worst, on records like "Jack and Jill" or "Jam Up Jelly Tight," Roe served up sophomoric, formula pop rock aimed at young teens. Tommy Roe's biggest sellers include:

"Sheila"	ABC/Paramount	#1	1962
"Susie Darlin'"	ABC/Paramount	#35	1962
"The Folk Singer"	ABC/Paramount	#84	1963
"Everybody"	ABC/Paramount	#3	1963
"Come On"	ABC/Paramount	#36	1964
"Carol"	ABC/Paramount	#61	1964
"Party Girl"	ABC/Paramount	#85	1964
"Sweet Pea"	ABC/Paramount	#8	1966
"Hooray for Hazel"	ABC	#6	1966
"It's Now Winter's Day"	ABC	#23	1966 +
"Dizzy"	ABC	#1	1969
"Heather Honey"	ABC	#29	1969
"Jack and Jill"	ABC	#53	1969
"Jam Up Jelly Tight"	ABC	#8	1969 +
"Stir It up and Serve It"	ABC	#50	1970
"Stagger Lee"	ABC	#25	1971

ROGERS, TIMMIE ("OH YEAH") He got his start as a stand-up comic at Harlem's Apollo Theater. In 1957 he recorded "Back to School Again" (Cameo, #36, 1957), which became a big favorite on "American Bandstand." With its "Stroll" dance beat and lyrics that complained about the end of summer vacation, the song appealed to teenagers.

THE ROLLERS This R & B rock group had a minor hit in 1961, "The Continental Walk" (Liberty, #80, 1961), a song about a new dance fad.

RONALD AND RUBY They had some success with "Lollipop" (RCA, #39, 1958). But, unfortunately for them, another version of the song by the Chordettes became the bigger seller, peaking at number two.

THE RONETTES Their sound, an excellent blend of R & B rock and pop rock, made them one of the most important girl groups of the early 1960s. Powered by Phil Spector's "Wall of Sound" production work, and Veronica "Ronnie" Bennett's rich lead vocals, the group recorded some of rock & roll's greatest hits. Their best sellers included the classics "Be My Baby" (Philles, #2, 1963) and "Baby I Love You" (Philles, #24, 1963+), as well as "The Best Part of Breakin' Up" (Philles, #39, 1964); "Do I Love You" (Philles, #34, 1964); and "Walking in the Rain" (Philles, #23, 1964). Phil Spector and Ronnie Bennett got married in the late 1960s. In 1986 Ronnie Spector made a cameo appearance on Eddie Money's number four record, "Take Me Home Tonight," which featured Ronnie singing the lead line from "Be My Baby."

RONNIE AND THE HI-LITES In 1962 they had a big hit with "I Wish That We Were Married" (Joy, #16, 1962), a maudlin R & B rock ballad that reflected traditional teen attitudes toward dating and marriage.

THE ROOFTOP SINGERS Their lead singer, Erik Darling, formerly played with the Tarriers and the Weavers. In 1963 the Rooftop Singers rode the rising tide of folk music to the top of the rock charts with "Walk Right In" (Vanguard, #1, 1963), followed by "Tom Cat" (Vanguard, #20, 1963).

THE ROOMMATES After backing Cathy Jean on "Please Love Me Forever," they had a hit of their own with "Glory of Love" (Valmor, #49, 1961).

ROSE, DAVID In 1962 this bandleader had a number one hit with a pop instrumental called "The Stripper" (MGM, #1, 1962). The record's obvious sexual theme made it especially popular among teens, and its great success showed that many members of the rock audience were still enjoying and buying records with a traditional pop sound.

ROSIE AND THE ORIGINALS They had one of the most interesting and biggest hits of 1961 with "Angel Baby" (Highland, #5, 1960+), an R & B–influenced ballad powered by Rosie's high-pitched lead vocal. The song reflected teen interest in dating and going steady. Their only other hit was "Lonely Blue Nights" (Brunswick, #66, 1961).

ROSS, JACK This comedian had two novelty hits, "Happy Jose" (Dot, #57, 1962) and "Cinderella" (Dot, #16, 1962).

ROSS, SPENCER This pop musician received airplay on many rock stations with "Tracy's Theme" (Columbia, #13, 1960), an instrumental from the television production of *The Philadelphia Story*, which also fit nicely into the rock & roll formula of songs about girls' names.

THE ROUTERS They made it big in 1962 with a rousing, hand-clapping pop rock instrumental called "Let's Go" (Warner, #19, 1962). The song, as they said on "American Bandstand," had a good beat you could dance to. And the "Let's Go" chant became an immediate favorite with cheerleaders at sporting events and pep rallies. Their follow-up was another instrumental, "Sting Ray" (Warner, #50, 1963).

THE ROVER BOYS This Canadian group's soft, pop rock harmonies earned them hits with ballads like "Graduation Day" (ABC/Paramount, #16, 1956) and "From a School Ring to a Wedding Ring" (ABC/Paramount, #79, 1956). Both reflected traditional teen attitudes toward high school and dating in the mid 1950s.

THE ROYAL TEENS   In the late 1950s this pop rock group had several hits about teenage interests. Their biggest was "Short Shorts" (ABC/Paramount, #3, 1958), a sassy and sexy song that dealt with a popular girls' fashion. Their next release, "Big Name Button" (ABC/Paramount, 1958), focused on the teenage fad of wearing big, pin-on buttons that displayed the wearer's name. Although it failed to make the national charts, it did become popular on "American Bandstand" and on various radio stations across the country. They followed up with a novelty song, "Harvey's Got a Girlfriend" (ABC/Paramount, #78, 1958), about teen dating practices. Their last hit was "Believe Me" (Capitol, #26, 1959), an excellent doo wop ballad which expressed teen agony over lost love. One of the group's members, Bob Gaudio, later joined the Four Seasons.

THE ROYALTONES   Their only big hit came in 1958 with a honking sax instrumental, "Poor Boy" (Jubilee, #17, 1958).

RUBY AND THE ROMANTICS   This R & B rock group from Akron, Ohio, with a sound closer to white pop than rhythm and blues, had three big hits in 1963: "Our Day Will Come" (Kapp, #1, 1963); "My Summer Love" (Kapp, #16, 1963); and "Hey There Lonely Boy" (Kapp, #27, 1963). All three dealt with teenage love and romance.

THE RUMBLERS   Their name tried to plug into popular images of rebellious teens. Their only hit was a pop rock instrumental called "Boss" (Dot, #87, 1963).

RUSS, LONNIE   He had a minor hit in 1963 with "My Wife Can't Cook" (4-J, #57, 1962+), a novelty song about a sexual stereotype of the early 1960s.

RYAN, CHARLIE   In 1960 he released "Hot Rod Lincoln" (4 Star, #33, 1960) at about the same time that Johnny Bond released his version. Both records reflected teen interest in hot rods and racing, and both became hits (with Bond's version doing a little better, coming in at number 26).

RYDELL, BOBBY   A perfect example of the teen idols of the early 1960s, Rydell was boyishly handsome, had a magnificent pompadour hairstyle, an ever-present smile, and a seemingly never-ending supply of beautiful sweaters. Like other teen idols of the early 1960s such as Frankie Avalon, Fabian, or Bobby Vee, he was the clean-cut All-American boy come to life. His image, songs, and the fact that he was a local boy from Philadelphia made him a favorite on "American Bandstand." He also co-starred with Ann-Margaret and Dick Van Dyke in the popular movie *Bye Bye Birdie*. His hit records dealt with romance, dancing, or other teen interests. At his best, he put out some good songs that captured the feel of authentic rock & roll, including "Wild One," "I've Got Bonnie," and "I'll Never Dance Again." Most of his hits, though, were formula pop rock aimed at the teen market. Bobby Rydell's biggest-selling records include:

"Kissin' Time"	Cameo	#11	1959
"We Got Love"	Cameo	#6	1959
"I Dig Girls"	Cameo	#46	1959
"Wild One"	Cameo	#2	1960
"Swingin' School"	Cameo	#5	1960
"Ding-A-Ling"	Cameo	#18	1960
"Volare"	Cameo	#4	1960
"Sway"	Cameo	#14	1960
"Good Time Baby"	Cameo	#11	1961
"That Old Black Magic"	Cameo	#21	1961
"The Fish"	Cameo	#25	1961
"I Wanna Thank You"	Cameo	#21	1961
"Jingle Bell Rock" (with Chubby Checker)	Cameo	#21	1961
"I've Got Bonnie"	Cameo	#18	1962
"I'll Never Dance Again"	Cameo	#14	1962
"The Cha-Cha-Cha"	Cameo	#10	1962
"Butterfly Baby"	Cameo	#23	1963
"Wildwood Days"	Cameo	#17	1963
"Forget Him"	Cameo	#4	1963+
"A World Without Love"	Cameo	#80	1964
"I Can't Say Goodbye"	Capitol	#94	1964

THE SAFARIS   This pop rock group from Los Angeles had a big hit in 1960 with "Image of a Girl" (Eldo, #6, 1960), a doo wop ballad about a boy dreaming of the perfect girl. The song reflected romantic and sexual stereotypes of the day.

SAKAMOTO, KYU   This Japanese pop singer made it to the top of the rock charts in 1963 with "Sukiyaki" (Capitol, #1, 1963), a pleasant-sounding pop record sung entirely in Japanese. The unlikely hit caught on in America not only because it was a novelty, but also because it had a catchy melody and unforgettable refrain.

SANDS, JODIE   She had one hit, "With All My Heart" (Chancellor, #20, 1957), a pop rock song that focused on teen romance.

SANDS, TOMMY   He catapulted to fame in 1957, after starring in a television special, "The Singing Idol," based loosely on Elvis Presley's career. One of the songs he sang on the show, "Teen-Age Crush" (Capitol, #3, 1957), became a major hit for him. Other hits followed, including "Goin' Steady" (Capitol, #19, 1957); "Sing Boy Sing" (Capitol, #46, 1958); and "Sinner Man" (Capitol, 1958). This good-looking pop performer (who later married Nancy Sinatra) is a prime example of a media-created teen idol. His brand of pop rock was imitative and lacked any real rock & roll feel. And his success shows that many teenagers would buy any product being marketed as rock & roll.

SANTAMARIA, MONGO   In 1963 this Cuban-born bandleader and bongo player had a Top 10 hit with "Watermelon Man" (Battle, #10, 1963). The song mixed Latin rhythms with jazz and a rock beat, foreshadowing the eclectic R & B rock sound of the late 1960s and early 1970s.

SANTO AND JOHNNY   These two brothers from Brooklyn had a number one record their first time out with "Sleepwalk" (Canadian/American, #1, 1959). The instrumental featured Santo's steel guitar on lead. Its beautiful sound was perfect for slow, cheek-to-cheek dancing. They followed with other instrumentals such as "Tear Drop" (Canadian/American, #23, 1959); "Caravan" (Canadian/American, #48, 1960); and "Twistin' Bells" (Canadian/American, #49, 1960).

THE SCHOOLBOYS   Their name reflects the strong connection between rock & roll and youth culture. They made the national charts one time, with an R & B rock song called "Shirley" (Okeh, #91, 1957).

SCOTT, FREDDY   His blend of R & B rock and pop led to a Top 10 hit in 1963, "Hey Girl" (Colpix, #10, 1963), a Carole King and Gerry Goffin composition about love and heartbreak.

SCOTT, JACK He did not look like a typical rock & roll singer. He was comparatively old—in his mid 20s when most rock & rollers were still in their teens—and powerfully built, unlike many adolescent-looking rock stars. Yet he could sing country rock with the best of them. His first record was a two-sided hit, a lively rocker called "Leroy's Back (In Jail Again)," backed with a country rock ballad, "My True Love." He followed up with other impressive hits such as "Goodbye Baby," "The Way I Walk," and "What in the World's Come Over You." Many of his songs dealt with tragedy and love gone wrong, themes to which many teens could relate. Jack Scott's biggest hits include

"Leroy's Back (In Jail Again)"	Carlton	#25	1958
"My True Love"	Carlton	#3	1958
"With Your Love"	Carlton	#28	1958
"Goodbye Baby"	Carlton	#8	1958 +
"The Way I Walk"	Carlton	#35	1959
"What in the World's Come Over You"	Top Rank	#5	1960
"Burning Bridges"	Top Rank	#3	1960
"Oh, Little One"	Top Rank	#34	1960

SCOTT, LINDA She enjoyed success in the early 1960s with "I've Told Every Little Star" (Canadian/American, #3, 1961); "Don't Bet Money Honey" (Canadian/American, #9, 1961); "I Don't Know Why" (Canadian/American, #12, 1961); and "Count Every Star" (Canadian/American, #41, 1962). Her records featured her perky, teenage voice singing about teen romance, and are good examples of early 1960s pop rock aimed at the white, suburban teen audience.

THE SECRETS This girl group from Cleveland had one hit, a pop rock song called "The Boy Next Door" (Philips, #18, 1963).

SEDAKA, NEIL One of the most successful pop rock performers of the late 1950s and early 1960s. Unlike most other singers from the era, Sedaka wrote most of his hits (collaborating with Howard Greenfield). He first made the rock charts in 1958 with a doo wop ballad called "The Diary." Over the next five years he collected 11 more Top 30 hits, including rock classics like "Oh! Carol" (written for Carole King), "Calendar Girl," "Happy Birthday, Sweet Sixteen," and "Breaking Up Is Hard to Do." Sedaka's cheery, upbeat records about teen romance and interests are good examples of early pop rock. After many years off the charts, he staged a remarkable comeback in the late 1970s with "Laughter in the Rain" and several additional hits, including a sloweddown remake of "Breaking Up Is Hard to Do." Sedaka's greatest hits include:

"The Diary"	RCA	#14	1958+
"I Go Ape"	RCA	#42	1959
"Oh! Carol"	RCA	#9	1959
"Stairway to Heaven"	RCA	#9	1960
"You Mean Everything to Me"	RCA	#17	1960
"Run Samson Run"	RCA	#28	1960
"Calendar Girl"	RCA	#4	1960+
"Little Devil"	RCA	#11	1961
"Happy Birthday, Sweet Sixteen"	RCA	#6	1961+
"Breaking Up Is Hard to Do"	RCA	#1	1962
"Next Door to an Angel"	RCA	#5	1962
"Alice in Wonderland"	RCA	#17	1963
"Let's Go Steady Again"	RCA	#26	1963
"Laughter in the Rain"	Rocket	#1	1974+
"The Immigrant"	Rocket	#22	1975
"That's When the Music Takes Me"	Rocket	#27	1975
"Bad Blood"	Rocket	#1	1975
"Breaking Up Is Hard to Do"	Rocket	#8	1975+
"Love in the Shadows"	Rocket	#16	1976
"Steppin' Out"	Rocket	#36	1976
"Amarillo"	Elektra	#44	1977
"Should've Never Let You Go" (duet sung with his daughter, Dara)	Elektra	#19	1980

THE SENSATIONS This group featured Yvonne Baker as the lead singer and had one big hit, "Let Me In" (Argo, #4, 1962), a bouncy R & B rock song. Its opening line, "Let me in—whee ooh/ Ooh whee ooh!" brought back memories of vintage 1950s rhythm and blues.

SEVILLE, DAVID His real name was Ross Bagdasarian. In 1951 he co-wrote Rosemary Clooney's hit "Come On-a My House," and in 1957 had his own hit record with "Armen's Theme" (Liberty, #42, 1956+) (named for his wife). Two years later, while experimenting on a tape recorder, he accidently hit upon the idea of speeding up the voice track to produce a weird but funny effect. It resulted in the novelty pop rock record, "Witch Doctor" (Liberty, #1, 1958), which became enormously popular on "American

Bandstand" and a number one record across the country. After several minor follow-up hits, such as "The Bird on My Head" (Liberty, #36, 1958) and "Judy" (Liberty, #86, 1959), Seville used his speeded-up "Witch Doctor" voice on another record. The result was "The Chipmunk Song" in 1958, followed by many other Chipmunk hits. *See* The Chipmunks.

THE SEVILLES They enjoyed some success in 1961 with "Charlena" (J.C., #84, 1961), a pop rock song which, like many others, focused on a girl's name.

THE SHANGRI-LAS This girl group was formed in the early 1960s. Though pop rockers, they had a punk sound and sexy style echoing 1950s R & B rock. They first reached the rock charts with "Remember (Walkin' in the Sand)" (Red Bird, #5, 1964), an offbeat song about lost love. They followed with their biggest hit, "Leader of the Pack" (Red Bird, #1, 1964), a teen tragedy about a motorcycle gang leader, complete with screeching tires, revved-up engines, and breaking glass. Additional hits followed, such as "Give Him a Great Big Kiss" (Red Bird, #18, 1964 +); "Give Us Your Blessings (Red Bird, #29, 1965); "I Can Never Go Home Anymore" (Red Bird, #6, 1965); and "Past, Present, and Future" (Red Bird, #59, 1966). The Shangri-Las' songs reflected teenage fears about love and rebellious attitudes toward adults.

SHANNON, DEL One of the most talented pop rockers of the early 1960s. In 1961 he made it to the top of the rock charts with "Runaway," an outstanding song about lost love. It featured Shannon's strong vocal, supported by a haunting melody and a marvelous electric organ solo played on a Musitron. Written by Shannon, the song is one of rock's all-time greatest hits. He followed up with additional hits playing to teen interests. In 1963, prior to the Beatles' arrival on the American charts, Shannon became the first American artist to have a hit with a Lennon-McCarthy composition, "From Me to You." In the early 1980s Shannon made a comeback with a hit single, "Sea of Love," and an album produced by Tom Petty (of the Heartbreakers). Del Shannon's greatest hits include:

"Runaway"	Big Top	#1	1961
"Hats Off to Larry"	Big Top	#5	1961
"So Long Baby"	Big Top	#28	1961

"Hey! Little Girl"	Big Top	#38	1961+
"The Swiss Maid"	Big Top	#64	1962
"Little Town Flirt"	Big Top	#12	1962+
"Two Kinds of Teardrops"	Big Top	#50	1963
"From Me To You"	Big Top	#77	1963
"Sue's Gotta Be Mine"	Berlee	#71	1963
"Handy Man"	Amy	#22	1964
"Do You Want to Dance?"	Amy	#43	1964
"Keep Searchin' (We'll Follow the Sun)"	Amy	#9	1964+
"Stranger in Town"	Amy	#30	1965
"The Big Hurt"	Liberty	#94	1966
"Sea of Love"	Network	#33	1981+

SHARP, DEE DEE This R & B rock singer had several hits in the early 1960s, including "Mashed Potato Time" (Cameo, #2, 1962); "Gravy (For My Mashed Potatoes)" (Cameo, #9, 1962); "Ride" (Cameo, #5, 1962); and "Do the Bird" (Cameo, #10, 1963). All were dance songs, reflecting teen interest in new dance steps.

SHARPE, RAY His only hit came in 1959, with an offbeat song he had written called "Linda Lu" (Jamie, #46, 1959). Not only did it follow the pop formula of focusing on a girl's name, but doubled it! Sharpe gave his girl two names, explaining that people called her Patty, but her real name was Linda Lu. Perhaps he thought that a girl with two names would appeal to twice as many people. At any rate, the gimmick did not work: the well-crafted pop rock record failed to make the Top 40.

THE SHELLS They had a hit with "Baby Oh Baby" (Johnson, #21, 1960+), an R & B rock song about teen romance.

SHEP AND THE LIMELITES Shep, as the lead singer of the Heart-beats, had a hit record in 1956 called "A Thousand Miles Away." In 1961, with his new group the Limelites, he recorded a sequel, "Daddy's Home" (Hull, #2, 1961), which became an even bigger hit. The group's 1950s doo wop style earned them additional hits such as "Ready for Your Love" (Hull, #42, 1961); "Three Steps from the Altar" (Hull, #58, 1961); and "Our Anniversary" (Hull, #59, 1962).

THE SHEPHERD SISTERS These pop singers had a Top 20 hit with "Alone (Why Must I Be Alone)" (Lance, #20, 1957).

SHERMAN, ALLAN He started in the entertainment business as a comedy writer for Jackie Gleason, and later wrote for TV shows such as *"I've Got a Secret"* and "The Steve Allen Show." In 1963 he released a comedy record, "Hullo Muddah, Hullo Fadduh!" (Warner, #2, 1963), which zoomed up the rock charts. The novelty record was narrated from the point of view of a little boy at summer camp writing to his mother and father. Both Baby Boomers and their parents could relate to the idea, and found it hilarious.

THE SHERRYS This girl group had two R & B rock hits singing about new dance steps: "Pop Pop Pop-Pie" (Guyden, #35, 1962) and "Slop Time" (Guyden, #97, 1963).

THE SHIELDS They had one of the outstanding records of 1958 with "You Cheated" (Dot, #15, 1958). The song was a classic example of R & B rock, with doo wop harmonies and soaring falsettos provided by Jesse Belvin.

THE SHIRELLES Composed of Shirley Alston, Beverly Lee, Doris Kenner, and Micki Harris, the Shirelles (named after lead singer Alston) were the quintessential girl group of the early 1960s. For three years, from 1960 until 1963, they dominated the rock charts with their their sexy, R & B rock sound. It earned them 12 Top 40 hits, including two number one records. The Shirelles produced some of the finest hits in rock & roll history, including "Will You Love Me Tomorrow" (a number one record written by Carole King and Gerry Goffin); "Baby It's You" (a sexually charged rendition of a song written by Burt Bacharach and Hal David); "Dedicated to the One I Love" (which later became a hit for the Mamas and Papas); "Soldier Boy" (a number one record that reflected the era's patriotic attitudes); and the vastly underrated "Tonight's the Night." Their authentic R & B rock style and intimate vocals combined to produced classic, folk-quality recordings. The Shirelles' greatest hits include:

"I Met Him on a Sunday"	Decca	#50	1958
"Tonight's the Night"	Scepter	#39	1960
"Will You Love Me Tomorrow"	Scepter	#1	1960+
"Dedicated to the One I Love"	Scepter	#3	1961
"Mama Said"	Scepter	#4	1961
"A Thing of the Past"	Scepter	#41	1961
"What a Sweet Thing That Was"	Scepter	#54	1961

"Big John"	Scepter	#21	1961
"Baby It's You"	Scepter	#8	1961 +
"Soldier Boy"	Scepter	#1	1962
"Welcome Home Baby"	Scepter	#22	1962
"Stop the Music"	Scepter	#36	1962
"Everybody Loves a Lover"	Scepter	#19	1962 +
"Foolish Little Girl"	Scepter	#4	1963
"Don't Say Goodnight and Mean Goodbye"	Scepter	#26	1963
"What Does a Girl Do"	Scepter	#53	1963
"It's a Mad, Mad, Mad, Mad World"	Scepter	#92	1963
"Tonight You're Gonna Fall in Love With Me"	Scepter	#57	1964

SHIRLEY AND LEE   This duo began singing rhythm and blues in the early 1950s. Their greatest success came with two R & B rock hits, "Let the Good Times Roll" (Aladdin, #27, 1956) and "I Feel Good" (Aladdin, #38, 1956 +).

SHONDELL, TROY   A perfect example of the one-hit rock artist. He had a Top 10 record in 1961 with "This Time" (Liberty, #6, 1961), a pop rock song about teen love gone wrong.

SHORR, MICKEY, AND THE CUTUPS   They had a minor hit with a novelty record, "Doctor Ben Basey" (Tuba, #60, 1962), a spoof on TV's popular medical drama, "Ben Casey."

THE SHOWMEN   This R & B rock group made the national charts in 1962 with "It Will Stand" (Minit, #61, 1961 +).

THE SILHOUETTES   Even though this Philadelphia quartet had only one hit, it turned out to be one of the greatest hits in rock & roll history. In 1958 they made it to number one with "Get a Job" (Ember, #1, 1958), a classic example of 1950s doo wop. The song also reflected 1950s attitudes about work, the economy, and marriage. One line in "Get a Job" later inspired the name for Sha Na Na, one of the most popular nostalgia groups of the 1970s.

SIMEONE CHORALE, HARRY   This veteran pop musician and arranger first hit the rock charts in 1958 with "The Little Drummer Boy" (20th Century Fox, #13, 1958). Every Christmas season for the next five years, the record was re-released and headed straight up the charts. His great success showed that even teenagers hooked on rock & roll took time off to listen to traditional pop songs around Christmas time.

SIMON & GARFUNKEL   These folk rock superstars got their start as pop rockers during rock & roll's first decade. When they began in the late 1950s, they billed themselves as "Tom and Jerry," named after the cartoon characters. Their first record, "Hey School Girl," was just a minor hit, but it did land them a guest appearance on "American Bandstand." The two performers then went their separate ways, with Simon landing on the charts two more times in the early 1960s, once as part of the group Tico and the Triumphs with the song "Motorcycle," and the other time as a solo artist, singing under the name Jerry Landis, with the song "The Lone Teen Ranger."

Inspired by the rise of folk music, Simon and Garfunkel reunited in the mid 1960s as a folk duo using their real names, and had a number one record in 1966 with "Sounds of Silence." Numerous other hit singles and albums followed as they became one of the top folk rock groups. They split up in 1971, each pursuing solo projects. Their greatest hits—as a group and as individuals—include:

A.   Simon and Garfunkel:

"Hey School Girl" (by Tom & Jerry)	Big	#54	1957+
"The Sounds of Silence"	Columbia	#1	1965+
"Homeward Bound"	Columbia	#5	1966
"I Am a Rock"	Columbia	#3	1966
"The Dangling Conversation"	Columbia	#25	1966
"A Hazy Shade of Winter"	Columbia	#13	1966
"At the Zoo"	Columbia	#16	1967
"Fakin' It"	Columbia	#23	1967
"Scarborough Fair/Canticle"	Columbia	#11	1968
"Mrs. Robinson"	Columbia	#1	1968
"The Boxer"	Columbia	#7	1969
"Bridge Over Troubled Water"	Columbia	#1	1970
"Cecilia"	Columbia	#4	1970
"El Condor Pasa"	Columbia	#18	1970
"For Emily, Whenever I May Find Her"	Columbia	#53	1972
"My Little Town"	Columbia	#9	1975
"Wake Up Little Susie"	Columbia	#27	1982

B. *Paul Simon*:

"Motorcycle" (as part of Tico and the Triumphs)	Amy	#99	1962
"The Lone Teen Ranger" (as Jerry Landis)	Amy	#97	1963
"Mother and Child Reunion"	Columbia	#4	1972
"Me and Julio Down By the School Yard"	Columbia	#22	1972
"Kodachrome"	Columbia	#2	1973
"Loves Me Like a Rock"	Columbia	#2	1973
"American Tune"	Columbia	#35	1973 +
"Gone At Last"	Columbia	#23	1975
"50 Ways To Leave Your Lover"	Columbia	#1	1975 +
"Still Crazy After All These Years"	Columbia	#40	1976
"Slip Slidin' Away"	Columbia	#5	1977 +
"Late in the Evening"	Columbia	#6	1980
"You Can Call Me Al"	Columbia	#23	1986 +
"Graceland"	Columbia	#81	1986 +

C. *Art Garfunkel*:

"All I Know"	Columbia	#9	1973
"I Shall Sing"	Columbia	#38	1973 +
"Second Avenue"	Columbia	#34	1974
"I Only Have Eyes for You"	Columbia	#18	1975
"Break Away"	Columbia	#39	1975 +
"Wonderful World" (with Simon & James Taylor)	Columbia	#17	1978
"Since I Don't Have You"	Columbia	#53	1979

SIMONE, NINA   Many rock & roll fans loved her bluesy "I Loves You, Porgy" (Bethlehem, #18, 1959), from *Porgy and Bess*.

THE SIMS TWINS   Had a minor hit in 1961 with an R & B rock song, "Soothe Me" (Sar, #42, 1961).

SINATRA, FRANK   His smooth crooner style continued to appeal to many members of the rock & roll audience throughout the 1950s and 1960s. Hits that made the rock charts during rock's first decade included "All the Way" (Capitol, #2, 1957), from the movie *The Joker Is Wild;* "High Hopes" (Capitol, #30, 1959), from the film *A Hole in the Head;* "Nice 'n' Easy" (Capitol, #60, 1960); and "Ol' MacDonald" (Capitol, #25, 1960). In the mid and late 1960s Sinatra frequently hit the rock charts with big sellers like "Softly,

As I Leave You" (Reprise, #27, 1964); "It Was a Very Good Year" (Reprise, #28, 1965 +); "Strangers in the Night" (Reprise, #1, 1966); "Summer Wind" (Reprise, #25, 1966); "That's Life" (Reprise, #4, 1966); "Somethin' Stupid" (Reprise, #1, 1967), a duet sung with his daughter, Nancy; "The World We Knew" (Reprise, #30, 1967); "Cycles" (Reprise, #23, 1968); and "My Way" (Reprise, #27, 1969), written by Paul Anka. Sinatra's continuing success proved that many teenagers had very traditional musical tastes.

THE SINGING NUN   In 1963 Sister Sourier had a big hit with "Dominique" (Philips, #1, 1963), a song she had written while in a Belgian convent. A movie about her life soon followed. The record by this novelty act, a Belgian nun singing a pleasant song in French accompanied only by her acoustic guitar, had an infectious melody and an authentic folk quality. With folk music on the rise in the United States, the Singing Nun and "Dominique" were at the right place at the right time.

THE SIX TEENS   The name of this R & B rock group demonstrated the tie between youth and rock & roll. They had two minor hits, "A Casual Look" (Flip, #25, 1956) and "Arrow of Love" (Flip, #80, 1957).

SKIP AND FLIP   This pop rock duo, with soft doo wop harmonies, had two Top 20 hits: "It Was I" (Brent, #11, 1959) and "Cherry Pie" (Brent, #11, 1960). The latter was a remake of Marvin & Johnny's R & B rock classic. Flip, whose real name was Gary Paxton, later joined the Hollywood Argyles and had a hit with "Alley-Oop."

THE SKYLINERS   Their first hit, "Since I Don't Have You" (Calico, #12, 1959), was one of the most popular records of 1959. The excellent pop rock ballad featured a fabulous lead vocal by Jimmy Beaumont and backup harmonies that blended traditional pop and doo wop. Their other hits, "This I Swear" (Calico, #26, 1959) and "Pennies from Heaven" (Calico, #24, 1960), used the same ingredients for success. All reflected teen interest in romance.

THE SLADES   In 1958 they recorded "You Cheated" (Domino, #42, 1958), a song written by their lead singer. But their record was soon bumped off the charts by the Shields' version which went on to become a major hit.

SMITH, HUEY "PIANO," AND THE CLOWNS   Huey Smith came out of the New Orleans rhythm and blues tradition to record several rollicking R & B rock songs. His biggest hits included "Rockin' Pneumonia and the Boogie Woogie Flu" (Ace, #52, 1957); "Don't You Just Know It" (Ace, #9, 1958); and "Don't You Know Yockomo" (Ace, #56, 1958 +). He also wrote and played on "Sea Cruise," which became a big hit for Frankie Ford in 1959.

SMITH, JIMMY   This long-time jazz organist had his only Top 30 hit with "Walk on the Wild Side" (Verve, #21, 1962), an instrumental taken from the movie of the same name. The record's success reflected the film's great popularity, and the eclectic tastes of many members of the rock audience.

SMITH, RAY   His only big hit was a pop rock single called "Rockin' Little Angel" (Judd, #22, 1960).

SMITH, ROGER   He starred as the suave, cool private eye on TV's "77 Sunset Strip." In 1959 he tried to transfer his television popularity to a recording career, and enjoyed moderate success with "Beach Time" (Warner, #64, 1959), a pop rock song that tried to take advantage of the beach party fad of the day.

SMITH, WARREN   This rockabilly singer came out of the Sun Records stable that produced other country rockers like Elvis Presley, Jerry Lee Lewis, and Carl Perkins. Smith's lone hit was "So Long I'm Gone" (Sun, #72, 1957).

SOMMERS, JOANIE   This perky pop singer from Buffalo, New York, had several pop rock hits in the early 1960s. Her first, "One Boy" (Warner, #54, 1960), came from the musical *Bye Bye Birdie*. She followed up with "Johnnie Get Angry" (Warner, #7, 1962), a melodramatic song about teen dating. Although her next release, "When the Boys Get Together" (Warner, #94, 1962), barely made the charts, her bouncy, adolescent voice and her teen-oriented songs helped type her as a rising pop star of the Baby Boom generation. Pepsi Cola tried to take advantage of her image by selecting her to sing several "We Are the Pepsi Generation" commercials.

SOUL, JIMMY   His first hit came in 1962 with Twistin' Matilda" (S.P.Q.R., #22, 1962), an R & B rocker that blended Latin rhythms with the Twist dance fad. After disappearing for nearly a year, he returned to the charts with another R & B rock hit, "If You Wanna Be Happy" (S.P.Q.R., #1, 1963). The lively Latin-influenced song made it to the top of the rock charts with its novel advice: If you want to be happy, marry an ugly girl who will be grateful, instead of a pretty one, who will only cause problems.

SOUTH, JOE He came out of a country and western background in the late 1950s with two minor hits, a novelty record called "The Purple People Eater Meets the Witch Doctor" (NRC, #71, 1958), and a country rock ballad, "You're the Reason" (Fairlane, #87, 1961). His greatest success came in the late 1960s and early 1970s with country-influenced hits like "Games People Play" (Capitol, #12, 1969); "Don't It Make You Want to Go Home" (Capitol, #41, 1969); and "Walk a Mile In My Shoes" (Capitol, #12, 1970). He also played as a Nashville studio musician in the mid 1960s and wrote several outstanding hits for other performers, including "Down in the Boondocks" for Billy Joe Royal; "Hush" for Deep Purple; "Rose Garden" for Lynn Anderson; and "These Are Not My People" for Johnny Rivers.

THE SPACEMEN By the late 1950s many Americans were gazing at the heavens in response to media coverage of Sputnik, Muttnik, UFOs, and the growing U.S. space program. A group calling themselves the Spacemen tried to capitalize on the trend with a novelty record called "The Clouds" (Alton, #41, 1959).

THE SPANIELS One of the original R & B rock groups of the early 1950s. Their first success came with rhythm and blues hits like "Baby It's You" (Chance, 1953) and "Goodnight, Sweetheart, Goodnight" (Vee Jay, 1954). The latter song became an early R & B rock classic. Their doo wop style earned them another hit in 1957, "Everyone's Laughing" (Vee Jay, #69, 1957).

SPECTOR, PHIL He got his start as part of the Teddybears, a group that had a soft, doo wop sound similar to the Fleetwoods'. Spector wrote their first release, the beautiful pop rock ballad "To Know Him Is to Love Him" (Dore, #1, 1958), and it shot to the top of the rock charts. Spector soon turned full-time to writing and producing records for other rock artists. His stunning creativity earned him the nickname "the boy genius," and his lush arrangements, dubbed the "Wall of Sound" because of their multi-layers of voices and instruments, resulted in some of rock & roll's all-time greatest hits. Those records represented the state of rock art in the early 1960s, and reflected teen interest in romance and music. Spector was inducted into the Rock & Roll Hall of Fame in 1988. Some of the greatest hits produced by Phil Spector include:

"To Know Him Is to Love Him" (sung by the Teddybears)
"Corrina, Corrina" (Ray Peterson)
"Be My Boy" (Paris Sisters)
"I Love How You Love Me" (Paris Sisters)
"He Knows I Love Him Too Much" (Paris Sisters)
"Pretty Little Angel Eyes" (Curtis Lee)
"Every Breath I Take" (Gene Pitney)
"There's No Other Like My Baby" (Crystals)
"Uptown" (Crystals)
"He's a Rebel" (Crystals)
"He Hit Me (And It Felt Like a Kiss)" (Crystals)
"He's Sure the Boy I Love" (Crystals)
"Da Doo Ron Ron" (Crystals)
"Then He Kissed Me" (Crystals)
"Second Hand Love" (Connie Francis)
"Zip-A-Dee-Doo-Dah" (Bob B. Soxx and the Blue Jeans)
"Today I Met the Boy I'm Going to Marry" (Darlene Love)
"Wait Til My Bobby Gets Home" (Darlene Love)
"A Fine Fine Boy" (Darlene Love)
"Be My Baby" (Ronettes)
"Baby I Love You" (Ronettes)
"The Best Part of Breakin' Up" (Ronettes)
"Do I Love You" (Ronettes)
"Walking in the Rain" (Ronettes)
"Spanish Harlem" (Ben E. King)
"Stand By Me" (Ben E. King)
"Deep Purple" (Nino Tempo and April Stevens)
"You've Lost That Lovin' Feelin'" (Righteous Brothers)
"Just Once in My Life" (Righteous Brothers)
"Unchained Melody" (Righteous Brothers)
"Ebb Tide" (Righteous Brothers)
"River Deep, Mountain High" (Ike and Tina Turner)
"The Long and Winding Road" (Beatles)

SPENCER & SPENCER They had a hit in 1959 with "Russian Bandstand" (Argo, #91, 1959). The pop record, which spoofed the very popular "American Bandstand," showed that teenagers, like adults, were preoccupied with the Soviets and the Cold War.

THE SPINNERS This R & B rock group from Detroit had their first hit with "That's What Girls Are Made For" (Tri-Phi, #27, 1961), a Top 30 hit that reflected sexual stereotypes of the day. Their greatest successes came later in the 1970s and 1980s with hits like "I'll Be Around" (Atlantic, #3, 1972); "Could It Be I'm Falling in Love" (Atlantic, #4, 1972+); "One of a Kind (Love Affair)" (Atlantic, #11, 1973); "Then Came You" (Atlantic, #1, 1974, a duet with Dionne Warwick); "They Just Can't Stop It" (Atlantic, #5, 1975); "The Rubberband Man" (Atlantic, #2, 1976); "Working My Way Back to You/Forgive Me Girl" (Atlantic, #2, 1979+); and "Cupid/I've Loved You for a Long Time" (Atlantic, #4, 1980).

THE SPRINGFIELDS They were one of the few English acts to find success in America prior to the Beatles' arrival. In 1962, they contributed to the rising wave of folk music with their Top 20 hit, "Silver Threads and Golden Needles" (Philips, #20, 1962), a country-influenced folk song. One of the group's members, Dusty Springfield, later had many solo pop rock hits such as "I Only Want to Be with You" (Philips, #12, 1964); "Stay Awhile" (Philips, #38, 1964); "Wishin' and Hopin'" (Philips, #6, 1964); "You Don't Have to Say You Love Me" (Philips, #4, 1966); "All I See Is You" (Philips, #20, 1966); "The Look of Love" (Philips, #22, 1967); "Son of a Preacher Man" (Atlantic, #10, 1968+); "The Windmills of Your Mind" (Atlantic, #31, 1969); and "A Brand New Me" (Atlantic, #24, 1969).

STACY, CLYDE His only hit was "So Young" (Candlelight, #68, 1957), an excellent rockabilly song about the anguish of teenage love.

STAFFORD, TERRY He made the rock charts just before the British rock invasion of 1964. His early 1960s' pop rock style and Elvis Presley–like voice earned him hits with "Suspicion" (Crusader, #3, 1964) and "I'll Touch a Star" (Crusader, #25, 1964). But like many pop rockers from the early 1960s, he was quickly buried in the avalanche of British rock singers.

STAPLETON, CYRIL This British orchestra leader had a big hit with "The Children's Marching Song" (London, #13, 1959), from the film *The Inn of the Sixth Happiness*. The fact that many members of the rock audience liked the song reflected the popularity of the movie and showed that teen interests were often quite traditional.

THE STARLETS They had a Top 40 hit with "Better Tell Him No" (Pam, #38, 1961), an R & B rock song about teen dating.

STARR, KAY A pop singer from the 1940s who had a number one record in 1956 with "Rock and Roll Waltz" (RCA, #1, 1955+). The song's great success was an indication of the rising teen market, and showed that any record geared to that new audience could sell. It became a prototype for formula pop rock.

STARR, RANDY In 1957 he had a hit with "After School" (Dale, #32, 1957), a pop rock song reflecting teen attitudes toward school. Two years later, as a member of the Islanders, he made the charts again with an instrumental called "The Enchanted Sea."

THE STEREOS This R & B rock group from Ohio made the national charts with "I Really Love You" (Cub, #29, 1961), an upbeat number about teen romance.

STEVE AND EYDIE Pop singers Steve Lawrence and Eydie Gorme joined together for two hits in 1963. The husband and wife team made the Top 30 with a Carole King composition, "I Want to Stay Here" (Columbia, #28, 1963). Their follow-up was "I Can't Stop Talking About You" (Columbia, #35, 1963+). Both were traditional pop songs about romance.

STEVENS, APRIL She had minor success in 1959 with "Teach Me, Tiger" (Imperial, #86, 1959), a pop rock song that reflected sexual stereotypes of the day. Later she would team up with her brother, Nino Tempo, to record smash hits like "Deep Purple" (1963) and "Whispering" (1963).

STEVENS, CONNIE This Hollywood starlet played Cricket Blake on TV's "Hawaiian Eye." She first tasted success in the recording field when she sang the female part on Edd Byrnes' 1959 hit,

"Kookie, Kookie, Lend Me Your Comb" (Warner, #4, 1959). One of her lines, "You're the utmost, the very utmost," caught on as a teen expression. She followed with several other records aimed at the teen audience, including "Sixteen Reasons" (Warner, #3, 1960); "Too Young to Go Steady" (Warner, #71, 1960); and "Mr. Songwriter" (Warner, #43, 1962).

STEVENS, DODIE When she was just 13 years old, she recorded "Pink Shoe Laces" (Crystalette, #3, 1959), which became one of the biggest hits of 1959. The novelty pop rock song told the story of a cool guy who wore tan shoes, pink shoe laces, a polka-dot vest, and a Panama hat with a purple hat band. Other hits included "Yes Sir-ee" (Crystalette, #79, 1959) and "Yes, I'm Lonesome Tonight" (Dot, #60, 1960+).

STEVENS, RAY He may not have been the greatest singer in the history of rock & roll, but he certainly had the longest song title: his first hit was "Jeremiah Peabody's Poly Unsaturated Quick Dissolving Fast Acting Pleasant Tasting Green and Purple Pills." The novelty song satirized TV commercials. His next hit, "Ahab the Arab," spoofed various pop culture stereotypes involving Arabs, women, and movies. For the next several years, Stevens was perhaps the most successful novelty song singer on the rock charts. His biggest hits include:

"Jeremiah Peabody's Poly Unsaturated Quick Dissolving Fast Acting Pleasant Tasting Green and Purple Pills"	Mercury	#35	1961
"Ahab the Arab"	Mercury	#5	1962
"Santa Claus Is Watching You"	Mercury	#45	1962
"Funny Man"	Mercury	#81	1963
"Hairy the Hairy Ape"	Mercury	#17	1963
"Speed Ball"	Mercury	#59	1963
"Freddie Feelgood (and His Funky Little Five Piece Band)"	Monument	#91	1966
"Unwind"	Monument	#52	1968
"Mr. Businessman"	Monument	#28	1968
"Gitarzan"	Monument	#8	1969
"Along Came Jones"	Monument	#27	1969
"Everything Is Beautiful"	Barnaby	#1	1970
"Bridget the Midget"	Barnaby	#50	1970
"The Streak"	Barnaby	#1	1974
"Misty"	Barnaby	#14	1975

STEWART, SANDY   This pop singer, a regular on the Eddie Fisher and Perry Como TV shows, had a Top 20 hit in 1962 with a ballad called "My Coloring Book" (Colpix, #20, 1962 +).

STITES, GARY   This pop rock singer had several minor hits in 1959 and 1960. His biggest was "Lonely for You" (Carlton, #24, 1959). He followed with "A Girl Like You" (Carlton, #80, 1959); "Starry Eyed" (Carlton, #77, 1959); and a pop rock cover of Lloyd Price's rhythm and blues classic, "Lawdy Miss Clawdy" (Carlton, #47, 1960).

THE STOREY SISTERS   They had one hit, "Bad Motorcycle" (Cameo, #48, 1958). The pop rock song reflected teenage interest in motorcycles, and played to a popular stereotype of rebellious gang leaders, a la Marlon Brando in *The Wild One.*

STORM, BILLY   Former lead singer of the Valiants. His teenage manifesto, "I've Come of Age" (Columbia, #28, 1959), reflected the relationship between rock music and teen identity.

STORM, GALE   She became famous starring in the "My Little Margie" and "Oh Susanna" TV shows in the 1950s, but was also quite successful singing pop rock. In 1955 she had a big hit with "I Hear You Knockin'" (Dot, #2, 1955), a cover version of Smiley Lewis' rhythm and blues classic. She followed up with a ballad called "Teen Age Prayer" (Dot, #9, 1955 +). Other hits included "Memories Are Made of This" (Dot, #16, 1955 +); "Why Do Fools Fall in Love" (Dot, #15, 1956), a cover of the Frankie Lymon and the Teenagers' hit; "Ivory Tower" (Dot, #10, 1956); and "Dark Moon" (Dot, #5, 1957). Her records showed how traditional pop artists tried to capitalize on the new rock & roll sound. The success of her cover records also showed that many record buyers preferred familiar-sounding pop versions to the more foreign-sounding R & B originals.

THE STRING-A-LONGS   They had big hit with "Wheels" (Warwick, #3, 1961), a pop rock instrumental written and produced by Norman Petty, who had gained earlier fame producing hits for Buddy Holly and the Crickets. Although the String-a-Longs never duplicated their initial success, they did reach the charts with instrumentals like "Brass Buttons" (Warwick, #35, 1961) and "Should I" (Warwick, #42, 1961).

STRONG, BARRETT   He only had one hit, "Money (That's What I Want)" (Anna, #23, 1960), but it was one of the best records of 1960. It was an authentic R & B rocker that captured American attitudes toward success and material goods. The song was later covered by the Kingsmen, the Beatles, Junior Walker and the All-Stars, and the Flying Lizards. Although Strong never had another hit record, he did co-write many hits for the Temptations, including "Papa Was a Rollin' Stone," "Cloud Nine," and "Ball of Confusion."

SUNNY AND THE SUNGLOWS   Their biggest hit came in 1963 with a remake of Little Willie John's rhythm and blues classic, "Talk to Me" (Tear Drop, #11, 1963). Their version, which was more pop than R & B rock, typified the bland pop rock that made the charts in the early 1960s.

THE SURFARIS   Anyone who listened to rock & roll in 1963 will never forget the opening of the Surfaris' "Wipe Out" (Dot, #2, 1963). It began with a long, maniacal laugh, punctuated by a crazed voice giggling, "Wipe Out." The group then launched into a driving instrumental, with fast-paced electric guitars and an explosive, rolling drum solo. The record effectively captured the feel of surfing and wiping out on huge waves. Its flip side, "Surfer Joe" (Dot, #63, 1962), developed a cult following thanks to lead singer Ron Wilson's contagious vocals done in Buddy Holly's hiccupping style. It featured lyrics about the perfect beach bum named Surfer Joe. Both songs appealed to hedonistic teens and reflected the surfing craze of the early 1960s. The Surfaris had two other hits on the charts: "Point Panic" (Decca, #49, 1963) and a reissue of "Wipe Out" (Dot, #16, 1966).

THE TAMS   Their only big hit was "What Kind of Fool (Do You Think I Am)" (ABC/Paramount, #9, 1963+), a soulful song that was a throwback to 1950s R & B rock.

THE TASSELS   In 1959 they had a minor hit called "To a Soldier Boy" (Madison, #55, 1959). The song reflected patriotic and conservative attitudes of the day, and shows that teenagers were not yet offended by the military—as many would be by the late 1960s after the Vietnam War heated up.

TAYLOR, LITTLE JOHNNY   His only big hit was an R & B rock song called "Part-Time Love" (Galaxy, #19, 1963). He is no relation to Johnnie Taylor, the successful R & B rocker of the late 1960s and early 1970s who had a string of hits, including "I Wanna Testify" and "Who's Makin' Love."

THE TECHNIQUES In 1957 they had a Top 40 hit with a pop rock song called "Hey! Little Girl" (Roulette, #33, 1957).

THE TEDDY BEARS: *See* Phil Spector.

TEDDY AND THE TWILIGHTS Pop rock often reflected and reinforced common beliefs and stereotypes of the day, as evidenced by this group's hit, "A Woman Is a Man's Best Friend" (Swan, #59, 1962). The song simply pushed the dog aside as man's most subservient creature, and substituted a woman, showing the sexist attitudes that were common in rock during the early 1960s.

THE TEEN QUEENS In the early days of rock & roll, white cover versions habitually became hit records over the original black rhythm and blues versions. A notable exception was the Teen Queens' "Eddie My Love" (RPM, #22, 1956). The white audience likely found the Teen Queens acceptable because their name lacked any identification with rhythm and blues, and their sound was more pop than R & B.

TEMPO, NINO, AND APRIL STEVENS This brother and sister act from the Buffalo, New York, area had several big hits in the early 1960s. Their smooth, pop rock style, highlighted by April's intimate and sexy vocals, led to such hits as "Deep Purple" (Atco, #1, 1963); "Whispering" (Atco, #11, 1963+); "Stardust" (Atco, #32, 1964); and "All Strung Out" (White Whale, #26, 1966).

THE TEMPOS When they blended their Four Freshman—type harmonies with a rock beat and lyrics geared to a young audience, the result was a pretty pop rock ballad, "See You in September" (Climax, #23, 1959). The song later became an even bigger hit for the Happenings in 1966.

THE TEMPTATIONS This all-white pop rock quartet from New York should not be confused with the Motown group that recorded "My Girl," "Since I Lost My Baby," and other R & B rock hits in the mid and late 1960s. These Temptations had only one hit, "Barbara" (Goldisc, #29, 1960).

THOMAS, CARLA She enjoyed moderate success throughout the 1960s. Her first hit, "Gee Whiz (Look at His Eyes)" (Atlantic, #10, 1961), was written by her father, R & B rock star Rufus Thomas. Although she had many other early soul hits on the Atlantic and Stax labels during the decade, her only other record to crack the Top 30 was "B-A-B-Y" (Stax, #14, 1966). She also sang two successful duets with Otis Redding: "Tramp" (Stax, #26, 1967) and "Knock on Wood" (Stax, #30, 1967).

THOMAS, JON He had a minor hit with "Heartbreak (It's Hurtin' Me)" (ABC/Paramount, #48, 1960).

THOMAS, RUFUS This R & B rock singer had some interesting dance records in the early 1960s with "The Dog" (Stax, #87, 1963) and "Walking the Dog" (Stax, #10, 1963). He returned in the 1970s with additional dance hits, including "Do the Funky Chicken" (Stax, #28, 1970) and "(Do the) Push and Pull, Part I" (Stax, #25, 1970 +).

THOMPSON, SUE Her sound was an interesting blend of country and pop. Thompson's first hit came in 1961 with "Sad Movies (Always Make Me Cry)" (Hickory, #5, 1961), a country-influenced ballad written by John D. Loudermilk. The tearjerker told the story of a young girl who catches her boyfriend at a movie show with another girl. Her unique, perky voice led to additional teen-oriented hits like "Norman" (Hickory, #3, 1961 +), also written by Loudermilk; "Two of a Kind" (Hickory, #42, 1962); "Have a Good Time" (Hickory, #31, 1962); "James (Hold the Ladder Steady)" (Hickory, #17, 1962); and "Paper Tiger" (Hickory, #23, 1965).

THORNTON, WILLIE MAE (BIG MAMA) This R & B singer had a rhythm and blues hit in 1953 with "Hound Dog" (Peacock, 1953). Three years later, the Lieber and Stoller composition became a huge hit for Elvis Presley, but Elvis' version was so different that it hardly qualifies as a cover. The two versions show how talented artists can start with the same song and end up with two entirely different, but equally good, records.

THE THREE G'S They had a minor hit in 1958 with "Let's Go Steady for the Summer" (Columbia, #55, 1958), a pop rock song that reflected teenage dating practices.

THUNDER, JOHNNY In 1963 this R & B rock singer had a smash hit with "Loop de Loop" (Diamond, #4, 1962 +), reflecting dance crazes of the early 1960s.

TICO AND THE TRIUMPHS *See* Simon & Garfunkel.

TILLMAN, BERTHA She had some success in 1962 with "Oh, My Angel" (Brent, #61, 1962).

TILLOTSON, JOHNNY Coming out of a country music background, he became a top teen idol in the late 1950s and early 1960s with songs that reflected teen interest in romance and dating. Unlike most pop rockers of that era, Tillotson wrote many of his biggest hits, including "Dreamy Eyes," "Without You," and "It Keeps Right On A-Hurtin'." His better efforts, like "Why Do I Love You So," "Poetry in Motion," and "It Keeps Right On A-Hurtin'," were well-crafted records, blending country and pop styles. Johnny Tillotson's greatest hits include:

"Dreamy Eyes"	Cadence	#63	1958 +
"True True Happiness"	Cadence	#54	1959
"Why Do I Love You So"	Cadence	#42	1960
"Earth Angel"	Cadence	#57	1960
"Pledging My Love"	Cadence	#63	1960
"Poetry in Motion"	Cadence	#2	1960
"Jimmy's Girl"	Cadence	#25	1961
"Without You"	Cadence	#7	1961
"Dreamy Eyes" (re-release)	Cadence	#35	1961 +
"It Keeps Right On A-Hurtin'"	Cadence	#3	1962
"Send Me the Pillow You Dream On"	Cadence	#17	1962
"I Can't Help It (If I'm Still In Love with You)"	Cadence	#24	1962
"Out of My Mind"	Cadence	#24	1963
"You Can Never Stop Me Loving You"	Cadence	#18	1963
"Talk Back Trembling Lips"	Cadence	#7	1963 +
"She Understands Me"	Cadence	#31	1964
"Heartaches by the Number"	Cadence	#35	1965

TODD, ART AND DOTTY These pop singers had a big hit with "Chanson D'Amour" (Era, #13, 1958). The traditional pop song became quite popular on "American Bandstand" as its refrain, "Chanson D'Amour, ra ta, ta, ta, ta," caught on with teens across the country.

TODD, NICK Pat Boone's younger brother, Todd had minor success with the pop rock song, "Plaything" (Dot, #41, 1957).

THE TOKENS They had several pop rock hits, including "Tonight I Fell in Love" (Warwick, #15, 1961); "The Lion Sleeps Tonight" (RCA, #1, 1961); "B'wa Nina" (RCA, #55, 1962); "I Hear Trumpets Blow" (B.T. Puppy, #30, 1966); "Portrait of My Love" (Warner, #36, 1967); and "She Lets Her Hair Down" (Buddah, #61, 1969 +). They had a sound very similar to the Beach Boys' with tight harmonies and falsettos.

TOM AND JERRY *See* Simon and Garfunkel.

TONY AND JOE Had some success in 1958 with a novelty dance record called "The Freeze" (Era, #33, 1958). At certain points during the song, the music would stop and dancers would freeze in their tracks.

TORMÉ, MEL This jazz and pop singer from the 1940s made the rock charts in 1962 with "Comin' Home Baby" (Atlantic, #36, 1962).

THE TORNADOES One of the few English acts to crash the American rock charts in the years before the Beatles. In 1962 they capitalized on the growing popularity of President Kennedy's space program by launching a hit record, "Telstar" (London, #1, 1962), named after the American satellite, that climbed all the way to the top of the charts.

TOROK, MITCHELL He had three pop rock hits: "Pledge of Love" (Decca, #26, 1957); "Caribbean" (Guyden, #27, 1959); and "Pink Chiffon" (Guyden, #60, 1960). All dealt with romance and were aimed at the teen market. For example, "Pink Chiffon" told the story of a guy who was jilted just before he was going to propose to his girlfriend at the senior prom. Teens loved it, and every spring around prom time it became one of the most requested songs on the radio.

TOWNSEND, ED He reached the Top 20 in 1958 with "For Your Love" (Capitol, #15, 1958), an expressive gospel-influenced R & B rock ballad.

THE TRASHMEN   At the end of 1963 they made the charts with
   "Surfin' Bird" (Garrett, #4, 1963 +). It managed to parody the
   surfing craze and two R & B rock hits by the Rivingtons—"Papa-
   Oom-Mow-Mow" and "The Bird's the Word." Their follow-up,
   "Bird Dance Beat" (Garrett, #30, 1964), also made the Top 30.
   Both novelty records featured highly amplified, staccato vocals.

TRAVIS AND BOB   Sounding very much like the Everly Brothers,
   they had a big hit in 1959 with a country-influenced song, "Tell
   Him No" (Sandy, #8, 1959).

THE TREE SWINGERS   They had a minor pop rock hit, "Kookie Little Paradise" (Guyden, #73, 1960), which became an even bigger
   hit for Jo Ann Campell.

TROY, DORIS   This R & B rock singer had a Top 10 record in 1963
   with "Just One Look" (Atlantic, #10, 1963). The song later became a big hit for the Hollies in the late 1960s and for Linda
   Ronstadt in the early 1980s. It also became the basis for a Toyota
   commercial in 1982.

THE TUNE ROCKERS   They had a hit in 1958 with a novelty song
   called "The Green Mosquito" (United Artists, #44, 1958). The instrumental, featuring an uptempo dance beat and an electric guitar that mimicked the sound of a mosquito, became quite popular
   on "American Bandstand."

THE TUNE WEAVERS   One more example of a one-hit group in the
   annals of rock & roll. Their moment of glory came in 1957 with
   "Happy, Happy Birthday, Baby" (Checker, #5, 1957), a dramatic
   birthday song about lost love. The song, which blended pop and
   R & B rock, became one of rock & roll's all-time greatest hits.

THE TURBANS   This Philadelphia quartet's biggest hit was "When
   You Dance" (Herald, #33, 1955 +), an early R & B rock song that
   reflected teen interest in dancing.

TURNER, IKE AND TINA   Ike began as a rhythm and blues musician
   in the 1950s. After teaming with Tina, he made the charts in 1960
   with the R & B rock single, "A Fool in Love" (Sue, #27, 1960).
   They followed up with "It's Gonna Work Out Fine" (Sue, #14,
   1961), and numerous other minor hits. By the mid-1960s they

perfected their act; it featured Tina's dynamic lead vocals, Ike's surly expression as he played various instruments, and flashy backup vocals and dancing by the Ikettes (three female vocalists who had a hit of their own, "I'm Blue," in 1962). At one point they recorded a version of "River Deep, Mountain High" (Philles, #88, 1966), produced by Phil Spector. But the song fizzled on the charts, despite Spector's contention that it was the finest record he ever made. Later Ike and Tina Turner hits included "I Want to Take You Higher" (Liberty, #34, 1970); "Proud Mary" (Liberty, #4, 1971); and "Nutbush City Limits" (United Artists, #22, 1973). After the couple split up, Tina Turner went on to record many other big hits, including "What's Love Got to Do with It" (Capitol, #1, 1984); "Better Be Good to Me" (Capitol, #5, 1984); "Private Dancer" (Capitol, #7, 1985); "We Don't Need Another Hero" (Capitol, #2, 1985); and "Typical Male" (Capitol, #2, 1986).

TURNER, JESSE LEE   The late 1950s were the days of Sputnik, UFOs, and America's rising space program. Jesse Lee Turner tapped these interests and came out with a Top 20 record, "The Little Space Girl" (Carlton, #20, 1959).

TURNER, JOE   This rhythm and blues singer was an important prototype for early rock & roll. His 1954 rhythm and blues hit, "Shake, Rattle, and Roll" (not Bill Haley's cover version, which became the hit on national pop charts), now stands as the definitive version of the song. His biggest commercial successes were "Corrine, Corrina" (Atlantic, #41, 1956) and "Honey Hush" (Atlantic, #53, 1959+). His stylistic influences on early rock led to his induction into the Rock & Roll Hall of Fame in 1986.

TURNER, SAMMY   He had one of the biggest hits of 1959 with "Lavender-Blue" (Big Top, #3, 1959), an R & B rock ballad based on an old English folk song. Turner's version contained the infectious line, "Lavender-blue, dilly, dilly," which became quite popular among teens. Although his next release, "Always" (Big Top, #19, 1959), did not match the popularity of "Lavender-Blue," it still became a Top 20 record.

TURNER, TITUS   In 1961 he had a hit with "Sound-Off" (Jamie, #77, 1961), a novelty record based on the military practice of counting soldiers by sounding off, "One two-three-four." Its popularity reflected the conservative times. By the end of the tumultuous 1960s, songs glorifying the army were few and far between.

THE TWIN-TONES These twins, Johnny and James Cunningham, had a minor hit with "Jo Ann" (RCA, 1958), a song they had written. It was quintessential pop rock, featuring Everly Brothers–style harmonies, a splendid sax solo, and teen-oriented lyrics about a special girl and lost love. Unfortunately for the Twin-Tones, their success was undercut by the Playmates' version of the song, which became the Top 20 record.

TWITTY, CONWAY He took the rock & roll world by storm in 1958 when "It's Only Make Believe" became the number one seller on the rock charts. Kids went wild over Twitty's name and his snarling voice, which sounded remarkably like Elvis Presley's. Although "Conway Twitty" was just a stage name (he was born Harold Jenkins), it caught the public's fancy. Many people thought it was the greatest name to come along since Elvis Presley. The musical *Bye Bye Birdie* satirized Twitty by naming its lead character, a rock & roll star, "Conrad Birdie" (as in twitty bird). Twitty racked up several more country-influenced hits during the late 1950s and early 1960s. When his rock & roll career began to fade, he switched to country and western music, becoming one of the field's top stars. His biggest hits include:

"It's Only Make Believe"	MGM	#1	1958
"The Story of My Love"	MGM	#28	1959
"Mona Lisa"	MGM	#29	1959
"Danny Boy"	MGM	#10	1959
"Lonely Blue Boy"	MGM	#6	1959+
"What Am I Living For"	MGM	#26	1960
"Is a Blue Bird Blue"	MGM	#35	1960
"C'est Si Bon"	MGM	#22	1960+
"You've Never Been This Far Before"	MCA	#22	1973

THE TYMES This R & B rock group from Philadelphia featured George Williams, who sounded very much like a young Johnny Mathis. Their style, pop with a trace of rhythm and blues, earned them several big hits, including "So Much in Love" (Parkway, #1, 1963); "Wonderful! Wonderful!" (Parkway, #7, 1963); "Somewhere" (Parkway, #19, 1963+); and "You Little Trustmaker" (RCA, #12, 1974).

UPCHURCH, PHIL, COMBO   Led by session guitarist Phil Up-church, this R & B rock group had a Top 30 hit in 1961 with an instrumental called "You Can't Sit Down, Part 2" (Boyd, #29, 1961). Two years later, the Dovells added lyrics to the song and their version made it all the way to number three on the charts. Both versions were lively, fast-paced dance songs, and for many teens, that's what rock & roll was all about in the early 1960s.

THE VALADIERS   The year was 1961. Cold War tensions were in the air, as President Kennedy and Soviet Premier Khrushchev squared off over the Bay of Pigs invasion and the Berlin crisis. The Valadiers had a pop rock hit, "Greetings (This Is Uncle Sam)" (Miracle, #89, 1961), reflecting the era's patriotism and the possible war clouds on the horizon.

VALENS, RITCHIE   He arrived on the rock scene in 1958 when he was 17 years old. His first hit was a bouncy country-influenced rocker called "Come On Let's Go" (Del-Fi, #42, 1958). His next release was "Donna" (Del-Fi, #2, 1958 +), a quintessential pop rock "name song" about teen love and a special girl. Although the record had unsophisticated lyrics and simple instrumenta-tion, the plaintive ballad captured the essence of early rock, and became one of rock & roll's classics. Its flip side, "La Bamba" (Del-Fi, #22, 1958 +), was a lively rocker that featured a frenzied guitar and wild-sounding lyrics sung entirely in Spanish. The songs quickly established Valens as one of rock & roll's rising young stars. But tragedy struck. Valens' promising career was cut short when he was killed, along with Buddy Holly and the Big Bopper, in an airplane crash on February 3, 1959. Don McLean, in his 1971 hit "American Pie," characterized the event as "the day the music died." In the late 1980s Ritchie Valens, like Buddy Holly, was memorialized in a motion picture about his life, *La Bamba*.

VALENTINO, MARK   The year 1962 witnessed many popular dance crazes like the Twist, the Pop-Eye, and the Mashed Potato. This pop rocker had a Top 30 hit describing another new dance, "The Push and Kick" (Swan, #27, 1962).

THE VALIANTS   Led by Billy Storm, they enjoyed some success in 1957 with an R & B rock song called "This Is the Night" (Keen, #69, 1957 +). *See also* Billy Storm.

VALJEAN A pop musician and arranger who made the rock charts with "Theme from 'Ben Casey'" (Carlton, #28, 1962). The success of the record reflected the great popularity of the TV show, which featured Vince Edwards as a young, caring doctor.

VALLI, FRANKIE He rose to fame as the lead singer of the Four Seasons. His success continued as a solo artist with such hits as "Can't Take My Eyes off You" (Philips, #2, 1967); "My Eyes Adored You" (Private S., #1, 1974+); "Swearin' to God" (Private S., #6, 1975); "Our Day Will Come" (Private S., #11, 1975); and "Grease" (RSO, #1, 1978). *See also* the Four Seasons.

VALLI, JUNE This pop singer from the 1950s attained some popularity with the young audience. In 1953 she had a Top 10 hit with "Crying in the Chapel" (RCA, 1953), a cover version of the Orioles' record. Other hits included "Unchained Melody" (RCA, #29 on the Best Sellers Chart, 1955); "The Wedding" (Mercury, #43, 1958+); and "Apple Green" (Mercury, #29, 1960).

VAN DYKE, LEROY This country and western singer reached the Top 30 charts with "Auctioneer" (Dot, #29, 1956+), a novelty record about auctions. Five years later he had a bigger hit with "Walk On By" (Mercury, #5, 1961), an interesting country-influenced song about infidelity. He used the same formula on his last hit, "If a Woman Answers (Hang Up the Phone)" (Mercury, #35, 1962).

VAUGHAN, SARAH She came out of a gospel background to become a jazz vocalist and one of the more successful pop singers of the 1950s. She crossed over to the rock charts with "Broken-Hearted Melody" (Mercury, #7, 1959).

VAUGHN, BILLY This pop musician began his career with the Hilltoppers and hits like "P.S. I Love You" (1953) and "Marianne" (1957). He later became a musical arranger for Dot Records (where he worked on Pat Boone's hits) and had additional hits on his own, including "Sail Along Silvery Moon" (Dot, #5, 1957+); "Raunchy" (Dot, #33, 1957); "Look for a Star" (Dot, #19, 1960); "Wheels" (Dot, #28, 1961); and "A Swingin' Safari" (Dot, #13, 1962). The success of his pop instrumentals showed that many members of the rock audience in the late 1950s and early 1960s were still enjoying and buying traditional pop records.

VEE, BOBBY One of the most underrated and overlooked pop rock stars of the late 1950s and early 1960s. Many critics have dismissed him as just another teen idol. But Vee, whose real name was Robert Velline, was actually a very talented rock & roller. He got his break after Buddy Holly's death in a plane crash. Holly was scheduled to do a concert in Vee's hometown of Fargo, North Dakota. When news of the tragedy reached Fargo, dee jays asked local talent to fill the bill. Sixteen-year-old Bobby Vee and his band, the Shadows, stepped forward and sang several songs as a tribute to Holly. Talent scouts were impressed with Vee's style, which compared favorably to Holly's, and he was signed to a recording contract. His first two national hits, "Suzie Baby" and "What Do You Want," were done in a vocal style reminiscent of Holly's. Vee's next release, a cover of the Clovers' 1956 rhythm and blues hit "Devil or Angel," became a Top 10 hit in 1960, and Vee was off and running.

Over the next few years Bobby racked up hit after hit, including "Rubber Ball" (co-written by Gene Pitney) and "Take Good Care of My Baby" (written by Carole King and Gerry Goffin). He also recorded two albums that reinforced his image as the heir to the Buddy Holly tradition: *Bobby Vee Meets the Crickets*, which featured Vee singing with Holly's band, and *I Remember Buddy Holly*, which featured Vee singing a collection of Holly's greatest hits. Vee's music blended country rock and pop, producing a folk quality teens could relate to. His many hits provide a good reflection of teen romance, interests, and values of the early 1960s. Bobby Vee's greatest hits include:

"Suzie Baby"	Liberty	#77	1959
"What Do You Want"	Liberty	#93	1960
"Devil or Angel"	Liberty	#6	1960
"Since I Met You Baby"	Liberty	#81	1960
"Rubber Ball"	Liberty	#6	1960 +
"Stayin' In"	Liberty	#33	1961
"More Than I Can Say"	Liberty	#61	1961
"How Many Tears"	Liberty	#63	1961
"Take Good Care of My Baby"	Liberty	#1	1961
"Run to Him"	Liberty	#2	1961
"Walkin' with My Angel"	Liberty	#53	1961 +
"Please Don't Ask About Barbara"	Liberty	#15	1962
"I Can't Say Goodbye"	Liberty	#92	1962
"Sharing You"	Liberty	#15	1962
"Punish Her"	Liberty	#20	1962

"Someday" (with the Crickets)	Liberty	#99	1962
"The Night Has a Thousand Eyes"	Liberty	#3	1962+
"Charms"	Liberty	#13	1963
"Be True to Yourself"	Liberty	#34	1963
"A Letter from Betty"	Liberty	#85	1963
"Yesterday and You (Armen's Theme)"	Liberty	#55	1963
"Never Love a Robin"	Liberty	#99	1963
"Stranger in Your Arms"	Liberty	#83	1964
"I'll Make You Mine"	Liberty	#52	1964
"Hickory, Dick, and Doc"	Liberty	#63	1964
"Every Little Bit Hurts"	Liberty	#84	1964+
"Pretend You Don't See Her"	Liberty	#97	1964
"Cross My Heart"	Liberty	#99	1965
"Keep On Tryin'"	Liberty	#85	1965
"Look At Me Girl"	Liberty	#52	1966
"Come Back When You Grow Up"	Liberty	#3	1967
"Beautiful People"	Liberty	#37	1967
"Maybe Just Today"	Liberty	#46	1968
"My Girl/Hey Girl"	Liberty	#35	1968
"Do What You Gotta Do"	Liberty	#83	1968
"I'm Into Lookin' for Someone to Love Me"	Liberty	#98	1968
"Let's Call It a Day Girl"	Liberty	#92	1969
"Sweet Sweetheart"	Liberty	#88	1970

THE VELAIRES They had some success with "Roll Over Beethoven" (Jamie, #51, 1961), a remake of Chuck Berry's classic.

THE VELOURS This R & B rock group had two minor hits, "Can I Come Over Tonight" (Onyx, #83, 1957) and "Remember" (Onyx, #83, 1958).

THE VELVETS An R & B rock group from Texas, whose biggest hit was a doo wop song called "Tonight (Could Be the Night)" (Monument, #26, 1961).

THE VENTURES One of the top instrumental rock groups of the 1960s. Their records featured outstanding guitar work and a danceable beat. The Ventures' biggest hits included "Walk, Don't Run" (Dolton, #2, 1960); "Perfidia" (Dolton, #15, 1960); "Ram-Bunk-Shush" (Dolton, #29, 1961); "Walk, Don't Run '64" (Dolton, #8, 1964); and "Hawaii Five-O" (Liberty, #4, 1969).

VERNE, LARRY He had one of the biggest hits on the rock charts in 1960 with "Please Mr. Custer (I Don't Wanna Go)" (Era, #1, 1960). The novelty song told the story of a cowardly cavalry soldier who pleaded with Custer to excuse him from the Last Stand. The record became a favorite on "American Bandstand" and reflected Indian stereotypes of the day. Verne's only other hit was another historical novelty record, "Mister Livingston" (Era, #75, 1960).

THE VIBRATIONS *See* the Marathons.

THE VIDELS This pop rock group had some success in 1960 with "Mr. Lonely" (JDS, #73, 1960), an interesting doo wop song that reflected teen interests and attitudes about dating.

THE VILLAGE STOMPERS With their trumpet, clarinet, trombone, and banjo, they were hardly a rock & roll band. But they did have a big hit on the rock charts in 1963 with a dixieland swing record called "Washington Square" (Epic, #2, 1963). Its success demonstrated the eclectic tastes of the rock audience.

VINCENT, GENE, AND THE BLUE CAPS One of rock & roll's many shooting stars. For a brief moment Gene Vincent, an innovative song writer, vocalist, and guitarist, was one of the hottest acts around. In 1956 his country-influenced "Be-Bop-A-Lula" (Capitol, #7, 1956) rose up the charts, becoming one of the greatest hits in rock history. His star burned out quickly, though. He managed only one more big hit, "Lotta Lovin'" (Capitol, #14, 1957), and several minor ones, "Race with the Devil" (Capitol, #96, 1956); "Bluejean Bop" (Capitol, #49 on the Coming Up charts, 1956); and "Dance to the Bop" (Capitol, #43, 1957+).

VINTON, BOBBY His first release, "Roses Are Red (My Love)," made it to the top of the rock charts in 1962. The song, dealing with high school yearbooks and lost love, was a perfect example of early 1960s formula pop rock. It was sentimental, syrupy, romantic, and unabashedly aimed at the teen market. Vinton followed with many other hits throughout the 1960s. In the 1970s he turned even more toward traditional pop, recording ethnic-flavored hits like "My Melody of Love" and "Beer Barrel Polka." His early success revealed that many members of the rock & roll audience craved music with traditional values and romantic lyrics. His later hits reflected the aging of the rock audience, and the rise of ethnicity in American society by the mid 1970s. Bobby Vinton's biggest hits include:

"Roses Are Red (My Love)"	Epic	#1	1962
"I Love You the Way You Are"	Diamond	#38	1962
"Rain Rain Go Away"	Epic	#12	1962
"Trouble Is My Middle Name"	Epic	#33	1962 +
"Over the Mountain (Across the Sea)"	Epic	#21	1963
"Blue on Blue"	Epic	#3	1963
"Blue Velvet"	Epic	#1	1963
"There! I've Said It Again"	Epic	#1	1963 +
"My Heart Belong to Only You"	Epic	#9	1964
"Tell Me Why"	Epic	#13	1964
"Clinging Vine"	Epic	#17	1964
"Mr. Lonely"	Epic	#1	1964
"Long Lonely Nights"	Epic	#17	1965
"L-O-N-E-L-Y"	Epic	#22	1965
"Satin Pillows"	Epic	#23	1965 +
"Coming Home Soldier"	Epic	#11	1966 +
"Please Love Me Forever"	Epic	#6	1967
"Just As Much As Ever"	Epic	#24	1967 +
"Take Good Care of My Baby"	Epic	#33	1968
"Halfway to Paradise"	Epic	#23	1968
"I Love How You Love Me"	Epic	#9	1968
"To Know You Is to Love You"	Epic	#34	1969
"Sealed with a Kiss"	Epic	#19	1972
"My Melody of Love"	ABC	#3	1974
"Beer Barrel Polka"	ABC	#33	1975

THE VIRTUES This Philadelphia group had a big hit in 1959 with "Guitar Boogie Shuffle" (Hunt, #5, 1959). Three years later they tried to cash in on the Twist craze with the "Guitar Boogie Shuffle Twist" (Sure, #96, 1962), but the song barely made the charts.

THE VISCOUNTS Their "Harlem Nocturne" (Madison, #52, 1959 +) may be the most erotic rock instrumental ever recorded. The throbing sax solo seemed to ooze sex and, in the vernacular of the day, sounded outright wicked. The song became an even bigger hit (Amy, #39, 1965 +) when it was re-released five years later. In between, the group had two other minor hits—"Night Train" (Madison, #82, 1960) and "Wabash Blues" (Madison, #77, 1960 +).

VITO AND THE SALUTATIONS These pop rockers had a minor hit with a doo wop version of "Unchained Melody" (Herald, #66, 1963).

THE VOLUMES This Detroit quintet made it into the Top 30 with an R & B rock song called "I Love You" (Chex, #22, 1962).

THE VOXPOPPERS Their sound was reminiscent of the pop harmony groups of the 1940s. In 1958 they had a hit with "Wishing for Your Love" (Mercury, #44, 1958).

WADE, ADAM Billed as the next Johnny Mathis, this pop singer with the smooth voice had three Top 10 hits in 1961: "Take Good Care of Her" (Coed, #7, 1961); "The Writing on the Wall" (Coed, #5, 1961); and "As If I Didn't Know" (Coed, #10, 1961).

THE WAILERS In 1959 they made the charts with two upbeat instrumentals: "Tall Cool One" (Golden Crest, #36, 1959) and "Mau Mau" (Golden Crest, #68, 1959). Five years later, "Tall Cool One" was re-released and again became a Top 40 hit (Golden Crest, #38, 1964).

WALLACE, JERRY Although his style was always closer to pop than rock, he usually managed to sell well to the rock & roll audience. His first hit, "How the Time Flies" (Challenge, #11, 1958), was an unusual country-influenced pop rock song. The following year he had an even bigger hit with a more traditional-sounding record, "Primrose Lane" (Challenge, #8, 1959). In 1960 he enjoyed some success with a novelty record, "Little Coco Palm" (Challenge, #36, 1960). He followed with "There She Goes" (Challenge, #26, 1960+), another interesting song with a country rock feel. His last two big hits were "Shutters and Boards" (Challenge, #24, 1962+) and "In the Misty Moonlight" (Challenge, #19, 1964). The key to Wallace's success with the rock & roll audience was that they perceived him to be someone recording for them, as opposed to someone recording for adults. Wallace received a lot of exposure on "American Bandstand," and even his records that were closer to pop than rock had romantic lyrics that appealed to teenagers.

WARD, BILLY, AND HIS DOMINOES One of the legendary rhythm and blues groups of the 1950s, their sound was a prototype for early R & B rock. At various times the group featured Clyde Mc-Phatter and Jackie Wilson as lead singers. Their biggest hits on the national charts included "St. Therese of the Roses" (Decca, #27, 1956); "Star Dust" (Liberty, #13, 1957); and "Deep Purple" (Liberty, #20, 1957).

WARD, DALE He first made the rock charts in 1958 singing lead for the Crescendos on "Oh Julie." Later he had his own hit with a pop rock song called "Letter from Sherry" (Dot, #25, 1963 +).

WARD, ROBIN Her hit, "Wonderful Summer" (Dot, #14, 1963), is a perfect example of the formula pop rock that was being mass-produced in the early 1960s for the teen market. The record featured waves slapping on the shore and seagulls screeching in the background, as Robin's quintessential teenage voice sang about the quintessential summer romance, promising never to forget "the most wonderful summer of my life."

WARWICK, DIONNE She began her professional career singing gospel music. At one point, Dionne, her sister Dee Dee, and her aunt, Cissy Houston (the mother of Whitney Houston), had their own gospel group, the Gospelaires. Dionne Warwick's career as a pop singer took off after she teamed up with pop music composers Burt Bacharach and Hal David, who wrote most of her early hits, including "Don't Make Me Over," "Anyone Who Had a Heart," "Walk On By," and "You'll Never Get to Heaven." Some of Dionne Warwick's biggest hits are:

"Don't Make Me Over"	Scepter	#21	1962 +
"Anyone Who Had a Heart"	Scepter	#8	1963 +
"Walk On By"	Scepter	#6	1964
"You'll Never Get to Heaven	Scepter	#34	1964
"Reach Out for Me"	Scepter	#20	1964
"Message to Michael"	Scepter	#8	1966
"Trains and Boats and Planes"	Scepter	#22	1966
"Alfie"	Scepter	#15	1967
"The Windows of the World"	Scepter	#32	1967
"I Say a Little Prayer"	Scepter	#4	1967
"(Theme From) Valley of the Dolls"	Scepter	#2	1968
"Do You Know the Way to San Jose"	Scepter	#10	1968
"Promises Promises"	Scepter	#19	1968
"This Girl's in Love with You"	Scepter	#7	1969
"I'll Never Fall in Love Again"	Scepter	#6	1969 +

"Then Came You" (with the Spinners)	Atlantic	#1	1974
"I'll Never Love This Way Again"	Arista	#5	1979
"Deja Vu"	Arista	#15	1979+
"Heartbreaker"	Arista	#10	1982+
"That's What Friends Are For"(sung with Friends, i.e., Elton John, Gladys Knight, and Stevie Wonder)	Arista	#1	1985+

WASHINGTON, BABY   This R & B rock singer began her career with the Hearts in the mid-1950s. She went on to record several minor hits on her own, such as "Nobody Cares" (Neptune, #60, 1961); "That's How Heartaches Are Made" (Sue, #40, 1963); and "Leave Me Alone" (Sue, #62, 1963).

WASHINGTON, DINAH   She got her start in the 1940s singing jazz and blues. Her biggest hit came in 1959 with "What a Difference a Day Makes" (Mercury, #8, 1959). After that she had additional R & B rock hits like "Unforgettable" (Mercury, #17, 1959); "This Bitter Earth" (Mercury, #24, 1960); and "September in the Rain" (Mercury, #23, 1961). Dinah Washington teamed up with Brook Benton for two additional hits, "Baby (You've Got What It Takes)" (Mercury, #5, 1960) and "A Rockin' Good Way" (Mercury, #7, 1960).

WATERS, MUDDY   Although this legendary Mississippi Delta bluesman never made the rock charts, his singing and guitar style greatly influenced early R & B rockers like Chuck Berry. Waters' best known rhythm and blues songs include "Louisiana Blues" (Chess, 1951); "I'm Your Hootchie Coochie Man" (Chess, 1954); and "Forty Days and Forty Nights" (Chess, 1956). Waters was inducted into the Rock & Roll Hall of Fame in 1986 in recognition of his influences on early rock.

WATTS, NOBLE   This saxophonist's only hit was in 1958 with an R & B rock instrumental called "Hard Times (The Slop)" (Baton, #48, 1957+).

WAYNE, THOMAS   He had a Top 5 record with "Tragedy" (Fernwood, #5, 1959), an excellent country rock ballad about lost love. Although the song later became a hit for the Fleetwoods, Wayne's plaintive vocal makes his the definitive version.

WELCH, LENNY This pop singer had one of the biggest hits of 1963 with a romantic ballad called "Since I Fell for You" (Cadence, #4, 1963). His only other Top 30 hit came with a remake of the pop standard "Ebb Tide" (Cadence, #25, 1964), from the film *Sweet Bird of Youth*. Welch's success proved that traditional pop music was still selling to many members of the rock generation in the early 1960s.

WELK, LAWRENCE This veteran pop musician and polka man actually had two hits on the rock charts in the early 1960s, showing that the tastes of many members of the rock audience differed little from the tastes of adults. His first was a cover version of Floyd Cramer's "Last Date" (Dot, #21, 1960). He followed up with "Calcutta" (Dot, #1, 1960+), a number one record.

WELLS, MARY One of the more successful R & B rock singers of the early 1960s. She was one of the first performers signed by Berry Gordy's Motown Records. Her early releases, slick mixtures of pop and R & B, contained many of the elements that later came to characterize the "Motown sound." Wells' smooth and sexy vocals brought her a long string of hits. Her best sellers include:

"The One Who Really Loves You"	Motown	#8	1962
"You Beat Me to the Punch"	Motown	#9	1962
"Two Lovers"	Motown	#7	1963+
"Laughing Boy"	Motown	#15	1963
"You Lost the Sweetest Boy"	Motown	#22	1963
"What's Easy for Two Is So Hard for One"	Motown	#29	1963+
"My Guy"	Motown	#1	1964
"Once Upon a Time" (duet with Marvin Gaye)	Motown	#19	1964
"What's the Matter with You Baby" (duet with Marvin Gaye)	Motown	#17	1964
"Use Your Head"	20th Century	#34	1965

WHITE, KITTY In 1956 she had a hit with "A Teen-Age Prayer" (Mercury, #68, 1955+), a song clearly aimed at the emerging youth market.

THE WILD-CATS Their only hit came in 1959 with a novelty pop rock instrumental called "Gazachstahagen" (United Artists, #57, 1959).

WILDE, MARTY He tried to capitalize on the rebellious image of teenagers in the late 1950s with his pop rock record, "Bad Boy" (Epic, #45, 1960). His daughter, Kim Wilde, had a series of pop rock hits in the 1980s.

WILLIAMS, ANDY The Perry Como of the 1960s and 1970s, he began his pop career in the early 1950s as a regular on Steve Allen's "Tonight Show." His first big hit came in 1956 with "Canadian Sunset," and over the next two decades he added many other hit singles to his credits. His smooth crooner style was straight pop, as were his hit records that reflected traditional values regarding God, love, marriage, and country. Add his TV specials, series, and many albums focusing on movie themes, Broadway shows, and holiday seasons, and his image as a pure pop performer grows even clearer. His extraordinary popularity among many teenagers during the 1950s and 1960s indicates that young tastes and values were often quite similar to those of adults. Andy Williams' greatest hits include:

"Canadian Sunset"	Cadence	#7	1956
"Butterfly"	Cadence	#1	1957
"I Like Your Kind of Love"	Cadence	#9	1957
"Are You Sincere"	Cadence	#10	1958
"Promise Me, Love"	Cadence	#17	1958
"The Hawaiian Wedding Song"	Cadence	#11	1958+
"Lonely Street"	Cadence	#5	1959
"The Village of St. Bernadette"	Cadence	#7	1959+
"Stranger on the Shore"	Columbia	#38	1962
"Can't Get Used to Losing You"	Columbia	#2	1963
"Days of Wine and Roses"	Columbia	#26	1963
"Hopeless"	Columbia	#13	1963
"A Fool Never Learns"	Columbia	#13	1964
"Dear Heart"	Columbia	#24	1964+
"Battle Hymn of the Republic"	Columbia	#33	1968
"Happy Heart"	Columbia	#22	1969
"(Where Do I Begin) Love Story"	Columbia	#9	1971
"Love Theme from *The Godfather*"	Columbia	#34	1972

WILLIAMS, BILLY His gospel-influenced pop style brought him some success on the rock charts with hits like "I'm Gonna Sit Right Down and Write Myself a Letter" (Coral, #6, 1957) and "Nola" (Coral, #39, 1959).

WILLIAMS, LARRY He ranks alongside Little Richard as one of early rock & roll's premier shouters and ravers. His first big hit,

"Short Fat Fannie" (Specialty, #6, 1957), was a spirited R & B rocker. His follow-up, "Bony Moronie" (Specialty, #18, 1957), was another lively number that became tremendously popular on "American Bandstand." Then, after two minor hits—"You Bug Me, Baby" (Specialty, #45, 1957) and "Dizzy Miss Lizzy" (Specialty, #69, 1958)—Williams dropped off the charts. Yet his memory lives on, for many critics now consider "Bony Moronie" one of rock & roll's all-time greatest hits.

WILLIAMS, MAURICE, AND THE ZODIACS   Like many groups in rock & roll history, this R & B rock group went through a series of name changes. They began as the Gladiolas and had a minor hit in 1957 with "Little Darlin'" (which became an even bigger hit for the Diamonds). They then changed their name to the Excellos, and in 1959 changed again to Maurice Williams and the Zodiacs. Their biggest hit was "Stay" (Herald, #1, 1960), which made it to the top of the charts in 1960. Other hits included "I Remember" (Herald, #86, 1961) and "Come Along" (Herald, #83, 1961). *See also* the Gladiolas.

WILLIAMS, OTIS, AND THE CHARMS   At first known simply as the Charms, they had several rhythm and blues hits such as "Hearts of Stone" (DeLuxe, 1954) and "Ling, Ting, Tong" (DeLuxe, 1955). After altering their name to showcase their lead singer, they made the rock charts with hits like "That's Your Mistake" (DeLuxe, #48, 1956); "Ivory Tower" (DeLuxe, #12, 1956); and "Little Turtle Dove" (King, #95, 1961).

WILLIAMS, ROGER   This popular pianist had several hits on the rock charts, including "Autumn Leaves" (Kapp, #2, 1955); "Almost Paradise" (Kapp, #15, 1957); "Till" (Kapp, #27, 1957); "Near You" (Kapp, #10, 1958); and "Born Free" (Kapp, #7, 1966).

WILLIS, CHUCK   One of the pioneers of early R & B rock. His hits "C.C. Rider" (Atlantic, #12, 1957) and "Betty and Dupree" (Atlantic, #33, 1958) inspired the Stroll dance craze. After he died in 1958, three more Willis records made the rock charts, with ironic titles like "What Am I Living For" (Atlantic, #9, 1958); "Hang Up My Rock and Roll Shoes" (Atlantic, #24, 1958); and "My Life" (Atlantic, #46, 1958).

THE WILLOWS This R & B rock group had one hit record, a doo wop song called "Church Bells May Ring" (Melba, #62, 1956).

WILSON, JACKIE One of the most dynamic R & B rock performers of the 1950s and 1960s. He was inducted into Rock & Roll's Hall of Fame in 1986. He began his career as the lead singer for Billy Ward's Dominoes. In 1957 he set out on his own and found success with "Reet Petite" and "To Be Loved," two songs co-written by Berry Gordy, the founder of Motown Records. But the hit that established him as a superstar was "Lonely Teardrops" (1958), also co-written by Gordy. It was the perfect vehicle for Wilson's explosive singing style. The up-tempo R & B rock song allowed him to shout and dance across his bluesy message. He became a big favorite on "American Bandstand," and followed with many other hits over the next several years. Jackie Wilson's biggest hits include:

"Reet Petite"	Brunswick	#62	1957
"To Be Loved"	Brunswick	#22	1958
"Lonely Teardrops"	Brunswick	#7	1958 +
"That's Why (I Love You So)"	Brunswick	#13	1959
"I'll Be Satisfied"	Brunswick	#20	1959
"Talk That Talk"	Brunswick	#34	1959 +
"Night"	Brunswick	#4	1960
"Doggin' Around"	Brunswick	#15	1960
"(You Were Made for) All My Love"	Brunswick	#12	1960
"A Woman, A Lover, A Friend"	Brunswick	#15	1960
"Alone At Last"	Brunswick	#8	1960
"My Empty Arms"	Brunswick	#9	1961
"Please Tell Me Why"	Brunswick	#20	1961
"I'm Comin' On Back to You"	Brunswick	#19	1961
"The Greatest Hurt"	Brunswick	#34	1962
"Baby Work Out"	Brunswick	#5	1963
"Shake! Shake! Shake!"	Brunswick	#33	1963
"Whispers (Gettin' Louder)"	Brunswick	#11	1966
"(Your Love Keeps Lifting Me) Higher and Higher"	Brunswick	#6	1967
"Since You Showed Me How to Be Happy"	Brunswick	#32	1967
"I Get the Sweetest Feeling"	Brunswick	#34	1968

WILSON, J. FRANK, AND THE CAVALIERS Technically, J. Frank Wilson's career comes during the second decade of rock & roll, since his only big hit, "Last Kiss" (Josie, #2, 1964), peaked on the charts several months after the arrival of the Beatles. But, for all practical purposes, both J. Frank Wilson and his song belong to rock & roll's first decade. Wilson's singing style was a carbon copy of Buddy Holly's, and "Last Kiss" was a continuation of the "Death Rock" sound popularized by Mark Dinning's "Teen Angel" (1959) and Ray Peterson's "Tell Laura I Love Her" (1960). Wilson's record told the story of a guy and girl involved in a tragic car crash. It had all the ingredients many teenagers loved: cars, screeching tires, busting glass, and tragic romance. At the end of the song, the driver scrambles to his girlfriend who has been tossed from the wreckage; he holds her dead body close to his, and gives her one "last kiss." The macabre scene was illustrated on the *Last Kiss* album cover, which had J. Frank Wilson holding in his arms an alleged corpse with a ghastly-looking face. While J. Frank Wilson and the Cavaliers may not have been the most successful performers in rock & roll history, their "Last Kiss" song and album cover scaled the pinnacle (or probed the depths, depending on one's viewpoint) of early 1960s' Death Rock.

WINDING, KAI This jazz trombonist had a Top 10 single with "More" (Verve, #8, 1963), the theme for the motion picture *Mondo Cane*.

WOLF, HOWLIN' Legendary blues performer from the 1940s and 1950s, whose style influenced many early R & B rock artists. Although he never had any hits on the pop or rock charts, he did have many rhythm and blues hits, including "How Many More Years" (Chess, 1951) and "Smoke Stack Lightning" (Chess, 1956).

WONDER, STEVIE He arrived on the rock music scene in 1963, billed by Motown Records as Little Stevie Wonder—a blind, 13-year-old musical genius. His first release, a live recording called "Fingertips, Part 2," became a number one record in 1963. The high-energy R & B rock song immediately established the youngster as a force to be reckoned with in the rock world. Over the next several years, he more than lived up to his potential, producing many critically acclaimed hit singles and albums that set the pace for rock music from the early 1960s through the 1980s. He was elected to Rock & Roll's Hall of Fame in 1988. Stevie Wonder's biggest hits include:

"Fingertips, Part 2"	Tamla	#1	1963
"Workout Stevie, Workout"	Tamla	#33	1963
"Hey Harmonica Man"	Tamla	#29	1964
"Uptight (Everything's Alright)"	Tamla	#3	1965 +
"Blowin' in the Wind	Tamla	#9	1966
"A Place in the Sun	Tamla	#9	1966
"I Was Made to Love Her"	Tamla	#2	1967
"I'm Wonderin'"	Tamla	#12	1967
"Shoo-Be-Doo-Be-Doo-Da-Day"	Tamla	#9	1968
"For Once in My Life"	Tamla	#2	1968
"My Cherie Amour"	Tamla	#4	1969
"Yester-Me, Yester-You, Yester-Day"	Tamla	#7	1969
"Signed, Sealed, Delivered I'm Yours"	Tamla	#3	1970
"Heaven Help Us All"	Tamla	#9	1970
"We Can Work It Out"	Tamla	#13	1971
"If You Really Love Me"	Tamla	#8	1971
"Superstition"	Tamla	#1	1972 +
"You Are the Sunshine of My Life"	Tamla	#1	1973
"Higher Ground"	Tamla	#4	1973
"Living for the City"	Tamla	#8	1973 +
"Don't You Worry 'Bout a Thing"	Tamla	#16	1974
"You Haven't Done Nothin'"	Tamla	#1	1974
"Boogie On Reggae Woman"	Tamla	#3	1974 +
"I Wish"	Tamla	#1	1976 +
"Sir Duke"	Tamla	#1	1977
"Send One Your Love"	Tamla	#4	1979
"Master Blaster (Jammin')"	Tamla	#5	1980
"I Ain't Gonna Stand for It"	Tamla	#11	1980 +
"That Girl"	Tamla	#4	1982
"Ebony and Ivory" (duet with Paul McCartney)	Columbia	#1	1982
"Do I Do"	Tamla	#13	1982
"I Just Called To Say I Love You"	Motown	#1	1984
"Love Light in Flight"	Motown	#17	1984 +
"Part-Time Lover"	Motown	#1	1985
"Go-Home"	Motown	#10	1985 +
"Overjoyed"	Motown	#24	1986

WONDER LAND, ALICE This pop rock artist with the high recognition name had a minor hit with "He's Mine (I Love Him, I Love Him, I Love Him)" (Bardell, #62, 1963), a song that reflected teen attitudes about romance and sexual stereotypes of the day.

WOOLEY, SHEB   He began his career as a country and western singer and acted in movies such as *Little Big Horn, Giant,* and *High Noon.* In 1958 he made it to the top of the rock charts with a song he had written, "The Purple People Eater" (MGM, #1, 1958). The novelty record dealt with a silly creature from outer space who came to Earth to join a rock & roll band. It became a big hit on "American Bandstand," and Dick Clark even held a contest to determine who could send in the best sketch of the Purple People Eater. Sheb Wooley later played the part of Pete Nolan, a cowboy on TV's successful series, "Rawhide." He also recorded numerous country and western novelty hits under the name Ben Colder.

WRAY, LINK, AND HIS RAY MEN   In 1958 they had a big hit with "Rumble" (Cadence, #15, 1958), an instrumental that reflected popular images of rebellious teenagers and gang fights. Their only other Top 30 hit came the following year with "Raw-Hide" (Epic, #23, 1959), an instrumental that tried to capitalize on the popularity of TV westerns.

WRIGHT, DALE   He had a Top 40 hit with "She's Neat" (Fraternity, #39, 1958), a pop rocker reflecting teenage slang.

YORK, DAVE   Surfing and beach party movies starring Annette, Frankie Avalon, or other young performers were the rage in the early 1960s. York tried to tap into these interests with his record, "Beach Party" (P-K-M, #95, 1962), which became a minor hit in 1962.

YOUNG, FARON   This country and western performer had several hits on the rock charts in the late 1950s and early 1960s, including "The Shrine of St. Cecelia" (Capitol, #96, 1957); "Alone with You" (Capitol, #51, 1958); and "Hello Walls" (Capitol, #12, 1961). His success evidenced country and western's continuing influence on the rock audience.

YOUNG, KATHY, AND THE INNOCENTS   Their biggest hit was "A Thousand Stars" (Indigo, #3, 1960). The romantic ballad, featuring Young's teenage voice on lead, was a well-produced pop rock song, with just a hint of 1950s doo wop. The same formula produced another Top 30 record, "Happy Birthday Blues" (Indigo, #30, 1961). Both are excellent examples of early 1960s formula

pop rock, mass-produced for the young audience. *See also* the Innocents.

YOUNG, VICTOR   This popular musician and orchestra leader
made the rock charts with "Around the World" (Decca, #26,
1957), the theme from the popular film, *Around the World in 80
Days.*

YURO, TIMI   She had a powerful voice and a sound similar to
Brenda Lee's. Her first and biggest hit was a tearful pop rock
ballad called "Hurt" (Liberty, #4, 1961). Other hit singles included "What's a Matter Baby" (Liberty, #12, 1962) and "Make
the World Go Away" (Liberty, #24, 1963).

ZACHERLE, JOHN   He first gained local fame as "The Cool Ghoul,"
hosting horror movies on a Philadelphia TV station. In 1958 he
released a novelty song entitled "Dinner with Drac—Part 1"
(Cameo, #6, 1958). The record featured Zacherle doing a Count
Dracula imitation, welcoming various ghouls to dinner. It became an instant hit with the local audience on "American Bandstand," and soon caught on nationwide with other teenagers
raised on horror films.

Notes

For the sake of brevity, I have used only abbreviated titles in notes. Full citations for each work can be found in the Bibliography.

Part I: Rock & Roll's First Decade

1. Miller, *Rolling Stone Illustrated History*, 3–13; Yorke, *History of Rock 'n' Roll*, 11, 12; Belz, *Story of Rock*, 16–20. The most recent, and best, comprehensive overview of the history of rock music is Ward, Stokes, and Tucker, *Rock of Ages*.
2. Gillett, *Sound of the City*, 12.
3. Gillett, *Sound of the City*, 1, 17; Miller, *Rolling Stone History*, 11; Yorke, *History of Rock 'n' Roll*, 11; Belz, *Story of Rock*, 34; Bill Haley interview in Gillett, *Sound of the City*, 30–31.
4. Alan Freed interview in *New Musical Express*, September 23, 1956, quoted in Chapple and Garofalo, *Rock 'n' Roll Is Here to Pay*, 56.
5. Shaw, *The Rockin' 50s*, 106.
6. Joe Turner, "Shake, Rattle, and Roll"; Bill Haley and His Comets, "Shake, Rattle, and Roll"; © 1954 UNICHAPPELL MUSIC, INC. (Renewed). Used by permission. All rights reserved.
7. Frank Zappa interview, *Life* magazine, quoted in Shaw, *The Rockin' 50s*, 122.
8. Chapple and Garofalo, *Rock 'n' Roll Is Here to Pay*, 40; Gillett, *Sound of the City*, 66. For more information on Elvis Presley, see Marcus, *Mystery Train: Images of America in Rock 'n' Roll*, 137–205; and Miller, *Rolling Stone History*, 19–34, as well as the Presley entry in Part III of this book. To determine when songs were hit records, I have relied upon personal knowledge and/or consulted *Billboard's* record charts from 1954 until 1964, as researched and compiled by Joel Whitburn in his excellent volume, *Top Pop Singles, 1955–1986*.

9. Gillett, *Sound of the City*, 12, 36, 37.

10. For positive remarks about "American Bandstand," see Dick Clark's autobiographical *Rock, Roll, & Remember*, and Shore (with Clark), *The History of American Bandstand*. Less kind is Chapple and Garofalo, *Rock 'n' Roll Is Here to Pay*, 28, 49–51, 63, 247.

11. For an interesting survey of rock films, see Jenkinson and Warner, *Celluloid Rock*.

12. Belz, *Story of Rock*, 36, 37; *Billboard*, May 28, 1955, 35.

13. Belz, *Story of Rock*, 25; Brown, *Art of Rock and Roll*, 26–49; and Miller, *Rolling Stone Illustrated History*, 61–62.

14. Much has been written about the impact of Kennedy's assassination on teenagers. For example, see Wolfenstein and Kliman, *Children and the Death of a President;* Ginsparg and Moriarity, "Reactions of Young People to the Kennedy Assassination"; and most recently, Hoffman, "Rock and Roll and JFK."

15. Jones, *Great Expectations*, 2, 3, and also chs. 1 and 2; Friedel and Brinkley, *America in the Twentieth Century*, 388.

16. Miller and Nowak, *The Fifties*, 270.

17. Richard Mabey, quoted in Denisoff, *Solid Gold*, 30.

18. Riesman, "Listening to Popular Music"; Denisoff, "What Is Popular Music? A Definition."

19. Shaw, *The Rockin' 50s*, 87, 88.

20. The Silhouettes, "Get a Job," Kae Williams Music, Inc. and Wildcat Music, Inc., © 1957.

21. Belz, *Story of Rock*, vii.

22. For a good discussion of subculture, see Willis, *Profane Culture;* Brake, *The Sociology of Youth Culture;* and, especially, Hebdige, *Subculture: The Meaning of Style.*

23. Miller and Nowak, *The Fifties*, 9.

24. Jones, *Great Expectations*, 72.

25. For descriptions of rock & roll as rebellion and conflict, see Denisoff, *Solid Gold*, 16–30; Hentoff, "Something's Happening"; Miller and Nowak, *The Fifties*, 291–313; Yorke, *History of Rock 'n' Roll*, 11, 12; Hentoff, "Popular Music," 23; and Belz, *Story of Rock*, 56–59.

26. Miller and Nowak, *The Fifties*, ch. 3.

27. Miller and Nowak, *The Fifties*, 139–142.

28. Chuck Berry, "Maybellene," Arc Music Corp., © 1955.

29. Barrett Strong, "Money," © 1960.

30. Boorstin, *The Americans*, 89, 90, 188, 552, 554.

31. Benzaquin, "The U.S. Teen-Age Consumer"; Leuchtenburg, *A Troubled Feast*, 65.

32. Miller and Nowak, *The Fifties*, 344, 345. For specific studies

about rock & roll and the media, see Clark and Robinson, *Rock, Roll, and Remember*, and Passman, *The Deejays*.

33. Miller and Nowak, *The Fifties*, 10, 11; Leuchtenburg, *A Troubled Feast*, 23–117; Degler, *Affluence and Anxiety*, 164–204; Gilbert, *Another Chance*, ch. 4; Rosenberg and Rosenberg, *In Our Times*, chs. 2 and 3.

34. Cochran and Capehart, "Summertime Blues," American Music, Inc., © 1958.

35. Jody Reynolds, "Endless Sleep," Johnstone-Montei/Elizabeth Music, © 1958. Denisoff attempts to link "Death Rock" with generational conflict and coming of age in his article, "Death Songs and Teenage Roles," 171–176, 214.

36. Information for the year-by-year historical records was drawn from numerous books and articles. The following were some of the most useful.

   For rock: Marsh and Stein, *Book of Rock Lists*; Roxon, *Rock Encyclopedia*; Peter Berry, *"And the Hits Just Keep On Comin' "*; Gilbert and Theroux, *The Top Ten, 1956–Present*; Macken, Fornatale, and Ayres, *The Rock Music Source Book*; Hendler, *Year by Year in the Rock Era*.

   For movies: Mast, *A Short History of the Movies*; Robert Sklar, *Movie-Made America*.

   For television: Brooks and Marsh, *The Complete Directory to Prime Time Network TV Shows*.

   For assorted information: *Information Please Almanac*; Linton, *The Bicentennial Almanac*; Friedel and Brinkley, *America in the Twentieth Century*; Miller and Nowak, *The Fifties*; and Obst, *The Sixties*.

Part III: The Performers, A To Z

1. Information for this section came from personal knowledge gained over the past 30 years, as well as details gleaned from numerous books and articles. All references to chart positions and dates of hit records are based on *Billboard* magazine's Top 100 and Hot 100 chart surveys, as researched and compiled by Joel Whitburn in his comprehensive volume, *Top Pop Singles, 1955–1986* (Menomonee Falls, Wisconsin: Record Research Inc., 1987). Whitburn has published books listing every entry to hit *Billboard's* Hot 100, Top Pop Albums, R & B, Country, and Adult Contemporary Charts, plus many more. Also useful were Berry, *"And the Hits Just Keep on Comin' "*; Miller, *Rolling Stone Illustrated History*; Gabree, *The World of Rock*; Roxon, *Rock Encyclopedia*; and various issues of *Billboard*.

Bibliography

1. Books

Belz, Carl. *The Story of Rock.* New York: Harper & Row, 1972.

Bergon, Frank, and Zeese Papnikolas, eds. *Looking Far West: The Search for the American West in History, Myth, and Literature.* New York: Mentor, 1978.

Berry, Peter E. *"And the Hits Just Keep On Comin'."* Syracuse, NY: Syracuse University Press, 1977.

Betroch, Alan. *Girl Groups: The Story of a Sound.* New York: Delilah Books, 1982.

Boone, Pat. *'Twixt Twelve and Twenty.* New York: Dell, 1958.

Boorstin, Daniel. *The Americans: The Democratic Experience.* New York: Vintage, 1973.

Brake, Mike. *The Sociology of Youth Culture and Youth Subcultures: Sex, Drugs, and Rock 'n' Roll.* London: Routledge & Kegan Paul, 1980.

Brooks, Tim, and Earle Marsh. *The Complete Directory to Prime Time Network TV Shows, 1946–Present.* New York: Ballantine, 1979.

Brown, Charles T. *The Art of Rock and Roll.* Englewood Cliffs, NJ: Prentice-Hall, 1983.

Brown, George Tindall. *America: A Narrative History.* New York: Norton, 1984.

Chapple, Steve, and Reebee Garofalo. *Rock 'n' Roll Is Here to Pay: The History and Politics of the Music Industry.* Chicago: Nelson-Hall, 1977.

Chipman, Bruce, ed. *Hardening Rock: An Organic Anthology of the Adolescence of Rock 'n' Roll.* Boston: Little, Brown, 1972.

Clark, Dick, and Richard Robinson. *Rock, Roll, & Remember.* New York: Popular Library, 1978.

Cohn, Nik. *Rock from the Beginning.* New York: Stein & Day, 1969.

Cooper, B. Lee. *Images of American Society In Popular Music.* Chicago: Nelson-Hall, 1982.

Davis, Clive. *Clive: Inside the Record Business.* New York: Ballantine, 1976.

Degler, Carl. *Affluence and Anxiety: America Since 1945.* Glenview, IL: Scott, Foresman, 1975.

Denisoff, R. Serge. *Solid Gold: The Popular Record Industry.* New Brunswick, NJ: Transaction Books, 1975.

Dixon, Robert, and John Godrich. *Blues and Gospel Records, 1902–1942*. New York: Stein & Day, 1970.

Eisen, Jonathan, ed. *The Age of Rock*. New York: Random House, 1969.

Farnham, Marynia, and Ferdinand Lundberg. *Modern Woman: The Lost Sex*. New York: Grosset & Dunlap, 1947.

Frank, Lawrence, and Mary Frank. *How To Be a Woman*. New York: Bobbs-Merrill, 1954.

Friedel, Frank, and Alan Brinkley. *America in the Twentieth Century*. New York: Knopf, 1982.

Frith, Simon. *Sound Effects: Youth, Leisure, and the Politics of Rock 'n' Roll*. New York: Pantheon, 1981.

Fuld, James T. *American Popular Music, 1875–1950*. Philadelphia: Musical Americana, 1955.

Gabree, John. *The World of Rock*. Greenwich, CT: Fawcett, 1968.

Gans, Herbert. *Popular Culture and High Culture*. New York: Harper & Row, 1974.

Gilbert, Bob, and Gary Theroux. *The Top Ten, 1956–Present*. New York: Simon & Schuster, 1982.

Gilbert, James. *Another Chance: Postwar America, 1945–1968*. New York: Knopf, 1981.

Gillett, Charlie. *The Sound of the City: The Rise of Rock and Roll*. New York: Dutton, 1970.

Goldrosen, John. *The Buddy Holly Story*. New York: Quick Fox, 1979.

Goldstein, Richard. *The Poetry of Rock*. Englewood Cliffs, NJ: Prentice-Hall, 1969.

Grossman, Loyd. *A Social History of Rock Music*. New York: David McKay, 1976.

Guralnick, Peter. *Feel Like Going Home: Portraits in Blues and Rock 'n' Roll*. New York: Dutton, 1971.

Haralambos, Michael. *Right On: From Blues to Soul in Black America*. New York: Drake, 1975.

Hardy, Phil, and Dave Laing. *Encyclopedia of Rock*. New York: Schirmer Books, 1988.

Hebdige, Dick. *Subculture: The Meaning of Style*. New York: Methuen, 1979.

Helander, Brock. *The Rock Who's Who*. New York: Schirmer Books, 1982.

Hendler, Herb. *Year by Year in the Rock Era: Events and Conditions Shaping the Rock Generation That Reshaped America*. Westport, CT: Greenwood Press, 1983.

Hodgson, Godfrey. *America in Our Time: From World War II to Nixon, What Happened and Why*. New York: Vintage, 1976.

Hoffman, Frank. *The Literature of Rock*. Metuchen, NJ: Scarecrow Press, 1981.

Hoffman, Frank, and B. Lee Cooper. *The Literature of Rock II*. Metuchen, NJ: Scarecrow Press, 1986.

Hopkins, Jerry. *Elvis*. New York: Simon & Schuster, 1971.

Information Please Almanac. New York: Information Please Publishing, 1979.

Jenkinson, Philip, and Alan Warner. *Celluloid Rock*. London: Lorrimer, 1974.

Jones, Landon Y. *Great Expectations: America and the Baby Boom Generation.* New York: Ballantine, 1981.

Lait, Jack, and Lee Mortimer. *U.S.A. Confidential.* New York: Crown, 1952.

Leuchtenburg, William. *A Troubled Feast: American Society Since 1945.* Boston: Little, Brown, 1983.

Linton, Calvin, ed. *The Bicentennial Almanac.* New York: Thomas Nelson, 1975.

Logan, Nick, and Bob Woffenden. *The Illustrated Encyclopedia of Rock.* New York: Harmony Books, 1977.

Lull, James, ed. *Popular Music and Communication.* Newbury Park, CA: Sage Publications, 1987.

Lydon, Michael. *Rock Folk: Portraits from the Rock 'n' Roll Pantheon.* New York: Dial Press, 1971.

Macken, Bob, Peter Fornatale, and Bill Ayres. *The Rock Music Source Book.* Garden City, NY: Anchor Books, 1980.

Marcus, Greil. *Mystery Train: Images of America in Rock 'n' Roll Music.* New York: Dutton, 1976.

Marsh, Dave, and Kevin Stein. *The Book of Rock Lists.* New York: Dell/Rolling Stone, 1981.

Mast, Gerald. *A Short History of the Movies.* Indianapolis: Bobbs-Merrill, 1981.

Miller, Douglas T., and Marion Nowak. *The Fifties: The Way We Really Were.* Garden City, NY: Doubleday, 1975.

Miller, Jim, ed. *The Rolling Stone Illustrated History of Rock & Roll.* New York: Random House/Rolling Stone, 1980.

Nachbar, Jack, Deborah Weiser, and John Wright, eds. *The Popular Culture Reader.* Bowling Green, OH: Bowling Green University Popular Press, 1978.

Nite, Norm N. *Rock On: The Illustrated Encyclopedia of Rock 'n' Roll.* New York: Popular Library, 1977.

Nugent, Stephen, and Charlie Gillett. *Rock Almanac.* Garden City, NY: Anchor/Doubleday, 1978.

Oakley, Giles. *The Devil's Music: A History of the Blues.* New York: Harcourt Brace Jovanovich, 1978.

Obst, Lynda Rosen. *The Sixties.* New York: Random House/Rolling Stone, 1977.

Pareles, Jon, and Patricia Romanowski, eds. *The Rolling Stone Encyclopedia of Rock and Roll.* New York: Summit Books, 1983.

Passman, Arnold. *The Deejays.* New York: Macmillan, 1971.

Pollock, Bruce. *When Rock Was Young.* New York: Holt, Rinehart, 1981.

Riesman, David, with Reuel Denney and Nathan Glazer. *The Lonely Crowd: A Study of the Changing American Character.* New Haven, CT: Yale University Press, 1950.

Rosenberg, Norman L., and Emily S. Rosenberg. *In Our Times.* Englewood Cliffs, NJ: Prentice-Hall, 1982.

Roxon, Lillian. *Rock Encyclopedia.* New York: Grosset & Dunlap, 1969.

Shaw, Arnold. *Honkers and Shouters: The Golden Years of Rhythm and Blues.* New York: Collier, 1978.

———. *The Rockin' 50s: The Decade That Transformed the Pop Music Scene.* New York: Hawthorne Books, 1974.

———. *The Rock Revolution.* New York: Paperback Library, 1971.

Shore, Michael, with Dick Clark. *The History of American Bandstand.* New York: Ballantine, 1984.

Sklar, Robert. *Movie-Made America.* New York: Vintage, 1975.

Smith, Henry Nash. *Virgin Land: The American West as Symbol and Myth.* Cambridge, MA: Harvard University Press, 1950.

Spock, Benjamin. *The Common Sense Book of Baby and Child Care.* New York: Pocket Books, 1946.

Starr, Kevin. *Americans and the California Dream, 1850–1915.* New York: Oxford University Press, 1973.

Tamke, Susan S., and William H. Cohn, eds. *History and Popular Culture.* Bowling Green, OH: Bowling Green University Popular Press, 1976.

Uslan, Michael, and Bruce Solomon. *Dick Clark's The First 25 Years of Rock & Roll.* New York: Greenwich House, 1981.

Ward, Ed, Geoffrey Stokes, and Ken Tucker. *Rock of Ages.* New York: Summit, 1986.

Whitburn, Joel. *Top Pop Singles, 1955–1986.* Menomonee Falls, WI: Record Research, Inc., 1987.

Whitcomb, Ian. *After the Ball: Pop Music from Rag to Rock.* New York: Simon & Schuster, 1972.

White, David Manning, and John Pendleton, eds. *Popular Culture: Mirror of American Life (Reader).* Delmar, CA: Publishers, Inc., 1977.

Williams, Paul. *Outlaw Blues.* New York: Dutton, 1969.

Willis, Paul E. *Profane Culture.* London: Routledge & Kegan Paul, 1978.

Wolfenstein, Martha, and Gilbert Kliman, eds. *Children and the Death of a President.* New York: Doubleday, 1965.

Yorke, Ritchie. *The History of Rock 'n' Roll.* Toronto: Methuen, 1976.

2. Articles

Aquila, Richard. "Images of the American West in Rock Music." *Western Historical Quarterly* 11 (October 1980): 415–432.

———. "Not Fade Away: Buddy Holly and the Making of an American Legend." *Journal of Popular Culture* 15 (Spring 1982): 74–81.

———. "Rock Music: A Source Guide for Collection Development." *Indiana Media Journal* 5 (Spring 1983): 6–15.

Bezaquin, Paul. "The U.S. Teen-Age Consumer." *Life*, August 31, 1959, 78—87.

Billington, Ray Allen. "The Plains and Deserts Through European Eyes." *Western Historical Quarterly* 10 (October 1979): 467–486.

Billboard. New York: Billboard Publications, Inc. Various issues.

Browne, Ray B. "Popular Culture: The World Around Us." In *The Popular*

Culture Reader, edited by Jack Nachbar et al. Bowling Green, OH: Bowling Green University Popular Press, 1978.

Burner, David, Robert D. Marcus, and Jorj Tilson. "Introduction To Popular Culture." In *America Through the Looking Glass: A Historical Reader in Popular Culture, vol. 2*, edited by David Burner et al. Englewood Cliffs, NJ: Prentice-Hall, 1974.

Cooper, B. Lee. "Teaching American History Through Popular Music." *AHA Newsletter*, no. 14 (October 1976): 3–5.

Denisoff, R. Serge. "What Is Popular Music? A Definition." In *Popular Culture: Mirror of American Life (Reader)*, edited by David Manning White and John Pendleton, 153–156. Delmar, CA: Publishers, Inc., 1977.

———. "Death Songs and Teenage Roles." In R. Serge Denisoff, *Sing a Song of Social Significance*. Bowling Green, OH: Bowling Green University Popular Press, 1972.

"The First Baby." *Life*, December 24, 1956.

Gallico, Paul. "You Don't Know How Lucky You Are to Be Married." *Reader's Digest*, July 1956, 134–136.

Ginsparg, Sylvia, and Alice E. Moriarity. "Reactions of Young People to the Kennedy Assassination." *Bulletin of the Minninger Clinic* 33 (September 1969): 295–309.

Graebner, William. "Teaching the History of Rock 'n' Roll." *Teaching History: A Journal of Methods* 9 (Spring 1984): 2–20.

Hentoff, Nat. "Popular Music: Sounds of the People." In *Popular Culture: Mirror of American Life (Article Booklet)*, edited by David Manning White and John Pendleton. Delmar, CA: Publishers, Inc., 1977.

———. "Something's Happening and You Don't Know What It Is." In *Popular Culture: Mirror of American Life (Reader)*, edited by David Manning White and John Pendleton, 163–168. Delmar, CA: Publishers, Inc., 1977.

Hoffman, Paul Dennis. "Rock and Roll and JFK: A Study of Thematic Changes in Rock and Roll Lyrics Since the Assassination of John F. Kennedy," *Popular Music and Society* 10, no. 2 (1985): 59–79.

Jeffries, John W. "The 'Quest for National Purpose' of 1960." *American Quarterly* 30 (Fall 1978): 451–470.

Junker, Howard. "As they used to say in the 1950s. . . ." In *Things In the Driver's Seat: Readings In Popular Culture*, edited by Henry Russell Huebel. New York: Rand McNally, 1972.

Mailer, Norman. "The White Negro." Reprinted in Mailer, *Advertisements for Myself*. New York: Putnam, 1959.

de Montalvo, Garci Rodriguez Ordonez. *Las Sergas de Esplandian*. Translated by E. Hale, "The Queen of California." *Atlantic Monthly* 13 (March 1864): 266–267.

Mooney, Hugh. "Just Before Rock: Pop Music 1950–1953, Reconsidered." *Popular Music and Society* 3 (1974): 65–108.

Morrow, Lance. "They're Playing Ur-Song." *Time*, March 7, 1983, 90.

Nye, Russel B. "Notes on a Rationale for Popular Culture." In *The Popular Culture Reader*, edited by Jack Nachbar et al. Bowling Green, OH: Bowling Green University Popular Press, 1978.

Riesman, David. "Listening to Popular Music." *American Quarterly* 2, no. 4 (Winter 1950): 359–371.

Robins, Wayne. "Teeny Boppers' Buying Power Declines." *Denver Post, Round-Up Section,* June 11, 1978, 75.

"The Ronettes." *Rolling Stone,* May 11, 1968.

White, David Manning. "Popular Culture: The Multi-Faceted Mirror." In *Popular Culture: Mirror of American Life (Reader),* edited by David Manning White and John Pendleton. Delmar, CA: Publishers, Inc., 1977.

Music in American Life

University of Illinois Press
1325 South Oak Street
Champaign, IL 61820-6903
www.press.uillinois.edu